Treaty Interpretation Under the Vienna Convention on the Law of Treaties

Chang-fa Lo

Treaty Interpretation Under the Vienna Convention on the Law of Treaties

A New Round of Codification

Springer

Chang-fa Lo
Judicial Yuan
Constitutional Court
Taipei
Taiwan

ISBN 978-981-10-6865-2 ISBN 978-981-10-6866-9 (eBook)
https://doi.org/10.1007/978-981-10-6866-9

Library of Congress Control Number: 2017955658

Printed on acid-free paper

This Springer imprint is published by Springer Nature
The registered company is Springer Nature Singapore Pte Ltd.
The registered company address is: 152 Beach Road, #21-01/04 Gateway East, Singapore 189721, Singapore

Preface

Treaty interpretation is a very important component in the operation of all treaties. It is governed by a set of rules provided in Articles 31–33 of the Vienna Convention on the Law of Treaties (VCLT). These rules were actually codified from the customary rules of treaty interpretation. But the current codified rules are relatively short and much simplified. International players and interpreters would not be able to apply them simply based on the wordings if they are not familiar with international practices and jurisprudence. However, the understanding and skill of treaty interpretation should not be the know-how exclusively possessed by those who are extremely familiar with international practices and jurisprudence. There should be a relatively detailed set of interpretation provisions, which are precise enough so that parties to any treaty and all potential interpreters should be able to understand the exact rules and apply them, but also flexible enough so that interpreters are still able to make their overall assessments in the course of interpretation in different cases. In addition, there are new situations (such as the increasing possibilities for different treaties to be in conflict with each other) which need to be addressed in the conduct of treaty interpretation. Certain rules governing the emerging situations should also be needed. The book argues that it is desirable to have a second round of codification so that certain existing international practices and jurisprudence concerning treaty interpretation as well as certain new rules addressing emerging issues can be codified into the VCLT to make treaty interpretation more predictable and transparent. I hope that my argument of a new round of codification will provide an input in the broader discussion of treaty interpretation and that the concrete suggestions in the book about the actual provisions to be incorporated into the new set of codified rules will serve as a useful basis for the ultimate result of codification.

In addition to explaining the purpose of this book, I like to take this opportunity to thank one of my best students at National Taiwan University College of Law, Yi-tzu Chen, who assisted me to edit the book, especially in checking the sources of citations and their formats. She has greatly helped expedite the publication of the book. I also like to thank the team from Springer. They are extremely efficient and professional. I enjoy very much working and cooperating with them for the publication of academic works.

Taipei, Taiwan
August 2017

Chang-fa Lo

Contents

About the Author

Chang-fa Lo has been Justice of the Constitutional Court of the ROC (Taiwan) since October 2011. Prior to his current judicial position, he was the Chair Professor and Lifetime Distinguished Professor at National Taiwan University (NTU); Dean of NTU College of Law; Director of Asian Center for WTO and International Health Law and Policy of NTU College of Law (ACWH); Director of Center for Ethics, Law and Society in Biomedicine and Technology of NTU; Commissioner of Taiwan's Fair Trade Commission; Commissioner of Taiwan's International Trade Commission; and legal advisor for Taiwan's GATT/WTO accession negotiations. In his capacity as the Director of ACWH, Prof. Lo launched two English journals, namely the *Asian Journal of WTO and International Health Law and Policy* and the *Contemporary Asia Arbitration Journal* (CAA) in 2006 and 2008, respectively. In his tenure as Dean of NTU College of Law, he also launched an English journal, the *NTU Law Review*. Prior to his teaching career, he practiced law in Taipei. He received his SJD degree from Harvard University Law School in 1989. He was appointed by the WTO as a panelist for *DS332 Brazil—Measures Affecting Imports of Retreaded Tyre* in 2006, *DS468 Ukraine—Definitive Safeguard Measures on Certain Passenger Cars* in 2014, and as a member of the Permanent Group of Experts under the SCM Agreement of WTO in 2008. He is also the Chairman of the Asia WTO Research Network (AWRN) since 2013. He is the author of 13 books (including the current one) and the editor of 6 books, and has authored about 100 journal papers and book chapters.

Part I
The Setting

Chapter 1
Revisiting the Essence of Treaty Interpretation

Contents

1.1 Legal Interpretation in General

1.1.1 Legal Interpretation as Opposed to Other Daily Interpretations

Interpretation of a writing is basically a hermeneutical task for the explanation, elucidation or understanding of the meanings in the writing. The term "interpretation" can be used in a very broad way. In our social life, we always have to give meanings to the communicated words which we receive from our counterparts so as to properly understand the socially perceivable messages. In linguistics, interpretation is about the analysis of languages in their forms and meanings. For religions, scriptures also need interpretation, but different views exist as to whether Bible scriptures should be interpreted literally. In domestic and international politics, readers of a political document or statement sometimes have to read out the hidden

C. Lo, *Treaty Interpretation Under the Vienna Convention on the Law of Treaties*,
https://doi.org/10.1007/978-981-10-6866-9_1

messages from it. When interpreting a poem, its readers sometimes have to adopt an imaginative interpretation so as to appreciate the beauty of the expression.

When it comes to the interpretation of a term in any legal document, either in a treaty, a constitution, a legislation or a contract, it is not merely a language or linguistic issue, although legal interpretation almost always starts from the textual language of the interpreted document. Also although a legal interpretation is not to specifically identify the socially perceivable message, it still needs to find the meaning which is "ordinary" in its usage. A legal document is not supposed to have a "hidden" message, but an interpreter cannot exclude the possibility that a meaning is not literally reflected from the surface of the interpreted term and hence a basic approach of considering the object-and-purpose of the legal document and the context of the interpreted term must be taken. Although a legal interpretation cannot be based on the interpreter's imagination, he/she still has to take into account a wider range of perspectives and to conduct an overall assessment and should not exclusively stick to the rigid wording in the interpreted document in isolation from the contextual reference. Hence, a legal interpretation is not like the interpretations which people encounter in their daily life. But there are still similarities in their essences.

If a legal interpretation is basically not like other daily interpretations, then what is the essence of legal interpretation? There are a number of necessary features/elements for an interpretation to be considered as legal interpretation. These features include that an interpretation is usually conducted within or under certain legal proceedings (which usually are judicial or quasi-judicial proceedings); that it is usually conducted by the an adjudicator, who usually is a judge, an arbitrator, or other kinds of judicial or quasi-judicial body; that the interpreted subject is a provision or a term in a legal document; that the functions and purposes of interpretation are to clarify the unclear and vague terms so to give a proper meaning to a legal provision to be applied to a dispute or in a legal proceeding, or to remove the incompleteness in the legal documents, especially the incompleteness in a law or a treaty; and that there must be certain pre-established rules provided in law or treaty or developed by jurisprudence to be based upon for conducting legal interpretation.

Among these, the key feature in a legal interpretation which is so vastly different from other interpretations in our daily life is that legal interpretation conducted by the interpreter must be based on certain pre-established rules. For the interpretation of treaties, such pre-established rules are the set of customary rules of treaty interpretation, which are far too "abridged" and need additional elements to be included to make the rules more comprehensive and operable.

1.1.2 *Treaty Interpretation Being a Process, a Method and a Mechanism*

Legal interpretations basically include treaty interpretation, constitutional interpretation, statutory interpretation and contractual interpretation. There will be some comparisons among these legal interpretations in the next chapter of this book so as to get better ideas of them.

For treaty interpretation, briefly speaking, it is a very important component of judicial or quasi-judicial process[1](hence treaty interpretation is in essence a "process") to clarify and determine the rights and obligations between relevant parties under a treaty through giving a proper meaning to its term or provision (hence treaty interpretation is a part of a dispute settlement "mechanism") based on some interpretation rules (hence it is a "method").

Specifically, treaty interpretation includes the features that the relevant legal process is "usually" conducted in an international legal proceeding (such as an international judicial or quasi-judicial dispute settlement proceeding)[2]; that the interpreter is usually an international judge or arbitrator in such legal proceeding, or, in the context of the World Trade Organization (WTO), a dispute settlement penal or the Appellate Body[3]; that the interpreted subject is a treaty provision or a term in the provision; that the functions/purposes are to clarify the uncertain and possibly disputed term or provision and to give a meaning to such term or provision or to remove the incompleteness of a treaty which is to be applied in an international dispute so as to determine the rights and obligations of the disputing parties and to resolve the dispute; that the rules to be based upon for the interpreter to conduct treaty interpretation are those provided in the Vienna Convention on the Law of Treaties (VCLT)[4] (which are the already codified customary international rules of treaty interpretation)[5] and, possibly, the jurisprudence developed by

---

[1]Some treaty interpretation activities are conducted by international or regional "courts", such as the International Court of Justice and the European Court of Human Rights. Some others are conducted by "quasi-judicial" bodies, such as the dispute settlement "panels" created for specific cases and the Appellate Body permanently created under the WTO, both of which can only be considered as quasi-judicial bodies because they only issue "reports" and their "reports" are to be adopted by the WTO's Dispute Settlement Body which is composed of all WTO Members.

[2]But it must be noted that sometimes domestic courts also have opportunities to interpret and directly international treaties if the treaties are self-executing to the jurisdictions where the domestic courts locate.

[3]If a treaty is directly interpreted and applied by a domestic court, the domestic court is also the treaty interpreter.

[4]The text of the Vienna Convention on the Law of Treaties, *opened for signature* 23 May 1969, 1155 U.N.T.S. 331, can be found at https://treaties.un.org/doc/publication/unts/volume%201155/volume-1155-i-18232-english.pdf.

[5]The contents of the VCLT concerning treaty interpretation being of the nature of customary rules of treaty interpretation will be explained in Chap. 3 of this book.

international dispute settlement mechanisms (which are uncodified interpretation rules).[6] So the "key difference" of treaty interpretation from other legal interpretations is that the rules of interpretation are those provided in the VCLT and those developed by international jurisprudence.

As shown in the title of this book, the main purpose of this writing is to argue the desirability of further codifying certain treaty interpretation rules. But a discussion on the need of possible codification of certain new rules for treaty interpretation would require a comprehensive understanding of the nature and features of treaty interpretation. Hence, in the next part of this chapter, discussions will be focused on these features of treaty interpretation.

1.1.3 Treaty Interpretation Being an Important Component of Treaty Operation

International legal instruments can be negotiated and drafted in a binding and non-binding manner. VCLT Article 2.1(a) defines "treaty" as "an international agreement concluded between States in written form and governed by international law, whether embodied in a single instrument or in two or more related instruments and whatever its particular designation". In other words, it is not part of the requirements for the purpose of being considered as a treaty under the VCLT concerning whether a written international instrument between States is binding or not. But the practice has been that basically only those international instruments which impose at least "some" binding obligations on the parties are concluded as treaties and treated as such. A purely non-binding international instrument is basically not considered as a treaty or is usually not concluded or adopted in the form of a treaty.

However, it must be borne in mind that within a treaty, there could still be many non-binding rules in addition to the binding provisions. For instance, in the WHO Framework Convention on Tobacco Control (FCTC), there are many mandatory provisions imposing legal obligations on its Parties. Article 5 of the FCTC is an example. It states: "Each Party shall develop, implement, periodically update and review comprehensive multisectoral national tobacco control strategies, plans and programmes in accordance with this Convention and the protocols to which it is a Party." The FCTC also has many non-binding provisions. An example is in Article 16.7, which provides: "Each Party should, as appropriate, adopt and implement effective legislative, executive, administrative or other measures to prohibit the sales of tobacco products by persons under the age set by domestic law, national law or eighteen."

---

[6]For instance, the "holistic interpretation" has been recognized by the jurisprudence of international tribunals and has achieved the status of customary rules of treaty interpretation. See the discussion in Chap. 17 of this book.

Hence, there could be purely non-binding international instruments, such as most "declarations" issued and most "guidelines" and "principles" adopted by members of international organizations or by the relevant parties. There could also be non-binding provisions under and within international treaties. Concerning such non-binding international instruments or those non-binding provisions under international treaties, the parties do not have a strict international obligation to implement them. The operation of such non-binding international instruments and non-binding provisions as well as the achievement of their goals could rely very much on consensus-building, peer pressure, periodic review and other mechanisms. For these non-binding instruments and non-binding rules, the "legal interpretation" of them is not an essential component for their operation.

However, for the binding provisions in international treaties, it is important that the parties' rights are preserved and their obligations are fulfilled so that the treaties will be able to properly function. To ensure the preservation of rights and the fulfilment of obligations as well as the compliance of treaty rules, the vast majority of treaties have either strict or "soft" dispute settlement procedures. Treaty interpretation is a very important component in the dispute settlement procedures (especially for the stricter dispute settlement procedures). Hence, it can be said that treaty interpretation is an important component for the overall operation of international treaties, especially for their binding provisions.

1.2 Features of Treaty Interpretation

1.2.1 As an Essential Component of International Judicial/ Quasi-judicial Legal Proceedings

As indicated above, the first important feature for treaty interpretation is that it is an essential component of international judicial and quasi-judicial legal proceedings. In this regard, it must be noted that international treaties or organizations do not always have the separation of powers into three branches (namely the executive, the legislative and the judiciary) similar to the domestic constitutional systems in many jurisdictions. However, it is very common for treaties to include dispute settlement mechanisms (DSMs) so as to resolve dispute arising from the application and implementation of the respective treaties. If a DSM is strictly rule-based conducted by a separate body which is to issue a binding decision, it can be seen as an international judicial proceeding. The essence of international judicial proceeding should be that the decisions of disputes are based on certain substantive and procedural rules and the decisions are legally binding and are supposed to be followed/ implemented by the disputing parties. In international judicial proceeding, the adjudicator usually has to find the facts, to interpret and apply the procedural and substantive applicable rules and to make a decision on the dispute. Interpreting an applicable provision or its term in the relevant treaty is an essential component of the international judicial process.

There are also other bodies or panels under certain international DSMs which perform similar functions in handling disputes, but do not issue binding decisions. For instance, the DSM under the Understanding on Rules and Procedures Governing the Settlement of Disputes (the DSU) of the WTO includes a panel proceeding and the Appellate Body proceeding. Both the panel and the Appellate Body are to issue their "reports" to be adopted by the Dispute Settlement Body (DSB)[7] (which is composed of representatives from WTO Members). The adoption mechanism makes the panel and Appellate Body reports of legally non-binding nature before the completion of the adoption process, although "practically" their reports are 100% adopted because of the "negative consensus" provision in the DSU.[8] Hence, strictly speaking, the DSM under the WTO cannot be legally considered as a purely international judicial proceeding, neither can the panel or the Appellate Body be considered as judicial branch of the WTO. At the most, the DSM is a quasi-judicial proceeding. However, the panel (created for each WTO dispute) and the standing Appellate Body still conduct treaty interpretation. This will be further explained in Chap. 8 of this book.

Also, as will be discussed in Chap. 8 of this book, not only the international judicial and quasi-judicial proceedings (conducted by international adjudicating and quasi-adjudicating bodies) include treaty interpretation as an important part of their activities, domestic judicial proceedings (conducted by domestic courts) sometimes could also involve treaty interpretation activities if a dispute in a domestic court concerns the direct application of a treaty. In other words, treaty interpretation sometimes can also be a component of domestic judicial process.

It has been mentioned above that treaty interpretation is a very important component in the rule-based international dispute settlement procedures. This is

---

[7]See the following provisions in the DSU concerning the issuance and adoption of panel and Appellate Body reports: Article 2.1: "… the DSB shall have the authority to establish panels, adopt panel and Appellate Body reports, maintain surveillance of implementation of rulings and recommendations, and authorize suspension of concessions and other obligations under the covered agreements." Article 12.7: "Where the parties to the dispute have failed to develop a mutually satisfactory solution, the panel shall submit its findings in the form of a written report to the DSB …" Article 16.4: "Within 60 days after the date of circulation of a panel report to the Members, the report shall be adopted at a DSB meeting unless a party to the dispute formally notifies the DSB of its decision to appeal or the DSB decides by consensus not to adopt the report …" Article 17.14: "An Appellate Body report shall be adopted by the DSB and unconditionally accepted by the parties to the dispute unless the DSB decides by consensus not to adopt the Appellate Body report within 30 days following its circulation to the Members …".

[8]The negative consensus requirement for the adoption of a panel or Appellate Body report is provided in Articles 16.4 and 17.14 of the DSU. Concerning the adoption of a panel report, Article 16.4 provides in part that: "Within 60 days after the date of circulation of a panel report to the Members, the report shall be adopted at a DSB meeting unless a party to the dispute formally notifies the DSB of its decision to appeal or the DSB decides by consensus not to adopt the report. …" Concerning the adoption of an Appellate Body report, Article 17.14 provides in part that: "An Appellate Body report shall be adopted by the DSB and unconditionally accepted by the parties to the dispute unless the DSB decides by consensus not to adopt the Appellate Body report within 30 days following its circulation to the Members. …".

because the ultimate purpose of such procedures is to have a proper understanding or meaning of the norm to be given to the interpreted provision for the interpreter to apply it so as to resolve a dispute. However, in a friendlier or "soft" dispute settlement procedure, such as mediation or conciliation, its purpose is to find their mutually acceptable solution and to amicably resolve the dispute. The focus of the proceeding of such kind is on finding or formulating a mutually agreeable solution. Hence the application and interpretation of a relevant treaty provision becomes far less important.

However, this does not mean that in a mediation or conciliation proceeding, treaty interpretation is never relevant. Sometimes in the mediation or conciliation proceeding, proper interpretation of the relevant treaty provisions could facilitate a successful conclusion of the proceeding. But in some other times, deliberately resorting to treaty interpretation could lead to extensive legalistic arguments in the mediation proceeding and could hamper the conclusion of a settlement agreement.

1.2.2 Treaty Interpreters Mostly Being International Adjudicators

It was mentioned above that treaty interpreters include international judges or arbitrators, and, in the context of the WTO, a dispute settlement penal and the Appellate Body. It is because these individuals or bodies are adjudicators or quasi-adjudicators to decide or help decide the dispute. This is different from the interpretation of constitutional provision or legal provision in domestic context, which is normally conducted by domestic courts.

However, there is an overlap between treaty interpretation and domestic legal interpretation (including constitutional and statutory interpretation) regarding the interpreters. As mentioned above, sometimes domestic courts have to directly interpret and apply international treaties to resolve disputes if such international treaties are directly governing and applicable to a legal relations to be decided by domestic courts. When domestic courts conduct treaty interpretation, they usually have to be bound by the VCLT as well, unless the applicable treaty is of such nature of handling/governing private matters. This will be further discussed in Chap. 8 of this book.

1.2.3 The Interpreted Subjects Being Treaty Provisions/ Terms Plus Certain Codified Customary Rules

Treaty interpretation is about the interpretation of treaties. According to the VCLT Articles 1 and 2.1(a), the VCLT (including its treaty interpretation part of Articles

31 to 33) applies to treaties between States in written form. Hence, treaty interpretation conducted under the VCLT is basically to interpret written treaties, including multilateral, regional and bilateral treaties. Other forms of international law, including customary international law and the general principles of law recognized by civilized nations, are "generally" not subject to treaty interpretation rules for their understanding.

But this does not mean that other forms of international law never need interpretation. Sometimes a customary international law rule can be codified. But a codified customary international law rule is still of the nature of customary law. A codified customary international law rule could sometimes be unclear and need clarification and interpretation. Although the interpretation rules provided in the VCLT do not directly apply to the interpretation of such codified customary international law rule, "similar interpretation rules" should still be there for the purpose of identifying or clarifying the meaning of the codified provision.

Example of the codified international rules which need interpretation is the VCLT itself. As will be explained in Chap. 3 of the book, the VCLT is a set of codified rules reflecting customary international law. For those States which have ratified the VCLT, it is of the nature of treaty as defined by VCLT Articles 1 and 2.1 (a). For those other States which have not ratified the VCLT, the rules provided in it is still of the nature of the customary international rules to them. But even the rules provided in the VCLT are merely of the nature of customary international law to such States, the provisions of the VCLT could still need further interpretation so as to understand their meanings. The need of interpretation also applies to VCLT Articles 31 to 33 which govern treaty interpretation. Hence, when we discuss the meanings and applications of VCLT Articles 31 to 33, actually we are engaging in the proper interpretation of these provisions.

The above mentioned "similar interpretation rules" for the interpretation of codified customary international law rules should mean that the interpretation would still start from looking for the "ordinary meaning" of the codified provision of the customary rule. The "context" within the codified rules should also be taken into consideration. There could be the "object-and-purpose" of "codification", but there might not be an "object-and-purpose" of "having certain substantive provisions drafted in certain way". Hence, the object-and-purpose element as provided in VCLT Article 31.1 might not be useful in clarifying a codified customary rule. But the preparatory work (which serves as the supplementary means for ordinary treaty interpretation purpose as provided in VCLT Article 32) could be very useful in understanding the proper meaning of a provision in the codified customary rules.

1.2.4 Clarifying Vagueness and Giving Meanings to the Term so as to Determine Rights and Obligations and to Resolve Dispute

"Law reading" and "treaty reading" basically includes two processes, namely identifying the proper provision to be applied (i.e. law and treaty *application*) and having the proper understanding for or giving a proper meaning to the applied provision (i.e. statutory and treaty *interpretation*). The distinction of these two processes will be further elaborated in Chap. 7 of this book. Here it must be noted that, concerning the interpretation aspect, treaty or statutory interpretation is about the interpretation of *codified norms*. If a norm is uncodified, it is not within the meaning of "interpretation" here. For an uncodified customary rule, there is no "textual language" to be based on for interpretation.

Article 31.1 of the Vienna Convention on the Law of Treaties (VCLT) also states that: "*A treaty* shall be interpreted in good faith in accordance with the ordinary meaning to be given to the terms of the treaty in their context and in the light of its object and purpose." (Emphasis added) Article 2.1(a) of the VCLT refers a treaty to "an international agreement concluded between States in written form". Hence, it is the written international instruments which need to be interpreted based on certain interpretation rules, not the uncodified customary international law to be interpreted.

For the uncodified customary rules, conceptually their "clarification" should not be considered as an "interpretation". When we use some terms to describe the proper understanding of the meaning, content, nature or scope of an uncodified customary rule, we are actually engaging in "defining", "explaining" and "discussing" its meaning, content, nature and scope. This activity does not fall within the contour of an "interpretation" activity.

Although many international disputes arise exclusively from the unclear fact, a large number of international disputes arise from the unclear or vague provision or term in the treaty, from its incompleteness, or even from its conflicting provisions. For an unclear or vague treaty provision or term, the adjudicator will have to properly understand its meaning before applying the provision. Even if a treaty provision or term is clear to one of the disputing parties, the other party could still suggest different understanding of the provision. The disputed provision still requires interpretation.

Sometimes, treaty provisions are incomplete and fail to address certain specific situations which fall within the scope of the treaty. The adjudicator still has to make decision for the dispute of such kind. So treaty interpretation is not merely to "read out" and to give appropriate meaning to a treaty term or provision so that it can be applied by an international adjudicator. Treaty interpretation is also to address the incompleteness.

In some other situations, there could even be conflicting provisions, both of which could be applicable to the same issue. Such conflicts include internal conflict (i.e. the conflict between different provisions in the same treaty) or external conflict (i.e. the conflict of a provision in one treaty with a provision in another treaty). Treaty interpretation is also to address such conflicts.

Hence, the functions and purposes of treaty interpretation are multiple: When an adjudicator encounters the objectively or subjectively uncertain and vague disputed terms or provisions, his/her role is to remove the unclear and vague aspect of the treaty so that the disputing parties can follow clear rules. When the adjudicator encounters incompleteness which create a gap between the rules and the regulated subject matters, his/her role is to interpret the rules so as to remove the gap or loophole. When he/she encounters internal conflict, the most constantly resorted means is to rely on contextual interpretation (which will be discussed in Chap. 12 of the book) so as to make the conflicting provisions consistent with each other. When he/she encounters external conflict, it is more complicated. Various interpretation methods might need to be combined so as to remove or coordinate the external conflict. The latter issue will be discussed in Chap. 19 of the book.

After having given the meaning to the terms or provisions or having removed the incompleteness of treaty provisions, the adjudicator will know how to apply relevant provisions to the case so as to determine the rights and obligations of the disputing parties and to resolve the dispute. Hence, the immediate functions and purposes of treaty interpretation are to remove the unclearness, vagueness and incompleteness in the treaty, but the ultimate function is to resolve dispute arising from the treaty.

In any event, a treaty interpreter must assume the role of addressing these incompleteness, vagueness and conflict issues. This is to maintain the proper operation of a treaty. Hence, it can be said that treaty interpretation is a necessary "operational mechanism" so as to ensure the proper operation of the interpreted treaty.

1.2.5 Interpretation Being Conducted Based on Certain Rules

As mention above, the fundamental difference between the interpretation that we encounter in our daily life and the legal interpretation is that legal interpretation must be based on certain rules. And the fundamental difference between treaty interpretation and other legal interpretations is that treaty interpretation is based on certain pre-established international rules of interpretation, whereas other legal interpretations (including statutory interpretation, constitutional interpretation and contractual interpretation) could be based on domestic legislations or local jurisprudence.

In order to have a proper understanding of an interpreted norm, an international adjudicator will have to carefully examine the text of the interpreted treaty and follow the explicit or implied instruction provided thereof so that the interpretation will not deviate from the legislative instruction. Hence the text of the legislation or treaty is the starting point for its interpretation. Also the international adjudicator will have to identify and look into some possible meanings of the interpreted provisions so that their interpretation will not be affected by their own preconceived notion. The adjudicator will further use other methods of interpretation (such as contextual, teleological and holistic approaches) to decide the most appropriate meaning for the interpreted term or provision so as to assist the application of a treaty. Hence in addition to the premise that the treaty interpretation is an important component of the judicial or quasi-judicial proceeding, it is also about the "method" to be developed or adopted so that an interpreter can properly discharge the duties vested to him/her under the treaty. These methods and rules are basically provided in VCLT Articles 31 to 33.

Treaty interpretation is similar to other legal interpretations in that their functions are both to secure a proper meaning being provided to an interpreted term or provision. But, as will be discussed, treaty interpretation and other legal interpretations are subject to different methods. Their focuses and results could also be quite different. The comparison of treaty interpretation on the one hand and statutory interpretation as well as contract and constitutional interpretations on the other hand will be further discussed in Chap. 2.

1.3 Treaty Interpretation Is not a Political or Legislative Process

1.3.1 Not a Political Process

It was explained above that treaty interpretation is a very important part of judicial or quasi-judicial proceeding. The distinctiveness of a judicial or quasi-judicial proceeding from other proceedings is that the former requires the adjudicators to be independent from political or other external influences, whereas the latter could still be subject to political or other influences. The levels of independence between a judicial and a quasi-judicial proceeding could still be different. Legally speaking, a judicial proceeding requires the adjudicator to be completely independent from any external influence. Whereas for a quasi-judicial proceeding, the adjudicator could still be subject to certain kind of influence. For instance, the dispute settlement panel and the Appellate Body of the WTO can only issue their reports to be adopted by the DSB, which is composed of representatives of WTO Members. Hence, theoretically WTO Members can collectively decide not to adopt a report. In this way, they can affect the result of the dispute settlement proceeding. This design follows the idea of Member-driven approach of the WTO's operation. But since DSU Articles 16.4 and 17.14 have similar provisions that their report shall be adopted by the DSB "unless the DSB decides by consensus not to adopt" the report (the consensus being considered as negative consensus or the "negative consenus"), the adoption of the report becomes semi-automatic. Therefore, WTO members do not have much influence in the outcome of the dispute settlement proceeding, although its DSM is not purely of the nature of judicial proceeding.

In any event, since treaty interpretation is a part of judicial or quasi-judicial proceeding and since such proceeding should be independent to certain extents, the treaty interpretation activity itself is a legal process, not a political process.

1.3.2 Not to Create New Norms

In Plato's words, "The legislator is a writer. And the judge is a reader."[9] Although this statement is an overly simplified description of the relations between the legislature and the judiciary, it still provides the core idea of judicial function to denote that judges are expected to read (i.e. to understand and to follow) the law and not to write (i.e. to create) a law. Oftentimes, reading the law and writing a law are dichotomically unclear. Their distinction could fall short of clarity and distinctness especially when there is a gap between the regulating norm and the regulated subject matters. In such situation, a judge might want to interpret the norm in a way to properly remove the gap. Whether or not this is reading the law or writing the law is not crystal clear. However, this does not reduce the value of the basic statement that judges' primary role is not to write the law.

Furthermore, the statement about reading/writing a law also denotes that judges are to read the law for the parties in connection to specific disputes so as to decide their cases. Reading the law by judges does not mean to vocalize the legal language for themselves. They read the law for the purpose of laying out the normative basis to resolve a dispute. Hence, judges are to read the law for the disputing parties to "listen" and for the disputes to be resolved. Judges must know what to read and how to read it properly. So their jobs include identifying the applicable norm (so as to know what to read) and properly interpreting the norm (so as to read it properly to ensure that the disputing parties can understand its meaning) for the ultimate solution of a dispute.

In domestic context, judges are to read the domestic law (and not to create a domestic law) not only for the disputing parties to resolve their dispute, but also for others in the same jurisdiction to follow. In international context, it is the international adjudicator to read the related treaty (and not to create a treaty norm) not only for the disputing States to settle their treaty dispute, but also for other States governed by the same treaty to understand how to implement their treaty obligations. Hence, from the perspective of the role played by a domestic court and an international adjudicator, there is no apparent difference. They are both readers of relevant rules.

[9]Derrida (2005), p. 663.

Having said this, it must be noted that a lot of time, an adjudicator cannot avoid creating certain rules through interpretation activity so as to fill the gap or loophole and to handle the dispute. The question to be asked is what should be the limit to constrain such rule-creating activities in conjunction with interpretation so as to avoid undesirable judicial activism. This issue will be further elaborated in Chap. 5 of this book.

Reference

Derrida J (2005) Deconstruction. In: Habib MAR (ed) A history of literary criticism and theory. Blackwell, Massachusetts, pp 649–666

Chapter 2
Treaty Interpretation as Opposed to Statutory, Constitutional and Contractual Interpretations

Contents

2.1 Interpretation of Different Legal Texts

2.1.1 Different Legal Texts Needed Interpretation

There are many types of legal documents/instruments which are of different natures. Some of the legal documents/instruments (such as a statute and a constitution of a jurisdiction) are domestic norms to govern relevant matters in a jurisdiction. Some others (such as bilateral, regional and multilateral treaties) are international norms to govern relevant matters beyond a specific jurisdiction. Still some other documents (such as contracts and articles of incorporation of companies) are private norms established by private parties to govern their private relations. No matter what their respective natures are, they all need interpretation when a controversy as to the "correct meaning" of a term or a provision in the documents/instruments arises.

The general issues of interpreting these documents/instruments are quite similar. They are basically interpreted by adjudicators. For statutory interpretation, the

C. Lo, *Treaty Interpretation Under the Vienna Convention on the Law of Treaties*,
https://doi.org/10.1007/978-981-10-6866-9_2

interpreters are domestic judges or arbitral tribunals. For constitutional interpretation, the interpreters are constitutional courts or the highest courts in relevant jurisdictions. For contractual interpretation, the interpreters are also judges or arbitral tribunals. For treaty interpretation, the interpreters are mainly international tribunals (such as the International Court of Justice and the panel or the Appellate Body of the WTO conducting interpretation for the Dispute Settlement Body). But, as will be further discussed in Chap. 8 of the book, sometimes the treaty interpreters could also be domestic courts. These interpreters are entrusted with the power to adjudicate disputes. So the interpretation activities of these documents are very important component of judicial function under various dispute settlement mechanisms.

Interpretations of all types of legal documents are always started with the texts of such documents. So the textual wording is the starting point of all interpretations, whether it is interpretation of a provision in a statute, in a constitution, in a contract or even in a treaty. However, as to when the textual wording can be avoided, what role should be given to context and what should be the scope of context, whether the intent of the drafter should be respected more or less, and to what extent the object-and-purpose of a legal document should guide its interpretation, there are still differences in these interpretations.

Another point worth mentioning is that treaty interpretation, statutory interpretation and constitutional interpretation are basically legal issues and the decisions can be appealed to a higher court or the highest court in charge of legal review, whereas contractual interpretation is a fact-finding activity performed by a court. Unless a rule of contractual interpretation has been breached by the fact-finding court, otherwise the result of contractual interpretation is an issue of fact and hence cannot be appealed to the court which is in charge of reviewing legal issues.

2.1.2 No Uniform Rules for Statutory, Constitutional and Contractual Interpretations, but International Constraints Still Exist

It was mentioned in Chap. 1 of the book that all legal interpretations are based on certain pre-established rules. But unlike treaty interpretation, which is governed by a pre-established set of international rules under the VCLT, there are no uniformed rules for statutory, constitutional and contractual interpretations for all jurisdictions. Different legal systems have their own rules and principles of statutory, constitutional and contractual interpretations either provided in their laws or developed through jurisprudence. However, there are some commonly found rules or principles in regard to these interpretations. They reflect the essence of these interpretation activities and are useful basis to be compared with treaty interpretation.

Another important aspect about statutory, constitutional and contractual interpretations concerns their possible international constraints. The fact that there is a lack of international rules deciding or governing the interpretation of statute, constitution and contract does not mean that these interpretation activities are entirely immune from international rules. Actually, international rules could affect such interpretations in a number of ways, although there are no comprehensive international rules to impose restraints on such interpretations.

An interpretation of domestic laws and regulation is a part of their "administration" of rules. Such administration can be subject to some international requirements. For instance, Article X:3(a) of the GATT 1994 provides that "Each contracting party shall *administer in a uniform, impartial and reasonable manner* all its laws, regulations, decisions and rulings of the kind described in paragraph 1 of this Article." (Emphasis added).[1] This is basically about the administration of domestic laws, regulations, decisions and rulings governing international trade in goods. The administration of such domestic trade rules can be conducted by government agencies in charge of administering and implementing such rules. But this is not the only situation. A domestic court can also affect the administration of such domestic trade rules through its interpretation activities. Hence, if the domestic courts are interpreting their domestic trade rules not in a uniform, impartial and reasonable manner, there could be a violation of such requirement under GATT Article X:3(a). In other words, although this GATT provision does not provide methods for statutory or constitutional interpretation, it actually sets a limit for such interpretation in the situation where the interpreted provision falls within the scope of domestic trade rules provided in Article X:1. The limits are that statutory or constitutional interpretation for domestic trade rules should be conducted in a uniform, impartial and reasonable manner. If the same statutory or constitutional provision governing international trade is interpreted by the court in an apparently different or capricious manner in different cases, it is possible for other WTO Members to argue that the provision is not administered in accordance with the requirements under GATT Article X:3(a).

However, sometimes it could be difficult to draw the line between the consistency and the inconsistency with the requirement of "a uniform, impartial and reasonable manner" arising from different interpretations of the same trade rules in different cases. This is because all judges are conducting their interpretation activities in accordance with their beliefs of correct understanding of the interpreted rules. By nature, it is possible (and even quite common) that different judges could have different views on the proper interpretation of certain governing rules. If

[1]Article X:1 of the GATT 1994 in turn provides in part: "Laws, regulations, judicial decisions and administrative rulings of general application, made effective by any contracting party, pertaining to the classification or the valuation of products for customs purposes, or to rates of duty, taxes or other charges, or to requirements, restrictions or prohibitions on imports or exports or on the transfer of payments therefore, or affecting their sale, distribution, transportation, insurance, warehousing inspection, exhibition, processing, mixing or other use, shall be published promptly in such a manner as to enable governments and traders to become acquainted with them…". Such laws, regulations, judicial decisions and administrative rulings of general application are collectively called in this Chapter as "domestic trade rules".

domestic courts' decisions are strictly required to be consistent with each other, it is actually requiring that all countries are required to adopt the doctrine of *stare decisis*. However, this should not be the situation. GATT's requirement in Article X:3(a) should not be interpreted in such way as to require WTO Members to adopt the doctrine of *stare decisis*. So the key basis to decide whether a domestic trade rule has not been interpreted in "a uniform, impartial and reasonable manner" should be whether the inconsistency is so capricious and systemic, and whether there is a mechanism in the judicial system to correct or reduce such inconsistency.

Another example of international rules affecting statutory, constitutional and contractual interpretation is that an interpretation of a domestic law provision can become a specific challenged measure. Let's assume that an interpretation of a domestic trade law provision by a domestic court is consistent with the requirement of "a uniform, impartial and reasonable manner". Let's further assume that the textual wording in trade law is not clear as to whether a specific kind of government measure to restrict international trade is mandatorily required by the trade law. If the court's "uniform, impartial and reasonable" interpretation leads to the result that the government authority is required to restrict certain trade activities, such interpretation has made a trade restriction mandatory. The interpretation becomes an integral part of the trade law to mandatorily restrict international trade. Hence the interpretation, together with the interpreted law, can become the challenged measure. Based on the same reason, a constitutional court's interpretation of a constitutional provision which affects international trade could also make such constitutional interpretation becoming a measure which restricts international trade and can thus be challenged by other WTO Members.

Domestic court's interpretation of investment contract between its government and a foreign investor can also become a challenged measure if, for instance, a court's interpretation leads to the nullification of this investment contract. Nullifying an investment contract would make the investor economically suffer. It is possible that such contractual interpretation leading to nullifying a contractual right is challenged as an expropriation of a foreign investment. Such contractual interpretation could be examined by an investor-to-State arbitral tribunal based on a bilateral investment treaty. Through this way, a domestic court's contractual interpretation could be constrained by the country's international obligations.

2.2 Statutory Interpretation and Its Comparison with Treaty Interpretation

2.2.1 Statutory Interpretation

Depending on the types and natures of law being interpreted, rules and methods for statutory interpretation could be vastly different. For instance, for statutory provisions governing civil matters, an extensive interpretation or an analogical interpretation could be permitted or even needed. For those statutory provisions governing the scope and extent of criminal punishment, they are always subject to the restrictive interpretation; no extensive or analogical interpretation so as to expand the scope and extent of punishment should be permitted. However, there are still some statutory interpretation rules (such as reliance on the plain meaning of the text, reliance on systemic/contextual interpretation, and, to different extents, reliance on the legislative intent and teleological interpretation) applicable or relevant to civil, administrative and criminal law provisions.

As mentioned above, there are no internationally uniform rules of statutory interpretation for all jurisdictions. Hence, statutory interpretation is subject to domestic rules, which could be quite diverse from jurisdiction to jurisdiction. However, there are still some rules commonly resorted to for statutory interpretation in many jurisdictions. From theoretical perspective, there are debates between textualist, intentionalist and purposivist. From practical perspective, textualism is almost always the fundamental element of statutory interpretation in all jurisdictions. Other elements (i.e. the legislative intent and the object-and-purpose of the interpreted statutory provision) are to supplement or modify the ordinary/plain meaning of textual wording. So the first common rule for statutory interpretation is the reliance on the textual wording and the interpretation of the text based on its ordinary/plain meaning. This is basically to require literal interpretation of an interpreted provision.

There are advantages of relying on ordinary/plain meaning of an interpreted statutory provision.[2] First, it provides certainty to the regulated parties about the contents of regulation, because the regulated parties will be able to predict what to expect from the provision based on their "ordinary understanding" of the norm. Second, the plain meaning rule also provides equality for all regulated parties, because they will have common "ordinary understanding" on the same provision and they are regulated by the same rule based on their same "ordinary understanding".

Although the ordinary/plain meaning rule seems to suggest that there must be a single ordinary/plain meaning of an interpreted term which is "clear and certain, not susceptible of doubt",[3] actually many terms could be very far from "plainness" or "ordinariness". A related issue is how to find or decide the ordinary/plain meaning. One criterion is to decide the ordinary/plain meaning based on the reasonable person's understanding of the meaning. But there could be problems of identifying the group of persons to serve for the benchmark and for deciding whether they are really reasonable persons.

There are some commonly used methods to identify the plain meaning of the word, including checking the statutory definition and looking for reference in case law or administrative regulations or decisions. As a secondary source, it is also

---

[2]Sullivan R, The Plain Meaning Rule and Other Ways to Cheat at Statutory Interpretation. http://aix1.uottawa.ca/~resulliv/legdr/pmr.html. Accessed 30 July 2017.

[3]Id.

possible, in many jurisdictions, for a judge to rely on a dictionary for the purpose of identifying the ordinary/plain meaning of a statutory provision. Legislative history or legislator's intent could be considered as a secondary source to identify the ordinary/plain meaning.[4] But in many jurisdictions, legislative history or legislator's intent is not necessarily a "secondary" source but a constantly relied-on source. It is not only used to identify the ordinary meaning of a statutory term, but also used as an independent method of statutory interpretation.

States could adopt different rules concerning the exceptions to the "plain meaning rule". For instance, in the United States, the "absurdity" rule allows a court to avoid the literal meaning of a statutory provision so as to obviate an absurd result arising from the ordinary meaning of the interpreted term.[5]

Concerning the case law for statutory interpretation, it should be noted that different States have different approaches concerning the reliance on previous court decisions for statutory interpretation. Generally speaking, common law countries have the *stare decisis* rule. Hence, previous interpretation of a particular statutory provision has binding force on later decisions. Whereas, civil law countries do not adopt the *stare decisis* rule. And hence the interpretation of a statutory provision does not have a binding force on the later court decisions. However, even in civil law countries, previous decisions on the interpretation of a statutory provision are always "useful references" for judges in later cases to interpret a statutory provision. The jurisprudence could even have a de facto binding force on later decisions in civil law countries.

In addition to the recognition of the importance of ordinary/plain meaning and precedent in virtually all jurisdictions, they also generally recognize the relevance of statutory purposes, the legislative works and the need to put a particular provision into its statutory context.[6]

2.2.2 Comparison with Treaty Interpretation

International treaties also have different categories. Except for those treaties relating to or governing civil/private matters (which will be discussed in Chap. 9), there are also treaties dealing with criminal matters (such as the *United Nations Convention against Transnational Organized Crime*, which criminalizes the participation in an organized criminal group, the laundering of proceeds of crime, and the corrupting practices) and treaties of other natures. They are all subject to the same interpretation rules under the VCLT, which does not distinguish the natures and categories of interpreted treaties. Whereas statutory interpretation for provisions governing

[4]Clark and Connolly (2006).

[5]Farber (1996), p. 514.

[6]Id. at p. 516.

civil matters and those governing criminal punishments could be subject to different interpretative approaches, although there are still common interpretation methods.

Concerning the issue of finding or deciding the ordinary/plain meaning, a domestic court which conducts statutory interpretation could look at the reasonable persons' understanding of the meaning, although sometimes there could still be problem of deciding the scope of reasonable persons. But in treaty interpretation, it is difficult to rely on "reasonable persons' understanding" because people in different States could have different understandings and it would not be possible for anyone to argue that the people in one country is more reasonable than those in another country for the purpose of deciding their understanding of an interpreted term. Hence, in treaty interpretation, the approach of "reasonable persons' understanding" is not used.

Also in domestic context, when deciding the ordinary meaning of a statutory term, the court usually looks for reference in case law as the primary means (no matter whether it is in a civil law or common law country) and checks dictionary as the secondly means. However, as will be discussed, in treaty interpretation, international adjudicators usually check the dictionaries as the first step to look for definitions to decide the ordinary meaning of a treaty term and then rely on jurisprudence to support their understanding of the ordinary meaning. But it must still be said that in statutory interpretation, countries rely on previous decisions quite extensively whether or not the doctrine of *stare decisis* is applied. This is similar to treaty interpretation, to the extent that previous interpretations are actually and extensively cited and constantly referred to.

In many jurisdictions, legislative history or legislator's intent is a very important source for interpreting statutory terms. It can be used to identify the ordinary meaning of a statutory term. It can also be used to identify the object-and-purpose of the legislation. It can even be used as an independent method of statutory interpretation. However, for treaty interpretation, the drafter's intent as reflected in the preparatory work is a secondary means. It is used only to confirm the meaning resulting from the application of VCLT Article 31, or to determine the meaning when the interpretation according to Article 31 leaves the meaning ambiguous or obscure or leads to a result which is manifestly absurd or unreasonable.[7] Preparatory work is not to be used to identify the object-and-purpose of a treaty.

In treaty interpretation, context can be very broad to refer not only to other parts of the treaty text, its preamble and annexes, but also to other treaties. This will be further discussed in Chap. 12 of the book. But in statutory interpretation, the method of contextual or systemic interpretation generally is not used so as to extend to other statues. Basically, the context is limited to relevant parts in the same statute.

[7]See Vienna Convention on the Law of Treaties, Art. 32, *opened for signature* 23 May 1969, 1155 U.N.T.S. 331.

2.3 Constitutional Interpretation and Its Comparison with Treaty Interpretation

2.3.1 Constitutional Interpretation

Constitutional interpretation is both similar to and different from statutory interpretation. Both of them are guided by the ordinary/plain meaning of the text and by the context of the norms. Prior judicial decisions are also important both in statutory interpretation and in constitutional interpretation, either serving as a binding source or as valuable reference (depending on the legal systems). But the unique aspects in constitutional interpretation are that social, political and economic/financial consequences could affect the interpretation and that the natural law could be brought into guide or assist constitutional interpretation.[8] Also it is not crystal clear concerning the weight to be given to the drafter's intention. The following points are some important issues specifically arising from constitutional interpretation.

First, social, political and economic/financial consequences have possible impact on or implication for constitutional interpretation. Since constitution is the highest norm in a jurisdiction, its operation will affect not only the legal system and practice there, but also the fundamental rights of the people in the jurisdiction. When interpreting a constitutional provision, judges in the constitutional court or in the highest court in the jurisdiction could not avoid considering various consequences, in addition to their beliefs in constitutional values (such as the democracy and the respect of human dignity). The most commonly identified consequences include social consequence (such as whether a certain way of interpretation will create positive or negative serious implications for the society), political consequence (such as whether certain interpretation will give rise to a political turmoil or whether it will help improve political stability) and economic/financial consequence (such as whether certain interpretation will lead to requiring the government to immensely reallocate the resource or to greatly increase spending). Although such consequences are not formally introduced as part of constitutional interpretation method, they definitely could affect individual judges' decisions.

Second, the natural law and certain external values can become the guidance in constitutional interpretation. This is because the main part in the constitutions of most countries is to ensure the protection of fundamental rights and human dignity. When a constitution is not sufficient in providing such protection or is not entirely in line with such expectation of full protection of the fundamental rights, the natural law could be introduced as the higher norm to guide the interpretation of the constitutional provisions. Also certain external values of high importance being universally recognized (especially those provided in human rights conventions) have the potential of being introduced into the operation of a constitution. There are two possible ways to bring external values required in human rights treaties into the

---

[8]Linder D, Exploring Constitutional Conflicts—Theories of Constitutional Interpretation. http://law2.umkc.edu/faculty/projects/ftrials/conlaw/interp.html. Accessed 30 July 2017.

operation of a constitutional system. One way is to directly apply such treaties by a constitutional court or the highest court in a jurisdiction. But there could be complicated legal/constitutional issues concerning whether or not a treaty can be directly applied by the court. Another possible way is to rely on constitutional interpretation so as to have such treaties shedding light to the constitutional provisions and helping understand their meanings. Through this way, the result of interpreting constitutional provision will be in line with relevant human rights treaties.

Third, a related issue is the desirability of ensuring a living constitution through constitutional interpretation so that it can keep up with the changes in different generations, without amending the text of the constitution.[9] Although the concept of living constitution can be controversial to some people, it is of high importance in the operation of a constitution. This is because constitution is a fundamental document concluded through complicated political and legal processes. Any change of a constitutional provision is a difficult task. In many countries, their constitutions are quite "old". If new elements cannot be brought into the constitutional framework through interpretation, it would transform the oldness of the constitution into obsoleteness of it.

Fourth, another related issue in this context is the possible adoption of an "evolutive interpretation" so as to give new meanings to an aged constitutional provision. This is particularly important if there are new contents of fundamental rights being developed or recognized at international level (such as a treaty recognizing a new kind of human rights being concluded) and if the contents of such rights are in contradiction with the intent of the drafter of the constitution, the new element must be brought into the process of constitutional interpretation. This approach will help a constitution adapt to new circumstances in the society of the State and will make sure that the constitution will not hinder the progress of the society. This approach will also ensure that a constitution will evolve and improve over time and would also reduce the need of amending the text of a constitution.

Fifth, the drafter's intent is important, but not critical, in constitutional interpretation. Constitution is not merely a legal document. It is definitely a political document. Drafting constitution is a political process. Its contents are the result of political decision. They need to be fully respected. Interpreters of constitutional provisions are not in a position to wilfully change the intents of the drafters. However, it is also true, as mentioned above, that a constitution can be "old" in its age and that it should be desirable to make the constitution a living one. Hence, a respect to the drafter's intent and the need of making it a living constitution must be properly balanced.

Sixth, when interpreting a constitutional provision, balancing various factors and competing rights/interests could be very important. In many countries, the principle of proportionality is explicitly provided or impliedly embedded in their constitutions to decide the constitutionality of a restriction of constitutional rights. In some

[9]Different perspectives on living constitution is explained in Rehnquist (2006), pp. 402–403.

other countries, there is a necessity requirement, which is quite similar to the principle of proportionality. This principle/requirement basically expects that the interpreter of the constitution must consider some related factors and must "weight and balance" these factors so as to decide the constitutionality of a measure or a law provision. In addition to the process of weighing and balancing these factors, the constitutional interpreter in many countries also develop different tests (such as rational basis test, heightened scrutiny test or strict scrutiny, depending upon the importance of the rights being infringed) to help interpret constitutional provisions.

2.3.2 *Comparison with Treaty Interpretation*

Treaty interpretation in a rule-based dispute settlement procedure is basically not affected by the possible social, political and economic/financial consequences in a jurisdiction. In this regard, treaty interpretation is quite different from the interpretation of a constitutional provision, the interpreter of which could be practically affected by the possible impact on or implication for the social, political or economic/financial situation.

Concerning constitutional interpretation, there are supports of maintaining or ensuring living constitution so that the constitution can either lead social development or at least is not to be left behind from the development of the society. Also it is desirable to incorporate important human values developed in international treaties (especially human rights treaties) into the constitution system through interpretation of the constitutional provisions. For treaty interpretation, although there is no apparent recognition of "living treaty", it is still desirable, as argued in Chap. 18 of this book, to introduce some eternal values of high importance into a treaty through its interpretation.

In constitutional interpretation, evolutive interpretation should be used so as to adapt to the new development or situation of the society. In treaty interpretation, especially for those treaties which govern State's behaviours (such as those for the protection of human rights) , evolutive interpretation could also be desirable. But it must be noted that for trade and economic treaties, it is also very important to maintain the balanced results (i.e. the results of "gives and takes" by the contracting parties) arising from negotiations.

For constitutional interpretation, the drafter's intent is important and must be properly respected. However, the intent should not be an "absolute guidance" because the constitution needs to be operated in a way to keep up with the new development of the society and the new values being widely recognized domestically or international. For treaty interpretation, the drafter's intent, as reflected in the preparatory work, is merely a secondary and supplementary means to assist treaty interpretation, as provided in Article 32 of the VCLT.

For constitutional interpretation, balancing competing rights and interests is a constant exercise. When deciding the constitutionality of a statute or a government measure, related public interests to be pursued by the statute or the measure, and the importance and extent of infringement to the fundamental right need to be weighted and balanced. For treaty interpretation, in many situations (for instance, when deciding whether a measure is necessary to protect human health or life under GATT Article XX (a) and (b)), it is also needed to balance related competing interests. The latter situation will be discussed further in Chap. 16 of this book.

2.4 Contractual Interpretation and Its Comparison with Treaty Interpretation

2.4.1 Contractual Interpretation

Contractual interpretation is different from statutory, constitutional and treaty interpretations in that the latter are to interpret the norms which are to be applied to decide the rights and obligations of the disputing parties, whereas the former is to interpret the private norm created by and for the disputing parties in private relations. Since the interpreted contractual provision is a written document, relying on the plain meaning (literal meaning) of the textual wording is still the key guiding principle. In addition to this, there are some unique aspects for contractual interpretation.[10]

First, there are situations where a contact term is ambiguous, unclear or reasonably susceptible to more than one interpretation. A court will have to rely on other methods to interpret the term. In many jurisdictions, the court is required by its law to look for the parties' intent so as to understand the meaning of the contract term to be interpreted. Parties' intent is usually identified by the negotiation history of the contract and the related documents associated with the negotiations. But if the term is clear, the court generally has no power to resort to the parties' intent so as to distort the clear literal meaning of the contract term.

Second, there could be limited situations where a contract term can be interpreted contrary to its literal meaning. For instance, if the literal meaning of a contract term would lead to absurdity in the circumstance or would be inconsistent with the key part or the majority part of the contract, such term should be interpreted in a way to avoid such absurd or inconstant result. One interpretation method to avoid such absurdity and inconsistency is to resort to the intent of the parties when they negotiated the contract.

Third, there is another situation where the literal meaning or the parties' intent can be disregarded. When parties to a contract are not in equal footing when negotiating their contract, especially when a party is apparently weak in its economic or negotiation position, a contract term can be interpreted in the weaker party's favor when a contractual provision is susceptible to two different interpretations. In such situation, the court should not rely on the party's intent so as to

[10]Martorana (2014).

decide the meaning of the provision. Otherwise, it would result in favoring the economically-stronger party because during the negotiation, the stronger party might dominate the process and hence the negotiating history could reflect the stronger party's intent. This is undesirable result. A similar situation is in the pre-drafted contract form. If a contract is pre-drafted by a party and if there is ambiguity in the term used in such "form contract", laws in many countries would require the adjudicator to also interpret the term in favor of the drafting party's opposing side, who are usually the weaker party. This is to avoid resorting to parties' intent, which usually turns out to be the intent of the drafter of the contract.

Fourth, since a private contract between parties of equal footings is basically an outcome of exchanged rights and obligations, it is of importance to maintain the balance of rights and obligations between the parties. Contract interpreters are not vested with the power to readjust the parties' rights and obligations through contractual interpretation, unless very high public interests justify readjusting such balance. In the latter situation, the readjustment of the balance could be conducted through contractual interpretation, as mentioned in the preceding paragraph. The readjustment can also be required by domestic legislation.

2.4.2 Comparison with Treaty Interpretation

In contractual interpretation, the drafter's intent is given much weight in deciding the meaning of a contract term when there is a doubt about the true meaning of the term. This means that subjective interpretation method is preferred in contractual interpretation. However, in treaty interpretation, drafter's intent as reflected in the preparatory work for a treaty is not given much weight. It only plays a supplementary and secondary role as explained above. Hence treaty interpretation prefers objective methods, including ordinary meaning of textual wording, context, and object-and-purpose.

For contractual interpretation, there are some situations where textual wording must be interpreted so as to provide better protection for the weaker party to the contract. But in treaty interpretation, there is no such principle or guidance of interpreting a treaty so as to provide better protection for the weaker contracting State. If a weaker party under a treaty is to be better protected or to be given favors or privileges, such favors or privileges must be reflected by textual wording.

For the interpretation of a private contract between parties who negotiated the deal based on equal footing, it is important to maintain the balanced result when a court is to interpret the contract provisions. This is quite similar to the interpretation of those treaties governing trade and other economic relations, which are basically the results of exchange of concessions. Interpretation of such treaties should not add to or diminish the rights and obligations of the parties, nor rebalance the concessions. But as mentioned above, if it is an interpretation of a treaty governing the behavior of its contracting parties, there is no such issue of balancing or rebalancing the rights and obligations between the parties.

References

Clark K, Connolly M (2006) A guide to reading, interpreting and applying statutes. https://www.law.georgetown.edu/academics/academic-programs/legal-writing-scholarship/writing-center/upload/statutoryinterpretation.pdf. Accessed 30 July 2017

Farber DA (1996) The hermeneutic tourist: statutory interpretation in comparative perspective. Cornell Law Rev 81:513–529

Linder D Exploring constitutional conflicts—theories of constitutional interpretation. http://law2.umkc.edu/faculty/projects/ftrials/conlaw/interp.html. Accessed 30 July 2017

Martorana VR (2014) A guide to contract interpretation. http://www.reedsmith.com/files/uploads/miscellany/A_Guide_to_Contract_Interpretation__July_2014_pdf. Accessed 30 July 2017

Rehnquist WH (2006) The notion of a living constitution. Harv J Law Public Policy 29(2):401–415

Sullivan R The plain meaning rule and other ways to cheat at statutory interpretation. http://aix1.uottawa.ca/~resulliv/legdr/pmr.html. Accessed 30 July 2017

Chapter 3
Meaning of Codification and VCLT as the First Round of Codification of Customary Rules of Treaty Interpretation

Contents

3.1 Meaning of Codification

Codification is usually understood as "the collection and systematic arrangement, usually by subject, of the laws of a state or country, or the statutory provisions, rules, and regulations that govern a specific area or subject of law or practice."[1] In connection with his proposal of codifying a set of rules to address and promote mediated settlement agreements by submitting the draft "*Convention on Cross-Border Enforcement of International Mediated Settlement Agreements*", the author of this book also explained in a paper he authored that "Codification is the process

[1]Definition suggested by Legal Dictionary, at The Free Dictionary. http://legal-dictionary.thefreedictionary.com/codification. Accessed 30 July 2017.

C. Lo, *Treaty Interpretation Under the Vienna Convention on the Law of Treaties*,
https://doi.org/10.1007/978-981-10-6866-9_3

of arranging and integrating various normative elements into a legal instrument in a systemic manner."[2] Hence, the essences of codification are that it involves a process of a collection and systematic arrangement of rules (normative elements) and that it must be in specific subject of law or practice.

The rules being systemically arranged can be case law of specific area of law in domestic context. For instance, in the United States, although sometimes it might be necessary to check the previous case law to understand the intrinsic meaning of a statutory provision, most of the criminal law rules have been codified into statutes and courts are to apply the statutory provisions.[3] The rules being systemically arranged can also be customary rules of specific field of law in international context. For instance, as will be discussed in the later part of this chapter, many VCLT provisions were the results of codification of previous customary international law rules. Also for instance, in the field of law of war, there are considerable amount of rules in the current international treaties (especially the four Geneva Conventions)[4] being the results of codification from customary international law.[5]

Most codifications are conducted by authorities. Actually, in international context, codification is supposed to be promoted by the United Nations. Article 13, paragraph 1 of the Charter of the United Nations provides in part that "The General Assembly shall initiate studies and make recommendations for the purpose of: a … encouraging the progressive development of international law and its codification …".[6]

[2]Lo (2011), p. 10.

[3]The Lectric Law Library. The Common Law. http://www.lectlaw.com/mjl/cm001.htm. Accessed 30 July 2017.

[4]They include: (1) the Geneva Convention for the Amelioration of the Condition of the Wounded and Sick in Armed Forces in the Field of August 12, 1949; (2) the Geneva Convention for the Amelioration of the Condition of Wounded, Sick and Shipwrecked Members of Armed Forces at Sea of August 12, 1949; (3) The Geneva Convention Relative to the Treatment of Prisoners of War of August 12, 1949; and (4) The Geneva Convention Relative to the Protection of Civilian Persons in Time of War of August 12, 1949. See American Red Cross (2011). The article is available at https://www.redcross.org/images/MEDIA_CustomProductCatalog/m3640104_IHL_SummaryGenevaConv.pdf. Accessed 30 July 2017.

[5]In this regards, the following explanation is useful: "There is considerable judicial and scholarly support, which is also endorsed by the International Committee of the Red Cross (ICRC), that the rules contained in the four Geneva Conventions of 1949 for the Protection of Victims of War and in the Hague Convention (IV) of 1907 on the Laws and Customs of War on Land (except for administrative, technical, and logistical provisions) reflect customary law. It is also widely recognized that many, perhaps even most, of the provisions, principles, and rules contained in Additional Protocol I to the Geneva Conventions and some, perhaps even many, of the provisions contained in Additional Protocol II reflect customary law. Several rules pertaining to types of weapons, and especially the prohibition on the use of chemical weapons, are regarded as customary." Quoted from Meron T, Customary Law. http://www.crimesofwar.org/a-z-guide/customary-law/. Accessed 30 July 2017.

[6]The text of the Charter of the United Nations can be found at United Nations. http://www.unorg/en/charter-united-nations/. Accessed 30 July 2017.

But the term "codification" can also be loosely used to denote the efforts put forth by individuals or private institutions in systematically arranging existing rules or creating new rules for a specific area of law. For instance, the *1961 Harvard Draft Convention on the International Responsibility of States for Injuries to Aliens*[7] and the *Draft Convention on the Prevention and Punishment of the Crime of Developing, Producing, Acquiring, Stockpiling, Retaining, Transferring or Using Biological or Chemical Weapons*[8] were private initiatives to codify certain international law rules. The above mentioned draft "*Convention on Cross-Border Enforcement of International Mediated Settlement Agreements*" proposed by the author of this book was also a private initiative of creating a codified international treaty by the international community so as to resolve the cross border enforcement issues of mediated settlement agreements and to ultimately promote the friendlier dispute settlement mechanism of mediation for commercial matters.

The codified rules (i.e. the existing normative elements) usually existed before they were codified in the instrument. For instance, in relation to the codification of the case law or the customary international law rules, the normative elements pre-existed the resulting instruments. However, it is also possible that new rules (i.e. the newly created normative elements) are formulated through the codification process. In the real world, the situation might not be so clear cut. Sometimes a codification is used for the purpose of integrating the existing uncodified rules into a text in the document. But at the same time, there could still be elements in the text which are actually not found or cannot be clearly identified in the pre-existing non-codified rules. Hence, the process of codifying the pre-existing rules could also partly involve the creation of certain new rules.

Concerning the result of codification, the final codified text can be a legal instrument formally adopted by the legislative body within a jurisdiction to make it become a legislation, or adopted by the contracting parties to the instrument to make it become a treaty. However, it must be noted that certain codified rules still maintain their nature of customary law. As will be explained in the later part of this chapter, for those States which have not ratified the VCLT, the contents of the VCLT are still of the nature of customary rules of international law to such States and they are still bound by such customary rules.

---

[7]1961 Harvard Draft Convention on the International Responsibility of States for Injuries to Aliens. http://readinglists.ucl.ac.uk/items/46B29567-93F9-31C3-293E-4CB55932CF47.html. Accessed 30 July 2017.

[8]Draft Convention on the Prevention and Punishment of the Crime of Developing, Producing, Acquiring, Stockpiling, Retaining, Transferring or Using Biological or Chemical Weapons. http://www.sussex.ac.uk/Units/spru/hsp/documents/Draft%20Convention%20-%20English.pdf. Accessed 30 July 2017.

3.2 Reasons to Discuss VCLT's Status as Customary International Law

There are basically two main branches of international law, namely international treaty between States (*jus inter gentes*) and the customary international law (*jus gentium* or law of nations). Customary international law, as opposed to international treaty, is a binding set of international norms arising from general and consistent State practice and has been followed by States as binding legal obligation (accepted as law or *opinio juris*). This is reflected in Article 38.1.b of the Statute of the International Court of Justice that "The Court, whose function is to decide in accordance with international law such disputes as are submitted to it, shall apply: … b. international custom, as evidence of a *general practice accepted as law* …".

The VCLT was adopted on 22 May 1969 and opened for signature on 23 May 1969 by the United Nations Conference on the Law of Treaties. The Convention entered into force on 27 January 1980 in accordance with Article 84, paragraph 1, which provides that: "The present Convention shall enter into force on the thirtieth day following the date of deposit of the thirty-fifth instrument of ratification or accession." The VCLT has 114 Parties as of March 2017.[9] For these Parties, the VCLT is a treaty to them and it binds them because of their treaty obligations.

Although the VCLT's Parties are quite many in number, they only represent a little less than 60% of the international community as a whole if it is calculated based on United Nations' 193 member States.[10] At least there are 79 countries which are UN Member States being not Parties to the VCLT. Many other international organizations or multilateral treaties have many more contracting parties than the VCLT. For instance, as of July 2017, the WTO has 164 Members[11] and the WHO Framework Convention on Tobacco Control (FCTC) has 181 Parties.[12] Hence there are still many members/parties to the United Nations and other international organizations or multilateral treaties which are not Parties to the VCLT.

Also there are some key countries which are yet to become Parties to the VCLT. For instance, although the United States signed the VCLT on 24 April 1970, its Senate did not give advice and consent to approve the Convention as required by the United States Constitution for the country to become Party to the Convention. Notwithstanding the fact that the United States has not become a Party to the VCLT, it generally considers "many provisions" of the VCLT to constitute to be

[9]United Nations Treaty Collection. https://treaties.un.org/Pages/ViewDetailsIII.aspx?src=TREATY&mtdsg_no=XXIII-1&chapter=23&Temp=mtdsg3&clang=_en. Accessed 30 July 2017.

[10]United Nations. Member States. http://www.un.org/en/members/index.shtml. Accessed 30 July 2017.

[11]World Trade Organization. Members and Observers. https://www.wto.org/english/thewto_e/whatis_e/tif_e/org6_e.htm. Accessed 30 July 2017.

[12]FCTC. Parties to the WHO Framework Convention on Tobacco Control. http://www.who.int/fctc/signatories_parties/en/. Accessed 30 July 2017.

customary law on the law of treaties.[13] France, India, Indonesia and South Africa played important roles in negotiating and concluding treaties and constantly engaged in dispute settlement procedures under various treaties. But they are also among the group of non-Parties to the VCLT.

A partial overlap of memberships not only exists between the VCLT and other multilateral treaties or international organizations, but also between the VCLT and many plurilateral or bilateral treaties. For instance, in the bilateral FTAs and investment treaties concluded between the United States and its partner countries, at least one of the contracting parties (i.e. the United States) is not Party to the VCLT. Now President Trump of the United States has withdrawn the US's participation in the plurilateral FTA of Trans Pacific Partnership (TPP, which is yet to become effective).[14] But when the TPP negotiations were concluded among the 12 negotiating countries (including Singapore, Brunei, New Zealand, Chile, United States, Australia, Peru, Vietnam, Malaysia, Mexico, Canada and Japan), there were three of them (Singapore, Brunei and the United States) not Parties to the VCLT.

So if a dispute is between two parties of a bilateral treaty and if both sides are Parties to the VCLT, the VCLT as a treaty to bind the Parties will apply to their relations under such bilateral treaty. But in the situations where the membership of a multilateral, plurilateral or bilateral treaty does not fully overlap with the membership of the VCLT, there is an issue about whether the VCLT should also bind the disputing parties *if* the VCLT is merely a treaty in nature and is not considered as customary international law. First, suppose a dispute arises between two parties to a multilateral or plurilateral treaty and suppose both parties are not VCLT Parties. Treaty interpretation provisions in the VCLT do not bind the Parties *as a treaty* and will not apply to their dispute *if* the VCLT is merely a treaty in its status and is not considered as customary international law. Second, suppose one of the disputing parties to a multilateral or plurilateral treaty is Party to the VCLT. Treaty interpretation provisions in the VCLT will not apply to their dispute either, *if* the VCLT is merely a treaty and is not considered as customary international law. Thirdly, suppose both of the disputing parties under a multilateral or plurilateral treaty are Parties to the VCLT. Treaty interpretation provisions in the VCLT will bind them and will apply to their dispute as a treaty, even it is not considered as customary international law.

However, the logical outcomes in these situations would create a very difficult issue concerning the justification of the *same provision* under a multilateral or plurilateral treaty being possibly interpreted either based on the VCLT (when both disputing parties are VCLT Parties) or not based on the VCLT (when one or both of the disputing parties are not VCLT Parties). It is rather unthinkable and undesirable that an exactly same treaty provision being decided under the exactly same dispute

[13]U.S. Department of State. Vienna Convention on the Law of Treaties. http://www.state.gov/s/l/treaty/faqs/70139.htm. Accessed 30 July 2017.

[14]Up to the completion of this book, the TPP's fate is still uncertain due to President Trump's withdrawal from it. It is yet to see whether the agreement will survive with some of the remaining 11 parties still being interested in having a TPP without the United States.

mechanism would be interpreted based on different rules when the disputing parties are different.

Nevertheless, if the VCLT represents the codified version of customary international law for treaty interpretation, the result of interpreting the same provision will be the same, no matter whether the membership of the VCLT fully overlaps with the membership of the interpreted treaty and no matter whether both of the disputing parties are Parties to the VCLT. This is because States are bound to follow customary international law rules as a matter of law. All disputes will be subject to the treaty interpretation rules under the VCLT which represents the contents of customary rules of international law. Hence, the status of the VCLT concerning whether it represents customary international law matters.

3.3 "Codifying" or "Developing" Customary International Law of Treaty Interpretation

3.3.1 VCLT Being the Result of Codification Process

Codification of customary international law is generally referred to as "the more precise formulation and systematization of rules of international law in fields where there already has been extensive State practice, precedent and doctrine."[15] So the essence is to transform the contents of *pre-existing uncodified international law rules* (i.e. State practice, precedent and doctrine) into a written instrument with the original contents of the customary rules being maintained.

It was in the middle of the twentieth century when "customary international law of treaties had grown to a fairly comprehensive body of rules".[16] It became mature for the international community to codify customary international law of treaties. The result of the codification process had been successful. The detailed provisions concerning international treaty law were enumerated in the text of the VCLT.

The VCLT was drafted by the International Law Commission of the United Nations (ILC) mainly based on previous practices, precedents and doctrines. As mentioned above, the VCLT was adopted in 1969 and opened for signature later in the same year by the United Nations Conference on the Law of Treaties, which was convened pursuant to General Assembly resolutions 2166 (XXI) 1 of 5 December 1966 and 2287 (XXII) 2 of 6 December 1967. The treaty entered into force on 27 January 1980 when the necessary threshold for putting the treaty into effect had been met.[17]

---

[15]Statute of the International Law Commission, Art. 15 (1947).

[16]Zemanekm K, Vienna Convention on the Law of Treaties Vienna, 23 May 1969—Historical Context. http://legal.un.org/avl/ha/vclt/vclt.html. Accessed 30 July 2017.

[17]United Nations Treaty Collection. https://treaties.un.org/pages/ViewDetailsIII.aspx?src=TREATY&mtdsg_no=XXIII-1&chapter=23&Temp=mtdsg3&lang=en. Accessed 30 July 2017.

If we can use the expression of the "King of the Kings" to denote a governor who are superior to other governors, we can use the similar expression "the treaty of all treaties" to describe the VCLT and to denote that all other treaties (including their conclusion, there effectiveness, their operation and their interpretation) are subject to the rules of the VCLT.

Hence, the VCLT is not merely a set of rules governing treaty interpretation. It has much broader coverage and application. It is for almost all aspects of international treaties. More specifically, it deals with conclusion, reservation, entry into force and provisional application of treaties.[18] It also governs observance, application and interpretation of treaties as well as rules regarding third States.[19] It addresses amendment, modification,[20] invalidity, termination and suspension of the operation of treaties.[21] Hence the rules governing treaty interpretation is only a small part of the VCLT. But this treaty interpretation part includes very important provisions in the Convention which are most constantly resorted to in international legal proceedings.

It must be noted that the VCLT limits its application to written treaties between States (excluding treaties concluded between international organizations).[22] Hence, literally it does not apply to agreements with a party being a non-State international entity (such as Hong Kong and Macau). For instance, Hong Kong and Macau are parties to the WTO agreements. Strictly speaking, the VCLT (including its treaty interpretation provisions) will not apply to these agreements because they do not fall into the scope of "treaties between States" under VCLT Article 1. However, there has not been any doubt in WTO jurisprudence that the same rules of treaty interpretation should be applied to the WTO agreements even non-States are being parties to these agreements. Actually, the panels and Appellate Body of the WTO always apply the treaty interpretation rules under the VCLT to interpret WTO agreements disregarding the fact that the parties to these agreements include non-State parties.

Also, since the VCLT only applies to written treaties, literally speaking, the codified customary rules (which are not treaties themselves) are not supposed to be interpreted under the VCLT. However, practically, the treaty interpretation part in the VCLT should still be the useful basis to understand and interpret such codified

[18]Vienna Convention on the Law of Treaties, Part II, opened for signature 23 May 1969, 1155 U.N.T.S. 331.

[19]Id. at Part III.

[20]Id. at Part IV.

[21]Id. at Part V.

[22]Id. at Art. 2.1(a). For treaties between States and International Organizations or between international organizations, there is a similar treaty "Vienna Convention on the Law of Treaties between States and International Organizations or between International Organizations" being concluded on 21 March 1986. But it is yet to become effective. See United Nations Treaty Collection. https://treaties.un.org/pages/ViewDetails.aspx?src=TREATY&mtdsg_no=XXIII-3&chapter=23&lang=en. Accessed 30 July 2017.

non-treaty rules of customary nature. The latter issue was discussed in Chap. 1 of this book. It will also be further elaborated in a later part (Sect. 3.4.4) of this chapter.

3.3.2 *"Codifying" the Already Existing Customary Rules or "Developing" New Customary Rules*

It is generally the situation that the VCLT was drafted so as to reflect the pre-existing practices, precedents and doctrines. But if it comes to the detailed rules provided in the Convention, it must be more precisely said that the provisions of the VCLT were not always based on the contents of the pre-existing customary international law rules. There had been some elements added to or created by the ILC for the purpose of transforming them into the components of customary international law or ensuring the application of such elements as treaty obligations.

A paragraph in the Preamble of the VCLT reads:

> Believing that the *codification* and *progressive development of the law of treaties* achieved in the present Convention will promote the purposes of the United Nations set forth in the Charter… (Emphasis added)

Hence there are two parts achieved in the VCLT, namely the part of "codification of the law of treaties" and the part of "progressive development of the law of treaties". It has been explained that "codification of international law" is about formulation and systematization of rules of international law in the fields "where there already has been extensive State practice, precedent and doctrine."[23] "Progressive development of international law", on the other hand, means "the preparation of draft conventions on subjects which have not yet been regulated by international law or in regard to which the law has not yet been sufficiently developed in the practice of States."[24] From the above quoted preambular paragraph in the VCLT, it can be seen that some parts of the VCLT were definitely codified from the pre-existing practices, precedents and doctrines. But some other parts of the Convention were the results of *progressive development of international law* through formulating written rules on certain subjects which had not been sufficiently developed in the practice of States at or prior to the time when the VCLT was drafted.

The apparent example of the VCLT to involve "progressive development of international law" is Article 9.2, which provides that: "The adoption of the text of a treaty at an international conference takes place by the vote of two-thirds of the States present and voting, unless by the same majority they shall decide to apply a different rule." In previous time, the adoption of a treaty text was almost always based on unanimity of the negotiating parties. The ILC considered that "it would be

---

[23]Statute of the International Law Commission, Art. 15, second part (1947).

[24]Id. at Art. 15, first part.

undesirable to lay down unanimity as the general rule for the adoption of the texts of treaties drawn up at conferences or within organizations."[25] Hence, the ILC created a rule which was not consistent with the common practice at the time when the VCLT was drafted. Obviously, the content of Article 9.2 of the VCLT was not codified from the pre-existing customary international law rules, but was formulated by the ILC.

In addition to Article 9.2 of the VCLT, actually most procedural rules provided in the Convention, such as Article 20.5 (concerning a reservation being considered to have been accepted by a State if it shall have raised no objection to the reservation), Article 65 (concerning procedure to be followed with respect to invalidity, termination, withdrawal from or suspension of the operation of a treaty) and Article 67 (concerning instruments for declaring invalid, terminating, withdrawing from or suspending the operation of a treaty), which require its Parties to observe when invoking certain legal effect under the VCLT, cannot be considered as the results of codification of customary international law. Neither can the dispute settlement provisions in Article 66 of the VCLT (concerning procedures for judicial settlement, arbitration and conciliation) be considered as the codification of the pre-existing customary international law.[26] These are basically created by the ILC.

3.4 Treaty Interpretation Rules in VCLT as Codified Customary International Law

3.4.1 The Decision About Which Parts Are Pre-existing Customary Rules Being Codified

So there are two categories of provisions in the VCLT which are differentiated from the perspective of whether they are codified from the pre-existing customary rules of international law. One category consists of the codification of pre-existing customary international law and the other category involves progressive development of international law.

A further issue here is whether both categories of VCLT provisions are now universally accepted as reflecting/representing the current customary rules of international law or only the category of codifying the "then pre-existing customary international law" can be considered as the current contents of customary international law at the present time.

As mentioned above, there have been 114 States having become Parties to the VCLT up to the present time. The fact that there are at least 79 countries being non-Parties to the VCLT *does not* necessarily lead to the conclusion that either the category of VCLT provisions (which were the result of codification from the

---

[25]Cited from Sinclair (1984), p. 13.

[26]Schmalenbach (2012), p. 85.

pre-existing customary international law) or the category of VCLT provisions (which involve progressive development of international law) has not become the contents of the overall consensus of international community and hence does not constitute the contents of customary international law.

For the category of VCLT provisions which reflect the codification of the pre-existing customary international law at the time when the Convention was drafted, apparently the provisions are still customary international law in nature. The fact that customary international law had been codified as a treaty does not undermine its status of being/maintaining customary international law nature.

But for the category of VCLT provisions which involve progressive development of international law, countries might still have problems accepting them as customary international law rules. Hence, it is possible that for those VCLT provisions which were not codified from customary international law, but were progressively developed during the drafting process, there could be Parties and non-Parties to the VCLT which might not accept them as being the contents of current customary international law.

As indicated above, the United States generally considers "many provisions" of the VCLT having constituted customary international law of treaties.[27] Apparently, the United States does not consider that "all" VCLT provisions constitute customary international law. There has not been a universal agreement as to whether the whole contents of the VCLT are all customary international law of treaties as of the present time. Neither is it clear as to which parts of the VCLT should constitute customary law of treaties and which parts should not.

There have been reservations and declarations made by the parties to the VCLT.[28] Many of the reservations were made in relation to VCLT Article 66 concerning procedures for judicial settlement, arbitration and conciliation.[29] But their reservations did not limit to this article. Hence, at least, Article 66 of the VCLT, or at the most, all articles being reserved by its parties, should not be considered as representing customary rules of international law.

Arguably, other parts in the VCLT which had not been reserved by its Parties could be considered as representing the *current* customary rules of international

[27]*Supra* note 13.

[28]The reservations and declarations can be seen at *supra* note 17.

[29]VCLT Article 66 (entitled "Procedures for judicial settlement, arbitration and conciliation") provides:

If, under paragraph 3 of article 65, no solution has been reached within a period of 12 months following the date on which the objection was raised, the following procedures shall be followed:

(a) any one of the parties to a dispute concerning the application or the interpretation of articles 53 or 64 may, by a written application, submit it to the International Court of Justice for a decision unless the parties by common consent agree to submit the dispute to arbitration;
(b) any one of the parties to a dispute concerning the application or the interpretation of any of the other articles in Part V of the present Convention may set in motion the procedure specified in the Annexe to the Convention by submitting a request to that effect to the Secretary-General of the United Nations.

law, either because they were from the pre-existing customary rules or because they have achieved the status of customary law *through the very wide use and application of these rules*. This is also because for those VCLT provisions which had not been reserved by its Parties, there were no expressed objections to the codified contents in the Convention and hence a likely presumption is that countries do not disagree with the ILC's views on the scope and contents of customary international law for treaties as reflected in the VCLT.

3.4.2 The Treaty Interpretation Part *Has Become Codified Customary Rules*

For the treaty interpretation provisions in VCLT Articles 31–33, the first issue to be asked is whether they were the result of codification of the pre-existing customary international law at the time when the Convention was drafted or whether they were formulated by the ILC. The second issue to be asked is whether these provisions should be applied as the current (now existing) customary international law *even if* it is unclear as to whether these provisions were the codified version of the pre-existing customary international law.

Concerning the first issue about whether these provisions were codified from the pre-existing customary international law or were formulated by the ILC, a commentator states that[30]:

> Another result of progressive development is the rule of interpretation in article 31, which establishes, inter alia, the object and purpose of a treaty and the latter's context as guidelines of interpretation. These are teleological elements which militate against a narrow literal construction of treaty texts. It is noteworthy that the International Court of Justice stated in the Judgment on the Arbitral Award of 31 July 1989 that "…[a]rticles 31 and 32 of the Vienna Convention on the Law of Treaties…may in many respects be considered as a codification of existing customary international law…" (I.C.J. Reports 1991, pp. 69–70, para. 48). Yet, *it is not clear whether the Court was of the opinion that the custom had existed before the Vienna Convention and had been codified in it, or that it had been generated by it and was by now "existing"*. (Emphasis added)

Apparently, there was no clear consensus as to whether the contents in VCLT Articles 31–33 precisely reflect the customary international law which existed before the codification of the VCLT.

Concerning the second issue about whether Articles 31–33 should still be applied as the current customary international law, notwithstanding the fact that it is unclear as to whether they were codified from the pre-existing customary international law, there are two reasons to confirm that the provisions in these articles should be applied to all treaties in all international disputes between all disputing parties (whether or not they are also Parties to the VCLT). First, there has not been

[30]*Supra* note 16.

any Party to the VCLT having made any reservation or declaration concerning the treaty interpretation provisions in Articles 31 to 33 in the VCLT when they accepted and acceded to the Convention.[31] This shows the high consensus on the contents in these articles.

Second, there have been many international dispute settlement cases confirming the current status of treaty interpretation provisions in the VCLT that they constitute customary international law and hence these provisions should be applied to interpret treaty provisions whether or not there is any one of the disputing parties not being Party to the VCLT.

In the *Case concerning Kasikili/Sedudu Island* of 1999 between Botswana and Namibia, the International Court of Justice noted that notwithstanding the fact that both disputing parties were not Parties to the VCLT, both of them considered that Article 31 of the VCLT is applicable inasmuch as it reflects customary international law.[32]

There are many more WTO cases in which the Appellate Body confirmed that the treaty interpretation provisions in the VCLT are customary rules of treaty interpretation. In *US—Gasoline* of 1996, the Appellate Body of the WTO confirmed the customary international law status of *the provision in VCLT Article 31.1*,[33] although it did not mention whether the provisions were codified from the pre-existing customary rules. The Appellate Body states that:

> … The general rule of interpretation [i.e. that provided in VCLT Article 31.1] *has attained the status of a rule of customary or general international law*. As such, it forms part of the "customary rules of interpretation of public international law" which the Appellate Body has been directed, by Article 3(2) of the *DSU*, to apply in seeking to clarify the provisions

---

[31] *Supra* note 17.

[32] See para 18 in the judgement; at http://www.icj-cij.org/docket/index.php?sum=505&code=bona&p1=3&p2=3&case=98&k=b7&p3=5. Accessed 30 July 2017.

[33] The full text of VCLT Article 31 (entitled General rule of interpretation) is quoted below:

1. A treaty shall be interpreted in good faith in accordance with the ordinary meaning to be given to the terms of the treaty in their context and in the light of its object and purpose.
2. The context for the purpose of the interpretation of a treaty shall comprise, in addition to the text, including its preamble and annexes:
   (a) Any agreement relating to the treaty which was made between all the parties in connexion with the conclusion of the treaty;
   (b) Any instrument which was made by one or more parties in connexion with the conclusion of the treaty and accepted by the other parties as an instrument related to the treaty.
3. There shall be taken into account, together with the context:
   (a) Any subsequent agreement between the parties regarding the interpretation of the treaty or the application of its provisions;
   (b) Any subsequent practice in the application of the treaty which establishes the agreement of the parties regarding its interpretation;
   (c) Any relevant rules of international law applicable in the relations between the parties.
4. A special meaning shall be given to a term if it is established that the parties so intended.

> of the General Agreement and the other "covered agreements" of the Marrakesh Agreement Establishing the World Trade Organization (the "WTO Agreement"). That direction reflects a measure of recognition that the General Agreement is not to be read in clinical isolation from public international law.[34] (Emphasis added)

In *EC—Chicken Cuts* of 2005, the Appellate Body explained that *the whole provisions in Article 31* of the VCLT is the codified customary international law. It indicates that:

> … Interpretation pursuant to *the customary rules codified in Article 31 of the Vienna Convention* is ultimately a holistic exercise that should not be mechanically subdivided into rigid components. …[35] (Emphasis added)

In *Japan—Alcoholic Beverages II* of 1996, the Appellate Body re-confirmed the customary international law status of VCLT *Articles 31.1 and 32*,[36] without mentioning whether the contents of the VCLT provisions were from the pre-existing customary rules. The Appellate Body states that:

> Article 3.2 of the DSU directs the Appellate Body to clarify the provisions of GATT 1994 and the other "covered agreements" of the WTO Agreement "in accordance with customary rules of interpretation of public international law". Following this mandate, in *United States - Standards for Reformulated and Conventional Gasoline*, we stressed the need to achieve such clarification by reference to the fundamental rule of treaty interpretation set out in Article 31(1) of the Vienna Convention. We stressed there that *this general rule of interpretation "has attained the status of a rule of customary or general international law". There can be no doubt that Article 32 of the Vienna Convention, dealing with the role of supplementary means of interpretation, has also attained the same status.*[37] (Emphasis added)

In *US—Carbon Steel* of 2002, the Appellate Body further confirmed the customary international law status of *not only Article 31 of the VCLT, but also Article 32 of the Convention*. It indicates that:

> … we recall that Article 3.2 of the DSU recognizes that interpretative issues arising in WTO dispute settlement are to be resolved through the application of customary rules of interpretation of public international law. It is well settled in WTO case law that *the*

[34] Appellate Body Report, *United States—Standards for Reformulated and Conventional Gasoline*, at 17, WTO Doc. WT/DS2/AB/R (adopted 20 May 1996).

[35] Appellate Body Report. *European Communities—Customs Classification of Frozen Boneless Chicken Cuts*, para. 176, WTO Doc. WT/DS269/AB/R, WT/DS286/AB/R, WT/DS269/AB/R/Corr.1, WT/DS286/AB/R/Corr.1 (adopted 27 Sept 2005).

[36] The text of VCLT Article 32 (entitled "Supplementary means of interpretation") is quoted below:

Recourse may be had to supplementary means of interpretation, including the preparatory work of the treaty and the circumstances of its conclusion, in order to confirm the meaning resulting from the application of article 31, or to determine the meaning when the interpretation according to article 31:

(a) Leaves the meaning ambiguous or obscure; or
(b) Leads to a result which is manifestly absurd or unreasonable.

[37] Appellate Body Report, *Japan—Taxes on Alcoholic Beverages*, at 10, WTO Doc. WT/DS8/AB/R, WT/DS10/AB/R, WT/DS11/AB/R (adopted 1 Nov 1996).

principles codified in Articles 31 and 32 of the Vienna Convention on the Law of Treaties (the "Vienna Convention") are such customary rules. …[38] (Emphasis added)

In *US—Softwood Lumber IV* of 2004, the Appellate Body further confirmed that *Article 33*[39] of the VCLT is also part of customary international law. It states that:

> … in accordance with the *customary rule of treaty interpretation reflected in Article 33(3) of the Vienna Convention on the Law of Treaties* (the "Vienna Convention"), the terms of a treaty authenticated in more than one language — like the WTO Agreement— are presumed to have the same meaning in each authentic text. It follows that the treaty interpreter should seek the meaning that gives effect, simultaneously, to all the terms of the treaty, as they are used in each authentic language.[40] (Emphasis added)

3.4.3 Two Ways to Bring VCLT Articles 31–33 into a Dispute Settlement Procedure

There are two ways to bring VCLT Articles 31–33 into the operation and process of a dispute settlement procedure under international treaties. One possible way is to have a "*connecting provision*" in the dispute settlement rules impliedly or explicitly requiring the adjudicating body to apply these provisions. Another way is through the adjudicating body's direct application of these VCLT provisions as applicable customary international law.

For the purpose of discussion here, the term "*connecting provision*" means a provision in the disputed treaty to explicitly or impliedly require its adjudicator to apply the treaty interpretation provisions in the VCLT so as to connect the disputed treaty with the VCLT. Most dispute settlement rules do not include such

[38]Appellate Body Report, *United States—Countervailing Duties on Certain Corrosion-Resistant Carbon Steel Flat Products from Germany*, para. 61, WTO Doc. WT/DS213/AB/R, WT/DS213/AB/R/Corr.1 (adopted 19 Dec 2002).

[39]The text of VCLT Article 33 (entitled "Interpretation of treaties authenticated in two or more languages") is quoted below:

1. When a treaty has been authenticated in two or more languages, the text is equally authoritative in each language, unless the treaty provides or the parties agree that, in case of divergence, a particular text shall prevail.
2. A version of the treaty in a language other than one of those in which the text was authenticated shall be considered an authentic text only if the treaty so provides or the parties so agree.
3. The terms of the treaty are presumed to have the same meaning in each authentic text.
4. Except where a particular text prevails in accordance with paragraph 1, when a comparison of the authentic texts discloses a difference of meaning which the application of articles 31 and 32 does not remove, the meaning which best reconciles the texts, having regard to the object and purpose of the treaty, shall be adopted.

[40]Appellate Body Report, *United States—Final Countervailing Duty Determination with Respect to Certain Softwood Lumber from Canada*, para. 59, WTO Doc. WT/DS257/AB/R (adopted 17 Feb 2004).

"*connecting provision*" to require the application of the VCLT treaty interpretation provisions. But the dispute settlement rules under the WTO do consist of such "*connecting provision*", which is to impliedly require the interpretation of WTO agreements based on the provisions in VCLT Articles 31–33.

Article 3.2 of the DSU provides in part that "…The Members recognize that it serves to preserve the rights and obligations of Members under the covered agreements, and to clarify the existing provisions of those agreements in accordance with *customary rules of interpretation of public international law.*" (Emphasis added). Although it does not explicitly mention the application of VCLT Articles 31–33, the facts that it requires interpreting WTO agreements in accordance with customary rules of interpretation of public international law and that the provisions in these VCLT articles are the codified interpretation rules imply that the treaty interpreters under the WTO are required to apply these VCLT articles. So under the WTO, the introduction of VCLT Articles 31–33 into the interpretation activities is based on a "*connecting provision*" in DSU Article 3.2.

It must be noted that the kind of "*connecting provision*" as provided in DSU Article 3.2 is "not necessary" for the purpose of bringing VCLT articles into the operation of the dispute settlement proceedings under other treaties. For many other international treaties of which dispute settlement provisions do not contain such *connecting provision*, their treaty interpreters will still have to use the same VCLT articles to interpret the related treaty provisions. The lack of a "*connecting provision*" does not prevent the VCLT from being a set of *mandatory rules* governing treaty interpretation and being directly applied by the adjudicators.

Under the circumstances where there is no "*connecting provision*" in the disputed treaty, the adjudicators still have to apply the VCLT's treaty interpretation rules for two reasons. First, these rules are binding to the parties to the treaty in dispute (either because of their treaty obligations under the VCLT or because of their customary international law obligations) and hence they are binding to the adjudicators who are to interpret the disputed treaty and to decide the parties' rights and obligations under the treaty. Second, when contracting parties conclude the treaty, the interpretation rules in the VCLT should be considered as inherently attached to the treaty. In essence, treaty interpretation is to "find out" the correct meaning for a disputed treaty provision. The interpretation rules in the VCLT is to help find out such correct meaning. Hence, the application of the interpretation rules under the VCLT is an inherent part of the process of understanding the disputed treaty provisions.

3.4.4 The Codified Treaty Interpretation Rules also Need Interpretation

Judicial interpretation activities are basically conducted in connection with a normative written legal document. For treaty interpretation, there must be a treaty to be interpreted. If it is not about a treaty, but about a customary international rule, there is no treaty interpretation issue. Customary international law might need an "explanation" concerning its contents, meanings and scopes. But it is not an "interpretation" of customary international law.

However, the VCLT is different. Some provisions of it were from the pre-existing customary rules. Other provisions which were non-previously existing but formulated by the drafters have achieved the status of customary international law after the conclusion of the Convention. No matter whether a VCLT provision falls within the scope of previously existing customary international law or not, it could need interpretation if there is a doubt about the correct meaning of a term.

For instance, Article 31.1 of the VCLT provides that "A treaty shall be interpreted in good faith in accordance with the ordinary meaning to be given to the terms of the treaty in their context and in the light of its object and purpose." The term "context" has been further elaborated in Articles 31.2 and 31.3. But whether or not this term can be understood based on its "ordinary meaning" so as to further decide the scope of the term "context" (in addition to the scope provided in Articles 31.2 and 31.3) could be an issue. Also there could be issues concerning what are the *ordinary meanings* for the term "good faith" and even for the term "ordinary meaning" itself and what is the meaning and scope of the term "object-and-purpose" . They could also need interpretation. These will be further discussed in later chapters of this book (Chaps. 10–12).

3.5 Further Development of Treaty Interpretation Rules

At this stage, the codified contents of customary rules of treaty interpretation are reflected in VCLT Articles 31–33. This does not mean that there are no other practices, precedents and doctrines which can be qualified as the contents of customary international law rules on treaty interpretation. Neither should an inference be made that there need not be any further codification process so as to update the treaty interpretation rules in the Convention through introducing new elements into it.

In the next chapter, the book will argue the desirability of having another round of codification of certain treaty interpretation rules into the VCLT. Also in the chapters in Part II of this book, the author will further argue that there are some specific additional rules or doctrines concerning treaty interpretation which have achieved the status of customary international law of treaty interpretation or which should be useful rules (even they have not achieved such customary law status), and that it should be suitable for the international community to conduct a second round of codification to include these practices, precedents and doctrines into the VCLT.

Also in Part III of this book, the author will argue that there are new circumstances which justify the formulation and systematization of certain interpretation rules so as to progressively develop new elements for treaty interpretation. The apparent new circumstances are that the treaties in different fields of law are getting more and more diverse and fragmented, that they may conflict with each other and that there is a need to make such potentially conflicting international treaties coherent through treaty interpretation. Also it is important to recognize certain human values of high importance and to introduce such values into different treaties through interpretation. New rules for treaty interpretation to address such issues should be needed and could be formulated and codified for predicable and consistent use by different dispute settlement mechanisms.

References

1961 Harvard draft convention on the international responsibility of states for injuries to aliens. http://readinglists.ucl.ac.uk/items/46B29567-93F9-31C3-293E-4CB55932CF47.html. Accessed 30 July 2017

American Red Cross (2011) Summary of the Geneva conventions of 1949 and their additional protocols. Int Humanitarian Law. https://www.redcross.org/images/MEDIA_CustomProductCatalog/m3640104_IHL_SummaryGenevaConv.pdf. Accessed 30 July 2017

Draft convention on the prevention and punishment of the crime of developing, producing, acquiring, stockpiling, retaining, transferring or using biological or chemical weapons. http://www.sussex.ac.uk/Units/spru/hsp/documents/Draft%20Convention%20-%20English.pdf. Accessed 30 July 2017

FCTC. Parties to the WHO framework convention on tobacco control. http://www.who.int/fctc/signatories_parties/en/. Accessed 30 July 2017

http://www.icj-cij.org/docket/index.php?sum=505&code=bona&p1=3&p2=3&case=98&k=b7&p3=5. Accessed 30 July 2017

Lo C (2011) A private initiative of codification in international law—some ideas of the draft "convention on cross-border enforcement of international mediated settlement agreements". Chin (Taiwan) Yearb Int Law & Affairs 29:10–26

Meron T Customary Law. http://www.crimesofwar.org/a-z-guide/customary-law/. Accessed 30 July 2017

Schmalenbach K (2012) Article 4. Non-retroactive of the present convention. In: Dörr O, Schmalenbach K (eds) Vienna convention on the law of treaties: a commentary. Springer, New York, pp 81–88

Sinclair I (1984) The Vienna convention on the law of treaties, 2nd edn. Manchester University Press, Manchester

The Free Dictionary. http://legal-dictionary.thefreedictionary.com/codification. Accessed 30 July 2017

The Lectric Law Library. The common law. http://www.lectlaw.com/mjl/cm001.htm. Accessed 30 July 2017

U.S. Department of State. Vienna convention on the law of treaties. http://www.state.gov/s/l/treaty/faqs/70139.htm. Accessed 30 July 2017

United Nations Treaty Collection. https://treaties.un.org/Pages/ViewDetailsIII.aspx?src=TREATY&mtdsg_no=XXIII-1&chapter=23&Temp=mtdsg3&clang=_en. Accessed 30 July 2017

United Nations Treaty Collection. https://treaties.un.org/pages/ViewDetails.aspx?src=TREATY&mtdsg_no=XXIII-3&chapter=23&lang=en. Accessed 30 July 2017

United Nations. http://www.un.org/en/charter-united-nations/. Accessed 30 July 2017

United Nations. Member states. http://www.un.org/en/members/index.shtml. Accessed 30 July 2017

World Trade Organization. Members and observers. https://www.wto.org/english/thewto_e/whatis_e/tif_e/org6_e.htm. Accessed 30 July 2017

Zemanekm K (1969) Vienna convention on the law of treaties Vienna, 23 May 1969—Historical Context. http://legal.un.org/avl/ha/vclt/vclt.html. Accessed 30 July 2017

Chapter 4
Desirability and Some Principles for a New Round of Codification

Contents

4.1 The Elapse of a Long Period of Time Justifies a Review

As explained in the preceding chapter, the VCLT was drafted and adopted in 1960s and became effective in 1980. In the past half century when the VCLT was in place, there were many developments in international treaties. One of the developments is the rapid increase of the number of treaties. This development can be called the "proliferation of treaties". Another development is the getting wider and wider coverages of new treaties, many of which overlap in their subject matters and in their applications. This can be called the "proliferation of treaty coverages". Yet another development is the rapid increase in the number of international disputes under various treaties. This can be called the "proliferation of international disputes".

Currently, there are thousands of treaties of different forms, including bilateral, regional and multilateral. At least hundreds of treaties are still in active operation. Many of the treaties currently in active operation were concluded in the past decades. Most notably, some human rights treaties, the WTO agreements, many bilateral and regional free trade agreements (FTAs) and economic cooperation

C. Lo, *Treaty Interpretation Under the Vienna Convention on the Law of Treaties*,
https://doi.org/10.1007/978-981-10-6866-9_4

agreements, many bilateral investment treaties (BITs), many regional and multilateral environmental protection treaties, and many international health treaties were conclude in the recent two decades. When ILC drafted the VCLT, it might not have envisaged the rapid development of international treaties concerning their huge number and their diverse but overlapping subject matters.

Although the rapidness of the increasing number of treaties does not necessarily affect the principles of treaty interpretation, at least such expended number of treaties creates the possibilities that the current rules might not be sufficient to address various interpretation issues arising from the newly emerged subject matters in the treaties or from the potential conflicts between different treaties.

Also in the past decades, there have been even more rapidly increasing number of international disputes arising from the application and interpretation of treaties. The apparent example reflecting such development of proliferation of disputes is the frequently-relied-on dispute settlement procedure under the WTO. The number of complaints raised under the WTO is remarkably high. Since the establishment of the WTO in 1995, there have already been more than 500 complaints raised by WTO Members. Against these complaints, over 350 rulings have been issued by the Dispute Settlement Body in accordance with the Panels' or Appellate Body's recommendations.[1]

The large number of international disputes having occurred in the past is both a challenge and a contribution to the treaty interpretation issues and practices. It is a challenge because that the disputing parties (often assisted by external legal counsels) are able to sophistically identify, bring up and argue various treaty interpretation issues to make the disputes more and more complicated. Many of these issues were new and innovative at the time when the disputes were conducted. The treaty interpreters had to decide the appropriate use of the provisions in Articles 31 to 33 of the VCLT to address such issues.

It is also a contribution because the adjudicators were pushed to make many of the uncertain aspects of treaty interpretation much more certain and clear. For instance, it was the Appellate Body of the WTO which clarified and confirmed the customary international law status of VCLT Articles 31 to 33, as explained in the preceding chapter of this book. The Appellate Body's view has contributed to a wider recognition of the status of the VCLT's treaty interpretation provisions.

In any event, it is timely for the international community to review whether there are certain new understandings of the VCLT provisions which need to be integrated into the current interpretation rules so as to make the current treaty interpretation norms clearer and more predictable.

Also even after fifty years of operation of the VCLT, there are still areas where the treaty interpretation provisions in Articles 31 to 33 of the Convention are considered not clear. From this perspective, the VCLT itself needs interpretation. This also justifies a review of the current rules to assess whether there is a proper

[1]Dispute Settlement 2017.

ground to further codify certain rules to help understand the current provisions in the VCLT.

4.2 Traditional Issues in Which Further Codifications Are Needed

4.2.1 Areas in Which the VCLT Is Still Uncertain

Treaty interpretation is guided by Articles 31 through 33 in Sect. 3 (entitled "Interpretation of Treaties") of the VCLT. The fundamental rule is provided in Article 31.1, which requires that a treaty shall be interpreted in good faith in accordance with the ordinary meaning to be given to the terms of the treaty in their context and in the light of its object and purpose. This rule lays the foundation for treaty interpretation. Throughout the discussions in the book (especially in Chaps. 10–12), there will be many more elaborations on the terms/phrases of "good faith" , "ordinary meaning" , "context" and "object-and-purpose".

Briefly, the book will argue that the meaning of the term "ordinary meaning" used in VCLT Article 31.1 needs interpretation; that the scope of the "context" as provided in Articles 31.1, 31.2 and 31.3 also needs clarification; that the method of identifying the "object-and-purpose" as required in Article 31.1 needs to be further developed; that the good faith principle and the hierarchical or holistic relation among the "ordinary meaning", the "context" and the "object-and-purpose" of an interpreted provision or of the interpreted treaty as a whole also need clarification. These are unclear aspects directly arising from the provisions of the VCLT.

A codification to include certain new rules to clarify these uncertain aspects will help treaty interpreters and the disputing parties to correctly and consistently apply provisions in Articles 31 to 33 so as to make the outcome of applying these rules more consistent and hence to make the result of the settlement of dispute more predictable.

4.2.2 Areas Where There Is a Need to Codify the Current Jurisprudence

In addition to the above, there are some other traditional interpretation problems which are not addressed by the VCLT. For instance, there are many vague and "indefinite legal concepts" used in different treaties, such as "necessary" and "public moral". When interpreting these vague and indefinite legal concepts, an adjudicator is not merely to look for other terms or phrases so as to help understand the meanings of these concepts. Treaty interpreters need to provide certain elements or to create some formulas to serve as the basis to ensure that the application of such indefinite concepts will be in line with the appropriate meanings given to them. Such practice of providing elements or creating certain formulas to decide the meaning and application of a treaty term in the interpretation process has been very common. In such formulas or elements, certain balancing schemes are usually built in.

For instance, concerning some paragraphs in Article XX of the General Agreement on Tariffs and Trade (GATT) 1994, the Appellate Body and some dispute settlement panels under the WTO have formulated detailed contents of "necessity test" for the purpose of deciding whether a challenged measure has been necessary for the protection of public moral or for the protection of human, animal or plant life or health.

The VCLT does not address this kind of issues. But there has been jurisprudence developed to require treaty interpreter to follow certain formula so as to interpret and apply treaty provisions. It should be useful to have some guidance in the VCLT so as to reflect the need of developing formulas to interpret some "indefinite legal concepts" .

This is only an example to show that certain jurisprudence could be of high value to help adjudicator interpret certain abstract treaty provisions. There could be other jurisprudence of similar value developed by other international tribunals which is qualified to become a set of written rules to help interpretation of treaty provisions. The related issues will be discussed in Chap. 16 of this book.

4.2.3 Areas Where VCLT Is not Sufficient to Address the Issues

The treaty interpretation rules provided in the VCLT are designed to address those treaties governing the relations between their contracting parties (such as trade and investment relations of the contracting parties) and governing their behaviours (such as contracting parties' practices of human rights protection). A treaty interpretation problem arising from the VCLT is its failure to consider the different natures of the interpreted treaties. For those treaties governing the relations between the contracting parties, maintaining the proper balance between them so as not to "restrike" a new balance through treaty interpretation is of high importance, whereas for those treaties governing the behaviours of the contracting parties (especially concerning human rights protection), it is sometimes more important to ensure the "living treaty" so that States will not be able to easily escape from their international obligations. The related issues will be further elaborated in Chap. 13 of the book.

Also the book will argue that there is a group of treaties which govern private (contractual) relations (such as those treaties governing international sales of goods) or procedural issues of private disputes (such as those treaties governing the choice of courts). The book calls them "treaties for private matters". These treaties are interpreted and applied by domestic courts or by commercial or civil arbitral tribunals. The book will explain in Chap. 9 that the VCLT is not a proper basis for domestic courts or for commercial or civil arbitral tribunals to interpret such treaties. There must be different rules deciding the proper interpretation of such treaties. The book is to develop the rules and considerations for their interpretation.

Also when a treaty is negotiated and concluded, it reflects the surrounding circumstances of the time of its negotiation and conclusion. As time goes by, society evolved and technology developed. Treaty interpretation issue involving a time factor arises concerning whether and when jurisprudence established in previous time should be revised due to the change of surrounding circumstances; whether a treaty must be interpreted "in the light of the circumstances at the time of its conclusion" ("contemporaneous interpretation") or "in the light of the circumstances at the time of its application" ("evolutive interpretation") . Although a change of circumstances might not necessarily be caused by technology development, actually technology evolution has caused the main problem. There are other interpretation issues arising from technology development, such as whether technological neutrality should play a role in deciding the ordinary meaning of a treaty term, in serving as the context, and in identifying the object-and-purpose for the interpreted provision. The related issues will be addressed in Chap. 15 of this book.

4.3 Issues Arising from Increasing Number of New Treaties

4.3.1 New Situations and the Associated Uncertainty

In addition to the traditional issues mentioned above, treaty interpretation encounters new situations (such as the diversification and fragmentation of international treaties) and challenges (such as the need of coordination between different treaties and the need of introducing external values into a treaty through treaty interpretation process).

In addition to the increasing number of treaties, as explained in the outset of this chapter, there are some other phenomena in the last couple of decades in the field of international law. These phenomena have apparent implications for treaty interpretation process.

The first widely identified phenomenon is the expansion of international law in the form of new treaties, which is reflected in the swiftly growing numbers of bilateral, regional and multilateral agreements in different fields, such as international trade, international investment, public health, environment, labor protection, and human rights, among others. Merely in these fields, there are already many thousands of treaties. They are still expanding. These keep government officials and international law professors very busy in engaging in negotiations, in implementing the new rules as well as in identifying and resolving their related problems.

The second phenomenon is the emerging new fields of international norms, which make international law more diverse. A salient example of the new international law rules is the international legislations for public health protection. The rules include the FCTC (including its protocol and many sets of its guidelines) as well as the International Health Regulations (IHR), all of which were concluded in the last decade or so. The expansion and diversification phenomenon is commonly called the "fragmentation" of international law. This term tends to be too negative in looking at the trend. The book sees the trend as a necessary and healthy development. It is necessary because new issues of international concern need collective efforts from international community and the most effective way of coordinating collective efforts is to create new international conventions, treaties or agreements. The expansion and diversification of international law through codification process is also a healthy development because creating international norms is a process of reaching consensus, which helps cooperation and coordination among countries.

The third phenomenon is a reverse trend of integration of international law in different fields through incorporating and bringing other international norms into a treaty system. This is occurring in the context of FTAs, especially in most of those concluded in the last two decades. In these FTAs, not only trade liberalizations and their respective trade rules are included, but also chapters or provisions to introduce international labor laws, investment rules, environmental treaties, competition rules, and even human rights protection into these agreements are their essential and important parts.

This is also a very positive development, because when different fields of international law are integrated into a single treaty of FTA, their respective rules can be mutually supportive in its operation and interpretation. This is not merely to avoid possible conflicts between different treaties, but also to incorporate important values (such as human rights and labour protection), which could originally be external to the FTA, into an FTA as its core components. For instance, when a matter concerning whether a trade measure for environmental purpose is justified under an FTA needs to be decided, a tribunal under the FTA will be able to apply or take into account those environmental rules which have been incorporated into this FTA. The outcome of the dispute can be reasonably expected to be consistent with both the trade provisions in the FTA and the cited or incorporated international environmental norms.

When there are expansion and diversification of international law rules, jurisdictional overlaps and normative inconsistences or conflicts occur more constantly. A trade measure authorized by an environmental or public health treaty may be challenged under a trade agreement. A public health measure may also be challenged under an investment treaty.

Such jurisdictional overlaps and normative conflicts are not merely theoretical possibilities. They have actually happened in recent years. For instance, Uruguay had been challenged by a big international tobacco company through investor-State arbitration under a BIT because of its adoption of extensive pictorial warning requirements on cigarette which are in line with the recommendation of the FCTC.[2] Australia had also been challenged by the same big tobacco company through investor-State arbitration under a BIT for its adoption of plain packaging requirements suggested by the FCTC and its guidelines. The tobacco company alleged that the packaging requirements violate Australia's obligations under the investment treaty.[3] Australia's plain packaging requirements are also challenged by Ukraine, Honduras, Cuba, the Dominican Republic, and Indonesia under the DSU of the WTO. These countries allege that the measures are in breach of the Agreement on the Trade-Related Aspects of Intellectual Property Rights (the TRIPS Agreement).[4] There could be more and more such conflicts. Unless certain rules to deal with the problem are clearly established, there will be uncertainties arising from these conflicts.

First, countries do not know what to follow if they have no idea about which rules prevail, jurisdictionally or substantively. Second, there will be hesitation for countries to engage in cooperate in new areas of common interest and to develop new rules in these fields. Third, there will be uncertainty in the enforcement and implementation of existing rules. To put it more straightforward, a major international law issue nowadays concerns the uncertainty arising from the vastly increasing diversity of international treaties.

Although it was mentioned above that there is a trend of integration of international law in different fields through incorporating or bringing other international norms into FTAs, such integration of international laws occurs only on bilateral and regional levels and is not sufficient. For instance, the FCTC and its protocol and guidelines are basically not integrated into FTAs. Also there is no such trend of "integrating different norms into a single treaty" at the multilateral level. For instance, the WTO has not been explicitly referring to international treaties in environment, public health and other fields to help decide its application and operation. The remaining possible way of addressing treaty conflict issues and to ease the uncertainty problem at the present time is to rely on treaty interpretation based on the existing rules.

Briefly, the treaty interpretation rules provide in Articles 31 and 32 of the VCLT could theoretically be relied on so as to coordinate the jurisdictional and substantive conflicts. The method is to take into account international norms in the fields of public health, environment and others which are external to a treaty system (such as the WTO and the related BITs), so as to help understand the ordinary meaning of WTO and BIT provisions and terms; or to take such external norms as "any relevant

---

[2]In its investment dispute with the tobacco company, Uruguay won the case in 2016. See Mander (2016).

[3]In its investment dispute with the tobacco company, Australia won the case in 2015. See Smyth (2015).

[4]In this WTO case, Australia further won the case at the Panel level. The Panel Report has not been make public at the time of writing of this chapter on 31 July 2017. But news report has indicated that the WTO's dispute settlement panel for this case has decided to support Australia's plain packaging cigarette requirement. See Miles and Geller (2017).

rules of international law applicable in the relations between the parties" as provided in Article 31.3(c). The related issues will be further addressed in Chap. 19 of this book.

4.3.2 Searching for Solutions Through Treaty Interpretation

For the purpose of this Chapter, it should be useful to briefly explain the use of treaty interpretation in the above example. The alleged violation by the five WTO Members against Australia for its plain package requirements for tobacco products is mainly in TRIPS Article 20 which requires that the use of a trademark in the course of trade shall not be unjustifiably encumbered by special requirements. This is understood as requiring countries to refrain from imposing requirements which could cause unjustifiable encumbrance. The problem is whether the packaging-related measure is "unjustifiable encumbrance" to the use of a trademark. The key issue here is the proper interpretation of "unjustifiability". Also TRIPS Article 8 provides in part that "Members may … adopt measures necessary to protect public health …" An important question is how to interpret the "necessity" requirement so as to decide whether a packaging-related regulatory measure is necessary to protect public health.

Another set of rules is the BITs, most of which require some minimum or heightened standards to be extended to investors and their investments, which include intellectual property rights. Some commonly found standards of protection in BITs include "fair and equitable treatment" and compensation for direct and indirect expropriation. An important question in this context is the proper understanding of "fair and equitable treatment" and the compensable "indirect expropriation" vis-à-vis the non-compensable state's right to regulation so as to decide whether the packaging-related regulatory measures are permitted or not under BITs.

The requirements and conditions of intellectual property protection in these two sets of rules are different. But they also have a similar issue, i.e. whether and to what extent the legitimate regulatory purpose and other relevant factors required or suggested by another treaty can be introduced into the interpretation of these terms and phrases.

The "unjustifiable encumbrance" or the "necessity to protect public health" under the TRIPS Agreement and the "fair and equitable treatment" as well as compensable or non-compensable exercise of State's right to regulate under BITs must be understood in consideration of the fundamental external values and rules established in other international treaties widely participated by WTO Members.

In other words, the contents in other international norms should be able to shed light to and to help understand the interpreted terms of "unjustifiability" or "necessity" in TRIPS and "fair and equitable", and State's right to regulate. More specifically, if a measure is required or recommended by a treaty (such as the packaging measure recommended by the FCTC), such measure should enjoy some kind of presumption of compliance with the requirements under the TRIPS Agreement and the BITs through treaty interpretation methods.

However, there are shortages in this treaty interpretation approach of inter-treaty coordination. First, there is uncertainty in expecting treaty interpreters to allow FCTC to shed light to the terms in the TRIPS Agreement and BITs. It is still the fact that the WTO, relevant BITs and other international dispute settlement mechanisms have not established such jurisprudence of allowing other treaty systems to systemically shed light to the interpreted treaty provisions.

Second, even if a treaty interpreter allows FCTC to shed light on these terms, the weight to be given to the FCTC in deciding the ordinary meaning of these terms is not predictable. Third, although there is a possibility to consider the FCTC and its protocol and guidelines as "any relevant rules of international law applicable in the relations between the parties" provided in VCLT Article 31.3(c), the uncertainty is still obvious, because FCTC's guidelines are not binding and might not be qualified as "rules of international law". Also the FCTC parties and WTO members are not exactly the same. So the FCTC might not be qualified as meeting the requirement "applicable in the relations between the parties". So we need to consider whether there must be new rules of treaty interpretation being introduced into a treaty system (such as the WTO or a specific BIT).

The book argues that it is desirable to have some interpretation rules to address such jurisdictional overlaps and normative conflicts and to remove the uncertainty.

4.4 The Desirability in Summary and Some Principles

4.4.1 The Desirability in Summary

For traditional interpretation issues, the current provisions in VCLT Articles 31 and 32 involve certain unclear and uncertain elements. These "interpretation provisions" themselves need interpretation. Also, the VCLT is not appropriate to address the interpretation issues of "treaties of private matters". The existing jurisprudence under the current rules is not sufficient to cope with the time factor and the issues related to technological development.

For new situations arising from the conflicting rules in different treaty systems, there is also a need to establish certain interpretation rules. First, conflicts between treaties are vastly undesirable. There must be coordination mechanism. Second, there are shortages to resolve such conflicts through current treaty interpretation rules as explained above. So treaty interpreters are not able to fully rely on the current interpretation rules. The book will argue that there is a desperate need to have some interpretation rules to address such jurisdictional overlaps and normative conflicts and to remove the uncertainty.

In addition, treaty interpretation is not a mechanical procedure to include inputs, processes and outputs so as to produce a mechanically consistent and standardized result. Treaty interpretation process involves various elements of evaluation and selections of values. For instance, there could be two or more "ordinary meanings" for a treaty term defined in the dictionary. A treaty interpreter will have to decide the "most appropriate ordinary meaning" to be applied to the text.

Since a treaty interpreter will have to make decisions in searching for and selecting the "right" meaning or the "most appropriate" understanding of a treaty term in fulfilling his/her job, it is not possible to exclude the situation that the values or positions regarding the subject matter held by the interpreter play a key role in the process. In other words, treaty interpretation is supposed to be objective and of value-neutrality, but it sometimes cannot avoid a choice of value.

Based on this premise, the author will further suggest in Chap. 18 of this book that there must be new rules to explicitly allow universally established fundamental human values (including human rights provided in human rights treaties, public health provided in widely accepted public health treaties, and sustainability provided in widely adopted environmental agreements) to be introduced into the interpretation of other treaties so that such values can be formally taken into account in the process, instead of introducing these values into the interpreted terms merely through relying on the understanding of their ordinary meaning.

4.4.2 Some Principles for the Next Round of Codification

The ultimate argument of this book is that there must be a new round of codification to address the treaty interpretation issues listed above. The book is of the view that there are some principles to be followed when conducting the new round of codification.

First, there must be much detailed and comprehensive rules to address treaty interpretation issues. Currently there are only three articles in the VCLT addressing the vastly wide range of treaty interpretation issues. Hence, many aspects of the treaty interpretation issues are not addressed in these articles. The results of the new round of codification should include a bigger set of rules so as to cover various aspects of interpretation issues.

Second, there must be a proper balance between detailed rules and the needed flexibility. The book is not arguing for an absolute and rigid set of rules for treaty interpretation. As will be explained in Chap. 17 of the book, a certain extent of flexibility to allow treaty interpreter to conduct an overall assessment should be necessary when he/she engages in the interpretation exercise. However, it must also be equally important that the flexibility should not undermine the need of certainty and predictability. A clearer rules to provide various factors of considerations and to help weigh the importance of various factors would help achieve a predictable outcome arising from treaty interpretation.

Third, there must be a mechanism to allow periodical review of the operation of existing treaty interpretation rules. It can be predicted that even if there could be a new round of codification, there will be new systemic issues occurred which need new interpretation rules to address the problem. Definitely codification should not be made as a simultaneous and constant response to new situations, because this would create an adverse effect of making treaty interpretation rules uncertain. So the intervals between different rounds of codification should not be too short. However, it might not be desirable either, if there will be another fifty years to wait for new clear rules to address new interpretation issues. After all, not all treaty interpreters are masters in the field of international law. Many of them (including international arbitrators who are appointed on a case-by-case basis and those domestic judges who encounter treaty interpretation issues only once or a couple of times in their entire careers) do not have much expertise and experience in sophisticatedly develop their theories and approaches to interpret treaty provisions when the VCLT provisions are not sufficient or unclear so as to provide basis for treaty interpretation. A clearer and more comprehensive set of codified rules, which are updated from time to time, should help the proper implementation of treaties.

References

Dispute settlement. https://www.wto.org/english/tratop_e/dispu_e/dispu_e.htm. Accessed 8 Aug 2017

Mander B (2016) Uruguay defeats Philip Morris test case lawsuit. Financ Times. https://www.ft.com/content/1ae33bc8-454e-11e6-9b66-0712b3873ae1. Accessed 8 Aug 2017

Miles T, Geller M (2017) Australia wins landmark WTO tobacco packaging case. http://www.reuters.com/article/us-wto-tobacco-australia-idUSKBN1801S9. Accessed 8 Aug 2017

Smyth J (2015) Australia wins legal battle over plain cigarette packs. Financ Times. https://www.ft.com/content/b0742d48-a542-11e5-9101-8718f09f6ece. Accessed 8 Aug 2017

Part II
Existing Issues to Be Subject to Codified Rules

Chapter 5
Boundary of Treaty Interpretation and the Possible Codification

Contents

5.1 Approaches/Schools of Treaty Interpretation and the Theoretical Boundary

5.1.1 Approaches/Schools of Treaty Interpretation

Adjudicators need to make the governing/applicable provisions clear to the disputing parties so as to resolve their dispute. But the problem is in what way they are to make the provisions clear. There are different schools or approaches for making clear (i.e. interpreting) a legal provision. Different interpretation approaches could lead to vastly different results. The difference mainly arises from their diverse focuses either on the textual wording of the interpreted provision, the context of it, the objective of the rule, or the drafter's intent.[1]

The first school of treaty interpretation is "textualism", which focuses on the text of the interpreted treaty. It pays less attention to other aspects (such as context and

[1]For the discussions of the schools of treaty interpretation, see International Judicial Monitor. Treaty Interpretation. http://www.judicialmonitor.org/archive_0906/generalprinciples.html. Accessed 8 Aug 2017. See also Baofu (2010), p. 148.

C. Lo, *Treaty Interpretation Under the Vienna Convention on the Law of Treaties*,
https://doi.org/10.1007/978-981-10-6866-9_5

objective of an interpreted provision). As will be discussed in Chap. 10 of the book, the textual wording of a treaty should be the starting point for its interpretation. It is because the textual wording is the interpreted subject matter and forms the basis of an interpretation activity. Whether or not an interpretation can or should go beyond the textual wording is another issue. But an interpretation activity can never ignore the existence of the textual wording and the essence of that has been implied from the wording. For instance, the intationalist approach (i.e. an approach to look at the drafter's intent) suggests to go beyond the words of a treaty. The purposive interpretation (i.e. an approach to look at the object-and-purpose of the interpreted provision) could go further beyond the textual wording. But they all begin with understanding and clarifying the textual meaning of the interpreted provision. Textualism puts a predominant weight to the wording of the interpreted provision and puts much less weight to other aspects of the interpreted provision (such as the context of the interpreted term, the object-and-purpose of the treaty, and the preparatory works of the interpreted term).

Narrowly speaking, textualism requires treaty interpreters to focus merely on the interpreted provision and to rely on the ordinary/plain meaning of such textual wording. Hence, textualism is basically an "objective approach", which is to rely on the objective appearance of the text of a treaty provision. Textualism is also a "restrictive interpretation" because it relies on the texts only or predominantly, and not others. The result would also lead to restrictiveness, because the context, the object-and-purpose, and the preparatory works will not be used to expand the scope of the interpreted provision.

Broadly speaking, textualism also expects treaty interpreter to look at different provisions in the same treaty. In other words, textualism can be seen as purely focusing on the interpreted text; it can also be perceived as embracing "contextualism" to see other part of the whole text so as to find the proper meaning of the interpreted provisions. But the contextual approach can also be seen as a part of "subjective approach", which takes into account not only the cause underlying the treaty, but also the context.

Both textual wording and contextual arrangement of a treaty are the main approaches required by Article 31.1 of the VCLT, which states in part that: "A treaty shall be interpreted … in accordance with the ordinary meaning to be given to the terms of the treaty in their context …" But in practice, Article 31 gives the highest weight to the textual wording.

The second school is "intentionalism", which expects treaty interpreters to look at the intent of the drafters. This is a "subjective approach" since it requires to look at the negotiators' intent at the time when the treaty was negotiated. One way of understanding the intent of the treaty negotiators is to look at the preparatory works (travaux préparatoires). However, it must be noted that intentionalism is not the main approach for treaty interpretation. Under the VCLT, preparatory works are only a secondary means for interpreting treaty provisions. They are used only when an interpretation based on Article 31 would lead to unclear or unreasonable results. VCLT Article 32 reads:

> Recourse may be had to supplementary means of interpretation, including *the preparatory work* of the treaty and the circumstances of its conclusion, in order to confirm the meaning resulting from the application of article 31, or to determine the meaning when the interpretation according to article 31:
>
> (a) leaves the meaning ambiguous or obscure; or
> (b) leads to a result which is manifestly absurd or unreasonable.
>
> (Emphasis added)

For multilateral and plurilateral treaties, textualism is definitely more preferred. This is due to the fact that multilateral and plurilateral treaties had been negotiated by some or many States, but not necessarily by all participating countries. Many parties to such treaties could be those which joined such treaties long after the conclusion of the negotiations. Since those countries which participated in or accede to a treaty at a later stage did not engage in the drafting process, they might not have access to the full scope of preparatory works and might not know the original intents of the drafters or negotiators. Their reasonable expectation is that they will be bound by the textual wording. Others can also only expect the acceding countries to observe the text of the treaty, not the preparatory documents. It would not be fair to the acceding countries if the operation of such treaties is still closely linked to the drafters' intent through treaty interpretation after (or even long after) their conclusions.

But for bilateral treaties, negotiators' intent becomes far more relevant and important. It is because the original intent of the negotiators was the reason and the cause to conclude such bilateral treaties and to formulate the provisions in certain ways. The drafters/negotiators were all from the contracting parties and were representing them in the negotiation process. Hence, in a dispute arising from a bilateral treaty, an adjudicator must (or is justified to) put more weight on the negotiators' intent through looking at the preparatory works for its negotiations. The VCLT fails to consider that the different types of treaties could justify or require different weights to be put on the drafters' intent.

The third school is the "teleological approach" or "purposivism", which expects treaty interpreters to look at the object-and-purpose of an interpreted treaty or an interpreted provision (i.e. the fundamental cause to conclude such treaty or such provision) or to look at the main underlying problem to be addressed by such treaty or by such provision. Since the approach is to look for an interpretation that best suits the goal of the interpreted treaty, it is also called "effective interpretation." This approach is also one of the main approaches required by VCLT Article 31.1 which states in part that; "A treaty shall be interpreted … in the light of its object and purpose."

5.1.2 The Theoretical Boundary

The above mentioned schools/approaches are not necessarily mutually exclusive. They overlap among each other in that basically each school still considers others as its supplementary. The difference among them is mainly that they emphasize one element over the other.[2]

From the perspective of the VCLT, no single one approach is exclusively relied on for treaty interpretation. Textualism, contextualism and purposivism are concurrently used in a holistic manner. But the intentionalism is used as a secondary means. However, the requirement of interpreting treaty in a good faith manner can also be interpreted as expecting the reliance on the drafters' intent. The specific meanings of these interpretation methods and their relations will be further discussed in Chaps. 10–12 and 17 of this book.

There are two aspects to further explain these approaches from the perspective of setting the boundary for treaty interpretation.

First, these approaches should serve as the main body of treaty interpretation rules. But there should also be other rules not directly related to these approaches. For instance, there are some Latin maxims which are applied as rules of "legal interpretation" and "legal application" both in domestic context for statutory interpretation and in international context for treaty interpretation, such as *lex specialis derogat legi generali* (meaning that the special law repeals the general laws),[3] *lex posterior derogat legi priori* (meaning that a later law repeals an earlier law),[4] and *expressio unius est exclusio alterius* (meaning that the inclusion of the one is the exclusion of the other),[5] *ut res magis valeat quam pereat* (meaning that law in general, and rights and obligations thereunder, should be effective rather than not),[6] *in dubio mitius* (meaning of more leniently in case of doubt),[7] and *exceptio est strictissimae applicationis* (meaning that an exception is of the strictest application).[8]

These rules are mainly for treaty interpretation. But many of them are also for treaty application because many of them are the rules for the adjudicator to decide

---

[2]Tumonis (2012), p. 114.

[3]Fellmeth and Horwitz (published on line, 2011) Guide to Latin in International Law. http://www.oxfordreference.com/view/10.1093/acref/9780195369380.001.0001/acref-9780195369380-e-1303 . Accessed 8 Aug 2017.

[4]Id. https://www.google.com.tw/webhp?sourceid=chrome-instant&ion=1&ie=UTF-8&rct=j#q=lex+posterior+derogat+legi+priori+oxford+reference&*. Accessed 8 Aug 2017.

[5]Id. http://www.oxfordreference.com/view/10.1093/acref/9780199664924.001.0001/acref-9780199664924-e-1494?rskey=S4FPOs&result=1638. Accessed 8 Aug 2017.

[6]Id. http://www.oxfordreference.com/view/10.1093/oi/authority.20110810104822397. Accessed 8 Aug 2017.

[7]Id. http://www.oxfordreference.com/view/10.1093/acref/9780195369380.001.0001/acref-9780195369380-e-910. Accessed 8 Aug 2017.

[8]Id. http://www.oxfordreference.com/view/10.1093/acref/9780195369380.001.0001/acref-9780195369380-e-731. Accessed 8 Aug 2017.

how to correctly define the relations between different treaty provisions and to decide which one of the relevant rules is applicable. The issue concerning the difference and relations between treaty application and treaty interpretation will be addressed in Chap. 6 of this book.

These interpretation rules to constitute additional treaty interpretation rules will further be discussed in Chap. 14 of this book. But these rules do not have much to do with the above mentioned textualism, contextualism, purposivism and intentionalism. In other words, although these schools or approaches of treaty interpretation are fundamental, they do not form an outer limit of scope or boundary for treaty interpretation.

Second, although there are theoretical debates about whether to adopt textualism, contextualism, purposivism, or intentionalism, apparently, the VCLT has already taken a position on such matter. The VCLT's approach is a mixture of various approaches. It relies more on the objective approaches (i.e. textualism and contextualism), but it also uses subjective approaches (i.e. purposivism and intentionalism) to support the objective interpretation. It is suggested that:

> They [VCLT Articles 31–33] give preference to objective over subjective interpretation, with Article 31 making a treaty's text the main source of its construction. This textualism, somewhat mitigated by the fact that Article 31 permits resort to context and subsequent practice, has been the primary cause of criticism levelled against the Vienna rules; proponents of a subjective method, focusing on the parties' intent, labelled it 'the grossest exercise of arbitrary formalism'. … arguably the holistic approach of Article 31 includes all major schools of interpretation, namely textualism ('ordinary meaning') , teleology ('object and purpose') and, less explicitly, intentionalism ('good faith').[9]

The bottom line is that an interpreter will have to conduct an overall or holistic assessment after taking all relevant subjective and objective factors into consideration so as to make a proper interpretation.

5.2 Internal Boundary for Treaty Interpretation

5.2.1 Constrained by a Meaning Decided by the Parties or by a Definition Provided in the Same Treaty or in a Separate Treaty

Treaties are basically interpreted by international adjudicators in connection with their exercise of judicial or quasi-judicial functions, such as the exercise of the dispute settlement function by the International Court of Justice or by the WTO's panel or Appellate Body. But this is not the only situation of treaty interpretation. A treaty can be interpreted by the contracting parties collectively through a separate mechanism, or interpreted by the treaty itself through providing definitions in the

[9]Aust et al. (2014), pp. 80–81.

text of the treaty or even interpreted by a separate treaty within the same treaty system. These defining mechanism and definitional provision serve as a boundary for treaty interpretation by the adjudicators. The book calls such situations as "internal boundary" because they are the limits set forth by the treaty itself, either through a mechanism created by the same treaty, or through a definition provided within the same treaty or within a related treaty in the same treaty system.

The first internal boundary is the limit set forth through a mechanism created by the same treaty. There are treaties under which their contracting parties collectively have the final determination on the meaning of their treaty provisions. If the contracting parties in a bilateral treaty jointly or the contracting parties in a plurilateral or multilateral treaty collectively decide the meaning of a treaty term, the treaty interpreter will have to be bound by such meaning when he/she exercises the treaty interpretation activities. The reason for such mechanism being built into a treaty is to ensure that the contracting parties, which created the treaty, should have the ultimate say, in a collective way, about the meaning of the treaty provision which affects the operation of the treaty as well as their rights and obligations thereunder.

A salient example of a treaty to include a mechanism to give the supreme authoritativeness to the contracting parties' collective interpretation of the treaty provision is in the Agreement Establishing the World Trade Organization, Article IX:2 of which provides in part that:

> The Ministerial Conference and the General Council shall have *the exclusive authority to adopt interpretations* of this Agreement and of the Multilateral Trade Agreements. In the case of an interpretation of a Multilateral Trade Agreement in Annex 1, they shall exercise their authority on the basis of a recommendation by the Council overseeing the functioning of that Agreement. The decision to adopt an interpretation shall be taken by a three-fourths majority of the Members… (Emphasis added)

If the Ministerial Conference or the General Council of the WTO has adopted an interpretation on a provision or term in any one of the WTO agreements, the WTO's dispute settlement panel or its Appellate Body will be bound by such interpretation when it handles a dispute and applies the relevant WTO provision. This topic will be further addressed in connection with the issue of non-adjudicating body's interpretation of treaty provisions in Chap. 8 of this book.

The second boundary is the limit set forth by a definition provided within the same treaty. In many treaties, there are definitional provisions. For instance, in the Agreement on Trade in Services (GATS), there is a definition on the phrase "trade in services". It provides in Article I:2 the following:

> For the purposes of this Agreement, trade in services is defined as the supply of a service:
>
> (a) from the territory of one Member into the territory of any other Member;
> (b) in the territory of one Member to the service consumer of any other Member;
> (c) by a service supplier of one Member, through commercial presence in the territory of any other Member;
> (d) by a service supplier of one Member, through presence of natural persons of a Member in the territory of any other Member.

It also defines "services" to include "any service in any sector" except "services supplied in the exercise of governmental authority", which in turn is defined as "any service which is supplied neither on a commercial basis, nor in competition with one or more service suppliers", as per Articles I:3(b) and (c) of the GATS.

When a panel or the Appellate Body of the WTO interprets the term "trade in services", it is bound by these interpreting provisions so as not to include the services supplied in the exercise of governmental authorities.

However, very often an interpreting provision itself needs interpretation. For instance, it might not be crystal clear concerning whether the definition of "services" which cover "any service in any sector" would include the "electrical power" or whether the "electrical power" should be considered as product (goods) to be governed by the General Agreement on Tariffs and Trade (GATT) 1994. This issue will be further touched upon in connection with the discussion of "ordinary meaning" in Chap. 10 of the book.

Since the definitional interpretation in a treaty binds the treaty interpreter, he/she will have no authority to exercise treaty interpretation in a way to deviate from the definitional provision, even when a definition provided in the treaty might not be in line with the ordinary meaning of the interpreted term. For example, there is a definition of the term "juridical person" in GATS Article XXVIII:(l) which states:

> 'juridical person' means any legal entity duly constituted or otherwise organized under applicable law, whether for profit or otherwise, and whether privately-owned or governmentally-owned, including any corporation, trust, partnership, joint venture, sole proprietorship or association.

However, there could be different views about whether, legally speaking, a partnership, joint venture and sole proprietorship can be considered as "juridical person", because in many jurisdictions, the term "juridical person" is used to refer to those incorporated legal persons, which do not include a partnership and a joint venture (which are merely considered as contractual relations with no legal personality) as well as a sole proprietorship (which is considered as a part of the natural person and not a separate legal person in such jurisdictions). Nevertheless, an interpreter of the GATS provisions will have to be bound by the definitional provision in the agreement so as to have its decision based on the premise that the term "juridical person" does include a partnership, a joint venture and a sole proprietorship.

It must be noted that the definitional provisions under a treaty are not always provided in an article with the title of "Definition". For instance, some treaty provisions governing the relations between different treaties could also affect or guide treaty interpretation. They are generally provided in separate parts or provisions in a treaty. For instance, the FCTC provides in a non-definitional provision of Article 2.1 that:

> "In order to better protect human health, Parties are encouraged to implement measures beyond those required by this Convention and its protocols, and nothing in these instruments shall prevent a Party from imposing stricter requirements that are consistent with their provisions and are in accordance with international law."

This provision is about the discretion giving to the Parties to adopt measures beyond those required by the FCTC. Of course, this non-definitional provision will also affect and guide the interpretation of the provisions which set forth the obligations of the Parties.

The third boundary is the limit set forth by a definition provided in a separate treaty which is within the same treaty system. It is very common that a treaty is interpreted by another treaty or another legal instrument. For instance, under the WTO, there is the "Understanding on the Interpretation of Article II:1(b) of the General Agreement on Tariffs and Trade 1994", which explains the requirements for the phrase "other duties or charges" provided in paragraph 1(b) of Article II of the GATT 1994. There is the "Understanding on the Interpretation of Article XVII of the General Agreement on Tariffs and Trade 1994", which explains the "state trading enterprises" provided in Article XVII of the GATT 1994. There is the "Understanding on the Interpretation of Article XXIV of the General Agreement on Tariffs and Trade 1994", which explains some requirements concerning customs unions, free-trade areas, and interim agreements leading to the formation of a customs union or a free-trade area as provided in GATT Article XXIV, paragraphs 5–8. These WTO agreements not only interpret relevant GATT provisions, but also set forth additional requirements for those interpreted GATT provisions. When a panel or the Appellate Body has to interpret these GATT provisions, it has to be bound by these "interpreting agreements".

Of course, the interpreting treaties definitely could require further interpretation. For instance, the above mentioned "Understanding on the Interpretation of Article II:1(b) of the General Agreement on Tariffs and Trade 1994" is mainly to decide how WTO Members should do with "other duties or charges" in their respective the Schedules of concessions annexed to GATT 1994. However, if there is any dispute as to the meaning and scope of the term "other duties or charges", an interpreter will still have to conduct treaty interpretation for this term based on the provisions in the VCLT.

5.2.2 Not to Add to or Diminish Rights and Obligations

Treaty interpretation is basically to give proper meaning to a treaty text. Hence the "intrinsic confinement" for treaty interpretation activities is the "treaty text" itself. In other words, the text itself serves as the boundary of treaty interpretation. But of course, there could be exceptions to this principle. For instance, when resorting to the ordinary meaning of a textual wording would lead to a result of manifestly absurd or unreasonable, it is possible, under VCLT Article 32, for an interpreter to rely on supplementary means of interpretation (including the preparatory work of the interpreted treaty) to decide the meaning of the term. This could lead to a deviation from the textual wording. Of course, such exceptions should be limited in certain strictly defined situations as provided in VCLT Article 32.

As indicated above, the textual wording is the intrinsic limit to confine treaty interpretation activities. It does not need any specific provision to indicate such intrinsic confinement. But this does not mean that a treaty cannot make it clear by itself that the textual wording serves as the limit of treaty interpretation. An example can be found in the DSU under the WTO, which provides in Article 3.2 in part that: "Recommendations and rulings of the DSB *cannot add to or diminish the rights and obligations* provided in the covered agreements." (Emphasis added) Although it states that the Dispute Settlement Body's recommendation and ruling are not to add to or diminish WTO Members' rights and obligations under the WTO, it also actually means that when interpreting WTO agreements, the Appellate Body and the panels (whose reports are to be adopted by the Dispute Settlement Body) are not to add to or diminish Members' rights and obligations. This is because DSB's recommendation and ruling are based on the adopted reports of the Appellate Body or the panels, which are responsible to interpret and apply the WTO agreements. Hence, DSU Article 19.2 further provides that: "In accordance with paragraph 2 of Article 3, in their findings and recommendations, the panel and Appellate Body *cannot add to or diminish the rights and obligations* provided in the covered agreements." (Emphasis added)

The requirement of not adding to or diminishing the rights and obligations applies to the panel and Appellate Body's treaty interpretation functions. The phrase "not adding to or diminishing the rights and obligations" is actually indicating that the textual wording is the limit and confinement which the treaty interpreter will have to abide by. This is particularly important in economic treaties which are the results of the negotiations to achieve the balanced concessions. The requirement of not adding to or diminishing the rights and obligations for treaty interpreters is also to keep the balanced result of such treaties.

5.2.3 Not to Rebalance the Negotiated Deals

As indicated earlier, international treaties are basically to govern the commercial and economic relations between contracting parties (such as trade and investment agreements being concluded to govern trade or investment relations) or to govern the behaviors or activities of contracting States (such as human rights treaties being concluded to govern States' activities or behaviors of human rights protection; environmental treaties being concluded to prevent pollution or to preserve environment). So there are basically two types of treaties from the perspective of their governed subject matters, namely "relations-governing treaties" (such as trade and investment agreements) and "behavior-governing treaties" (such as human rights treaties). This distinction is not precise enough because "relations-governing treaties" are also to govern contracting parties' behaviors or activities. However, this distinction could be useful in understanding the nature of an international deal.

For the "relations-governing treaties", the respective rights and obligations of the contracting parties are the outcome of a series of negotiations and compromises.

They represent the reciprocal and balanced results of the give-and-take or request-and-offer process. Many provisions in a treaty might look peculiar. But they could be the result of balanced compromises. Interpreting a provision or a concession under a treaty in a certain way might break the balance. A very important approach for the interpretation of such treaties is to maintain the balanced results of the negotiated packages. Treaty interpretation is not a means to break the balance. Neither should it be used to "rebalance" the negotiated package.

The United States had indicated the following during the negotiation of the DSU's amendment. The statement is useful in understanding the achievement of a balanced and compromised result in the negotiation process:

> The covered agreements [of the WTO] are the result of negotiations among sovereign nations and autonomous customs territories. Negotiations inherently entail a number of compromises. Agreement by participants on particular terms in a covered agreement does not mean that all WTO Members have agreed on the same underlying approach or rationale for those terms. Some participants may have wanted stronger rules or disciplines that went further in a particular area, while other participants may not have wanted rules as strong or disciplines that went as far. It is for this reason that the text of the covered agreements is the best representation of the expectations of WTO Members.[10]

Hence, in order to ensure not to rebalance a negotiated package, a treaty interpreter would have to look at and to give more weights to the preparatory works concerning the process making concessions or forming the balanced results so as to understand the background the concessions and the reason of using such terms in the interpreted treaty.

For the "behavior-governing treaties", on the other hand, although there could also be compromises during the negotiations, the focus is that States are required to follow certain uniformed disciplines. Such uniform rules represent certain human values of high importance (such as human dignity in relation to human rights treaties, labor protection in relation to labor protection treaties, and sustainability in relation to environmental treaties). When interpreting such treaties, the focus should be on how the proper achievement of the object-and-purpose of these treaties, and not too much on what had been said by the drafters at the time of their negotiations.

Sometimes a treaty can embrace both types of provisions. For instance, in many FTAs there are chapters to govern trade and investment relations and other chapters to govern labor and environmental protections. When interpreting these provisions of different natures, an adjudicator will have to consider their respective natures. If the interpreted provision is in the trade and investment chapters in the FTAs, he/she should focus more on maintaining the balanced results; whereas if the interpreted provision is in or related to the labor and environmental chapters in the FTAs, he/she should give more weight on the object-and-purpose of the provisions.

---

[10]United States, Negotiations on Improvements and Clarifications of the Dispute Settlement Understanding—Further Contribution of the United states on Improving Flexibility and Member Control in WTO Dispute Settlement, Addendum. The document can be found at https://ustr.gov/sites/default/files/asset_upload_file777_10410.pdf. Accessed 8 Aug 2017.

5.3 External Boundary for Treaty Interpretation

5.3.1 Judicial Activism—The Line to Be Drawn

In the preceding section, the discussion was about the boundary set forth by the interpreted treaty itself. In this section, the discussion will be turned to the boundary that is not set forth by the interpreted treaty, but by some general principles. In this regard, the concept of judicial activism is brought into the discussion as to whether it should serve as constrain for treaty interpretation. The book considers refraining from practicing judicial activism as an "external" boundary because such constrain does not arise directly from the interpreted treaty, but from the operation of judicial or quasi-judicial function under the treaty.

The term "judicial activism" was first used by a non-lawyer Arthur Schlesinger Jr. in a Fortune magazine article in 1947 to describe the respective positions of the nine United States Federal Supreme Court justices at that time and to explain their alliances and divisions. He described Justices Black, Douglas, Murphy, and Rutlege as the "Judicial Activists"; Justices Frankfurter, Jackson, and Burton as the "Champions of Self Restraint"; and Justice Reed and Chief Justice Vinson as in the middle. He explained the United States Supreme Court's split on the interpretation of legislation and "the proper function of the judiciary in a democracy"[11]:

> This conflict may be described in several ways. The Black-Douglas group believes that the Supreme Court can play an affirmative role in promoting the social welfare; the Frankfurter-Jackson group advocates a policy of judicial self-restraint. One group is more concerned with the employment of the judicial power for their own conception of the social good; the other with expanding the range of allowable judgment for legislatures, even if it means upholding conclusions they privately condemn. One group regards the Court as an instrument to achieve desired social results; the second as an instrument to permit the other branches of government to achieve the results the people want for better or worse. In brief, the Black-Douglas wing appears to be more concerned with settling particular cases in accordance with their own social preconceptions; the Frankfurter-Jackson wing with preserving the judiciary in its established but limited place in the American system.[12]

Hence the concept of "judicial activism" was not created to imply that the term was negative and that the judicial activists were to be blamed. The term was just used to describe an "attitude" or "approach" toward the role or function of the judicial branch. Today, the term is used in vastly different ways with different meanings.[13] It is commonly used to criticize judges who are not merely interpreting or applying legal text in an active way, but are deciding cases without plausible connection to the law they purport to apply.[14] It is also commonly used in a milder way, to blame judges acting in bad faith or in a dishonest way when making their

---

[11]Kmiec (2004), pp. 1445–1446.

[12]Arthur Schlesinger Jr.'s paragraph is quoted from id. at pp. 1446–447.

[13]Id. at pp. 1442–1443.

[14]Dernbach and Prokopchak (2015), p. 343.

judgments as well as those judges relying on implausible and unconvincing reasoning.[15]

Here the book is not to engage in the debate of a proper definition of the term "judicial activism" or the assessment of its positive values or negative implications, but to use the term as a general parameter to indicate the boundary of treaty interpretation. For the purpose of discussions in this book, there are the following points to elaborate.

First, the essence of not resorting to an undesirable "judicial activism" is to expect that a treaty interpreter will respect the textual wording, the context and its object-and-purpose and that he/she will not create law. If an interpreter is not exercising such "undesirable" judicial activism, certain extent of activism could be allowed or even desirable. For instance, when a textual wording is vastly unclear concerning its meaning, an interpreter should be expected to engage in a more liberal interpretation so as to meet the object-and-purpose of the treaty.

Second, "judicial activism" is mainly about the interpretation of rules governing the disputes. Although the term "judicial activism" can be broadly used to address the full functions of an adjudicator, including the fact finding function and the functions of interpretation and application of the governing rules, the key concern is still on the possible undesirable deliberate deviation from the plausible interpretation of the applicable rules.

Third, the term "judicial activism" is not merely applied with respect to national courts. The issue of judicial activism also relates to international adjudication. When an international adjudicator decides a case, it must find facts and decide the interpretation and application of the governing treaty. When an international adjudicator conducts interpretation and application of the applicable treaty, it must be bound by the general principle of not deviating from the mandate of the treaty.

Fourth, there must be limits for international adjudicators to exercise their treaty interpretation power. Such limits include conducting the interpretation of the text of applicable treaty in a good faith manner and doing it with plausible and convincing reasoning. In the situation where the text of the applicable treaty is clear, treaty interpreters must respect the textual wording. There would be little room for a treaty interpreter to elaborate and to broaden, narrow or modify the scope of the interpreted text. But in the situation where the text is not so clear, the room should be made more widely available for treaty interpreters to have more liberal interpretation so as to meet the object-and-purpose of the treaty.

Fifth, treaty interpretation should not be limited to purely interpreting a treaty text. It should be given the function of filling the gap or loophole of a treaty, if it is needed *for the purpose of making the treaty operable*. Treaty interpretation should also be permitted to introduce external values into the operation of a treaty. It would be apparently undesirable to negatively use the concept of "judicial activism" for the purpose of preventing an international adjudicator to interpret a treaty so as to fill the gap or for the purpose of requiring the adjudicator to leave the gap or

---

[15]Allan (2015), p. 74.

loophole as it is without regard to the possibility that such gap or loophole could jeopardise the operation of the treaty. It would also be undesirable to rely on the concept of "judicial activism" to prevent the introduction of external values of high importance into the operation of a treaty so as to isolate its operation. The issue of introducing fundamental human values into treaty interpretation will be further discussed in Chap. 18 of the book.

Sixth, whether or not an interpretation can be considered as judicial activism is closely related to the treaty text itself. Concerning anti-dumping cases under the WTO, there had been many discussions about whether the Appellate Body had been practicing judicial activism in relation to their decisions on "zeroing"[16] issues. A related provision is in Article 17.6(ii) of the Agreement on Implementation of Article VI of the General Agreement on Tariffs and Trade 1994 (the Anti-Dumping Agreement), which reads:

> In examining the matter referred to in paragraph 5:
>
> …
>
> (ii) the panel shall interpret the relevant provisions of the Agreement in accordance with customary rules of interpretation of public international law. Where the panel finds that *a relevant provision of the Agreement admits of more than one permissible interpretation*, the panel shall find the authorities' measure to *be in conformity with the Agreement* if it rests upon one of those permissible interpretations.
>
> (Emphases added)

Many commentators consider that "zeroing" practice is not explicitly prohibited in the Anti-Dumping Agreement and therefore the agreement admits of more than one permissible interpretation concerning whether an investigating authority could rely on the "zeroing" method to calculate the dumping margin. Many of them challenged the Appellate Body of the WTO as judicial activist.[17] The Appellate Body took the position that the "zeroing" practice is not permitted by the Anti-dumping Agreement. So the issues of whether the Appellate Body was practicing "judicial activism" should be (1) whether a relevant provision concerning the calculation of dumping margins in the Anti-dumping Agreement admits of more than one permissible interpretation (admitting zeroing and not admitting zeroing) and (2) whether the Appellate Body has been interpreting the text of applicable provisions in the Agreement in a good faith manner and with plausible and convincing reasoning. These issues concern textual wording of the Anti-dumping Agreement and hence will be further discussed in relation to the textual words and their ordinary meaning in Chap. 10 of the book.

---

[16]Zeroing is a calculation method to decide whether there is a dumping margin (home price minus export price) so as to further decide the imposition of an anti-dumping duty. The United States anti-dumping authority aggregated the results of each margin of each sub-product category of the product under investigation, but to delete the negative margins so that they will not offset the positive margins so as to come up with a higher average margin.

[17]See the discussions in Cho (4 May 2006).

In this chapter, it is worth exploring the possibility of having the following "elements" included in a codified treaty interpretation rules: First, a treaty interpreter should only engage in interpreting the law, not engage in creating the law. In this regard, "judicial activism" could generally serve as an external boundary for treaty interpretation and a treaty interpreter should avoid practicing undesirable "judicial activism". But it does not mean that an interpreter does not have an overall power to prevent loopholes and to introduce certain important human values into treaty interpretation activities. Second, the ultimate line to be drawn is whether an interpretation of a treaty provision is conducted with plausible and convincing reasoning. If the reasoning is objectively plausible and convincing, the related interpretation should not be considered as the result of "judicial activism". Whether the reasoning is objectively plausible and convincing should be decided whether the VCLT and certain other treaty interpretation rules are relied on in the reasoning.

5.3.2 Previous Jurisprudence as a Boundary?

In domestic context, there is the doctrine of *stare decisis* (the doctrine of precedent) applied in many jurisdictions to require the court to defer to its previous decisions or the decisions of a higher court.[18] In such jurisdictions, a previous court decision (concerning its interpretation and application of law) has a binding effect on the same issue in later cases to be decided by the same court or by the lower courts. In many other jurisdictions, there is a different doctrine of "jurisprudence constante". In such jurisdictions, a single decision by the court in the past does not have binding force. But when there are repeated decisions in a series of cases accepting the same legal position, such legal position should be respected and should be given a greater weight.[19]

These doctrines are not about the fact-finding aspect of the previous decisions, but about the interpretation and application of a law. Hence, the doctrine of *stare decisis* would severely constrain the interpretation of a specific law provision by a domestic court. But the doctrine of "jurisprudence constante" would only expect judges in later decisions to take previous decisions into serious consideration.

In international context, there is no such rule of *stare decisis*. International tribunals are not bound by previous jurisprudence of the same dispute settlement mechanism or of another dispute settlement mechanism. For instance, Article 59 of the Statute of International Court of Justice (the ICJ Statute) provides: "The decision of the Court has no binding force except between the parties and in respect of that particular case." Hence, the previous decisions of the Court cannot bind the

[18]Legal Information Institute of Cornell University Law School. Stare Decisis. https://www.law.cornell.edu/wex/stare_decisis. Accessed 8 Aug 2017.

[19]USLegal. Jurisprudence Constante Law and Legal Definition. https://definitions.uslegal.com/j/jurisprudence-constante/. Accessed 8 Aug 2017.

disputing parties in a later case before the Court. Also Article 38.1 of the ICJ Statute lists the sources of law to be applied by the Court. The first three sources of law (including international conventions establishing rules expressly recognized by the contesting states, international customs as evidence of a general practice accepted as law, and the general principles of law recognized by civilized nations) apparently do not include previous decisions of the ICJ as the source of law to be applied by the Court. The fourth source of law is: "subject to the provisions of Article 59, judicial decisions and the teachings of the most highly qualified publicists of the various nations, as subsidiary means for the determination of rules of law." Hence, previous judicial decisions do not have binding force in the ICJ, but only serve as secondary source for the Court to determine cases. This is similar to the doctrine of "jurisprudence constante" in that the repeated decisions in a series of cases accepting the same legal position will be respected and given a greater weight in a later decision.

In practice, previous jurisprudence (although non-binding in nature) of interpreting a treaty under the same dispute settlement mechanism has been influential for later cases. A very good reason is provided by an International Centre for Settlement of Investment Disputes (ICSID) tribunal. In *AES Corp v. Argentine Republic*, the tribunal states:

> Each tribunal remains sovereign and may retain, as it is confirmed by ICSID practice, a different solution for resolving the same problem; but decisions on jurisdiction dealing with the same or very similar issues *may at least indicate some lines of reasoning of real interest*; this Tribunal *may consider them in order to compare its own position with those already adopted by its predecessors* and, if it shares the views already expressed by one or more of these tribunals on a specific point of law, it is free to adopt the same solution.[20]
>
> (Emphasis added)

For the WTO, the situation is the same as those in other areas of international law concerning the inexistence of the doctrine of *stare decisis* and concerning previous jurisprudence still being practically influential for later cases. The WTO Secretariat has noted the following[21]:

> … there is no rule of *stare decisis* in WTO dispute settlement according to which previous rulings bind panels and the Appellate Body in subsequent cases. This means that a panel is not obliged to follow previous Appellate Body reports even if they have developed a certain interpretation of exactly the provisions which are now at issue before the panel. Nor is the Appellate Body obliged to maintain the legal interpretations it has developed in past cases…
>
> If the reasoning developed in the previous report in support of the interpretation given to a WTO rule is persuasive from the perspective of the panel or the Appellate Body in the subsequent case, *it is very likely that the panel or the Appellate Body will repeat and follow*

[20]AES Corp. v. Argentine Republic, ICSID Case No.ARB/02/17, Decision on Jurisdiction, para. 30 (26 Apr 2005), http://www.italaw.com/documents/AES-Argentina-Jurisdiction_002.pdf.

[21]World Trade Organization. Legal Effect of Panel and Appellate Body Reports and DSB Recommendations and Rulings. https://www.wto.org/english/tratop_e/dispu_e/disp_settlement_cbt_e/c7s2p1_e.htm. Accessed 8 Aug 2017.

> *it*. This is also in line with a key objective of the dispute settlement system which is *to enhance the security and predictability of the multilateral trading system* (Article 3.2 of the DSU). In the words of the Appellate Body, these GATT and WTO panel reports — and equally adopted Appellate Body reports[22] – "*create legitimate expectations among WTO Members, and, therefore, should be taken into account where they are relevant to any dispute*."[23]
>
> (Emphases added)

As mentioned above, previous jurisprudence under a dispute settlement mechanism is influential in later cases within the same dispute settlement mechanism. It could also be a useful reference for an adjudicator under a separate dispute settlement mechanism. For instance, in the ICSID arbitration case of *Emilio Agustín Maffezini v. The Kingdom of Spain*, the arbitral tribunal referred to the decision of the ICJ on *Anglo-Iranian Oil Company Case* (Jurisdiction)[24] concerning its discussion on the most-favored-nation clause. The arbitral tribunal states:

> In addressing these issues, it must first be determined which is the basic treaty that governs the rights of the beneficiary of the most favored nation clause. This question was extensively discussed in the Anglo-Iranian Oil Company Case, where the International Court of Justice determined that the basic treaty upon which the Claimant could rely was that "containing the most-favored-nation clause". The Court then held that:
>
> "It is this treaty which establishes the juridical link between the United Kingdom and a third-party treaty and confers upon that State the rights enjoyed by the third party. A third party treaty, independent of and isolated from the basic treaty, cannot produce any legal effect as between the United Kingdom and Iran: it is *res inter alios acta*".
>
> This discussion has practical consequences for the application of the most favored nation clause...[25]
> (Emphasis added)

There are many other examples showing that in ICSID disputes, the ICJ's previous decisions have influence on the ICSID tribunals' decisions.[26]

It can be summarized from the above the following points: First, previous decisions do not have binding force on the later decisions under the same or different dispute settlement mechanisms because there is no such doctrine of *stare decisis*. But this does not mean that previous decisions are not relevant. Actually,

---

[22]Id. at Note 1 (citing Appellate Body Report, *United States—Import Prohibition of Certain Shrimp and Shrimp Products—Recourse to Article 21.5 of the DSU by Malaysia*, para. 109, WTO Doc. WT/DS58/AB/RW (adopted 21 Nov 2001).

[23]Id. at Note 2 (quoting Appellate Body Report, *Japan—Taxes on Alcoholic Beverages*, pp. 107–108, WTO Doc. WT/DS8/AB/R, WT/DS10/AB/R, WT/DS11/AB/R (adopted 1 Nov 1996).

[24]International Court of Justice (1952), p. 93. See also Fitzmaurice (1955–1956), p. 84.

[25]Emilio Agustín Maffezini v. The Kingdom of Spain, ICSID Case No. ARB/97/7, Award, paras. 44–45 (25 Jan 2000), http://www.italaw.com/documents/Maffezini-Jurisdiction-English_001.pdf.

[26]Gorbylev (2013), p. 351.

previous jurisprudence is always relevant and could be vastly influential in later cases.

Second, the jurisprudence of the same dispute settlement mechanism would have a higher practical value to be followed by later decisions. For instance, in the panel and Appellate Body reports, previous decisions on each legal issue are always thoroughly cited as the basis for further elaboration. But this is due to the practical need of consistency and predictability of the dispute settlement procedure, not due to any specific and explicit legal requirement.

Third, the jurisprudence under a different dispute settlement mechanism is also a useful reference. Since there involve two treaty systems and two dispute settlement mechanisms, there are no consistency and predictability issues. A reference to the jurisprudence of another dispute settlement system is because of the practical need. Citing the jurisprudence of another dispute settlement mechanism could enhance the credibility and persuasiveness concerning the need of a treaty provision to be interpreted in certain way.

Having elaborated the above, it should be useful to explore whether to include the following elements into a set of codified treaty interpretation rules: First, the ICJ Statute only applies to the ICJ cases. It would be useful to make clear that previous decisions do not have binding force for later cases and to make the above mentioned Article 38.1 of the ICJ Statute (concerning previous decisions being a subsidiary but useful means to assist treaty interpretation) generally applicable to other international dispute settlement mechanisms. This is to ensure consistency and predictability within the same dispute settlement system. Second, before citing jurisprudence of another dispute settlement mechanism, the interpreter will have to discuss whether the interpretation adopted under that other dispute settlement mechanism is plausible and convincing in serving as a secondary means to assist interpretation.

References

Allan J (2015) Chapter 6 The activist judges—vanity of vanities. In: Coutinho LP, La Torre M, Smith SD (eds) Judicial activism: an interdisciplinary approach to the American and European experiences. Springer, Switzerland, pp 71–88

Aust HP, Rodiles A, Staubach P (2014) Unity or uniformity? Domestic courts and treaty interpretation. Leiden J Int Law 27(1):75–112

Baofu P (2010) The future of post-human law—a preface to a new theory of necessity, contingency and justice. Cambridge Scholars, Newcastle

Cho S (2006) The WTO appellate body strikes down the U.S. zeroing methodology used in antidumping investigations. ASIL Insights, USA

Dernbach JC, Prokopchak M (2015) Recognition of environmental rights for Pennsylvania citizens: a tribute to chief justice castille. Duquesne Law Rev 53:335–369

Fellmeth AX, Horwitz M (2011). http://www.oxfordreference.com/view/10.1093/acref/9780195369380.001.0001/acref-9780195369380-e-1303. Accessed 8 Aug 2017

Fitzmaurice G (1955–1956) The law and procedure of the international court of justice, 1951–1954: points of substantive law

Gorbylev S (2013) The use of ICJ case law in investment treaty arbitration. Arbitration 79(4):349–356

International Court of Justice (1952) Reports

International Judicial Monitor. Treaty Interpretation. http://www.judicialmonitor.org/archive_0906/generalprinciples.html. Accessed 8 Aug 2017

Kmiec KD (2004) the origin and current meaning of “judicial activism”. Calif Law Rev 92:1441–1477

Legal Information Institute of Cornell University Law School. Stare Decisis. https://www.law.cornell.edu/wex/stare_decisis. Accessed 8 Aug 2017

Tumonis V (2012) Judicial creativity an constraint of legal rules: dueling cannons of international law. Univ Miami Int Comp Law Rev 20:93–133

United States, Negotiations on Improvements and Clarifications of the Dispute Settlement Understanding—Further Contribution of the United states on Improving Flexibility and Member Control in WTO Dispute Settlement, Addendum. https://ustr.gov/sites/default/files/asset_upload_file777_10410.pdf. Accessed 8 Aug 2017

USLegal. Jurisprudence Constante Law and Legal Definition. https://definitions.uslegal.com/j/jurisprudence-constante/. Accessed 8 Aug 2017

World Trade Organization. Legal Effect of Panel and Appellate Body Reports and DSB Recommendations and Rulings. https://www.wto.org/english/tratop_e/dispu_e/disp_settlement_cbt_e/c7s2p1_e.htm. Accessed 8 Aug 2017

Chapter 6
Difference and Relations Between Interpretation and Application of Treaties and the Possible Codification

Contents

6.1 Treaty Application Issues

6.1.1 Meaning of and Situations to Decide Treaty Application

Treaty interpretation and treaty application are of different natures with different functions.[1] "All interpretation pursues meaning within a penumbra of discursive formations."[2] Thus, treaty interpretation is a process of finding out the proper

[1]Lo (2012), p. 25.
[2]Desierto (2010).

C. Lo, *Treaty Interpretation Under the Vienna Convention on the Law of Treaties*, https://doi.org/10.1007/978-981-10-6866-9_6

meanings of treaty terms through various interpreting methods, whereas treaty application is a process of properly identifying the specific source of applicable law (i.e. the governing norm) and applying it to a set of facts.[3]

Some might argue that there is not much difference between a treaty interpretation and a treaty application. For instance, it is argued that:

> The distinction between application and interpretation is not concrete and it may in some cases be difficult to determine whether a WTO Tribunal is applying international law or simply using international law to interpret a WTO provision. The answer to this question may not make a large difference from a practical perspective.[4]

This is partly true because sometimes the distinction between treaty application and treaty interpretation co-exist and their difference in the whole dispute settlement stages is not very clear. However, for the following reasons, the distinction is still necessary. First, the VCLT has already distinguished treaty application and treaty interpretation in its text, as will be explained below. Second, although application and interpretation of treaties are interrelated and intertwined, their respective logics are still clearly different. When deciding the selection of an applicable rule for a dispute, it concerns treaty application issue. When deciding the proper understanding of the applicable rule (or the "possible" applicable rule), it concerns treaty interpretation issues.

Most of the time, treaty application is not a problem in a dispute settlement proceeding. For instance, whether or not a trade measure constitutes a breach of a WTO Member's MFN obligation under the GATT should be decided by Article I of the GATT. Whether or not an FTA meets the requirements of economic integration under the GATT should be based upon the provisions in Article XXIV of the GATT. The governing norms are clear in such situations and hence there is no problem arising from treaty application.

But there are situations where an applicable treaty (i.e. the treaty application issue) needs to be decided based on certain rules or based on certain considerations. These situations include: (1) the scope of application of a treaty provision in terms of time (whether to allow retroactive application); (2) the scope of application of a treaty provision in terms of territory (whether to apply to the entire territory of a contracting party); (3) the application of the previous or successive treaty; (4) the application of one of the conflicting treaties or treaty provisions; and (5) the application of one of the co-existing treaties or treaty provisions.

Treaty application and treaty interpretation are considered as separate issues and are dealt with in separate sections under the VCLT. In the VCLT, there is a section to govern treaty application issues. Part III of the VCLT covers three subject matters, namely observance of treaties, application of treaties and interpretation of treaties. Section 2 (entitled "Application of Treaties") under Part III of the VCLT includes the non-retroactive application of treaties in Article 28, the territorial

[3]For discussions of sources of law under WTO dispute settlement procedure, please see Palmeter and Mavroidis (2004), pp. 49–79.

[4]Mitchell and Heaton (2010), p. 570.

application of treaties in Article 29 and the application of successive treaties relating to the same subject matter in Article 30. So the VCLT has addressed the first three types of treaty application issues mentioned in the preceding paragraph.

6.1.2 Treaty Application Issues Addressed in VCLT—Non-retroactivities, Territorial Application and Successive Treaties

Article 28 of the VCLT follows the general doctrine of non-retroactivity of treaties.[5] It provides: "Unless a different intention appears from the treaty or is otherwise established, its provisions do not bind a party in relation to any act or fact which took place or any situation which ceased to exist before the date of the entry into force of the treaty with respect to that party."

There are two situations under this article to require a treaty not to be applied so as to avoid a retroactive application: First, the act or the related fact occurs before the effective date of a treaty. Second, if it is a continuous act, it has ceased to exist before such date. An exception to this principle is the intention of such retroactive application of a treaty which has appeared from the treaty or can be established through other means.

Article 29 of the VCLT is about the territorial application of a treaty. It requires that a treaty is to be applied to the whole territories of its contracting parties. Article 29 provides: "Unless a different intention appears from the treaty or is otherwise established, a treaty is binding upon each party in respect of its entire territory."

Article 30 of the VCLT is more complicated. It addressees the application issues of successive treaties and clarifies the application of an earlier or later treaty. Its text is quoted below:

1. Subject to Article 103 of the Charter of the United Nations, the rights and obligations of States parties to *successive treaties relating to the same subject-matter* shall be determined in accordance with the following paragraphs.
2. When a treaty specifies that *it is subject to*, or that it is not to be considered as incompatible with, *an earlier or later treaty, the provisions of that other treaty prevail.*
3. When all the parties to the earlier treaty are parties also to the later treaty but the earlier treaty is not terminated or suspended in operation under article 59, *the earlier treaty applies only to the extent that its provisions are compatible with those of the later treaty.*
4. When the parties to the later treaty do not include all the parties to the earlier one:

[5]Boda (1973), p. 341; the article is available at http://www.revistas.usp.br/rfdusp/article/viewFile/66677/69287. Accessed 8 Aug 2017.

(a) *As between States parties to both treaties* the same rule applies as in paragraph 3;
(b) *As between a State party to both treaties and a State party to only one of the treaties*, the treaty to which both States are parties governs their mutual rights and obligations.

5. Paragraph 4 is without prejudice to article 41, or to any question of the termination or suspension of the operation of a treaty under article 60 or to any question of responsibility which may arise for a State from the conclusion or application of a treaty the provisions of which are incompatible with its obligations towards another State under another treaty.

(Emphases added)

The application of Article 30 of the VCLT is premised on the condition that the two treaties must be "*successive treaties relating to the same subject-matter*". If a treaty is revised to a new version, the original and the new versions are successive treaties relating to the same subject matter.

But there are so many situations in which it is not crystal clear about whether the relevant treaties relate to the "same subject matter". For instance, the GATT and the North American Free Trade Agreement (NAFTA) "cover much of the same subject-matter, although GATT covers many other subjects as well." It is argued that "[w]hile a case could be made either way, the stronger argument is that these treaties would meet any reasonable test for 'same subject matter.'"[6] But, definitely there could be different views concerning the GATT and the NAFTA being related to the "same subject matter", because there are quite many chapters and provisions in the NAFTA the subject matters of which are not addressed in the GATT. And even though the GATT and the NAFTA are concerning the same subject matter on certain issues, the later treaty (which could be the NAFTA as opposed to the GATT 1947, or could be the GATT 1994 as opposed to the NAFTA) will not necessarily apply. It is because if a dispute settlement procedure is conducted under the WTO, the GATT 1994 will be exclusively applied; whereas if it is conducted under the NAFTA dispute settlement mechanism, the provisions in the NAFTA will be exclusively applied.

Article 30.2 of the VCLT basically says that if a treaty has indicated that it is subject to another treaty, the provisions of that other treaty prevail. This is basically prioritizing another treaty (either the later one or the earlier one) by the wording of a treaty. Articles 30.3 and 30.4 of the VCLT respectively deal with different situations. The first situation is when all of the parties to the earlier treaty are also parties to the later treaty. The second situation is when the later treaty does not embrace all the parties to the earlier one. Article 30.3 of the VCLT basically says that if all the parties to the earlier treaty are parties also to the later treaty but the earlier treaty is not terminated or suspended, the later treaty will apply; for the earlier treaty, it

[6]Borgen (2005), p. 580.

applies only to the extent that its provisions are compatible with those of the later treaty. In other word, if the earlier treaty is terminated or suspended, the earlier treaty does not apply.

6.1.3 Difference Between Conflicting and Co-existing Treaties Affecting Treaty Application

In the above-mentioned five situations where treaty application issues are involved, two important situations are not addressed in the VCLT. The first situation is where there are conflicting treaties or conflicting treaty provisions. The second situation is where there are co-existing treaties or coexisting treaty provisions.

Article 30 of the VCLT also addresses conflicting or co-existing treaties when the conflicting or co-existing obligations arise from the differences between an old and a successive treaties. But, the discussion in this section is not about the issues arising from successive treaties. The discussion here is about two existing parallel treaties or two parallel treaty provisions, the obligations concurrently imposed by which could be conflicting or co-existing in nature.

The book distinguishes the conflicting treaties (or treaty provisions) from the co-existing treaties (or treaty provisions) to describe different situations. In the situation of conflicting treaties or conflicting treaty provisions, a contracting party cannot practically and simultaneously comply with the obligations arising from both treaties or from both provisions in a treaty. The issue here is whether one treaty or treaty provision should apply over the other one. The obligations imposed by these two conflicting treaties or treaties provisions are contradictory to each other and cannot co-exist.

In the situation of co-existing treaties or co-existing treaty provisions, the respective obligations are not consistent but can co-exist. The issue is whether a contracting party is to fulfil its obligations under one or both of the co-existing treaties or treaty provisions. In other words, it is practically possible that a party assumes dual obligations under these co-existing treaties or treaty provisions.

These two situations are discussed below.

6.2 Conflicting Treaties and Their Application/Interpretation Issues

6.2.1 Conflicting Provisions in a Treaty—Intertwined Relation Between Interpretation and Application

There are many types of conflicting treaties or conflicting treaty provisions. The first type is reflected in conflicting provisions in a treaty. The above-mentioned example of GATT Articles I and XXIV is a proper illustration. Article I requires that a WTO Member must not discriminate like products originating from the territories of different WTO Members. But Article XXIV allows a WTO Members to establish economic integration with other countries (either WTO Members or non-WTO Members) so as to give favors to the products from such other countries (the constituent parties) and to discriminate products from the territories of non-parties (which could be WTO Members). Also for instance, GATT Article XI prohibits WTO Members from imposing import restrictions. But GATT Article XX allows WTO Members to adopt such trade restrictive measures, as long as the requirements in Article XX are met.

The treaty itself might have already provided solutions for such conflicting obligations. For instance, paragraph 5 of Article XXIV of the GATT provides in part that "the provisions of this Agreement *shall not prevent*, as between the territories of contracting parties, the formation of a customs union or of a free-trade area or the adoption of an interim agreement necessary for the formation of a customs union or of a free-trade area…" (Emphasis added) It is clear that Article I of the GATT does not prevent WTO Members to create such economic integrations. Hence the permitted discriminations against non-parties to an FTA or non-parties to a customs union under GATT Article XXIV prevail over the non-discrimination obligations under GATT Article I.

Also for instance, Article XX of the GATT provides in part that "Subject to the requirement that such measures are not applied in a manner which would constitute a means of arbitrary or unjustifiable discrimination between countries where the same conditions prevail, or a disguised restriction on international trade, *nothing in this Agreement shall be construed to prevent the adoption or enforcement by any contracting party of measures…*" (Emphasis added) In other words, if the requirements provided in Article XX are met, WTO Members are entitled to adopt trade restrictive measures, notwithstanding that such measures could otherwise be against the obligations of WTO Members under other GATT provisions.

If there is no explicit provision addressing the conflicting and incompatible provisions under a treaty, an adjudicator will have to resort to "both" the appropriate treaty application methods and the treaty interpretation methods to reconcile the conflicts. In this regard, the contextual interpretation of treaty provisions as well as the object-and-purpose of the whole treaty could be more relevant. The purpose is to decide which one of the conflicting provisions should apply in a specific situation.

So there is an intertwined relation between treaty interpretation and treaty application in this regard. The adjudicator will have to identify the relevant provisions which are the "possible" candidates to be applied in a dispute. He/she might need to interpret the meaning of the provisions, to look into the object-and-purpose and even to look at the context so as to decide the proper understanding of the respective provisions. After having properly understood the relevant provisions, the adjudicator would then be able to decide which one of the conflicting provisions should apply. If, after having properly interpreted the relevant provisions, the adjudicator is still unable to decide the application, then he might need to resort to some other treaty application/interpretation principles, such as the principle of a specific provision prevailing over a general provision (*Generalia Specialibus Non Derogant*).

6.2.2 *Conflicting Provisions in Two Treaties Under One Treaty System—Intertwined Relation Between Interpretation and Application*

The second type is reflected in conflicting provisions in two treaties under one treaty system. For example, in the WTO context, there could be conflicts between the Agreement Establishing the WTO and other WTO agreements as well as conflicts between different WTO agreements. Article XVI, paragraph 3, of the Agreement Establishing the WTO has a provision to address the conflict between itself and other WTO agreements and to prioritize the application of the Agreement Establishing the WTO: "In the event of a conflict between a provision of this Agreement and a provision of any of the Multilateral Trade Agreements, the provision of this Agreement shall prevail to the extent of the conflict."

Also under WTO, there is the DSU providing for the dispute settlement mechanism for the general use of WTO Members and there are a number of other WTO agreements also providing their specific dispute settlement procedures. Article 1.2 of the DSU addresses such conflict and prioritizes the application of the dispute settlement procedures provided in other WTO agreements:

> The rules and procedures of this Understanding shall apply subject to such special or additional rules and procedures on dispute settlement contained in the covered agreements as are identified in Appendix 2 to this Understanding. To the extent that there is a difference between the rules and procedures of this Understanding and the special or additional rules and procedures set forth in Appendix 2, the special or additional rules and procedures in Appendix 2 shall prevail…

Also for example, Article XXXIII of the GATT provides the accession procedures: "A government not party to this Agreement, or a government acting on behalf of a separate customs territory possessing full autonomy in the conduct of its external commercial relations and of the other matters provided for in this Agreement, may accede to this Agreement, on its own behalf or on behalf of that territory, on terms to be agreed between such government and the CONTRACTING PARTIES. Decisions of the CONTRACTING PARTIES under this paragraph shall be taken by a two-thirds majority." This provision has been modified and replaced by Article XII of the Agreement Establishing the WTO, which provides in paragraphs 1 and 2: "Any State or separate customs territory possessing full autonomy in the conduct of its external commercial relations and of the other matters provided for in this Agreement and the Multilateral Trade Agreements may accede to this Agreement, on terms to be agreed between it and the WTO. Such accession shall apply to this Agreement and the Multilateral Trade Agreements annexed thereto." "Decisions on accession shall be taken by the Ministerial Conference. The Ministerial Conference shall approve the agreement on the terms of accession by a two-thirds majority of the Members of the WTO."

Also for instance, GATT Article II sets forth market access commitments in the form of tariff reductions. But the Agreement on Agriculture (AoA) contains different disciplines and market access commitments. There are conflicting obligations arising from the provisions in the GATT and those in the AoA concerning market access obligations. The AoA basically prioritizes its application over the GATT provisions and the provisions in other WTO agreements.

Article 4.1 of the AoA provides: "Market access concessions contained in Schedules relate to bindings and reductions of tariffs, and to other market access commitments as specified therein." Article 21.1 of the AoA provides further that: "The provisions of GATT 1994 and of other Multilateral Trade Agreements in Annex 1A to the WTO Agreement shall apply subject to the provisions of this Agreement." In *EC—Bananas III*, the Panel rejected the European Communities' argument which suggests that Articles 4.1 and 21.1 of the AoA provided a justification for an inconsistency of the European Communities import scheme for bananas with Article XIII of GATT 1994.[7] The Appellate Body agreed with the Panel by stating the following:

> The preamble of the *Agreement on Agriculture* states that it establishes 'a basis for initiating a process of reform of trade in agriculture' and that this reform process 'should be initiated through the negotiation of commitments on support and protection and through the establishment of strengthened and more operationally effective GATT rules and disciplines'. The relationship between the provisions of the GATT 1994 and of the *Agreement on Agriculture* is set out in Article 21.1 of the *Agreement on Agriculture*:
>
> …
>
> Therefore, the provisions of the GATT 1994, including Article XIII, apply to market access commitments concerning agricultural products, except to the extent that the *Agreement on Agriculture* contains specific provisions dealing specifically with the same matter.
>
> …
>
> In our view, Article 4.1 does more than merely indicate where market access concessions and commitments for agricultural products are to be found. Article 4.1 acknowledges that significant, new market access concessions, in the form of new bindings and reductions of tariffs as well as other market access commitments (i.e. those made as a result of the tariffication process), were made as a result of the Uruguay Round negotiations on agriculture and included in Members' GATT 1994 Schedules. These concessions are fundamental to the agricultural reform process that is a fundamental objective of the *Agreement on Agriculture*.

Another example of conflicting obligations arising from different treaties under one treaty system is the conflicting obligations under the Agreement on Subsidies and Countervailing Measures (the SCM Agreement) and those under the AoA. Both agreements contain subsidies provisions. The subsidies rules in the SCM Agreement and those in the AoA might be contradicting with each other. For instance, export subsidies are prohibited under the SCM Agreement. But agricultural export subsidies are not prohibited under the AoA. They are only subject to certain extent of reduction. In this regard, the SCM Agreement provides in Article 3.1 the following to indicate that those export subsidies provided in the AoA are exceptions to the prohibited subsidies requirement:

---

[7] Panel Report, *European Communities—Regime for the Importation, Sale and Distribution of Bananas*, para. 7.127, WTO Doc. WT/DS27/R/ECU (adopted 25 Sept 1997).

Except as provided in the Agreement on Agriculture, the following subsidies, within the meaning of Article 1, shall be prohibited:

(a) subsidies contingent, in law or in fact, whether solely or as one of several other conditions, upon export performance, including those illustrated in Annex I;
(b) subsidies contingent, whether solely or as one of several other conditions, upon the use of domestic over imported goods.

Article 5 of the SCM Agreement imposes the obligation of not causing adverse effects to the interests of other WTO Members:

No Member should cause, through the use of any subsidy referred to in paragraphs 1 and 2 of Article 1, adverse effects to the interests of other Members, i.e.:

(a) injury to the domestic industry of another Member;
(b) nullification or impairment of benefits accruing directly or indirectly to other Members under GATT 1994 in particular the benefits of concessions bound under Article II of GATT 1994;
(c) serious prejudice to the interests of another Member.

But Article 13 of the AoA has due restraint provisions to require WTO Members refraining from resorting to the provisions of the SCM Agreements. Article 13 of the AoA reads:

> During the implementation period, notwithstanding the provisions of GATT 1994 and the Agreement on Subsidies and Countervailing Measures (referred to in this Article as the "Subsidies Agreement"):

(a) domestic support measures that conform fully to the provisions of Annex 2 to this Agreement shall be:
    (i) non-actionable subsidies for purposes of countervailing duties[8];
    (ii) exempt from actions based on Article XVI of GATT 1994 and Part III of the Subsidies Agreement; and
    (iii) exempt from actions based on non-violation nullification or impairment of the benefits of tariff concessions accruing to another Member under Article II of GATT 1994, in the sense of paragraph 1(b) of Article XXIII of GATT 1994;

(b) domestic support measures that conform fully to the provisions of Article 6 of this Agreement including direct payments that conform to the requirements of paragraph 5 thereof, as reflected in each Member's Schedule, as well as domestic support within *de minimis* levels and in conformity with paragraph 2 of Article 6, shall be:

---

[8]"Countervailing duties" where referred to in this Article are those covered by Article VI of GATT 1994 and Part V of the Agreement on Subsidies and Countervailing Measures.

(i) exempt from the imposition of countervailing duties unless a determination of injury or threat thereof is made in accordance with Article VI of GATT 1994 and Part V of the Subsidies Agreement, and due restraint shall be shown in initiating any countervailing duty investigations;
(ii) exempt from actions based on paragraph 1 of Article XVI of GATT 1994 or Articles 5 and 6 of the Subsidies Agreement, provided that such measures do not grant support to a specific commodity in excess of that decided during the 1992 marketing year; and
(iii) exempt from actions based on non-violation nullification or impairment of the benefits of tariff concessions accruing to another Member under Article II of GATT 1994, in the sense of paragraph 1(b) of Article XXIII of GATT 1994, provided that such measures do not grant support to a specific commodity in excess of that decided during the 1992 marketing year;

(c) export subsidies that conform fully to the provisions of Part V of this Agreement, as reflected in each Member's Schedule, shall be:

(i) subject to countervailing duties only upon a determination of injury or threat thereof based on volume, effect on prices, or consequent impact in accordance with Article VI of GATT 1994 and Part V of the Subsidies Agreement, and due restraint shall be shown in initiating any countervailing duty investigations; and
(ii) exempt from actions based on Article XVI of GATT 1994 or Articles 3, 5 and 6 of the Subsidies Agreement.

Another example is found in the conflicting obligations under the Agreement on Technical Barriers to Trade (the TBT Agreement) and the Agreement on Sanitary and Phytosanitary Agreement (the SPS Agreement). There could be a measure which meets the definition of a TBT measure (technical regulation) as provided in Annex 1 of the TBT Agreement: "Document which lays down product characteristics or their related processes and production methods, including the applicable administrative provisions, with which compliance is mandatory. It may also include or deal exclusively with terminology, symbols, packaging, marking or labelling requirements as they apply to a product, process or production method." The same measure could at the same time fall within the scope of SPS measures as provided in Annex A, paragraph 1, of the SPS Agreement:

Any measure applied:

(a) to protect animal or plant life or health within the territory of the Member from risks arising from the entry, establishment or spread of pests, diseases, disease-carrying organisms or disease-causing organisms;

(b) to protect human or animal life or health within the territory of the Member from risks arising from additives, contaminants, toxins or disease-causing organisms in foods, beverages or feedstuffs;
(c) to protect human life or health within the territory of the Member from risks arising from diseases carried by animals, plants or products thereof, or from the entry, establishment or spread of pests; or
(d) to prevent or limit other damage within the territory of the Member from the entry, establishment or spread of pests.

Article 1.5 of the TBT Agreement states: "The provisions of this Agreement do not apply to sanitary and phytosanitary measures as defined in Annex A of the Agreement on the Application of Sanitary and Phytosanitary Measures." In other words, even if a measure falls simultaneously within the scope of application under the TBT Agreement and the SPS Agreement, the SPS Agreement prevails.

There are other provisions addressing the conflicts between two WTO agreements. The General Interpretative Note to Annex 1A to the Agreement Establishing the WTO also provides that: "In the event of conflict between a provision of the General Agreement on Tariffs and Trade 1994 and a provision of another agreement in Annex 1A to the Agreement Establishing the World Trade Organization (referred to in the agreements in Annex 1A as the "WTO Agreement"), the provision of the other agreement shall prevail to the extent of the conflict." This is to prioritize other agreements on trade in goods (which include addition and special rules for trade in goods) over the text of the GATT.

In the above examples, one of the agreements will apply over the other agreement because of the specific provisions in one of these conflicting agreements. But if there is no explicit provision addressing the conflicting and incompatible provisions under a treaty, an adjudicator will have to resort to appropriate treaty application and treaty interpretation methods to reconcile the conflicts. In this regard, the contextual interpretation of treaty provisions and the overall objective of the whole treaty system could be more relevant. The purpose is to decide which one of the conflicting provisions should apply in a specific situation through proper interpretation of the relevant provisions. So the intertwined situation is similar to the situation in relation to the conflicting provisions in one treaty.

6.2.3 Conflicting Provisions Under Two Treaty Systems—It Being Interpretation Issue, Not Application Issue

The third situation is shown in the conflicting treaties in two separate treaty systems. It is more and more likely that different treaty systems impose directly opposite and conflicting obligations. For instance, the WTO requires the proper protection of intellectual property rights, whereas the FCTC encourages or even expects its parties to impose plain packaging requirements, which in essence limit the use of trademark. Also for instance, BITs basically require a proper protection of foreign investment, whereas the FCTC expects its parties to impose strict regulations on tobacco products, which could affect tobacco investors' rights.

In such situation, basically there is no treaty application issue. Because a DSM established under a treaty system (such as the WTO) is designed to resolve disputes arising from the treaty. The adjudicator is vested with the power to apply such treaty. He/she does not have the power to apply a treaty not covered by the DSM. For instance, Article 1.1 of the DSU provides in part that: "The rules and procedures of this Understanding shall apply to disputes brought pursuant to the consultation and dispute settlement provisions of the agreements listed in Appendix 1 to this Understanding (referred to in this Understanding as the 'covered agreements') …" Hence, a panel or the Appellate Body does not have the power to directly apply the FCTC because the FCTC is not a covered agreement under the WTO and hence not an applicable treaty for a WTO dispute. Neither can a WTO Member bring a WTO dispute pursuance to the FCTC. The only possibility for a panel and for the Appellate Body to take the FCTC into consideration is to rely on treaty interpretation methods.

For instance, the Appellate Body in its Report on *US—Shrimp* relied on other international instruments to decide the ordinary meaning of the term 'exhaustible natural resources' in Article XX(g) of the GATT 1994. It states:

> From the perspective embodied in the preamble of the WTO Agreement, we note that the generic term 'natural resources' in Article XX(g) is not 'static' in its content or reference but is rather 'by definition, evolutionary'. It is, therefore, pertinent to note that modern international conventions and declarations make frequent references to natural resources as embracing both living and non-living resources.[9]

In *EC—Approval and Marketing of Biotech Products*, the panel held even more clearly about the reliance on other treaties to decide the ordinary meaning of a treaty term:

> The ordinary meaning of treaty terms is often determined on the basis of dictionaries. We think that, in addition to dictionaries, other relevant rules of international law may in some cases aid a treaty interpreter in establishing, or confirming, the ordinary meaning of treaty terms in the specific context in which they are used. Such rules would not be considered because they are legal rules, but rather because they may provide evidence of the ordinary meaning of terms in the same way that dictionaries do. In the light of the foregoing, we consider that a panel may consider other relevant rules of international law when interpreting the terms of WTO agreements if it deems such rules to be informative. But a panel need not necessarily rely on other rules of international law, particularly if it considers that the ordinary meaning of the terms of WTO agreements may be ascertained by reference to other elements.[10]

---

[9]Appellate Body Report, *United States—Import Prohibition of Certain Shrimp and Shrimp Products*, para. 130, WTO Doc. WT/DS58/AB/R (adopted 6 Nov 1998).

[10]Panel Report, *European Communities—Measures Affecting the Approval and Marketing of Biotech Products*, paras. 7.92–7.93, WTO Doc. WT/DS291/R, WT/DS292/R, WT/DS293/R, Add.1 to Add.9, and Corr.1 (adopted 21 Nov 2006).

The Appellate Body confirmed in *EC—Chicken Cuts* that the Harmonized System (HS) constituted relevant "context" to interpret a Member's schedule of concessions and that the "broad consensus" among WTO Members to rely on such non-WTO rules helps confirm the needed relations:

> The Harmonized System is not, formally, part of the *WTO Agreement*, as it has not been incorporated, in whole or in part, into that Agreement. Nevertheless, the concept of 'context', under Article 31, is not limited to the treaty text—namely, the *WTO Agreement*—but may also extend to 'any agreement relating to the treaty which was made between all the parties in connection with the conclusion of the treaty', within the meaning of Article 31 (2)(a) of the *Vienna Convention*, and to 'any instrument which was made by one or more parties in connection with the conclusion of the treaty and accepted by the other parties as an instrument related to the treaty', within the meaning of Article 31(2)(b) of the *Vienna Convention*. Moreover, should the criteria in Article 31(3)(c) be fulfilled, the Harmonized System may qualify as a 'relevant rule of international law applicable in the relations between the parties'.
>
> The above circumstances confirm that, prior to, during, as well as *after* the Uruguay Round negotiations, there was broad consensus among the GATT Contracting Parties to *use* the HS as the basis for their WTO Schedules, notably with respect to agricultural products. In our view, this consensus constitutes an 'agreement' between WTO Members 'relating to' the WTO Agreement that was 'made in connection with the conclusion of' that Agreement, within the meaning of Article 31(2)(a) of the Vienna Convention. As such, this agreement is 'context' under Article 31(2)(a) *for the purpose of interpreting the WTO agreements*, of which the EC Schedule is an integral part. In this light, we consider that the HS is relevant for purposes of interpreting tariff commitments in the WTO Members' Schedules.[11]

The Panel Report on *EC—Tariff Treatment of Certain Information Technology Products* also confirms that the HS can be the context for interpreting WTO agreements because of its "close link" with the WTO agreements and the "close link" is shown by the relevant WTO agreements referring to the HS for the purpose of defining product coverage:

> In establishing that the HS provided relevant 'context' for the interpretation of a Member's schedule, the Appellate Body took into consideration a number of factors. While noting that the HS was not formally part of the WTO Agreement and was not incorporated, in whole or in part, into that Agreement, the Appellate Body observed that the vast majority of WTO Members are also contracting parties to the HS and identified what it considered was a 'close link' between the HS and the WTO Agreement. Specifically, the Appellate Body observed that a number of WTO agreements resulting from the Uruguay Round, including

---

[11]Appellate Body Report, *European Communities—Customs Classification of Frozen Boneless Chicken Cuts*, paras. 195, 199, WTO Doc. WT/DS269/AB/R, WT/DS286/AB/R, and Corr.1 (adopted 27 Sept 2005). See also Appellate Body Report, *European Communities—Customs Classification of Certain Computer Equipment*, para. 89, WTO Doc. WT/DS62/AB/R, WT/DS67/AB/R, WT/DS68/AB/R (adopted 22 June 1998): "We are puzzled by the fact that the Panel, in its effort to interpret the terms of [the EC Schedule], did not consider the Harmonized System and its Explanatory Notes. We note that during the Uruguay Round negotiations, both the European Communities and the United States were parties to the Harmonized System. Furthermore, it appears to be undisputed that the Uruguay Round tariff negotiations were held on the basis of the Harmonized System's nomenclature and that requests for, and offers of, concessions were normally made in terms of this nomenclature."

the Agreement on Rules of Origin (in Article 9), the Agreement on Subsidies and Countervailing Measures (in Article 27), and the Agreement on Textiles and Clothing (in Article 2 and the Annex thereto), refer to the HS for purposes of defining product coverage within the agreement or the products subject to particular provisions.[12]

6.3 Co-existing Treaties and Their Application/Interpretation Issues

It is very common that treaties in different treaty systems impose separate obligations which can perfectly co-exist. But there can also be separate obligations imposed by one treaty or by different treaties in one treaty system, the obligations in which might not be consistent with each other. But they are not contradictory to each other either. It is possible for a contracting party to fulfil these separate obligations simultaneously.

One issue is about the proper decision on whether the related treaties are in conflict with each other or whether they can co-exist. It is argued that:

> Ultimately, only when there is a conflict between two treaty provisions must one of them be set aside (either as suspended or abrogated). In all other situations, because good faith is to be presumed and States are obliged to implement their international obligations accordingly, it can be concluded that all States' obligations are cumulative and must be complied with simultaneously.[13]

In *Guatemala—Anti-Dumping Investigation Regarding Portland Cement from Mexico*, the Appellate Body has a statement concerning the decision of whether two provisions are in conflict against each other:

> In our view, it is only where the provisions of the DSU and the special or additional rules and procedures of a covered agreement *cannot* be read as *complementing* each other that the special or additional provisions are to *prevail*. A special or additional provision should only be found to *prevail* over a provision of the DSU in a situation where adherence to the one provision will lead to a violation of the other provision, that is, in the case of a *conflict* between them.[14]

Although the Appellate Body's view is about the relations between the dispute settlement provisions in the DSU and those in other WTO agreements, the principle can be extended to the relations between two "potentially" conflicting provisions in different treaties. The Appellate Body's view can be seen as a "presumption" against a treaty conflict when deciding the relations between two treaties. This is an

---

[12]Panel Report, *European Communities and its Member States—Tariff Treatment of Certain Information Technology Products*, para. 7.440, WTO Doc. WT/DS375/R, WT/DS376/R, WT/DS377/R (adopted 21 Sept 2010).

[13]Marceau (2001), p. 1084.

[14]Appellate Body Report, *Guat—Anti-Dumping Investigation Regarding Portland Cement from Mexico*, para. 65, WTO Doc. WT/DS60/AB/R (adopted 25 Nov 1998).

appropriate view because when the same countries concluded two treaties, their reasonable expectation should be to give full effects to these treaties unless they have expressed different expectations in any one of the treaties or unless the rights and obligations in the respective treaties logically cannot co-exist. Since different treaty provisions or different treaties in a treaty system should be presumed to co-exist, their contracting parties are supposed to cumulatively comply with these obligations.

In regard to the nature of deciding cumulative application, it is both the issue of treaty interpretation and that of treaty application. It is about treaty interpretation because the adjudicator will have to decide the nature of the respective obligations (through the textual wording, its context and the object-and-purpose of the treaty) so as to decide whether they can co-exist and should be cumulatively applied. It is also about treaty application because there involves a decision about which one of the rules should be applicable to a dispute.

6.4 Revisiting the Interrelated Relations Between Application and Interpretation of Treaties and Possible Codification

Based on the above explanation, the relations between treaty interpretation and treaty application can be described as the following:

First, as a general rule, an adjudicator will have to identify a relevant treaty provision which is the possible candidate to be applied in a dispute. So treaty application is "usually" the first step to decide a dispute. After an applicable treaty provision is identified, the adjudicator will then engage in treaty interpretation of such provision. But sometimes it could be very unclear as to whether a provision (or which provision) is relevant and applicable to a dispute. In such situation, an adjudicator will have to interpret the "potentially" applicable provision so as to decide its legal applicability. Hence, sometimes treaty interpretation will be first conducted before the interpreted provision is actually applied.

Second, when a conflict exists between two separate treaties or separate treaty systems, there is no real treaty application issue. A treaty outside the scope of applicable norm under a dispute settlement forum does not have a status to be directly applied. For instance, an environmental treaty (which is outside of the scope of the WTO) cannot be directly applied by the WTO panel or the Appellate Body. There is no real "treaty application" issue concerning which one (a WTO agreement or the environmental treaty) should be applied by the panel or the Appellate Body. In such situation, the eternal treaty (such as the environmental treaty being an external treaty to the WTO) can be "taken into consideration" only through treaty interpretation. This issue will be further discussed in Chap. 19 of the book.

Third, when a difference exists between two provisions in a treaty or between two treaties in a treaty system, an adjudicator will have to look into whether there have already been provisions in the treaty or in another treaty within the treaty system to address such difference or conflict. If there is such provision, then the adjudicator will have to "apply" it to resolve the difference or conflict. The issue of "treaty interpretation" is not apparent. But if there is no such provision addressing such difference, the adjudicator will have to rely on treaty interpretation to decide the nature of the respective obligations to see whether the two provisions are in conflict with each other or whether they can co-exist. A presumption should be given against conflict. There involve both treaty interpretation and treaty application here.

Fourth, if there is a conflict, the adjudicator might need to interpret the meaning of the conflicting provisions or to look at the context and the overall objective of the treaty so as to decide which one of the conflicting provisions should prevail and apply. If, after having properly interpreted the relevant provisions, the adjudicator is still unable to decide the application, then he/she might need to resort to some other principles for treaty application or treaty interpretation (such as the principle of the special law repeals the general laws). Here both treaty interpretation and treaty application are involved also.

Fifth, treaty interpretation and treaty application are also involved with respect to the VCLT. For instance, when interpreting WTO rules, a dispute settlement panel or the Appellate Body would have to apply the VCLT for the purpose of interpreting various WTO agreements so as to take into account non-WTO treaties. There are three conceptual steps in this process, namely applying the VCLT (this being "treaty application" or "application of customary international law"); possibly taking into account non-WTO treaties (this being "treaty interpretation"); and interpreting a WTO agreement (this being "treaty application"). Thus "treaty application" (the application of non-WTO rules, i.e. the VCLT; which is the only situation for the DSU to explicitly require applying non-WTO rules) and "treaty interpretation" (the interpretation of WTO agreement) are interrelated in this context.

Having elaborated the above, it should be useful to explore whether to include the following elements into a set of codified treaty interpretation rules: First, it could be useful to identify the situation where it is unclear as to whether a provision is relevant and applicable to a dispute and to expect an adjudicator to conduct interpretation of the "potentially" applicable provision so as to decide its legal applicability. Second, when there are different provisions in a treaty or within a treaty system, there must be a presumption against treaty conflict. In other words, different treaty provisions or different treaties in a treaty system should be presumed to co-exist and hence parties are supposed to cumulatively comply with these obligations. Third, if there is a real conflict between two provisions in a treaty or within a treaty system, the adjudicator will have to resort to the treaty interpretation rules to resolve such conflict. In such situation, the mutual contexts of the conflicting provisions and the ultimate object-and-purpose of the whole treaty or the whole treaty system should play important roles in the interpretation of the respective provisions.

References

Boda JG (1973) The doctrine of non-retroactivity of international treaties. Revista da Faculdade de Direito, Universidade de São Paulo 68:341–360. http://www.revistas.usp.br/rfdusp/article/viewFile/66677/69287. Accessed 8 Aug 2017

Borgen CJ (2005) Resolving treaty conflicts. George Wash Int Law Rev 37:573–648

Desierto DA (2010) Necessity and "supplementary means of interpretation" for non-precluded measures in bilateral investment treaties. Univ Pa J Int Law 31:827–934

Lo C (2012) Difference between treaty interpretation and treaty application and the possibility to account for non-WTO treaties during WTO treaty interpretation. Indiana Int Comp Law Rev 22 (1):1–25

Marceau G (2001) Conflicts of norms and conflicts of jurisdictions—the relationship between the WTO agreement and MEAs and other treaties. J World Trade 35:1081–1131

Mitchell AD, Heaton D (2010) The inherent jurisdiction of WTO tribunals: the select application of public international law required by the judicial function. Mich J Int Law 31:561–621

Palmeter D, Mavroidis PC (2004) Dispute settlement in the world trade organization: practice and procedure, 2nd edn. Cambridge University Press, Cambridge

Chapter 7
Relations Between Treaty Interpretation and Finding/Assessment of Facts and the Possible Codification

Contents

7.1 An Adjudicator's Finding and Assessment of Facts

7.1.1 Fact Finding/Assessment Being a "Question of Fact" as Opposed to a "Question of Law"

Just like domestic dispute settlement procedures, which commonly involve factual and legal issues, international dispute settlement procedures also often have factual and legal aspects. Factual issues include the finding of facts (i.e. collecting/gathering the factual information and evidence, allocating the burden of proof, assessing the collected evidence and drawing the conclusion as to the existence of certain facts) and the proper assessment of facts (i.e. assessing the nature of and the

C. Lo, *Treaty Interpretation Under the Vienna Convention on the Law of Treaties*,
https://doi.org/10.1007/978-981-10-6866-9_7

weight to be given to the found facts in the context of governing norm). The finding and the assessment of facts can be collectively treated as the fact finding activities of the adjudicator. The issues involved are commonly called the question of fact. On the other hand, legal issues include the interpretation and application of a normative rule. These are commonly called the question of law.

The distinction is similar in the international context. Fact finding in an international dispute settlement procedure is about the proper identification, collection or gathering of facts (i.e. the factual information and evidence) which are relevant to the dispute. For instance, an export subsidy is prohibited by the SCM Agreement of the WTO. In order to decide whether there is an export subsidy adopted by a WTO Member, a dispute settlement panel will have to find the existence of certain facts (such as the existence of a governmental program to support the domestic industry of the exporting country) which can be considered as "financial contribution by a government or any public body within the territory of a Member" and "a benefit is thereby conferred" (as required by Article 1.1 of the SCM Agreement) as well as the subsidy being "contingent, in law or in fact, whether solely or as one of several other conditions, upon export performance" (as provided in Article 3.1 of the same agreement). Whether or not there are facts to be considered as a "financial contribution", a "benefit being conferred" and a "contingency upon export performance" needs to be identified in the dispute settlement procedure.

An assessment of fact in international dispute is about the proper evaluation of an identified fact so that the governing treaty can be applied to such fact. In the above example, the WTO's dispute settlement panel will have to engage in evaluating whether the program to support domestic industry actually leads to providing financial contribution by the government or by a public body, whether such program actually leads to a benefit being conferred to an industry, and whether a contingency relationship exists between the provision of financial contribution and the export performance.

The distinction between a factual and a legal dispute is different from the distinction between the *de facto* and *de jure* existences of certain practice. For instance, Article 3.1 of the SCM Agreement provides in part that "… the following subsidies, within the meaning of Article 1, shall be prohibited: (a) subsidies contingent, *in law* or *in fact* …" (Emphasis added) Footnote 4 to the SCM Agreement further elaborates the *de facto* and *de jure* contingency by stating that: "This standard is met when the facts demonstrate that the granting of a subsidy, without having been made legally contingent upon export performance, is in fact tied to actual or anticipated exportation or export earnings. The mere fact that a subsidy is granted to enterprises which export shall not for that reason alone be considered to be an export subsidy within the meaning of this provision." The decision about whether there exists *a contingency in law* or *a contingency in fact* is an exercise of a "fact finding authority". This is not a legal issue.

It is possible that an international dispute procedure only involves factual issues. If the disputing parties do not have any different views on the application and interpretation of a relevant treaty provision, but have diverse views on the existence of certain facts or on the evaluation of the factual aspect, then there is no genuine legal issue involved in the dispute. In such case, the adjudicator will have to find the facts and to make necessary assessment of the found facts and to apply the undisputed treaty provision so as to come to a conclusion. For instance, if both parties in a WTO dispute do not have different views on the application and interpretation of Article 1 of the SCM Agreement, but the responding party of the dispute denies the existence of a program which is alleged by the complaining party to have provided financial contribution and conferred benefit to an industry, the factual dispute is apparent. The dispute settlement panel will have to decide whether the alleged program exists.

It is also possible that an international dispute only involves legal issues. If the disputing countries do not have different views on the factual background but have different views on the proper application or interpretation of a treaty provision, then there is no factual issue involved. In such case, the adjudicator will still have to indicate in its adjudication the undisputed facts for the purpose of applying the law to such facts. For instance, if both parties do not have a dispute on the existence of a program (which is set up and operated by a fund jointly contributed by the government and the related industry). The complaining party alleges that such program has provided financial contribution and conferred benefit to an industry. But both parties have different views about whether the concept of the term "public body" provided in Article 1.1 of the SCM Agreement covers such fund. The dispute settlement panel's main task is to decide the proper interpretation of the term "public body" so as to make clear about its scope and about its applicability to the fund.

In most situations, international disputes involve both the question of fact (including the finding of fact and the assessment of the fact) and the question of law (including treaty application and treaty interpretation), the latter of which have been discussed in the preceding chapter concerning their relations (i.e. the relations between treaty interpretation and treaty application). An adjudicator should be expected to clearly indicate both the facts that it has found and the application (and, possibly, the interpretation) of the relevant treaty provision. A clear example of a set of dispute settlement rules to indicate the adjudicator's duties of addressing factual and legal issues is provided in Article 12.7 of the DSU, which states in part that:

> Where the parties to the dispute have failed to develop a mutually satisfactory solution, the panel shall submit its findings in the form of a written report to the DSB. In such cases, the report of a panel *shall set out the findings of fact, the applicability of relevant provisions and the basic rationale behind any findings and recommendations that it makes*...
>
> (Emphasis added)

7.1.2 *Fact Finding/Assessment Can Also Become a "Question of Law"*

The distinction between the question of law and the question of fact is important, because the former is decided by the rules governing treaty applications and treaty interpretation, and the latter is decided by the rules governing fact finding and fact assessment. Also the adjudicators (i.e. the courts or the tribunals of different kind) in most DSMs are basically vested with the power to decide both the factual disputes and the legal disputes involved in the case. However, if a DSM has an appeal system to allow the disputing parties to make an appeal to the court/tribunal of higher instance and if such court/tribunal of higher instance requires that the appeal is limited to the question of law, then the factual issue cannot be appealed to the court/tribunal of higher instance. For instance, the DSM under the WTO created the Appellate Body to provide functions of second instance. The jurisdiction of the Appellate Body only extends to the question of law. Article 17.6 of the DSU provides that: "An appeal shall be limited to *issues of law* covered in the panel report and *legal interpretations* developed by the panel." (Emphasis added).

As will be explained below, an adjudicator's "fact finding" and "fact assessment" activities are governed by certain rules. A genuine error in the finding and assessment of fact is a factual issue. Under the DSU, such error cannot be appealed to the Appellate Body because it is not an issue of law as provided in Article 17.6 of the DSU. But an error in the finding or the assessment of facts can also arise from an incorrect application or interpretation of rules governing the finding or the assessment of facts. For instance, if a panel incorrectly allocates the burden of proving the existence of certain facts due to an incorrect interpretation or application of WTO provisions, it becomes an issue of law. Such issue can be appealed to the Appellate Body for review.

7.1.3 *The "Interpretation" of Domestic Law by a Domestic Court Is a Factual Issue in the Context of an International Dispute*

A domestic dispute can directly or indirectly involve foreign parties or foreign interest. For instance, one of the disputing parties in a domestic legal proceeding can be a foreign party. It is also possible that although "formally" there is no foreign "party" in a dispute, there could still be foreign interest involved.

For instance, a company registered and established under a domestic law (a "domestic" company) could be wholly invested and owned by a foreign investor. If this "domestic" company is involved in a court proceeding with a government agency concerning an investment agreement, formally speaking, this is a dispute between two domestic parties and hence the court is handling a domestic dispute. The court has *to find the fact* and *to interpret and apply* relevant domestic law governing the investment agreement between the company and the government agency. So from the perspective of domestic court with regard to the governing rules, it is interpreting and applying the domestic norms. But the foreign investor which owns the "domestic" company could be entitled to the protection under a bilateral investment treaty. Hence, it is possible that the domestic court's decision could be reviewed by an international arbitral tribunal established under the bilateral investment treaty (which governs the related investment and provides protection to this investor) to see whether the obligation of protecting a foreign investment has been breached. When the international arbitral tribunal decides the case, the "*interpretation and application of the domestic law by the domestic court*" becomes a "*factual element*" for the international arbitral tribunal to decide whether, based on the existence of such "fact", there is a breach of the related bilateral investment treaty which governs this foreign investment.

Also for instance, a domestic company alleges that a foreign product is being introduced into the domestic market at a "dumped price" (i.e. the export price which is lower than the normal value (i.e. the domestic price in the exporting country)) and asks the authorities of the importing country to conduct an investigation against such dumping practice and to impose an anti-dumping duty on the dumped product. In the domestic legal proceeding, the main parties are the applicant (which has initiated the proceeding) and the importer (which is supposed to pay the anti-dumping duty if relevant anti-dumping requirements are met). The exporters and manufacturers from the exporting country could be merely the "interested parties". But the foreign interests involved in such dispute (including the potential profits that can be earned by the foreign manufacturers and foreign exporters) are apparent and hence the domestic decision concerning the imposition of an anti-dumping duty can be reviewed by an international dispute settlement mechanism, especially by the DSM under the WTO. When a WTO's dispute settlement panel decides the case, the "*interpretation and application of the importing country's domestic anti-dumping laws by the importing country's domestic authorities*" becomes a "*fact*" or a "*factual element*" for it to decide whether, based on the existence of such fact, there is breach of the related provisions in the Anti-Dumping Agreement under the WTO, which governs the anti-dumping practice of WTO Members.

7.1.4 The Administration (Including the "Interpretation") of Domestic Law is Also a Factual Issue in the International Context

Let us use the GATT and the GATS as the examples to explain the issue. Not all international treaties have a similar provision like that provided in Article X:3(a) of the GATT, which reads: "Each contracting party shall *administer* in a uniform, impartial and reasonable manner all its laws, regulations, decisions and rulings of the kind described in paragraph 1 of this Article." (Emphasis added) Article VI:1 of the GATS also has similar provision: "In sectors where specific commitments are undertaken, each Member shall ensure that all measures of general application affecting trade in services *are administered* in a reasonable, objective and impartial manner." (Emphasis added) These unique treaty provisions also show that the "*interpretation and application of domestic law in local context*" can become *a matter of fact* in international context.

The key question here is whether the term "administer" should include the activities of "interpreting" and "applying" domestic laws and regulations in domestic context. If it does include the interpretation and application of domestic laws and regulations in domestic context, it would mean that the domestic interpretation and application of domestic rules are also subject to a review under GATT Article X:3 (a) or GATS Article VI:1. In this regard, the WTO dispute settlement Panel in *Thailand—Cigarettes (Philippines)* positively indicated that the "application of domestic laws and regulations" falls within the scope of the "administration of laws and regulations"[1]:

> … the guidance provided by the Appellate Body suggests that Article X:3(a) dictates the disciplines governing the administration of the legal instruments of the kind described in Article X:1. The scope of administration that is subject to a challenge under Article X:3(a) includes both *the manner in which the legal instruments* of the kind falling under Article X:1 *are applied or implemented* in particular cases as well as a legal instrument that regulates such application or implementation…
>
> (Emphasis added)

From the view expressed in the above panel report, it is apparent that under the GATT, the WTO Member's "*application* of its domestic laws and regulations" could be subject to review within a WTO dispute settlement proceeding to see whether the "*application* of domestic laws and regulations" is conducted in a uniform, impartial and reasonable manner.

Although the above panel report did not specifically indicate that the "*interpretation* of domestic laws and regulations" also falls within the scope of "*administration* of domestic laws and regulations", it is indicated in the same panel report that the scope of "administration" of laws and regulations is practically broad to even cover the "appointment of an administer" of laws and regulations[2]:

> Considered against the standard of 'administration' under Article X:3(a) as set out by the Appellate Body, we understand that the appointment of dual function officials as TTM directors may not be an application of the Thai customs and fiscal laws and regulations because it is not an act of applying the substance of the customs and tax provisions. Nonetheless *the broad scope of administrative processes falling within the scope of Article X:3(a)* suggests that the appointment of government officials to the director position of TTM (the only domestic company competing against imported cigarettes in the Thai

[1]Panel Report, *Thailand—Customs and Fiscal Measures on Cigarettes from the Philippines*, para. 7.873, WTO Doc. WT/DS371/R (adopted 15 July 2011).

[2]Id. at para. 7.886.

> market) may well be considered as part of the administrative process leading to *the application and implementation of the customs and fiscal measures* insofar as these government officials are sufficiently involved in *applying or implementing* the Thai customs and tax laws. (Emphasis added)

Since the concept of "*administration* of domestic laws and regulations" conducted by WTO Members is broad in scope, the term "administration" in this context should be able to include the "*interpretation* of domestic laws and regulations" by WTO Members, in addition to the "*application* of domestic laws and regulations". Also the interpretation and application of domestic laws and regulations are theoretically and practically closely connected. In many situations, there must be a proper interpretation of a domestic provision before a decision can be made as to whether it is applicable. In some other situations, the application of a domestic law provision is not a problem, but the way of interpreting it is an issue. Hence, the interpretation and application of domestic laws and regulations cannot be practically divided.

In sum, the "*interpretation* of domestic laws and regulations" by domestic courts or domestic administrative agencies is a "matter of fact" that can be reviewed in international context (by the WTO dispute settlement procedure) from the perspective of whether the interpretation is conducted in a uniform, impartial and reasonable manner.

7.2 Fact Finding and Treaty Interpretation

7.2.1 Procedural Rules for Fact-Finding and Their Relations with Treaty Interpretation

Whether specifically and comprehensively or generally and loosely designed, there are always procedural rules governing the fact-finding authorities of an adjudicator under various DSMs. Since these rules are parts of the treaty governing the procedural aspects of a dispute, there could be treaty application and interpretation issues involved in relation to the procedural rules when the adjudicator exercises his/her power under such rules.

In other words, treaty application and treaty interpretation issues are not limited to the application and interpretation of the "substantive provisions" in the governing treaty. The issues also include the application and interpretation of "procedural rules" in the governing treaty. So under the procedural rules, there could be the fact-finding activities conducted by the adjudicator in accordance with such rules; there could also be the adjudicator's activities of treaty application and interpretation so as to decide the proper understanding and application of such "procedural rules".

To use the WTO dispute settlement procedure as an example, there are many rules provided in the DSU to govern the fact-finding as well as the treaty application and interpretation activities of a panel and the Appellate Body. Some of the rules are provided in Appendix 3 "Working Procedures" to the DSU. For instance, paragraph 2 of the "Working Procedure" in the Appendix provides that: "The panel shall meet in closed session. The parties to the dispute, and interested parties, shall be present at the meetings only when invited by the panel to appear before it." Under such rule, all other WTO Members (which are neither the disputing parties, nor the third parties) are basically not permitted to be present at the meeting. In the close sessions, the panel is to hear the factual and legal arguments by the parties (and sometimes by the third parties). But Article 12.1 of the DSU provides that "Panels shall follow the Working Procedures in Appendix 3 unless the panel decides otherwise after consulting the parties to the dispute." In other words, it is possible for a panel to permit non-parties to be present after having consulted the disputing parties. However, it is also provided in Article 12.2 of the DSU that "Panel procedures should provide sufficient flexibility so as to ensure high-quality panel reports, while not unduly delaying the panel process." Suppose a panel decides to allow WTO Members which are neither the disputing parties nor the third parties to "observe" the conducting of a panel's "close session" in a *separate* room at the WTO building *via* a closed circuit broadcast. Issues arise as to whether such meeting is still a closed session; whether the disputing parties have to be consulted by the panel before the panel decides the broadcasting; and whether the broadcasting is the flexibility as expected by Article 12.2 of the DSU. These are issues concerning the proper interpretation and application of the procedural rules in the DSU.

The issues concerning the proper "interpretation and application of procedural rules" affect two other activities of an international adjudicator: (1) They affect the fact-finding activities of the adjudicator. It is because the adjudicator has to conduct its fact-finding duties based on the procedural rules as interpreted. For instance, the interpretation of the provision in DSU Article 11 (which requires a panel to make an "objective assessment of facts") definitely would affect the manner adopted by the panel in "objectively assessing the facts" in the dispute. (2) They also affect the activities of treaty interpretation of "substantive rules". It is because many dispute settlement rules directly or indirectly relate to the interpretation of "substantive" treaty provisions. For instance, DSU Article 11 requires that a panel should make an "objective assessment of the matter before it". The requirement of an "objective assessment of the matter" would definitely include the objective "assessment of the legal issues". Hence, the proper interpretation of the "objectiveness" of assessing the matter could decide whether an interpretation of a governing WTO provision is "objective" and hence could affect the manner of treaty interpretation adopted by the panel. Also for instance, DSU Article 3.2 provides in part that: "The Members recognize that it serves to preserve the rights and obligations of Members under the covered agreements, and to clarify the existing provisions of those agreements in accordance with *customary rules of interpretation of public international law*." The interpretation of this "procedural" rule concerning the scope of "customary rules of interpretation" would definitely affect the interpretation of "substantive" WTO rules. If DSU Article 3.2 is interpreted broadly so as "not" to exclude those other rules of interpretation not specifically enumerated and provided in the VCLT, then many other possible rules can be brought into the treaty interpretation activities conducted by the panel and the Appellate Body. This would definitely affect the result of the interpretation of the substantive WTO rules.

7.2.2 *Evidential Rules for Fact-Finding Activities Under the WTO Which Need Interpretation*

An important set of procedural rules which affect the fact-finding activities is the rules of evidence. The rules of evidence are rules to decide the allocation of burden of proof and the admissibility, relevance, weight and sufficiency of evidence.[3] Among these, the burden of proof is a constant dispute in international dispute settlement procedures, especially in the WTO procedures.

The Appellate Body and the dispute settlement panels have formulated quite a number of rules so as to interpret and supplement the provisions in the DSU. The following are the main principles established or clarified by the Appellate Body and by some dispute settlement panels:

First, the party asserting a fact bears the burden of providing proof: The Appellate Body has set forth the general principle of requiring the party (whether it is the claimant or the respondent) who asserts a fact to bear the burden of providing proof thereof. In *US—Wool Shirts and Blouses*, the Appellate Body has expressed a clear rule in this regard[4]:

> [W]e find it difficult, indeed, to see how any system of judicial settlement could work if it incorporated the proposition that the mere assertion of a claim might amount to proof. It is, thus, hardly surprising that various international tribunals, including the International Court of Justice, have generally and consistently accepted and applied the rule that *the party who asserts a fact, whether the claimant or the respondent, is responsible for providing proof thereof.*[5] Also, it is a generally-accepted canon of evidence in civil law, common law and, in fact, most jurisdictions, that *the burden of proof rests upon the party, whether complaining or defending, who asserts the affirmative of a particular claim or defence*. If that party adduces evidence sufficient to raise a presumption that what is claimed is true, the burden then shifts to the other party, who will fail unless it adduces sufficient evidence to rebut the presumption.[6] (Emphasis added)

[3]What are the Rules of Evidence?. http://hirealawyer.findlaw.com/choosing-the-right-lawyer/evidence-law.html. Accessed 8 Aug 2017.

[4]Appellate Body Report, *United States—Measures Affecting Imports of Woven Wool Shirts and Blouses from India*, p. 14, WTO Doc. WT/DS33/AB/R (adopted 23 May 1997) [hereinafter US—Wool Shirts and Blouses Appellate Body Report].

[5]Id. (citing Kazazi (1996), p. 117).

[6]Id. (citing Howard et al. (1990), p. 52 ("The burden of proof rests upon the party, whether plaintiff or defendant, who substantially asserts the affirmative of the issue."); Rutherford and Bone (eds) (1993), p. 266; Jowitt and Walsh (1977), p. 263; Curzon (1983), p. 47; Nouveau Code de Procédure Civile, Art. 9; Carbonnier (1991), p. 320; Chevalier and Bach (1995), p. 101; Guillien and Vincent (1995, p. 384); Samyn et al. (1986, p. 250); Pérez (1992, p. 311); Bianca et al. (1991, p. 550), Galgano (1994, p. 873); and Trabucchi (1991), p. 210.

> In the context of the GATT 1994 and the *WTO Agreement*, precisely how much and precisely what kind of evidence will be required to establish such a presumption will necessarily vary from measure to measure, provision to provision, and case to case.

Second, the initial burden lies on the complaining party, which must establish a *prima facie* case of inconsistency. This is the extent of proof needed to satisfy and discharge the initial burden assumed by the complainant. In *EC—Hormones*, the Appellate Body indicated the following criterion of establishing a *prima facie* case[7]:

> The initial burden lies on the complaining party, which must establish a *prima facie* case of inconsistency with a particular provision of the *SPS Agreement* on the part of the defending party, or more precisely, of its SPS measure or measures complained about. When that *prima facie* case is made, the burden of proof moves to the defending party, which must in turn counter or refute the claimed inconsistency. This seems straightforward enough and is in conformity with our ruling in *United States – Shirts and Blouses,*[8] which the Panel invokes and which embodies a rule applicable in any adversarial proceedings.

In *EC—Hormones*, the Appellate Body further stated the following concerning the establishment of a *prima facie* case:

> …The general rule in a dispute settlement proceeding requiring a complaining party to establish a *prima facie* case of inconsistency with a provision of the *SPS Agreement* before the burden of showing consistency with that provision is taken on by the defending party, is *not* avoided by simply describing that same provision as an 'exception'. In much the same way, merely characterizing a treaty provision as an 'exception' does not by itself justify a 'stricter' or 'narrower' interpretation of that provision than would be warranted by examination of the ordinary meaning of the actual treaty words, viewed in context and in the light of the treaty's object and purpose, or, in other words, by applying the normal rules of treaty interpretation. It is also well to remember that a *prima facie* case is one which, in the absence of effective refutation by the defending party, requires a panel, as a matter of law, to rule in favour of the complaining party presenting the *prima facie* case.[9]

Third, a panel has a wide discretion to require information so as to determine whether there is a *prima facie* case. In *Canada—Aircraft*, the panel expressed:

> …A *prima facie* case, it is well to remember, is a case which, in the absence of effective refutation by the defending party (that is, in the present appeal, the Member requested to provide the information), requires a panel, as a matter of law, to rule in favour of the complaining party presenting the *prima facie* case. There is, as noted earlier, nothing in either the DSU or the *SCM Agreement* to support Canada's assumption. To the contrary, a panel is vested with ample and extensive discretionary authority to determine *when* it needs information to resolve a dispute and *what* information it needs. A panel may need such information before or after a complaining or a responding Member has established its complaint or defence on a *prima facie* basis. A panel may, in fact, need the information sought in order to evaluate evidence already before it in the course of determining whether

[7]Appellate Body Report, *European Communities—Measures Concerning Meat and Meat Products (Hormones)*, para. 98, WTO Doc. WT/DS26/AB/R, WT/DS48/AB/R (adopted 13 Feb 1998) [hereinafter EC—Hormones Appellate Body Report].

[8]Id. (citing US—Wool Shirts and Blouses Appellate Body Report, *supra* note 4, at p. 14).

[9]Id. at paras. 102, 104. See also Panel Report, *Brazil—Export Financing Programme for Aircraft (Article 21.5—Canada)*, para. 6.22, WTO Doc. WT/DS46/RW (adopted 4 Aug 2000).

> the claiming or the responding Member, as the case may be, has established a *prima facie* case or defence. Furthermore, a refusal to provide information requested on the basis that a *prima facie* case has not been made implies that the Member concerned believes that it is able to judge for itself whether the other party has made a *prima facie* case. However, no Member is free to determine for itself whether a *prima facie* case or defence has been established by the other party. That competence is necessarily vested in the panel under the DSU, and not in the Members that are parties to the dispute.[10]

Fourth, the requirements of an affirmative defence raised by the responding party are to be proven by this party, whereas the violation of a positive obligation is to be proven by the complaining party. In *Brazil—Aircraft*, the Appellate Body stated the following in this regard:

> On reading paragraphs 2(b) and 4 of Article 27 together, it is clear that the conditions set forth in paragraph 4 are *positive obligations* for developing country Members, *not* affirmative defences. If a developing country Member complies with the obligations in Article 27.4, the prohibition on export subsidies in Article 3.1(a) simply does not apply. However, if that developing country Member does *not* comply with those obligations, Article 3.1(a) *does* apply.
>
> For these reasons, we agree with the Panel that the burden is on the complaining party (*in casu* Canada) to demonstrate that the developing country Member (*in casu* Brazil) is not in compliance with at least one of the elements set forth in Article 27.4. If such non-compliance is demonstrated, then, and only then, does the prohibition of Article 3.1(a) *apply* to that developing country Member.[11]

Fifth, the party applying a proviso is responsible to prove that the requirements in the proviso have been met. In *India—Quantitative Restrictions*, the Appellate Body explained:

> Assuming that the complaining party has successfully established a *prima facie* case of inconsistency with Article XVIII:11 and the Ad Note, the responding party may, in its defence, either rebut the evidence adduced in support of the inconsistency or invoke the proviso. In the latter case, it would have to demonstrate that the complaining party violated its obligation not to require the responding party to change its development policy. This is an assertion with respect to which the responding party must bear the burden of proof. We, therefore, agree with the Panel that the burden of proof with respect to the proviso is on India.[12]

Sixth, the benefit of the doubt should be given to the defending party in the dispute when evidence remains in equipoise. In *US—Section 301 Trade Act*, the Panel expressed:

---

[10] Appellate Body Report, *Canada—Measures Affecting the Export of Civilian Aircraft*, para. 192, WTO Doc. WT/DS70/AB/R (adopted 20 Aug 1999) [hereinafter Canada—Aircraft Appellate Body Report]. See also id. at paras. 217–219.

[11] Appellate Body Report, *Brazil—Export Financing Programme for Aircraft*, paras. 140–141, WTO Doc. WT/DS46/AB/R (adopted 20 Aug 1999).

[12] Appellate Body Report, *India—Quantitative Restrictions on Imports of Agricultural, Textile and Industrial Products*, para. 136, WTO Doc. WT/DS90/AB/R (adopted 22 Sept 199) [hereinafter India—Quantitative Restrictions Appellate Body Report].

> Since, in this case, both parties have submitted extensive facts and arguments in respect of the EC claims, our task will essentially be to balance all evidence on record and decide whether the EC, as party bearing the original burden of proof, has convinced us of the validity of its claims. *In case of uncertainty, i.e. in case all the evidence and arguments remain in equipoise, we have to give the benefit of the doubt to the US as defending party.*[13]

Seventh, the application of burden of proof is an issue of law. It can be appealed to the Appellate Body. In *India—Patents (US)*, the Appellate Body mentioned:

> … it is not sufficient for a panel to enunciate the correct approach to burden of proof; a panel must also apply the burden of proof correctly. A careful reading of paragraphs 7.35 and 7.37 of the Panel Report reveals that the Panel has done so in this case. These paragraphs show that the United States put forward evidence and arguments that India's "administrative instructions" pertaining to mailbox applications were legally insufficient to prevail over the application of certain mandatory provisions of the Patents Act. India put forward rebuttal evidence and arguments. India misinterprets what the Panel said about "reasonable doubts". The Panel did not require the United States merely to raise "reasonable doubts" before the burden shifted to India. Rather, after properly requiring the United States to establish a *prima facie* case and after hearing India's rebuttal evidence and arguments, the Panel concluded that *it* had "reasonable doubts" that the "administrative instructions" would prevail over the mandatory provisions of the Patents Act if a challenge were brought in an Indian court.
>
> For these reasons, we conclude that the Panel applied the burden of proof correctly in assessing the compliance of India's domestic law with Article 70.8(a) of the *TRIPS Agreement.*[14]

Eighth, the assessment of evidence is a matter of fact, but of course such assessment should be subject to DSU Article 11 which requires such assessment to be objective. In *India—Quantitative Restrictions*, the Appellate Body restated again that "weighing and assessing of the evidence" was not an issue of law and hence cannot be reviewed by it:

As to the second alleged mistake, namely, that the evidence introduced by the United States could not, as a matter of law, have constituted a *prima facie* case that India's balance-of-payments restrictions were not justified under the Ad Note, we recall that in *European Communities—Hormones*, the Appellate Body stated:

> Determination of the credibility and weight properly to be ascribed to (that is, the appreciation of) a given piece of evidence is part and parcel of the fact finding process and is, in principle, left to the discretion of a panel as the trier of facts …

Similarly, in *Korea—Taxes on Alcoholic Beverages*, the Appellate Body stated:

---

[13]Panel Report, *United States—Sections 301–310 of the Trade Act 1974*, para. 7.14, WTO Doc. WT/DS152/R (adopted 27 Jan 2000).

[14]Appellate Body Report, *India—Patent Protection for Pharmaceutical and Agricultural Chemical Products*, paras. 73–75, WTO Doc. WT/DS50/AB/R (adopted 16 Jan 1998).

> The Panel's examination and weighing of the evidence submitted fall, in principle, within the scope of the Panel's discretion as the trier of facts and, accordingly, outside the scope of appellate review. …

We believe that this second mistake alleged by India relates to the weighing and assessing of the evidence adduced by the United States, and is, therefore, outside the scope of appellate review.[15]

7.2.3 Relation Between the Rules of Burden of Proof and Treaty Interpretation

The rules of burden of proof have two functions. They allocate the onus of presenting the necessary evidence so that the party carrying the onus will have to put efforts in presenting evidence to persuade the adjudicator about the real factual aspects in the case. The rules also decide the final result of a disputed issue if the party carrying the onus is unable to submit the necessary evidence to discharge its burden. Hence such rules are a key component in a rule-based DSM. However, in most international dispute settlement rules, the burden of proof is not explicitly provided. Even in the very detailed DSU, the burden of proof is not specifically mentioned.

The Appellate Body was able to develop many useful rules to decide which party is to carry such onus, as mentioned above. Since these rules of burden of proof (such as the party asserting a fact to bear the burden of proof; the complaining party bearing the initial burden to establish a *prima facie* case of inconsistency; the requirements of an affirmative defence being proven by the responding party and a violation of a positive obligation being proven by the complaining party) are not found in the DSU, a question which arises in this context is about the "nature" of the rules.

The book considers that the rules are created by the Appellate Body and some panels as a result of their *interpretation of the DSU*. But it must be borne in mind that this is not an interpretation of a specific provision or a specific term of the DSU. It is rather to look at the "overall context" of the whole DSU and to interpret the DSU as a whole.

To further explain: A panel's function under the DSU, as proved in Article 11 of it, is to assist the DSB in discharging its responsibilities under the DSU and the covered agreements by making an objective assessment of the matter before it, including an objective assessment of the facts of the case and the applicability of and conformity with the relevant covered agreements, and by making such other findings as will assist the DSB in making the recommendations or in giving the rulings provided for in the covered agreements. In order to conduct the assessment of the facts of the case for the purpose of applying a related WTO agreement, the

---

[15] India—Quantitative Restrictions Appellate Body Report, *supra* note 12, at paras. 143–144.

facts must have been established and found by the panel. For a panel to find the facts, there must be rules to be based on. Hence the above rules of burden of proof created by the Appellate Body and by some panels are the result of *interpreting the DSU as a whole* and interpreting DSU Article 11 specifically so that the dispute settlement procedure can be conducted properly and the function of a panel under Article 11 of the DSU can be performed.

From the above explanation, we can also understand that although treaty interpretation is mostly about the interpretation of a specific term or a specific provision in a treaty so as to find the proper meaning of the interpreted term or provision, it is also possible that an interpreter will have to look at the "treaty at issue as a whole" so as to fill the legislative vacuum and to make the mechanism function. This aspect of treaty interpretation is particularly important for treaties of procedural nature. Things to be filled are additional rules governing the procedures. These rules must be essential elements for the purpose of making the mechanism properly function.

7.2.4 *Amicus Curiae* Submission and Its Relations with Treaty Interpretation

An *amicus curiae* submission is a submission from the "friend of the court". It is a submission presented by non-parties to a dispute. Such submissions are often presented by NGOs, the related industries, and even university professors for the purpose of pursuing certain causes or objectives (such as human rights or environmental protection).

There are two aspects concerning the relations between the *amicus curiae* submission on the one hand and the treaty interpretation on the other hand. The first aspect is that an *amicus curiae* submission can affect treaty interpretation conducted by the adjudicator. The second aspect is that whether or not an international dispute settlement procedure allows an *amicus curiae* submission depends on the interpretation of the procedural rules governing such DSM.

Concerning the first aspect, the views presented by an *amicus curiae* submission can include the general views or comments on the dispute, the specific views on the factual background (such as scientific evidence relevant to the dispute) and even the specific views on the proper interpretation and application of a specific treaty. In this regard, the *amicus curiae* submission is not only related to fact-finding activities of the adjudicator, but also relevant to the treaty interpretation and application. If such submission concerns treaty interpretation, the adjudicator might find it useful to consider the views expressed in the submission when it conducts treaty interpretation activities.

Concerning the second aspect, in the WTO context, there is no specific rule under the DSU and under its Working Procedures in Appendix 3 to the DSU for a panel or for the Appellate Body to decide whether to accept an *amicus* submission.

But Article 13.1 of the DSU indicates that each panel shall have the right to seek information and technical advice from any individual or body which it deems appropriate. Although an *amicus* submission is not solicited by the panel, still it can be considered as "information or technical advice from an individual or body", because Article 13.1 of the DSU does not limit to solicited information and advice.

Also Article 12.1 of the DSU provides that a panel shall follow the Working Procedures in Appendix 3 unless it decides otherwise after consulting the parties to the dispute. Article 12.2 provides that panel procedures should provide sufficient flexibility so as to ensure high-quality panel reports, while not unduly delaying the panel process. These provisions have provided flexibility for the panel to decide the acceptance of an *amicus curiae* submission.

Although the issue of whether to accept an *amicus* submission is still controversial under the WTO,[16] the Appellate Body has made clear that a panel and the Appellate Body itself have the right to decide the acceptance of an *amicus* submission. In *US—Shrimp*, the Appellate Body said[17]:

> 106. The thrust of Articles 12 and 13, taken together, is that the DSU accords to a panel established by the DSB, and engaged in a dispute settlement proceeding, ample and extensive authority to undertake and to control the process by which it informs itself both of the relevant facts of the dispute and of the legal norms and principles applicable to such facts. That authority, and the breadth thereof, is indispensably necessary to enable a panel to discharge its duty imposed by Article 11 of the DSU to "make an objective assessment of the matter before it, including an *objective assessment of the facts of the case and the applicability of and conformity with the relevant covered agreements* ...." (Emphasis added)
>
> 107. Against this context of broad authority vested in panels by the DSU, and given the object and purpose of the Panel's mandate as revealed in Article 11, we do not believe that the word "seek" must necessarily be read, as apparently the Panel read it, in too literal a manner. That the Panel's reading of the word "seek" is unnecessarily formal and technical in nature becomes clear should an "individual or body" first ask a panel for permission to file a statement or a brief. In such an event, a panel may decline to grant the leave requested. If, in the exercise of its sound discretion in a particular case, a panel concludes *inter alia* that it could do so without "unduly delaying the panel process", it could grant permission to file a statement or a brief, subject to such conditions as it deems appropriate. The exercise of the panel's discretion could, of course, and perhaps should, include consultation with the parties to the dispute. In this kind of situation, for all practical and pertinent purposes, the distinction between "requested" and "non-requested" information vanishes.
>
> 108. In the present context, authority to seek information is not properly equated with a prohibition on accepting information which has been submitted without having been requested by a panel. A panel has the discretionary authority either to accept and consider or to reject information and advice submitted to it, *whether requested by a panel or not*. The fact that a panel may *motu proprio* have initiated the request for information does not, by itself, bind the panel to accept and consider the information which is actually submitted. The amplitude of the authority vested in panels to shape the processes of fact-finding and

---

[16]Participation in Dispute Settlement Proceedings. https://www.wto.org/english/tratop_e/dispu_e/disp_settlement_cbt_e/c9s3p1_e.htm#txt2. Accessed 8 Aug 2017.

[17]Appellate Body Report, *United States—Import Prohibition of Certain Shrimp and Shrimp Products*, paras. 106–108, WTO Doc. WT/DS58/AB/R (adopted 6 Nov 1998).

legal interpretation makes clear that a panel will *not* be deluged, as it were, with non-requested material, *unless that panel allows itself to be so deluged.*

The Appellate Body's decision on whether to accept an *amicus* submission is actually the result of treaty interpretation of Articles 11, 12 and 13 of the DSU. These articles serve as *mutual contexts* to each other to allow the Appellate Body to come up with a conclusion that a panel has a wide discretion to decide the acceptance or rejection of an *amicus curiae* submission.

7.3 An Assessment of Facts and Treaty Interpretation

7.3.1 Objective Assessment of Facts and Its Relations with Treaty Interpretation

For an adjudicator which has responsibility to decide the factual issues, its responsibility is not merely to collect evidence to establish a factual background. The adjudicator is also to make proper assessment of the facts that he/she finds. In WTO context, there are some rules in the DSU to be based upon by the panel to properly assess the facts.

Article 11 (entitled "Function of Panels") provides in part that:

> … a panel should make an *objective assessment of the matter* before it, including an *objective assessment of the facts* of the case and the applicability of and conformity with the relevant covered agreements, and make such other findings as will assist the DSB in making the recommendations or in giving the rulings provided for in the covered agreements…

The requirement of an *objective assessment of the matter* should include the *objective assessment of facts* and the *objective assessment of applicable rules* (i.e. the proper interpretation of the governing provisions and the proper application of these rules to the found facts).

There are a number of aspects concerning an *objective assessment of facts*. First, an objective assessment of facts would require sufficient evidences to establish the factual background. If the evidence is insufficient, the adjudicator will not be able to make any objective assessment of the facts. In case the insufficiency is the result of a party's failure to discharge its burden of proof, the adverse result should be given to such party.

Second, an objective assessment of facts includes *drawing inferences* from the facts on the record. The Panel in *US—Large Civil Aircraft (2nd complaint)* quoted some statements of the Appellate Body in *Canada—Aircraft*: "… we note that the Appellate Body, in *Canada —Aircraft*, indicated that *drawing inferences from facts on the record is a routine and inherent aspect* of a panel's discharging its obligation under Article 11 of the DSU."[18] (Emphasis added)

Also in *US—Wheat Gluten*, the Appellate Body explained the need of drawing inference from the facts by the panel and stated that[19]:

> We … characterized the *drawing of inferences as a 'discretionary' task falling within a panel's duties under Article 11 of the DSU*. In *Canada — Aircraft*, which involved a similar factual situation, the panel did not draw any inferences 'adverse' to Canada's position. On appeal, we held that there was no basis to find that the panel had improperly exercised its discretion since 'the full ensemble of the facts on the record' supported the panel's conclusion.[20]
>
> In its appeal, the European Communities places considerable emphasis on the failure of the Panel to *draw 'adverse' inferences* from the refusal of the United States to provide information requested by the Panel. As we emphasized in *Canada — Aircraft*, under Article 11 of the DSU, *a panel must draw inferences on the basis of all of the facts of record relevant to the particular determination to be made*. Where a party refuses to provide information requested by a panel under Article 13.1 of the DSU, that refusal will be one of the relevant facts of record, and indeed an important fact, to be taken into account in determining the appropriate inference to be drawn. However, if a panel were to ignore or disregard other relevant facts, it would fail to make an 'objective assessment' under Article 11 of the DSU. In this case, as the Panel observed, there were other facts of record that the Panel was required to include in its 'objective assessment'. Accordingly, we reject the European Communities' arguments to the extent that they suggest that the Panel erred in not drawing 'adverse' inferences simply from the refusal of the United States to provide certain information requested from it by the Panel under Article 13.1 of the DSU. (Emphasis added)

Third, a deliberate rejection of an evidence by a panel is not in line with requirement of an objective assessment of fact. The Appellate Body indicated in *EC—Hormones* that[21]:

> The duty to make an objective assessment of the facts is, among other things, an obligation to consider the evidence presented to a panel and to make factual findings on the basis of that evidence. The deliberate disregard of, or refusal to consider, the evidence submitted to a panel is incompatible with a panel's duty to make an objective assessment of the facts. The wilful distortion or misrepresentation of the evidence put before a panel is similarly inconsistent with an objective assessment of the facts.

[18]Panel Report, *United States—Measures Affecting Trade in Large Civil Aircraft—Second Complaint*, para. 7.1820, WTO Doc. WT/DS353/R (adopted 23 Mar 2012).

[19]Appellate Body Report, *United States—Definitive Safeguard Measures on Imports of Wheat Gluten from the European Communities*, paras. 173–174, WTO Doc. WT/DS166/AB/R (adopted 19 Jan 2001).

[20]Id. (citing Canada—Aircraft Appellate Body Report, *supra* note 10, at paras. 204–205).

[21]EC—Hormones Appellate Body Report, *supra* note 7, at para. 133.

Fourth, the panel enjoys a margin of discretion in its objective assessment of facts. In *Japan—Apples*, the Appellate Body stated[22]:

> Since EC-Hormones, the Appellate Body has consistently emphasized that, within the bounds of their obligation under Article 11 to make an objective assessment of the facts of the case, *panels enjoy a "margin of discretion" as triers of fact*. Panels are thus "not required to accord to factual evidence of the parties the same meaning and weight as do the parties" (983) and may properly 'determine that certain elements of evidence should be accorded more weight than other elements'.
>
> Consistent with this margin of discretion, the Appellate Body has recognized that "not every error in the appreciation of the evidence (although it may give rise to a question of law) may be characterized as a failure to make an objective assessment of the facts." When addressing claims under Article 11 of the DSU, the *Appellate Body does not "second-guess the Panel in appreciating either the evidentiary value of ... studies or the consequences*, if any, of alleged defects in [the evidence]". (Emphasis added)

The above rules governing an objective assessment of facts are developed by the Appellate Body in *its treaty interpretation activities* in relation to Article 11 of the DSU. The rules are developed in connection with and given to the meaning of the phrase the "objective assessment of facts". Whether or not an assessment of facts is complying with the objectiveness requirement is a matter to be decided based on the interpretation results of the term "objective". This is one of the relations between the assessment of facts on the one hand and the treaty interpretation on the other hand.

Another relation between the assessment of facts and the treaty interpretation is in their respective sequence. In principle, there must be facts being found so that a panel is able to make assessment of the found facts. But sometimes the finding of facts and the assessment of facts are not so clearly distinguished. As mentioned above, the submission of evidence is part of the fact-finding process. But a deliberate rejection of relevant evidence can be considered as non-objective assessment of facts. After the facts are found and objectively assessed, there will be the application of treaty provisions to the facts and, if necessary, the interpretation of the relevant provisions. So the sequence is to find the fact, then to assess the fact, and then to interpret the rule and to apply it to the found and assessed fact.

7.3.2 **De Novo** ***Review or Total Deference to Decide the Fact and Its Relations with Treaty Interpretation***

The issue of an objective assessment of facts includes the decision of the standard of review under the DSU. If a panel is requested to review a measure which has been decided under a domestic mechanism, an issue arises as to whether the panel should

[22]Appellate Body Report, *Japan—Measures Affecting the Importation of Apples*, paras. 221–222, WTO Doc. WT/DS245/AB/R (adopted 10 Dec 2003).

start deciding the facts all overall again or whether it should respect the decision on the facts under the domestic mechanism. In this regard, the Appellate Body has indicated that a panel is not to engage in a "*de novo* review". Neither is a panel to pay "total deference" to the domestic decision. It must be in between these two extremes.

In *EC—Hormones*, the Appellate Body indicted that the standard of review under Article 11 of the *DSU* is neither "de novo review", nor "total deference", but rather the "objective assessment of facts". It stated[23]:

> So far as fact-finding by panels is concerned, their activities are always constrained by the mandate of Article 11 of the DSU: the applicable standard is neither *de novo* review as such, nor "total deference", but rather the "objective assessment of the facts".

The standard of review (i.e. not being a de novo review, nor a total deference) is to guide the assessment of facts. It is set forth by the Appellate Body and is also the result of its interpretation of the provision of "objective assessment of facts" stated in Article 11 of the DSU. In other words, treaty interpretation could affect the decision of the standard of review under a DSM. This is one of the relations between the standard of review and treaty interpretation. Another relation between these two aspects is also in their respective sequence. This is similar to the above-mentioned relations between the assessment of facts and treaty interpretation. In other words, there must be an assessment of fact made by the panel based on the standard of review in the first place, before the application and interpretation of substantive rules can be exercised by the panel.

To conclude the discussions in this chapter and from the perspective of codification, the book is of the view that it would be useful to make it clear in a codified set of rules of treaty interpretation to the adjudicator that he/she has a broader and more flexible latitude to interpret the procedural rules which govern the dispute before him/her (including the rules for the fact finding and for the fact assessment as well as for the evidential rules) and that when he/she has to decide the range of authorities in conducting the dispute settlement proceeding, an interpretation of the procedural rules governing the handling of dispute should be conducted in consideration of the treaty as a whole so as to make the dispute settlement mechanism envisaged by the contracting parties properly function.

References

Bianca CM, Patti S, Patti G (1991) Lessico di Diritto Civile. Giuffrè, Milano
Carbonnier J (1991) Droit civil, introduction, 20th edn. Presses Universitaires de France, Paris
Chevalier J, Bach L (1995) Droit civil, vol 1, 12th edn. Sirey, Paris
Curzon LB (1983) A directory of law, 2nd edn. Macdonald and Evans, London
Galgano F (1994) Diritto Privato, 8th edn. Casa Editrice Dott. Antonio Milani, Padova

[23]EC—Hormones Appellate Body Report, *supra* note 7, at para. 117.

Guillien R, Vincent J (1995) Termes juridiques, 10th edn. Dalloz, Paris
Howard MN, Crane P, Hochberg DA (1990) Phipson on evidence, 14th edn. Sweet & Maxwell, London
Jowitt E, Walsh C (1977) Jowitt's dictionary of english law, vol 1, 2nd edn. Sweet & Maxwell, London (ed. by J. Burke)
Kazazi M (1996) Burden of proof and related issues: a study on evidence before international tribunals. Kluwer Law International, Hague
Participation in Dispute Settlement Proceedings. https://www.wto.org/English/tratop_e/dispu_e/disp_settlement_cbt_e/c9s3p1_e.htm#txt2. Accessed 8 Aug 2017
Pérez JG (1992) Manual de Derecho Procesal Administrativo, 2nd edn. Civitas, Madrid
Rutherford L, Bone S (eds) (1993) Osborn's concise law dictionary, 8th edn. Sweet & Maxwell, London
Samyn O, Simonetta P, Sogno C (1986) Dictionnaire des Termes Juridiques. Editions de Vecchi, Paris
Trabucchi A (1991) Istituzioni di Diritto Civile. Casa Editrice Dott. Antonio Milani, Padova
What are the Rules of Evidence? http://hirealawyer.findlaw.com/choosing-the-right-lawyer/evidence-law.html. Accessed 8 Aug 2017

Chapter 8
International Adjudicating and Non-adjudicating Bodies as Treaty Interpreters and the Possible Codification

Contents

8.1 Clarification Between Dispute Settlement Mechanism, Adjudicators and Interpreters

A DSM is a set of procedures created under a legal system for handling disputes arising from and within the legal system. A DSM in domestic context mainly includes domestic court systems, arbitration and mediation/conciliation. A DSM in international context includes the mechanisms under permanent international tribunals, international arbitration, and international mediation/conciliation. Among these DSMs, mediation/conciliation is considered as a friendly DSM.

A DSM could be rule-based, power-based or negotiation-based. A rule-based DSM is to have the mechanism designed in a way so that a dispute is resolved strictly based on certain pre-established procedural and substantive rules. So a rule-based DSM includes two aspects. A set of pre-established procedural rules must be there so that the proceedings will be conducted in accordance with such rules. Also a set of pre-established or designated substantive rules must exist so that the resolution will be substantively based on such rules. Since a rule-based DSM will have to rely on the pre-established or designated procedural and substantive

C. Lo, *Treaty Interpretation Under the Vienna Convention on the Law of Treaties*,
https://doi.org/10.1007/978-981-10-6866-9_8

rules, it is possible that there are conflicts of views about the proper meaning of a provision in such rules. A rule-based DSM would definitely require interpretations of the applicable procedural and substantive norms. In the context of the WTO, the applicable procedural rules are mainly provided in the DSU and the applicable substantive rules are provided in various multilateral and plurilateral trade agreements under the WTO. Both the DSU and other substantive multilateral and plurilateral trade agreements under the WTO will have to be interpreted based on the VCLT and other treaty interpretation rules.

Under a mechanism for a friendly settlement of dispute, there will be the third neutral party (a mediator or conciliator) helping the parties to settle their dispute. The mediator or conciliator in the procedure is not an adjudicator. They only assist the parties and facilitate the conclusion of a settlement agreement between the disputing parties. Their duty does not include deciding the rights and obligations between the disputing parties. Generally, they are not expected to apply a substantive norm for the purpose of conducting mediation or conciliation. Hence, they basically do not have to interpret a governing norm.

In principle, only courts and arbitral tribunals, which are not considered as mechanisms for friendly settlement of disputes, will have to decide the application of a substantive norm and hence will have to interpret the provisions in the written norm.

But of course, this is only a general explanation. Depending on the design of a DSM, it is possible that a mediator or a conciliator will also have to interpret a written norm. For instance, prior to the establishment of the WTO, the GATT 1947 was operated with a dispute settlement procedure under GATT Article XXIII, which required disputing parties to engage in consultation. If not satisfactory, the contracting parties acting jointly shall promptly investigate any matter so referred to them and shall make appropriate recommendations or give a ruling on the matter. In earlier years of GATT 1947, disputes were decided by rulings of the Chairman of the GATT Council. Later, disputes were referred to the "working parties" composed of representatives from all interested GATT contracting parties, which included the disputing parties. In the late years of the GATT 1947, the working parties approach was replaced by *ad hoc* panels composed by three or five independent experts unrelated to the disputing parties. They prepared independent reports with recommendations and rulings to be submitted to the GATT Council, which decided the approval of the reports so as to make them binding on the disputing parties.[1] The panels in the age of the GATT 1947 actually had the function of promoting negotiated settlements through conciliation. But the panels also actually interpreted GATT provisions.

It must be also noted that a set of dispute settlement mechanism could concurrently include friendly and unfriendly settlement of disputes. For instance, the

[1]World Trade Organization. Historic Development of the WTO Dispute Settlement System. https://www.wto.org/english/tratop_e/dispu_e/disp_settlement_cbt_e/c2s1p1_e.html. Accessed 8 Aug 2017.

DSU under the WTO makes the panel and Appellate Body procedures (the more legalistic procedures), the good offices, mediation and conciliation (the friendlier procedure), and the arbitration procedures (the more legalistic procedures) available for the disputing parties to choose. Also prior to resorting to any procedure, the disputing parties will have to try mutually settling their dispute through consultation. In the panel and Appellate Body procedures, the panel and the Appellate Body are treaty interpreters. They have to interpret WTO agreements. But in the good offices, mediation and conciliation, the third neutral party is supposed to bring the disputing parties together for mutual settlement of their dispute. The third neutral party is not a treaty interpreter. Also in the consultation procedure, the parties are expected to settle their dispute on their own, without any third party's assistance. The disputing parties themselves are not treaty interpreters in the sense that the interpretation outcome will serve as the basis of deciding the dispute.

8.2 International Adjudicating Bodies to Interpret Treaties

8.2.1 Some Traditional International Adjudicating Bodies and Their Treaty Interpretation Functions

There are a number of traditional international adjudicating bodies whose constant works include treaty interpretation. Some permanent adjudicating bodies are established to handle all kinds of international disputes without regard to their natures and fields of law. Some others are created for some specific types of cases. In the latter situation, the adjudicating bodies are basically created by some specialized treaties.

The ICJ is the most authoritative adjudicating body at the international level. It was created in 1945 under Article 92 of the U.N. Charter (which provides in part that the ICJ shall be the principal judicial organ of the United Nations) and the Statute of the International Court of Justice (the ICJ Statute) (Article 1 of which provides in part that the ICJ established by the Charter of the United Nations as the principal judicial organ of the United Nations shall be constituted). The matters handled by the ICJ are not limited to any specific category or any specific nature of issues. Article 36.1 of the ICJ Statute states that the jurisdiction of the Court comprises all cases which the parties refer to it and all matters specially provided for in the Charter of the United Nations or in treaties and conventions in force. Hence the ICJ's jurisdiction can be extremely broad to cover all types of cases. All international disputes (whether concerning human rights, trade, investment, war and other conflicts, arms, territories and any other international disputes) can be submitted to the ICJ as long as its jurisdiction can be established. The ICJ also conducts advisory proceedings to provide advisory opinions on legal questions referred to it by UN organs or specialized agencies.[2] In both proceedings (i.e. the legal disputes between States and the advisory proceeding), the ICJ needs to conduct treaty interpretation so as to resolve a dispute or to provide its advisory opinion.

Also the Permanent Court of Arbitration (PCA) was established in 1899 and is an intergovernmental organization to provide a variety of dispute resolution services to the international community.[3] It provides services for the resolution of disputes involving various combinations of states, state entities, intergovernmental organizations, and private parties.[4] But the PCA itself is not an adjudicating body. It only facilitates arbitration and other forms of dispute resolution. So the "arbitral tribunals" established under the assistance of the PCA (not the PCA itself) serve as the adjudicating body.

Many international adjudicating bodies are created by special treaties for special types of disputes. For instance, the International Tribunal for the Law of the Sea (ITLOS) is an independent judicial body created by the 1982 United Nations Convention on the Law of the Sea (CLS) to adjudicate disputes arising from of the interpretation and application of the Convention.[5] According to Article 21 of the Statute of the International Tribunal for the Law of the Sea, the ITLOS has jurisdiction over any dispute concerning the interpretation or application of the Convention, and over all matters specifically provided for in any other agreement which confers jurisdiction on the Tribunal. Hence the ITLOS has its major duty of interpreting the CLS.

Treaty interpretation is mainly conducted by international adjudicating bodies. But most international adjudicators do not decide many cases each year, mainly because the number of disputes submitted to them is not large. For these international adjudicators, their treaty interpretation functions are not enormous in their amounts and in their wide-spread influence. Professor Detlev Vagts had the following explanation:[6]

> The International Court of Justice decides only a handful of cases a year and only a limited number of them can be said to hinge upon the interpretation of a treaty. Thus it cannot serve the function that domestic courts have of casting a shadow within which private parties can dispose of cases that do not go to court. For one thing it does not have the flow of 'easy cases' that bolster the authority of national tribunals. Those easy cases are then reflected in dozens of disputes that are settled extra-judicially in the light of their guidance and which confirm judicial authority. Nor do other arbitral tribunals do much to fill the gap. This comment does not, however, fully apply to the work of a few regional tribunals that regularly interpret the constitutive documents of the international organization to which they belong, namely: the European Court of Justice, the European Court of Human Rights and the Inter-American Court of Human Rights.

[2]http://www.icj-cij.org/court/index.php?p1=1&p2=6. Accessed 8 Aug 2017.

[3]http://www.pca-cpa.org/showpage37e7.html?pag_id=363. Accessed 8 Aug 2017.

[4]http://www.pca-cpa.org/showpage1d71.html?pag_id=1027. Accessed 8 Aug 2017.

[5]The Tribunal. https://www.itlos.org/en/the-tribunal/. Accessed 8 Aug 2017.

[6]Vagts (1993), p. 481.

8.2.2 *Proliferated International Adjudicating Bodies and Their Implications to Treaty Interpretation*

In recent decades there is a vastly increasing number of adjudicating mechanisms being created. This phenomenon can be considered as a "proliferation" of international adjudicating mechanisms.[7] These mechanisms are mostly highly specialized. Examples of such international adjudicating mechanisms include the various investment tribunals acting under the International Centre for Settlement of Investment Disputes (ICSID) Convention or other arbitration rules as well as the WTO's DSM. All of them interpret and apply their respective treaties.

The ICSID is also an international organization specializing in the settlement of investment disputes. It administers proceedings under the ICSIC rules as well as other rules (such as the UNCITRAL Arbitration Rules) and other *ad hoc* investor-State and State-State cases.[8] But the ICSID itself is not the adjudicating body. It is the arbitral tribunals established and administered under the ICSID being the adjudicating body and having the treaty interpretation duties.

In the field of international trade, there is the DSM under the WTO. The Appellate Body of the WTO is very active in applying the VCLT to interpret various WTO agreements. It is an active interpreter not necessarily because it takes such active position, but very importantly because it is encountering a very large number of cases, many of which have been controversial and were fiercely argued by the disputing parties and hence the related WTO provisions need detailed interpretations.

The dispute settlement procedures under the WTO are based on the DSU. Under the DSU, if the disputing parties cannot mutually agree on a solution to settle their dispute, they can resort to the adjudication procedure. The procedure includes a panel and the Appellate Body (if appealed) to issue their reports, which become binding if they are adopted by the DSB. DSU Article 11 provides in part that:

> The function of panels is to assist the DSB in discharging its responsibilities under this Understanding and the covered agreements. Accordingly, a panel should make an objective assessment of the matter before it, including an objective assessment of the facts of the case and the applicability of and conformity with the relevant covered agreements, and make such other findings as will assist the DSB in making the recommendations or in giving the rulings provided for in the covered agreements …

A panel's report has to be adopted by the DSB under DSU Article 16 to become effective. An Appellate Body report also has to be adopted by the DSB under DSU Article 17.14 to become effective. According to DSU Article 2.1, the DSB is to administer the rules and procedures under the DSU and to establish panels, adopt panel and Appellate Body reports, maintain surveillance of implementation of

[7]Reinisch (2008), p. 107.

[8]https://icsid.worldbank.org/apps/ICSIDWEB/services/Pages/Case-Administration.aspx. Accessed 8 Aug 2017.

rulings and recommendations, and authorize suspension of concessions and other obligations under the covered agreements.

Hence, from the perspective of the functions respectively played by a panel, the Appellate Body and the DSB, it is apparent that the DSB is the adjudicating body to finally decide a dispute. A panel and the Appellate Body are to assist the DSB to discharge its adjudicating function. Their reports need to be adopted by the DSB to become binding. However, the DSB can only decide to adopt or not to adopt the reports issued by the panels and the Appellate Body. Also the adoption is made through a negative consensus. That is to say that the reports will be adopted unless there is consensus not to adopt the reports. There is little likelihood for the DSB not to adopt the reports. In other words, it is the panels and the Appellate Body which *actually interpret* the provisions in WTO agreements. The legal adjudicator (legally being the DSB) is different from the treaty interpreters (practically being the panels and the Appellate Body) under the DSU.

There are also *ad hoc* adjudicators to decide international disputes. They also interpret the respective treaties. For instance, many FTAs require their disputes to be resolved by *ad hoc* arbitral tribunals, which are entrusted with the function of interpreting and applying FTA provisions to decide regional trade differences.

These newly created adjudicating bodies are actively engaging in handling and resolving disputes. Their treaty interpretations have greatly enriched the jurisprudence. The most apparent example is the WTO. The Appellate Body has already issued 140 reports as of March 2017.[9] And the number is still increasing. Many of these reports elaborate the rules provided in Articles 31 to 33 of the VCLT. Because of the larger number of cases being handled and because the treaty interpretation is more frequently conducted under the WTO's DSM, the range of treaty interpretation issues being dealt with by the Appellate Body is wide and comprehensive. The Appellate Body's reports have become a very important source of and constantly cited jurisprudence. The Appellate Body's treaty interpretation activities have turned the VCLT into a very important assisting tool to resolve dispute.

8.3 Other Players to Interpret Treaties

8.3.1 Interpretation by Non-adjudicating Body on the International Level

It was briefly mentioned in Chap. 5 of this book that a treaty interpreter's authority could be restricted by the "interpretation" issued by a separate authoritative body as provided by the relevant treaty. This has to do with non-adjudicative bodies/mechanisms also exercising *treaty interpretation of different nature.*

---

[9]See the WTO website at Appellate Body Reports. https://www.wto.org/english/tratop_e/dispu_e/ab_reports_e.html. Accessed 8 Aug 2017.

There are situations where non-adjudicative bodies also engage in treaty interpretation. A salient example is the Ministerial Conference and the General Council under the WTO, which are vested with the power of "authoritative interpretation". As quoted in Chap. 5 of the book, Article IX:2 of the Agreement Establishing the WTO provides the following:

> The Ministerial Conference and the General Council shall have *the exclusive authority to adopt interpretations* of this Agreement and of the Multilateral Trade Agreements. In the case of an interpretation of a Multilateral Trade Agreement in Annex 1, they shall exercise their authority on the basis of a recommendation by the Council overseeing the functioning of that Agreement. The decision to adopt an interpretation shall be taken by a three-fourths majority of the Members. This paragraph shall not be used in a manner that would undermine the amendment provisions in Article X.
>
> (Emphasis added)

The authoritative interpretation within the WTO was not exercised very often. The first formal request for an authoritative interpretation under this article was made in 1999 concerning DSU Articles 3.7, 21.5, 22.2, 22.6, 22.7 and 23. Although there were some Members considered an authoritative interpretation to be appropriate, most other Members expressed their concerns. Countries preferred to reach a negotiated solution in the discussions on review of the DSU.[10]

Also there was the Declaration on the TRIPS Agreement and Public Health, adopted on 14 November 2001. It states that the TRIPS Agreement "does not and should not prevent Members from taking measures to protect public health …, in particular, to promote access to medicines for all." Although the declaration did not mention the provision in Article IX:2 of the WTO Establishing Agreement, by its nature, it was actually an authoritative interpretation issued by the Ministerial Conference to address the relations between the TRIPS Agreement and the public health.

According to the Appellate Body, the fact that Article IX:2 of the Agreement Establishing the WTO vests the exclusive interpreting authority to the Ministerial Conference and the General Council implies that such authority is not available for any other body (including the DSB) under the WTO. It is in *Japan—Alcoholic Beverages II* where the Appellate Body rejected the Panel's finding that panel reports adopted by the CONTRACTING PARTIES under the GATT 1947 and those adopted by the DSB constitute a "definitive interpretation" within the meaning of Article IX:2 of the Agreement Establishing the WTO:[11]

> We do not believe that the CONTRACTING PARTIES, in deciding to adopt a panel report, intended that their decision would constitute a definitive interpretation of the relevant provisions of GATT 1947. Nor do we believe that this is contemplated under GATT 1994. There is specific cause for this conclusion in the WTO Agreement. Article IX:2 of the WTO

---

[10]WTO Analytical Index: Marrakesh Agreement. https://www.wto.org/english/res_e/booksp_e/analytic_index_e/wto_agree_03_e.htm#fnt348. Accessed 8 Aug 2017.

[11]Appellate Body Report, *Japan—Taxes on Alcoholic Beverages*, p. 13, WTO Doc. WT/DS8/AB/R, WT/DS10/AB/R, WT/DS11/AB/R (adopted 1 Nov 1996).

> Agreement provides: 'The Ministerial Conference and the General Council shall have the exclusive authority to adopt interpretations of this Agreement and of the Multilateral Trade Agreements'. Article IX:2 provides further that such decisions' shall be taken by a three-fourths majority of the Members'. *The fact that such an 'exclusive authority' in interpreting the treaty has been established so specifically in the WTO Agreement is reason enough to conclude that such authority does not exist by implication or by inadvertence elsewhere.* (Emphasis added)

There are three fundamental differences between the *authoritative interpretation* conducted by the Ministerial Conference and the General Council under Article IX:2 of the WTO Establishing Agreement on the one hand and the "treaty interpretation" conducted by the Appellate Body and that conducted by the dispute settlement panels on the other hand.

The first difference is in that the "treaty interpretation" conducted by the Appellate Body and the panels is restricted by the requirement of "not adding to or diminishing the parties' rights and obligations", whereas the authoritative interpretation conducted by the Ministerial Conference and the General Council is less restricted so that the result of authoritative interpretation could lead to adding to or diminishing the rights and obligations. In this regard, the Appellate Body stated in *US—FSC*:

> Under the WTO Agreement, an authoritative interpretation by the Members of the WTO, under Article IX:2 of that Agreement, is to be distinguished from the rulings and recommendations of the DSB, made on the basis of panel and Appellate Body Reports. In terms of Article 3.2 of the DSU, the rulings and recommendations of the DSB serve only 'to clarify the existing provisions of those agreements' and 'cannot add to or diminish the rights and obligations provided in the covered agreements.'[12]

The second difference is in the respective natures of these interpretations. Concerning the nature of the *authoritative interpretation* conducted by the Ministerial Conference and the General Council, the Appellate Body considers that such authoritative interpretation constitutes a "subsequent agreement" under VCLT Article 31.3(a) (which requires "Any subsequent agreement between the parties regarding the interpretation of the treaty or the application of its provisions" to be taken into account together with the context), whereas the treaty interpretation conducted by the Appellate Body or by a dispute settlement panel does not constitute a "subsequent agreement". The Appellate Body indicated in its report on *EC—Bananas—III*:[13]

> Article IX:2 of the *WTO Agreement* sets out specific requirements for decisions that may be taken by the Ministerial Conference or the General Council to adopt interpretations of provisions of the Multilateral Trade Agreements. Such multilateral interpretations are meant

[12]Appellate Body Report, *United States—Tax Treatment for "Foreign Sales Corporations"*, fn. 127, WTO Doc. WT/DS108/AB/R (adopted 20 Mar 2000).

[13]Appellate Body Report, *European Communities—Regime for the Importation, Sale and Distribution of Bananas EC—Bananas III (Article 21.5—US)/ (Article 21.5—Ecuador II)*, para. 383, WTO Doc. WT/DS27/AB/RW/USA, WT/DS27/AB/RW2/ECU (adopted 12 Dec 2008/ 11 Dec 2008).

> to clarify the meaning of existing obligations, not to modify their content. Article IX:2 emphasizes that such interpretations 'shall not be used in a manner that would undermine the amendment provisions in Article X'. A multilateral interpretation should also be distinguished from a waiver, which allows a Member to depart from an existing WTO obligation for a limited period of time. We consider that a multilateral interpretation pursuant to Article IX:2 of the *WTO Agreement* can be likened to a subsequent agreement regarding the interpretation of the treaty or the application of its provisions pursuant to Article 31(3)(a) of the *Vienna Convention*, as far as the interpretation of the WTO agreements is concerned.

The third difference is in whether the VCLT should be applied. In treaty interpretation conducted by the Appellate Body and the panels, the provisions in VCLT Articles 31 to 33 should serve as the basis of the exercise of interpretation and should be directly applied. Whereas the *authoritative interpretation* conducted by the Ministerial Conference and the General Council is not restricted in any way by the VCLT. Article 3.9 of the DSU provides clearly in this regard that: "The provisions of this Understanding are without prejudice to the rights of Members to seek *authoritative interpretation* of provisions of a covered agreement through decision-making under the WTO Agreement or a covered agreement which is a Plurilateral Trade Agreement." (Emphasis added) Since WTO Members' right to seek authoritative interpretation is not governed or restricted by the DSU (including DSU Article 3.2 which requires treaty interpretation to be based on customary rules of interpretation of public international law, i.e. the VCLT), the actual decision of an *authoritative interpretation* by the Ministerial Conference or the General Council should not be governed or bound by the DSU (including DSU Article 3.2) either. Hence although the term "interpretation" is also used in connection with the "*authoritative interpretation*", such interpretation does not fall within the scope of meaning of treaty interpretation as provided in the VCLT.

8.3.2 Domestic Courts to Interpret Treaties

The commonly seen situation which requires interpretation of a treaty provision is in the context of dispute settlement procedure conducted under a treaty governing the relations between its contacting parties (such as a bilateral, regional or multilateral trade agreement or a bilateral investment treaty) or a treaty governing the contracting parties' behaviors or activities (such as a human rights treaty). In such situation, disputes normally occur between the contracting parties to a related treaty. They sometimes occur between a contracting party and a private party from another contracting party (such as those disputes occurred between the host State and a foreign investor). International adjudicators in the context of such treaty disputes will have to interpret relevant treaty provisions and apply them. Their treaty interpretation activities are bound by the VCLT either because the disputing parties are contracting States to the VCLT or because the treaty interpretation rules in Articles 31 through 33 of the VCLT are part of the customary international law which binds the disputing parties.

There are situations where a domestic court will also have to apply and interpret a provision in a treaty which governs the relations between its contacting parties or governs the contracting parties' behaviors or activities. The premise for a treaty to be interpreted by a domestic court is that the treaty must be "self-executing" and it must have direct domestic effect. In dualist countries, international treaties must be textually incorporated and transformed into domestic law through domestic legislative process before their contents can be directly applied domestically. In such countries, treaties are not self-executing in the sense that they do not have a direct effect within these jurisdictions. But in monist countries, international treaties also have the force of law in the domestic legal system and hence they can be directly applied by the domestic courts.[14] Many countries adopt various hybrid systems under which whether a treaty can be directly applied depends upon whether a treaty is of the self-executing nature, which in turn is based on the contents of such treaty.

Only under the situation where a treaty is self-executing, a domestic court is in a position to directly apply a treaty provision and hence will have to interpret a disputed treaty provision when such provision is susceptible to possible two or more different interpretations.

For example, there are tax treaties to prevent double taxation of an income arising in one contracting party earned by the resident of another contracting party. In a domestic case concerning a tax dispute between the State (where the court is located) and a foreign taxpayer, the domestic court might need to directly apply and interpret a tax treaty of such kind so as to decide whether a tax should not be collected.

For instance, there are many BITs to grant foreign investors the non-discrimination treatment and the fair and equitable treatment, and to protect them against unlawful direct or indirect expropriations. In a domestic dispute concerning a foreign investor's treatment or protection, the domestic court might need to apply and interpret a BIT provision so as to decide whether a government's measure should be considered as unfavorable treatment which is prohibited by the treaty.

Also for instance, the International Covenant on Civil and Political Rights (ICCPR) provides in part in Article 14.1 that: "All persons shall be equal before the courts and tribunals. In the determination of any criminal charge against him, or of his rights and obligations in a suit at law, everyone shall be entitled to a fair and public hearing by a competent, independent and impartial tribunal established by law…" When deciding a criminal remedy or an access to court issue for a foreigner, a domestic court might need to directly apply and interpret the term "equal" provided in the ICCPR (especially concerning whether the term includes the situation where the formality in the domestic legislation is unequal for foreigners but the substantive provision is alleged to be equal), if the ICCPR is self-executing and directly applicable in such jurisdiction. Also when deciding a criminal charge

---

[14]The Peace and Justice Initiative. How Does International Law Apply in a Domestic Legal System? Dualist and Monist Systems. http://www.peaceandjusticeinitiative.org/implementation-resources/dualist-and-monist. Accessed 8 Aug 2017.

against a foreigner, a domestic court might need to interpret the term "fair hearing" provided in this article of the Convention so as to decide whether the accused has been provided with the required procedural treatment.

In these examples, domestic courts are not interpreting domestic legislations and hence are not conducting a "statutory interpretation". The methods for "statutory interpretation" in domestic context should not serve as the based for the domestic courts' interpretation of an applicable international treaty. Domestic courts will have to apply the VCLT because of its binding nature either as a treaty or as customary international law.

In addition to those treaties which govern the relations between the contracting parties and/or their behaviors, there is another group of treaties substantively governing or procedurally dealing with commercial or civil disputes, such as those treaties governing the contractual relations of buyers and sellers of goods, and those governing the selection of courts. The adjudicators of such treaties are most likely domestic courts or commercial/civil arbitrators. An issue arises as to whether in commercial or civil disputes dealt with by a treaty of such kind and resolved by domestic courts or commercial/civil arbitrators, there are also issues of treaty interpretation of similar nature and whether such interpretation is also bound by the VCLT or whether it should be based on other principles.

Since domestic courts and civil and commercial arbitral tribunals are mostly used to handle disputes between private parties and since the treaties being applied are those related to private issues, so the treaty interpretation function of domestic courts and commercial and civil arbitrators should be conducted in a way different from the treaty interpretation by international adjudicators. This will be further elaborated in the next chapter of the book.

8.4 Reasons for International Adjudicators and Interpreters Being Bound by the VCLT

It was mentioned in the preceding chapter that there is a "connecting provision" in Article 3.2 of the DSU to connect the interpretation of the WTO agreements and the provisions in VCLT Articles 31–33 (i.e. to require the clarification of the WTO agreements in accordance with the customary rules of treaty interpretation). It was also mentioned that a lack of a "connecting provision" does not prevent a treaty interpreter's application of the VCLT.

To explain further, an adjudicator basically has two sets of obligations. One set of obligations for the adjudicator is to conduct the dispute settlement procedure based on the agreed-upon procedural rules. If the treaty interpretation rules are already provided in the procedural rules (such as the situation of DSU Article 3.2), the adjudicator will have to use the VCLT's treaty interpretation rules as incorporated in DSU Article 3.2. The application of the VCLT becomes the duty of the interpreter in the fulfilment of its procedural duties.

Another set of obligations for an adjudicator to follow is to conduct the procedure based on the substantive governing law. The substantive governing law includes the proper meanings embedded in the provisions. Identifying the proper meanings to be given to the substantive governing law is the premise of properly applying such law. So the proper interpretation of a treaty provision based on the VCLT becomes the obligation of an adjudicator, notwithstanding the fact that the adjudicator itself is neither a party to the VCLT nor a party to the substantive governing norm.

To conclude the discussions in this chapter and from the perspective of codification, it should be useful to indicate in the codified set of provisions that the rules of treaty interpretation apply to the interpretation of all categories of treaties (except the kind of treaties governing private matters, which will be discussed in the next chapter of the book) conducted by all international adjudicating bodies and by national courts. If there is any authoritative interpretation mechanism created under a treaty, the substantive and procedural requirements as well as the effect of such interpretation will be decided based on the treaty which creates such interpretation. The treaty interpretation rules will not apply to such interpretations.

References

Appellate body reports https://www.wto.org/english/tratop_e/dispu_e/ab_reports_e.html. Accessed 8 Aug 2017

http://www.pca-cpa.org/showpage37e7.html?pag_id=363. Accessed 8 Aug 2017

http://www.icj-cij.org/court/index.php?p1=1&p2=6. Accessed 8 Aug 2017

http://www.pca-cpa.org/showpage1d71.html?pag_id=1027. Accessed 8 Aug 2017

https://icsid.worldbank.org/apps/ICSIDWEB/services/Pages/Case-Administration.aspx. Accessed 8 Aug 2017

Reinisch A (2008) The proliferation of international dispute settlement mechanisms: the threat of fragmentation versus the promise of a more effective system? Some reflections from the perspective of investment arbitration. In: Buffard I, Crawford J, Pellet A, Wittich S (eds) International Law between Universalism and Fragmentation: Festschrift in Honor of Gerhard Hafner. Leiden, Brill, pp 107–126

The Peace and Justice Initiative (2017) How does international law apply in a domestic legal system? Dualist and monist systems. http://www.peaceandjusticeinitiative.org/implementation-resources/dualist-and-monist. Accessed 8 Aug 2017

The Tribunal (2017) https://www.itlos.org/en/the-tribunal/. Accessed 8 Aug 2017

Vagts DF (1993) Treaty interpretation and the New American Ways of Law Reading. Eur J Int Law 4:472–505

World Trade Organization (2017) Historic Development of the WTO Dispute Settlement System. https://www.wto.org/english/tratop_e/dispu_e/disp_settlement_cbt_e/c2s1p1_e.html. Accessed 8 Aug 2017

WTO (2017) Analytical index: Marrakesh Agreement. https://www.wto.org/english/res_e/booksp_e/analytic_index_e/wto_agree_03_e.htm#fnt348. Accessed 8 Aug 2017

Chapter 9
Interpreting Treaties for Private Matters and the Possible Codification

Contents

C. Lo, *Treaty Interpretation Under the Vienna Convention on the Law of Treaties*,
https://doi.org/10.1007/978-981-10-6866-9_9

9.1 Situations and Premises

9.1.1 Commercial/Civil Adjudicators Interpreting Treaties Governing Private Matters

In the preceding chapter, there have been explanations about international adjudicators and domestic courts serving as interpreters of those treaties governing the relations between the contracting parties and/or governing states' behaviors. It was also mentioned that there is another group of treaties substantively governing or procedurally dealing with private matters, including commercial and other civil matters.[1]

There are two kinds of disputes that could arise from such treaties for private matters. One kind of disputes is about whether a contracting party to a treaty of such nature has fulfilled its treaty obligations, such as the obligation to require its domestic courts to apply the treaty provision. This is a State-to-State dispute which should be dealt with by international adjudicators. For such disputes, the VCLT will decide the interpretation of the contracting party's obligation under the treaty. It will be discussed in the later part of this chapter that the 1980 *Convention on Contracts for the International Sale of Goods* (CISG)[2] is mostly interpreted by domestic court or commercial/civil arbitrators. But there could also be a State-to-State dispute arising from the CISG. For instance, Article 1(1) of the CISG requires its Contracting States to apply the Convention to contracts of sale of goods between parties whose places of business are in different States when these States are Contracting States. If a Contracting State's domestic law prohibits such application or if its domestic court fails to apply the Convention, there could be a breach of the State's obligation under the CISG. This could be subject to the State-to-State DSM and hence an international adjudicator under such DSM will have to interpret the CISG according to Articles 31 to 33 of the VCLT.

Another kind of disputes arising from the treaties procedurally or substantively governing or dealing with commercial or civil matters is the disputes between private parties. The adjudicators of such disputes are either domestic courts or international or domestic commercial/civil arbitrators. The discussions in this chapter will focus on the situations where domestic courts and commercial/civil arbitrators will have to interpret treaties governing commercial or civil matters. It will explain the different nature of such treaty interpretation from other "ordinary treaty interpretation" and discuss whether domestic courts and commercial/civil arbitrators should be bound by the VCLT. This chapter will use the CISG as an example to discuss the elements of considerations for interpreting such treaties. It

[1]The main contents of this chapter are basically revised from Lo C (2015) Should Domestic Court's and Commercial Arbitral Tribunal's Interpretation of "Treaties for Private Matters" Be Based on the VCLT or Other Rules? Contemp Asia Arbitration J 9:1–32.

[2]The text of the CISG is available at http://www.uncitral.org/pdf/english/texts/sales/cisg/V1056997-CISG-e-book.pdf . Accessed 8 Aug 2017.

will elaborate the appropriateness of expanding the use of these elements to the interpretation of other treaties of similar nature.

9.1.2 *Premise for a "Domestic Court" to Interpret International Treaties*

As explained in the preceding chapter of the book, the premise for a domestic court to directly apply and interpret a treaty is that the treaty must be self-executing so as to directly bind the domestic court. If a treaty is not self-executing and hence the domestic court is not directly bound by a treaty, the court will not have the power and opportunity to "directly" apply and interpret provisions of such treaty.

On the other hand, it is also possible that the legislature has already incorporated the contents of a treaty into a domestic legislation. If it is the case that the treaty has been textually incorporated and transformed into domestic law through a domestic legislative process, the domestic court will be actually applying and interpreting the domestic law, the content of which has been transformed from a treaty. So the interpretation of domestic courts in such context is *statutory interpretation*, not treaty interpretation.

Only when a domestic court is directly bound by a treaty and accordingly is obligated to directly apply the treaty provision, the court is of the power and has the opportunity to interpret the treaty which is the governing law of a disputed commercial or civil relation. In such situation, a domestic court is conducting "treaty interpretation" and "treaty application". But, of course, as argued below in this chapter, if the relevant treaty is for private matters (including the matters of civil and commercial relations), the nature of treaty interpretation under such circumstance is different from that of the "ordinary treaty interpretation" by international and domestic adjudicators under the VCLT.

9.1.3 *Premise for a "Commercial/Civil Arbitrator" to Interpret International Treaties*

In the situation where a commercial/civil arbitration is a domestic one and where the arbitral tribunal conducts arbitration proceedings under a monism jurisdiction (in which an international treaty does not need to be transformed into domestic legislation so as to be directly applied by the adjudicator), the arbitral tribunal will also be bound by an international treaty which has the force of law in such jurisdiction, if such treaty is the applicable norm governing the substantive or procedural issues. Even when it is an international commercial/civil arbitration, arguably the arbitral tribunal will also have to directly apply a treaty which is part of the applicable law, if its applicable law is that of a monism country. Also in hybrid systems, if a treaty is considered as self-executing, the situation is the same as that in the monism countries concerning the directly applicability of the treaty.

When a commercial/civil arbitrator is to directly apply a treaty as the governing law of a commercial/civil relation, actually it is also conducting "treaty interpretation". The issue here is similar to the issue in the domestic court's context as to whether the arbitral tribunal is bound by the VCLT or should be bound by other appropriate principles. The book will argue that if the relevant treaty is for private matters, the nature of treaty interpretation conducted by a commercial/civil arbitrator under such circumstance is different from that of the "ordinary treaty interpretation" by international and domestic adjudicators under the VCLT.

9.2 Commercial/Civil Adjudicators Not Bound by VCLT When Interpreting Treaties for Private Matters

9.2.1 The Group of Treaties for Private Matters

As explained above, most international treaties are concluded to govern the relations between States or to govern States' behaviors. But there are many other international treaties which are concluded to address/govern private matters between transaction counterparts or between individuals and are intended or supposed to be applied by domestic courts and commercial/civil arbitrators.

For instance, there are treaties concerning jurisdiction of domestic courts, such as the 1965 *Convention on the Choice of Court* (Article 2, paragraph 1, provides that this Convention shall apply to agreements on the choice of court concluded in civil or commercial matters in situations having an international character)[3] and the 2005 *Convention on Choice of Court Agreements* (Article 1(1) of which states that this Convention shall apply in international cases to exclusive choice of court agreements concluded in civil or commercial matters).[4] These conventions can possibly be (and are usually) directly applied and interpreted by domestic courts.

For instance, there are treaties concerning recognition and enforcements of foreign arbitral awards or foreign judgments, such as the 1958 *Convention on the Recognition and Enforcement of Foreign Arbitral Awards* (i.e. the "New York Convention",[5] which allows its Contracting States to make "commercial

[3]The text of the Convention on the Choice of Court can be found at https://www.hcch.net/en/instruments/conventions/full-text/?cid=77. Accessed 8 Aug 2017.

[4]The text of the Convention on Choice of Court Agreements can be found at https://www.hcch.net/en/instruments/conventions/full-text/?cid=98. Accessed 8 Aug 2017.

[5]The text of the New York Convention can be found at http://www.newyorkconvention.org/english. Accessed 8 Aug 2017.

reservations" to limit its application to commercial relationships)[6] and the 1971 Convention on the Recognition and Enforcement of Foreign Judgments in Civil and Commercial Matters (Article 1, paragraph 1, of which states that this Convention "shall apply to decisions rendered in civil or commercial matters by the courts of Contracting States").[7] These type of treaties can also be (and are usually) directly applied and interpreted by a domestic court.

For instance, there are treaties concerning choice of law rules, such as the 1986 *Convention on the Law Applicable to Contracts for International Sale of Goods*, Article 1 of which states that this Convention "determines the law applicable to contracts of sale of goods (a) between parties having their places of business in different States; (b) in all other cases involving a choice between the laws of different States, unless such a choice arises solely from a stipulation by the parties as to the applicable law, even if accompanied by a choice of court or arbitration."[8] This treaty can be (and is usually) applied and interpreted by a domestic court and an arbitral tribunal regarding commercial/civil sales of goods.

Also for instance, there are treaties concerning substantive norms of transactions, such as the CISG, Article 1(1) of which provides that this Convention "applies to contracts of sale of goods between parties whose places of business are in different States: (a) when the States are Contracting States; or (b) when the rules of private international law lead to the application of the law of a Contracting State". Hence, this convention can also be (and is usually) applied and interpreted by a domestic court and an arbitral tribunal.

---

[6]Article I:3 of the New York Convention provides in part that: any State "may also declare that it will apply the Convention only to differences arising out of legal relationships, whether contractual or not, which are considered as commercial under the national law of the State making such declaration." But it must be noted that if a Contracting State to the New York Convention does not make such "commercial reservation", it is possible that the New York Convention can be applied to the enforcement of an "investor-to-State arbitration" which is not subject to the International Centre for Settlement of Investment Disputes (ICSID) Convention. The text of the ICSID Convention can be found at https://icsid.worldbank.org/en/Documents/icsiddocs/ICSID%20Convention%20English.pdf. Accessed 8 Aug 2017. The main difference between the New York Convention and the ICSID Convention concerning the enforcement of an "investor-to-State" arbitral award is in that the New York Convention allows the domestic courts to refuse enforcement of an arbitral award based on, for instance, the award being contrary to the public policy of the enforcing country, the subject matter being not capable of settlement by arbitration under the law of the enforcing country, or the arbitration agreement being invalid. See Article V of the New York Convention. But The ICSID Convention does not allow such non-enforcement of an arbitral award.

[7]The text of the Convention on the Recognition and Enforcement of Foreign Judgments in Civil and Commercial Matters can be found at https://www.hcch.net/en/instruments/conventions/full-text/?cid=78. Accessed 8 Aug 2017.

[8]The text of the Convention on the Law Applicable to Contracts for the International Sale of Goods can be found at https://www.hcch.net/en/instruments/conventions/full-text/?cid=61. Accessed 8 Aug 2017.

There are also substantive international norms to govern other civil matters. For instance, the 1980 Convention on the Civil Aspects of International Child Abduction, Article 1 of which provides that:

The objects of the present Convention are–

(a) to secure the prompt return of children wrongfully removed to or retained in any Contracting State; and
(b) to ensure that rights of custody and of access under the law of one Contracting State are effectively respected in the other Contracting States.

The United States Supreme Court in the case *Abbott v. Abbott*[9] has to interpret the Convention on the Civil Aspects of International Child Abduction so as to decide whether the *ne exeat* rights are rights of custody. After having referred to international case law and scholars' views, the United States Supreme Court confirmed that there is a broad acceptance of the rule that *ne exeat* rights were rights of custody, even though the Convention does not specifically mention such rights.[10] This is a very good example to show that domestic court's duty of interpreting international treaty to decide private matters.

With the exception of the New York Convention, the above treaties are exclusively designed to directly or indirectly govern private relations or their resulting legal procedures. For those provisions in such treaties which can be directly applied by the court or by an arbitral tribunal to address such private relations (for instance, the provisions in these treaties deciding the validity of a choice of court agreement or deciding the applicable law for a contract), they are similar to the domestic substantive and procedural law in their respective natures. As to the New York Convention, the main provisions to be directly applied and interpreted by a domestic court are those provides in Article V, which reads:

1. Recognition and enforcement of the award may be refused, at the request of the party against whom it is invoked, only if that party furnishes to the competent authority where the recognition and enforcement is sought, proof that:

   (a) The parties to the agreement referred to in article II were, *under the law applicable to them*, under some incapacity, or the said agreement is not valid under the law to which the parties have subjected it or, failing any indication thereon, *under the law of the country where the award was made*; or
   (b) The party against whom the award is invoked was not given proper notice of the appointment of the arbitrator or of the arbitration proceedings or was otherwise unable to present his case; or
   (c) The award deals with a difference not contemplated by or not falling within the terms of the submission to arbitration, or it contains decisions on matters beyond the scope of the submission to arbitration, provided that, if the decisions on matters

[9]Abbott v. Abbott, 130 S. Ct. 1983 (2010).

[10]Hague Conference on Private International Law case law search website at http://www.incadat.com/index.cfm/themas/cluster/index.cfm?act=search.detail&cid=1029&lng=1&sl=2. Accessed 8 Aug 2017.

submitted to arbitration can be separated from those not so submitted, that part of the award which contains decisions on matters submitted to arbitration may be recognized and enforced; or

(d) The composition of the arbitral authority or the arbitral procedure was not in accordance with the agreement of the parties, or, failing such agreement, was not *in accordance with the law of the country where the arbitration took place*; or

(e) The award has not yet become binding on the parties, or has been set aside or suspended by a competent authority of the country in which, or *under the law of which*, that award was made.

2. Recognition and enforcement of an arbitral award may also be refused if the competent authority in the country where recognition and enforcement is sought finds that:

(a) The subject matter of the difference is not capable of settlement by arbitration *under the law of that country*; or

(b) The recognition or enforcement of the award would be contrary to *the public policy of that country*.

(Emphasis added)

There are indications in these provisions that when determining the recognition and enforcement of a foreign arbitral award, the court will have to make its decision based on the law applicable to the disputing parties, the law of the country where the award was made, or the law or the public policy of the country where the arbitration took place. Hence, although the New York Convention can be applied to decide the recognition of not only the commercial arbitral awards, but also the non-ICSID investor-to-State arbitral awards, it is apparent that a critical task for the domestic court is to interpret such domestic law applicable to the disputing parties, the domestic law of the country where the award was made, and the domestic law or the public policy of the country where the arbitration took place. The interpretation of such domestic laws or domestic public policy is more similar to the interpretation of domestic law and public policy in the context of domestic disputes.

The above treaties can be categorized and collectively called "*treaties for private matters*" for the convenience of discussion in this chapter. The following discussions are to focus on this type of treaties. Their interpretation should be subject to certain rules which should not be identical to the rules for the ordinary treaty interpretation under the VCLT.

9.2.2 Reasons for Commercial/Civil Adjudicators not Bound by VCLT

There could be different perspectives concerning whether domestic courts and commercial/civil arbitrators are bound by the VCLT when interpreting "treaties for private matters". The positive view could be that the provisions of VCLT Articles 31 and 32 should be self-executing and therefore, domestic courts as well as commercial/civil arbitrators (which are subject to a domestic jurisdiction) are bound by the treaty interpretation rules set forth in these provisions when interpreting "treaties for private matters". It can be further argued that even though such provisions might not be self-executing treaty provisions, the contents of these provisions are still part of customary international rules of treaty interpretation. Since customary international law is basically of binding nature and is supposed to be universally applied, it thus has force of law to directly bind domestic adjudicators.

The negative views could be that since the VCLT is intended to deal with international agreement "governed by international law",[11] but "treaties for private matters" are dealing with private law matters, such treaties are not suitable of being governed by international law. Hence, "treaties for private matters" are arguably not subject to VCLT rules of treaty interpretation.

It must be noted that the phrase "governed by international law" is included in the VCLT not without controversies in its meaning and function. Some consider that this is not an ingredient for making a treaty; some others rely on this to distinguish treaties from other forms of agreement; still some others require that a treaty must establish a *relationship under international law* or must *intend* to create legal rights and obligations.[12] In other words, the element "governed by international law" in VCLT's definition of treaty does not necessarily lead to the conclusion that the VCLT does not apply to treaties for private matters. The non-application of the interpretation rules under the VCLT must be based on other reasons.

The most apparent reason for not requiring the interpretation of this category of treaties (i.e. the treaties for private matters) being based on the VCLT is the unique nature of such treaties. Since "treaties for private matters" (except the provisions governing the contracting States' rights and obligations in such treaties) are to govern procedural or substantive issues of private disputes, they are similar to other applicable domestic law for the resolution of private disputes. For instance, the 1965 *Convention on the Choice of Court* and the 2005 *Convention on Choice of Court Agreements* are part of or are to replace some provisions of domestic civil procedure rules; the *New York Convention* (especially concerning the provisions in the above quoted Article V of the Convention) and the 1971 *Convention on the Recognition and Enforcement of Foreign Judgments in Civil and Commercial Matters* are also part of or are to replace some provisions in domestic civil procedure or arbitration law; the 1986 *Convention on the Law Applicable to Contracts for International Sale of Goods* is part of or is to supplement or replace some provisions of the domestic choice of law rules; the CISG is part of or is to supplement or replace some provisions of domestic contract law or of domestic code governing civil matters.

---

[11]See the definition of treaty in VCLT Article 2(a): "'treaty' means an international agreement concluded between States in written form and *governed by international law*, whether embodied in a single instrument or in two or more related instruments and whatever its particular designation". (Emphasis added).

[12]Hollis (2012), pp. 25–26.

When domestic courts or commercial/civil arbitrators interpret these treaties, they are actually interpreting the applicable procedural or substantive law governing private matters. Therefore, such interpretation activity is similar to the interpretation of domestic procedural or substantive law provisions. Their nature is more similar to the "statutory interpretation". But, as will be further explained, although the nature of such treaty interpretation is more similar to the statutory interpretation, the interpreted provisions being enacted in a treaty makes it of international nature and makes it somewhat different from the ordinary "statutory interpretation".

Also as will be further discussed below, the CISG has its interpretation rules to govern the interpretation of this Convention. Although other "treaties for private matters" do not include similar interpretation provisions in their texts, the fact that the CISG containing interpretation rules specifically for the interpretation of this particular treaty shows that the drafter of the CISG does not intend to have the treaty interpretation rules under the VCLT applied to the CISG.

There is another possibility for a "treaty of substantive private law nature" to be applied by the domestic court or by an arbitral tribunal. That is: to have it applied through a contractual provision agreed upon by the parties in the transaction. CISG Article 1(1) provides that the Convention applies to contracts of sale of goods between parties whose places of business are in different States: (a) when the States are Contracting States; or (b) *when the rules of private international law lead to the application of the law of a Contracting State*. In other words, the CISG is still applicable even though the parties of the transaction are not in different Contracting States to the VCLT, as long as the governing *private international law rules* (the choice of law rules) require that the dispute is subject to the law of a Contracting Party. Since basically the private international law rules in all jurisdictions allow parties to mutually select the governing law for their international sale of goods contract, it is possible for the parties to a sale of goods contract to mutually decide the CISG to be the governing law for their contract. If a dispute arises from such contract, a domestic court or a commercial/civil arbitrator responsible to decide the dispute will have to use the CISG as the applicable law.

Hence, the CISG can be applied not only because of the treaty's binding force imposed on the domestic court or the arbitral tribunal, but also because of the treaty being an applicable law chosen by the parties. The substantive contents of the CISG are of not much difference from the contents of a domestic law from the perspective that they are the substantive law governing the contractual relations between the parties or they are chosen by the parties as the applicable law for their contractual relations. Accordingly, the interpretation of the CISG is similar to "statutory interpretation". But, again, since such interpretation involves a treaty, this makes it of international nature and makes it different from the "ordinary statutory interpretation".

9.3 The Interpretation of CISG as an Example

9.3.1 Self-Executing Nature of CISG

Most "treaties for private matters" do not contain their interpretation rules. But the CISG is different. Hence, it is worthwhile to review the CISG's interpretation provisions and to see how they can be understood and how they differ from the treaty interpretation rules under the VCLT, and whether similar principles can be developed and applied to the interpretation of "other treaties for private matters" .

It must be noted that the CISG is generally considered as self-executing. The main reason is that during the drafting session of the UNCITRAL Working Group, it was decided that the provisions of the intended treaty should be drafted in a way so that it would be applicable to international sales contracts without parallel domestic legislation.[13] Also the provisions of the CISG strongly suggest that the Convention is self-executing. Article 1(1) reads in part: "This Convention applies to contracts of sale of goods between parties whose places of business are in different States…" This provision indicates that the Convention is designed for directly applying to contracts of sale of goods under certain conditions. Article 4 reads: "This Convention governs only the formation of the contract of sale and the rights and obligations of the seller and the buyer arising from such a contract…" This provision suggests that the CISG is to be directly applied to govern the formation of contract of sale and the related rights and obligations. Article 6 further reads: "The parties may exclude the application of this Convention or, subject to article 12, derogate from or vary the effect of any of its provisions." The premise is that the Convention is directly applicable to a contract so that the parties of the contract will have the opportunity to exclude its application or to derogate from the effect.

Since the whole substantive content in the CISG is self-executing, its interpretation provisions (as discussed below) are also of self-executing nature. Domestic courts and commercial/civil arbitrators should be able (and are bound) to directly apply such provisions. They do not have to rely on any textual incorporation and transformation of such rules into domestic legislation before applying them.

Another reason to allow or to require domestic courts and arbitral tribunals to apply the CISG's interpretation provisions is that such provisions are an integral part of the governing law (i.e. the CISG) of the disputed contract of sale of goods which is subject to the Convention. Domestic courts and arbitral tribunals are obligated to apply this governing law in its totality, including the substantive rules and the interpretation rules provided in the CISG. It is not imaginable that a domestic court or an arbitral tribunal only partly applies the governing law, i.e. only applying the substantive part of the governing law but not applying the interpretative part of the governing law.

---

[13]Bailey (1999), p. 280.

9.3.2 Interpretation Provisions in CISG

As indicated above, a very unique feature of the CISG (that is not found in other treaties for private matters) is that there are "interpretation rules" provided in the Convention. The interpretation provisions are included in Article 7 of the CISG. It sets forth some elements to be considered when interpreting the Convention. It reads:

> (1) In the interpretation of this Convention, regard is to be had to its *international character* and to the need to promote *uniformity* in its application and the observance of *good faith* in international trade.
> (2) Questions concerning matters governed by this Convention which are not expressly settled in it are to be settled in conformity with *the general principles on which it is based* or, in the absence of such principles, in conformity with the law applicable by virtue of the rules of private -international law. (Emphases added)

The "Explanatory Note by the UNCITRAL Secretariat on the United Nations Convention on Contracts for the International Sale of Goods" (hereinafter "Explanatory Note")[14] clearly indicates that the related elements of interpreting the CISG are to be followed by domestic courts and arbitral tribunals. It states in paragraph 13 the following:

> This Convention for the unification of the law governing the international sale of goods will better fulfil its purpose if it is interpreted *in a consistent manner in all legal systems*. Great care was taken in its preparation to make it as clear and easy to understand as possible. Nevertheless, disputes will arise as to its meaning and application. When this occurs, all parties, including *domestic courts and arbitral tribunals, are admonished to observe its international character and to promote uniformity in its application and the observance of good faith in international trade*. In particular, when a question concerning a matter governed by this Convention is not expressly settled in it, the question is to be settled in conformity with *the general principles on which the Convention is based*. Only in the absence of such principles should the matter be settled in conformity with the law applicable by virtue of the rules of private international law. (Emphases added)

There are a number of "elements of consideration" which can be identified from the above provisions and the Explanatory Note. They are: the CISG's international character, the promotion of uniformity and consistency, the observance of good faith, and the general principle based by the CISG. These "elements of consideration" can be operated as principles of interpretation of the CISG so as to guide the interpreters.

Although it was explained above that the application of the CISG (as the governing law) by a domestic court or an arbitral tribunal is similar to its application of domestic law (as the governing law), there are still some fundamental differences in the international character of the CISG. Practically, it is possible that a domestic court or an arbitral tribunal still applies a "domestic statutory interpretation

---

[14]The text of the Explanatory Note is available at http://www.uncitral.org/pdf/english/texts/sales/cisg/V1056997-CISG-e-book.pdf. Accessed 8 Aug 2017.

approach or tradition" or applies "its domestic jurisprudence" in interpreting the CISG. But such interpretation will be strictly constrained by the elements of consideration discussed in the following sections of this chapter. The Secretariat Commentary to the 1978 draft indicates in paragraph 1 that the following elements of consideration work to restrict the application of domestic interpretation approaches:

> National rules on the law of sales of goods are subject to sharp divergencies [sic] in approach and concept. Thus, it is especially important to avoiding differing constructions of the provisions of this Convention by national courts, each dependent upon the concepts used in the legal system of the country of the forum. To this end Article 7 emphasizes the importance, in the interpretation and application of the provisions of the Convention, of having due regard for the international character of the Convention and of need to promote uniformity.[15]

9.3.3 The First Element of Consideration—CISG's International Character

When interpreting a domestic law which is the governing law of a contract, there is no apparent issue of international character with respect to the law itself because the domestic law is supposed to govern matters which are subject to its prescriptive jurisdiction. Even when there involves an international dispute, as long as it is governed by a domestic law, it indicates that such dispute is to be handled based on such domestic law. It means that the parties of such international dispute concede and submit themselves to a domestic regime. So when interpreting applicable domestic law (whether in the context of a purely domestic dispute or in the context of an international dispute), there is no apparent need of considering the applicable domestic law itself as having any international character.

But when interpreting the CISG as the governing law of a contract, the issue of its international character is apparent. It is the dispute being governed by the internationally accepted rules and being subject and conceding to such rules of international character. The element of international character of the CISG provided in Article 7[16] is of high importance.

The consideration of CISG's international character is purely a general indication. The CISG and its Explanatory Note do not provide clear guidance as to how to consider and how to give weight to such international character of the CISG. "Without an explicit explanation of how to implement the command to interpret the

---

[15] U.N. Secretariat, *Commentary on the Draft Convention on Contracts for the International Sale of Goods*, art. 6, cmt. 1. 7, U.N. Doc. A/CONF.97/5 (1979 (1978 Draft)) (cited from Bailey, *supra* note 3, at p. 293).

[16] CISG Article 7(1) provides in part that: "In the interpretation of this Convention, regard is to be had to its *international character* …" (Emphasis added).

Convention according to its international character, Article 7 fosters inconsistency because some courts will be more zealous than others in their recognition of the Convention's international character."[17] Hence an important task is to establish some further contents to guide the application of the consideration of CISG's international character.

In this regard, the following considerations should be relevant. First, the consideration of CISG's international character is closely relevant to the second element of promoting uniformity and consistency (as discussed below) and should be applied in a way to facilitate this second element. Hence, any interpretation approach which could clearly undermine the achievement of uniformity and consistency of interpreting the CISG should also be considered as not conforming to the consideration of CISG's international character. In contrast, any interpretation approach which could help the uniformity and consistency should be preferred.

Such preferred approach includes the consideration of the general practice of interpreting specific CISG's provisions in other jurisdictions. This does not mean that any particular jurisdiction's practice/jurisprudence should bind and absolutely guide the interpretation of the CISG in another jurisdiction. But if a CISG's provision is interpreted in a certain way generally by many jurisdictions, the consideration of the general practice in such jurisdictions should serve as a guidance under the required consideration of CISG's international character.

Second, and more specifically, if a statutory interpretation approach is unique in a jurisdiction and is not commonly found in most other jurisdictions, the use of such interpretation approach is not in line with the consideration of CISG's international character and is not preferred.

Third, since the CISG is an international treaty, the consideration of documents and materials related to the Convention is itself the consideration of CISG's international character. Hence the consideration of the legislative history of the CISG and the consideration of the Secretariat Commentaries to the 1978 Draft of the Convention[18] are in line with the required consideration of the Convention's international character.

9.3.4 The Second Element of Consideration—Promotion of Uniformity and Consistency

The terms uniformity (used in the text of CISG Article 7[19] and in the Explanatory Note) and consistency (used in the Explanatory Note) are of similar nature. The expectation from this element of consideration is that the results of interpreting the

---

[17]Bailey, *supra* note 3, at p. 291.

[18]Id. at p. 289.

[19]CISG Article 7(1) provides in part that: "In the interpretation of this Convention, regard is to be had… to the need to promote *uniformity* in its application…" (Emphasis added).

same CISG provisions by domestic courts or arbitral tribunals in different jurisdictions should not be divergent, disparate and in conflict with each other.

A common way of achieving the uniformity and consistency is to expect a court or an arbitral tribunal in a jurisdiction to consider existing interpretation of the same term or provision by domestic courts or arbitral tribunals in other jurisdictions. But a related problem is whether an individual jurisdiction's interpretation should have such guiding force or should be given a higher reference value. It is mentioned above that if an interpretative approach has been commonly adopted by some other jurisdictions, such interpretation definitely has a higher value of guidance or reference. But this does not mean that an individual jurisdiction's jurisprudence does not have any value of guidance or reference. It would still depend on the experience and reputation of jurisprudence of such jurisdiction so as to decide the "reference value".

Another way of achieving the uniformity and consistency is to expect a court or an arbitral tribunal to resort to authoritative writings or commentaries of the CISG. Although such publications do not enjoy a legal status for the purpose of interpreting the CISG, they are useful tools in helping achieve the uniformity and consistency purpose.

9.3.5 The Third Element of Consideration—Observance of Good Faith

The CISG requires that the Convention is to be interpreted in observance of good faith in international trade. But the text of the CISG and its Explanatory Note fail to provide any guidance in this regard. The book is of the view that the good faith requirement is of high importance in interpreting the CISG and it can be understood in an operable way.

First, since the good faith requirement is linked to international trade,[20] it is reasonable to understand that it is not to require that a court or an arbitral tribunal is to act in a good faith manner, but to require that the result of interpretation will recognize and implement the honest intent of the parties to a contract and will not result in a party taking obviously unfair advantages over another party in the transaction. Hence, the good faith requirement is to guide and to secure the proper result of CISG's interpretation.

Second, since the good faith requirement is to guide and to secure the proper result of CISG's interpretation, it is supplementary in nature. In other words, the good faith requirement comes to operate after interpretation activities have been initially conducted based on the required considerations of CISG's international character and the required consideration of the uniformity and consistency. The

---

[20]CISG Article 7(1) states in part that: "In the interpretation of this Convention, regard is to be had … to … the observance of *good faith in international trade*." (Emphasis added).

good faith requirement should be used to examine whether the result of CISG's interpretation would lead to recognizing a dishonest intent of a party and whether it would result in one party taking apparent unfair advantages over another party in the transaction.

9.3.6 The Fourth Element of Consideration—General Principles Based by the CISG

It must be noted that the CISG and its Explanatory Note do not instruct a court or an arbitral tribunal to look at the "general principles of law", but require *conforming the general principles on which it is based.*[21] However, the CISG does not specify the meaning and the contents of the general principles based by the Convention. The hints which can be drawn from the Convention are in its Preamble. Three elements can be seen in the Preamble in this regard. Although the Preamble of the CISG does not have a binding force, it is a useful reference to understand the broader and general backgrounds/principles on which the Convention is based. The relevant parts of the Preamble are quoted below:

> Considering that the *development of international trade* on the basis of equality and mutual benefit is an important element in promoting friendly relations among States,
>
> Being of the opinion that the adoption of *uniform rules* which govern contracts for the international sale of goods and take into account the different social, economic and legal systems would contribute to *the removal of legal barriers in international trade* and *promote the development of international trade,*

One element that can be found in the Preamble is the intention of the CISG to serve as uniform rules. This has been emphasized above concerning the Convention to be interpreted based on uniformity and consistency consideration.

The second element found in the Preamble is the promotion and development of international trade. The interpretation of the CISG should aim at promoting international transaction in goods, and should not work to hinder the development of international trade. The third element found in the Preamble is the removal of legal barriers. CISG's interpretation should ultimately lead to the result of reducing legal technicality and unnecessary complexity or diversity so that traders will be able to rely on friendlier governing rules for their transactions.

These elements are not the main interpretation principles, but should be considered as supplementing the interpretation of the Convention.

---

[21]CISG Article 7(2) provides in part that: "Questions … not expressly settled in it are to be settled in conformity with *the general principles on which it is based…*" (Emphasis added) Although this provision was not drafted in a way to indicate that this is to decide CISG's interpretation, in practice, this is also for CISG's interpretation to fill the gap when the Convention fails to address a disputed issue.

9.3.7 Similarity and Difference Between CISG Article 7 and VCLT Articles 31–32

As mentioned in previous chapters, treaty interpretation by international adjudicators are bound by the provisions in VCLT Articles 31 and 32. The relevant rules include the good faith requirement, the ordinary meaning of the textual wording, the context (including subsequent practice) of the interpreted provision, the object-and-purpose of the interpreted treaty and the supplementary means of preparatory work. Many of these principles will be further elaborated in the later chapters. For the purpose of comparison at this juncture, it should be said that there are aspects which are similar to or different from the elements of consideration provided in CISG Article 7.

Concerning the good faith requirement, VCLT Article 31 requires that treaty provisions shall be interpreted "in good faith". This is to expect treaty interpreters to perform their treaty interpretation duty in a good faith manner, i.e. treating the disputing parties fairly and conducting the activities impartially through treaty interpretation. But the good faith element to be considered by a domestic court or an arbitral tribunal in the context of interpreting the CISG is different. As mentioned above, the good faith requirement in CISG Article 7 is linked to international trade and hence it is to require that the interpretation will not result in a party in the transaction taking obviously unfair advantages over the other party.

Concerning the textual/ordinary meaning, it is the general rule of interpretation (either treaty interpretation or statutory interpretation) that the ordinary and plain meaning should be given to an interpreted treaty term. Although it is not indicated in CISG Article 7, the interpretation of the CISG should not deviate from such basic principle. In this regard, treaty interpretation under the VCLT and under the CISG is similar. But it must be noted that the considerations of CISG's international character and of the uniformity and consistency must still be used to guide and to restrict the search and the identification of the plain meanings of the CISG terms. When there are two or more plain meanings, one of them which could assist such considerations should be preferred. From this perspective, treaty interpretation and the interpretation of the CISG is different.

Concerning the context, the CISG does not mention such interpretation rule either. In statutory interpretation, the systemic interpretation is a common rule of interpreting a legal term or requirement. A domestic court or an arbitral tribunal should not be prevented from considering the context of a CISG provision for interpretation purpose. But again, the contextual interpretation should be subject to the considerations of CISG's international character and of the uniformity and consistency as required by CISG Article 7.

It should be a useful note that under the VCLT, subsequent practice of contacting parties can be taken into consideration as a context. This coincides with the uniformity and consistency consideration under the CISG, because, in order to achieve uniformity and consistency, the practices/jurisprudence in other jurisdictions is expected to be taken into consideration when interpreting the Convention.

Concerning the object-and-purpose of an interpreted treaty, the CISG does not explicitly mention this as an interpretation consideration. But the CISG requires interpretation to be in conformity with the general principles on which it is based. In practice, such CISG requirement is similar to VCLT's object-and-purpose requirement, because when deciding the conformity with the general principles on which the CISG is based, an interpreter will also have to look at the overall objectives of the Convention so as to identify the contents of such general principles.

Concerning preparatory work being used as a supplementary means of interpretation under the VCLT, this also coincides with the general practice of CISG's interpretation. For instance, the above mentioned Secretariat Commentary to the 1978 draft was the preparatory work of the CISG and is a useful material to understand the meaning of terms and provisions in the Convention.

9.4 Interpretation Rules for Other "Treaties for Private Matters"

9.4.1 Desirability of Establishing Interpretation Rules for All "Treaties for Private Matters"

As mentioned above, "treaties for private matters" usually do not include interpretation provisions (except the interpretation provisions in Article 7 of the CISG). But there are some reasons to support the idea of not applying the VCLT, but establishing some general interpretation rules or considerations for such treaties.

First, the treaty interpretation rules in the VCLT are not suitable for interpreting "treaties for private matters" mainly because such treaties are to govern procedural or substantive issues of private disputes and hence they are similar to other applicable domestic law for the resolution of private disputes. But the VCLT is designed to regulate and interpret public international law relations. Hence, it is not appropriate to apply VCLT Articles 31 and 32 for the interpretation of "treaties for private matters". There must be some other considerations or rules for interpreting such treaties.

Second, the general statutory interpretation rules in different countries could be vastly different. If "treaties for private matters" are subject to various different interpretation approaches of different contracting jurisdictions, it could result in extremely diverse outcomes, which apparently contradict to the original idea of concluding such treaties to unify or coordinate practices of contracting parties. Also, the interpretation of "treaties for private matters" is different from statutory interpretation concerning the international character and the need of uniformed and consistent interpretation of such treaties.

Third, considering the practice and experience of the CISG, it is possible and feasible to have certain elements of consideration to be established so as to properly interpret other "treaties for private matters" and to achieve the purpose of unifying private law rules.

9.4.2 *Contents of Interpretation Rules for Other "Treaties for Private Matters" That Can Be Codified*

The elements of consideration in relation to the interpretation of the CISG are very useful basis to establish the interpretation elements of consideration for other "treaties for private matters". Most interpretation elements of consideration set forth in the CISG should also be applicable to other "treaties for private matters".

More specifically, the international character and the promotion of uniformity and consistency of the interpreted treaties are very important elements to guide the interpretation of such kind of treaties. This is to achieve the main idea of unifying the private law rules of the contracting parties through concluding such treaties. Also the good faith requirement is a useful supplementary means to be used to secure the proper result of the interpretation of "treaties for private matters". The general principles based upon by the interpreted treaties for private matters should also be considered so as to supplement the interpretation of the interpreted treaties and to help clarify the proper meaning of their provisions.

In addition to the above elements to guide the interpretation of "treaties for private matters", it should also be desirable to incorporate some other elements of consideration for the interpretation of such treaties. For instance, the reliance of plain meaning of the interpreted terms and the systemic interpretation approach should all be helpful. When developing interpretation rules, such elements should be included. This is particularly important for a treaty in its initial stage of operation after its conclusion when there has not been jurisprudence in other jurisdictions or when the jurisprudence is not authoritative due to different reasons.

To conclude, this chapter basically argues the following points: First, the VCLT is not suitable for interpreting "treaties for private matters" by domestic courts and arbitral tribunals mainly because the contents of such treaties are designed to directly and indirectly govern private relations. Second, the CISG's elements of consideration for its interpretation are useful starting points for the establishment of general interpretation rules for interpreting all "treaties for private matters". These include the consideration of the international character, the promotion of uniformity and consistency of the interpreted treaties, the good faith requirement, and the general principles based by the interpreted "treaties for private matters". This chapter further suggests that it is desirable to incorporate some other considerations for the interpretation of such treaties, including the reliance of the plain meaning of the interpreted terms and the systemic interpretation approach. This chapter considers that it is desirable and feasible to formulate a set of general rules of interpretation for all "treaties for private matters". These rules can be codified so that when domestic courts and arbitral tribunals have to apply such treaties, there will be consistent interpretation rules to be followed and there will be more consistent outcomes for the disputes under such treaties.

References

Bailey JE (1999) Facing the truth: seeing the convention on contracts for the international sale of goods as an obstacle to a uniform law of international sales. Cornell Int Law J 32(2):273–317

Hollis DB (2012) Defining Treaties. In: Hollis DB (ed) The oxford guide to treaties. Oxford University Press, Oxford, pp 11–45

http://www.incadat.com/index.cfm/themas/cluster/index.cfm?act=search.detail&cid=1029&lng=1&sl=2. Accessed 8 Aug 2017

http://www.newyorkconvention.org/english. Accessed 8 Aug 2017

http://www.uncitral.org/pdf/english/texts/sales/cisg/V1056997-CISG-e-book.pdf. Accessed 8 Aug 2017

http://www.uncitral.org/pdf/english/texts/sales/cisg/V1056997-CISG-e-book.pdf. Accessed 8 Aug 2017

https://icsid.worldbank.org/en/Documents/icsiddocs/ICSID%20Convention%20English.pdf. Accessed 8 Aug 2017

https://www.hcch.net/en/instruments/conventions/full-text/?cid=61. Accessed 8 Aug 2017

https://www.hcch.net/en/instruments/conventions/full-text/?cid=77. Accessed 8 Aug 2017

https://www.hcch.net/en/instruments/conventions/full-text/?cid=78. Accessed 8 Aug 2017

https://www.hcch.net/en/instruments/conventions/full-text/?cid=98. Accessed 8 Aug 2017

U.N. Secretariat (1979) Commentary on the draft convention on contracts for the international sale of goods. U.N. Doc. A/CONF.97/5 (1978 Draft)

Chapter 10
Methods of Searching for the Ordinary Meaning and the Possible Codification

Contents

10.1 Meaning of a Treaty Term Can Be Very Controversial—The Meaning of "Goods" in Trade Agreements as an Example

The distinction between the two concepts of "goods" and "services" provided in many WTO agreements is a very good example to illustrate the difficulty of deciding the appropriate meaning for a treaty term.

C. Lo, *Treaty Interpretation Under the Vienna Convention on the Law of Treaties*,
https://doi.org/10.1007/978-981-10-6866-9_10

It is possible that the agreements for trade in "goods" (especially the GATT) and the agreement for trade in "services" (specifically the GATS) can be concurrently applied in the same dispute. For instance, the Appellate Body indicates in its Report on *Canada—Certain Measures Relating to Periodicals* that "The ordinary meaning of the texts of GATT 1994 and GATS as well as Article II:2 of the WTO Agreement, taken together, indicates that the obligations under GATT 1994 and GATS can co-exist and that one does not override the other."[1] The Appellate Body also indicates in its Report on *EC—Regimes for the Importation, Sale, and Distribution of Bananas* that "Certain measures could be found to fall exclusively within the scope of the GATT 1994, when they affect trade in goods as goods. Certain measures could be found to fall exclusively within the scope of the GATS, when they affect the supply of services as services. There is a third category of measures that could be found to fall within the scope of both the GATT 1994 and the GATS."[2] Having explained the above, it is still important to know, in many situations, whether a challenged measure is adopted in relation to goods or services so as to know whether the GATT 1994 or the GATS should apply.

A salient example of such kind is about whether the electrical power should be considered as "goods" so as to have the respective measure subject to the rules under the GATT and other agreements governing the trade in goods or whether it should be considered as "service" so as to have the respective measure subject to the rules provided in the GATS.

Although many WTO agreements use the term "goods", there is basically no definition for such term. It is theoretically possible to broadly understand the term "goods" as anything of economic utility. Under this meaning, electricity is definitely "goods". But this meaning could be so broad so as to cover all services and to blur the distinction between goods and services. It is also possible to less broadly understand the term as those things that are movable, but not necessarily tangible. Under this meaning, electricity is still a "goods". It is still possible to very narrowly understand the term as all tangible items. Under this meaning, electricity is not "goods", but a service.

The issue of whether electricity should be considered as goods or service under the WTO has been debated for a long time. As indicated by a commentator:

> …historically, the GATT's negotiators considered electricity a service rather than a good. … While some scholars support the idea that the GATT rules are applicable to every type of energy product, others argue that, although it can be assumed that under the GATT energy is generally considered a good, hydroelectric power has to be deemed a service. Furthermore, for some academics GATT rules do not apply to electricity due to its intangible nature. Nevertheless, as has been argued by some scholars, on several occasions domestic and other legal systems have commonly considered electricity a good. For

[1] Appellate Body Report, *Canada—Certain Measures Concerning Periodicals*, p. 19, WTO Doc. WT/DS31/AB/R19 (adopted 30 July 1997).

[2] Appellate Body Report, *European Communities—Regime for the Importation, Sale, and Distribution of Bananas*, para. 221, WTO Doc. WT/DS27/AB/R (adopted 25 Sept 1997).

example, in the landmark decision *Costa v. Enel*, the Court of Justice of the European Union (CJEU) confirmed implicitly that electricity is a good…"[3]

In the recent WTO case of *Canada—Renewable Energy/Feed-In Tariff Program*, the Panel found that the Feed-In Tariff (FIT) contract constituted "investment measures related to trade in goods" within the meaning of Article 1 of the Agreement on Trade Related Investment Measures (TRIMS Agreement)[4] and that the challenged trade-related investment measures concerning electricity and electricity generators were inconsistent with GATT Article III:4 and TRIMS Article 2.1,[5] both of which are trade rules to govern trade in "goods". The Appellate Body agreed with the Panel's finding in this regard with different reasons and considered that such measures do not fall within the scope of exceptions provided in GATT Article III:8(a). In other words, both the Panel and the Appellate Body in this case clearly considered that electricity is "goods" for the purpose of applying those trade rules governing trade in goods, without much explanation. But the meaning and scope of goods in relation to "electricity" is a great example to show that although it might be clear to some people that the term "goods" should be interpreted to only mean the tangible items, it might conversely be clear to other people that the "tangibility" is not the element to understand the meaning of this term.

The above example not only shows the result of interpretation of a single term could decisively affect whether to apply one or the other agreement, but also indicates that the terms that we are familiar with (i.e. goods, services, and electricity) might not necessarily mean the thing we ordinarily thought.

10.2 Ordinary Meaning as One of the Means

10.2.1 "Ordinary Meaning" as One of the Elements in VCLT Art. 31.1

Article 31.1 of the VCLT is the main part of the rules for treaty interpretation. It provides: "A treaty shall be interpreted in good faith in accordance with the *ordinary meaning* to be given to the terms of the treaty in their context and in the light of its object and purpose."[6] (Emphasis added) Certainly, the term "ordinary meaning" itself needs interpretation.

There are two fundamental instructions under this article concerning the interpretation "in accordance with the ordinary meaning to be given to the term". The

[3]Leal-Arcas et al. (2016), pp. 61–62.

[4]Panel Reports, *Canada—Certain Measures Affecting the Renewable Energy Generation Sector/ Measures Relating To The Feed-In Tariff Program*, paras. 7.108–7.112, WTO Doc. WT/DS412/R, WT/DS426/R (adopted 24 May 2013).

[5]Id. at paras. 7.155–7.166.

[6]Much of the discussion in this chapter is based on the following articles: Lo (2010, 2012).

first instruction from this part of Article 31 is that "the terms of the treaty" is the starting point of treaty interpretation, because the ordinary meaning is to be given to the textual terms (indicating that the treaty term is the basis of interpretation) and the context is the treaty terms' context (indicating that the treaty term serves as the basis to decide the context). Hence, the textualism is the primary means/method for treaty interpretation. The second instruction is that the terms of a treaty are to be given with the ordinary meaning, instead of an unusual, uncommon or distinctive meaning. Also the context of the interpreted term and the object-and-purpose of the interpreted treaty are the elements to be based upon for the interpretation of treaty terms. Although all these three elements (ordinary meaning of the terms, their context and the object-and-purpose of the treaty) and are keys for the interpretation of a treaty, identifying the ordinary meaning of the textual wording is always the starting point for treaty interpretation.

The idea of identifying the ordinary meaning of the textual wording being the starting point of treaty interpretation has been confirmed in the cases decided by the Appellate Body and the dispute settlement panels.[7] For instance, the Appellate Body in its Report on *US—Shrimp* indicated:[8]

> … *A treaty interpreter must begin with, and focus upon, the text of the particular provision to be interpreted.* It is in the words constituting that provision, read in their context, that the object and purpose of the states parties to the treaty must first be sought. Where the meaning imparted by the text itself is equivocal or inconclusive, or where confirmation of the correctness of the reading of the text itself is desired, light from the object and purpose of the treaty as a whole may usefully be sought.
>
> (Emphasis added)

In addition to these three elements, there is also the good faith requirement in the same paragraph. The relation between "good faith" and these three elements are thus of importance. The panel on *US—Section 301 Trade Act* states that "the elements referred to in Article 31—text, context and object-and-purpose as well as good faith—are to be viewed as one holistic rule of interpretation rather than a sequence of separate tests to be applied in a hierarchical order."[9]

Since all these elements are to be viewed in one holistic rule, it would be a reasonable understanding that these three elements should all be subject to the good faith principle. This conclusion can also be drawn from the sentence of Article 31.1, which not only requires a treaty to "be interpreted in good faith", but also "in accordance with the ordinary meaning to be given to the terms of the treaty in their context and in the light of its object and purpose". If the giving of certain "meaning" to the terms of the treaty or if the reliance of the context and the

---

[7]Knox (2004), p. 50.

[8]Appellate Body Report, *United States—Import Prohibition of Certain Shrimp and Shrimp Products*, para. 114, WTO Doc. WT/DS58/AB/R (adopted 6 Nov 1998) [hereinafter US—Shrimp Appellate Body Report].

[9]Panel Report, *United States—Sections 301–310 of the Trade Act 1974*, para. 7.22, WTO Doc. WT/DS152/R (adopted 27 Jan 2000) [hereinafter US—Section 301 Trade Act Panel Report].

object-and-purpose is not made in good faith, it would not meet the requirement that the treaty should be interpreted in good faith. A writer also held similar view and commented: "All of those elements are operating within the boundaries of the good faith safeguard of giving effect to the treaty terms."[10]

The good faith principle and the holistic interpretation will be further discussed in Chap. 17 of this book.

10.2.2 Distinction from and Relation with Other Interpretation Elements as Well as the "Grammatical Interpretation"

As will be explained in Chaps. 11 and 12 of this book, the object-and-purpose of the interpreted treaty and the context of the interpreted provision also need to be taken into account when conducting treaty interpretation. The main purpose of relying on the object-and-purpose and the context is to decide or select the most appropriate ordinary meaning from among many possible ordinary meanings. Hence, these two other elements are to support the decision of the ordinary meaning for the interpreted term.

There is another issue concerning the distinction between the reliance of textual wording's ordinary meaning and the contextual interpretation. Let's use the sentence of Article 31.1 of the VCLT as an example. It provides that: "A treaty shall be interpreted in good faith in accordance with the ordinary meaning to be given to the terms of the treaty in *their* context and in the light of *its* object and purpose." When the provision refers to "context", it uses the *plural form* of possessive pronoun "their". Hence grammatically, the word "context" in Article 31.1 must refer to the context of the "interpreted terms".

On the other hand, when Article 31.1 refers to the phrase "object-and-purpose", it uses the *singular form* of pronoun "it". Hence, grammatically, the phrase "object-and-purpose" in Article 31.1 must refer to the "object-and-purpose" of the "entire interpreted treaty", not the "object-and-purpose" of the "interpreted provision in the treaty". This distinction is meaningful. Because sometimes a treaty's overall object-and-purpose could be very different from a specific provision's object-and-purpose. This will be further explained in the next chapter of this book.

Such "grammatical interpretation" can be considered as an inherent ingredient in the textual interpretation of giving ordinary meaning to the textual wording in the treaty provision.

---

[10]Ruse-Khan (2010), p. 164.

10.2.3 Why to Rely on Ordinary Meaning

There are some functions that we can identify for the reasons of using and predominantly relying on the ordinary meaning to interpret treaty terms. The first function for the use of and reliance on the ordinary meaning of an interpreted treaty term is to prevent a treaty interpreter's possible subconscious prejudice or deliberate misuse of interpretation power arising from his/her political and other positions or arising from external influences (such as political influences). If an interpreter is not strictly bound by the ordinary meaning of an interpreted textual term, it is more likely that the interpretation could be used to serve some particular political or other purposes. The ordinary meaning of a treaty term sets forth the boundary of treaty interpretation so that the interpreter will have to elaborate and apply the interpreted term within such constraint and boundary.

The second function for treaty interpretation to rely on the ordinary meaning of a treaty term is to prevent a treaty interpreter from becoming a law maker. It is a matter of course that the line between interpretation and law-making could sometimes be unclear and that an interpretation to fill a vacuum created by the treaty maker is sometimes necessary. But there is still a boundary within which the treaty interpreters are to exercise its power so as not to make themselves treaty makers. The requirement of interpreting a treaty term based on its ordinary meaning helps confine the adjudicatory function so as not to turn to exercising a legislative function.

Third, a related function of relying on the ordinary meaning of a treaty term is to ensure achievement of the legitimate expectation of the parties to a treaty. The Appellate Body has stated in *India—Patents* (*US*) that: "The legitimate expectations of the parties to a treaty are reflected in the language of the treaty itself."[11] If an interpreted term is provided with a meaning that is not ordinary, it goes beyond the actual language used in the treaty and could lead to surprising one or both of the disputing parties, who have not had the idea that a treaty provision is to be interpreted in a way to depart from their legitimate expectations.

The fourth function from relying on the ordinary meaning is to ensure consistency and objectiveness in treaty interpretation. Although there are still problems concerning the identification the ordinary meaning of an interpreted term, the ordinary meaning is still the most objective element in deciding the treaty interpretation. Due to its potential objectiveness, the reliance on the ordinary meaning to interpret a treaty term could lead to a more predictable, stable and consistent outcome from interpreting the same treaty term under the same DSM in different cases (or even under different DSMs).

The fifth function is in its "confining role" in deciding the use of "other treaty interpretation methods". Again, Article 31.1 is the main part for treaty interpretation. It provides: "A treaty shall be interpreted in good faith *in accordance with* the

[11]Appellate Body Report, *India—Patent Protection for Pharmaceutical and Agricultural Chemical Products*, para. 45, WTO Doc. WT/DS50/AB/R (adopted 16 Jan 1998).

ordinary meaning to be given to the terms of the treaty in their context and in the light of its object and purpose." (Emphasis added) It requires that a treaty term shall be interpreted "in accordance with" the ordinary meaning. So the ordinary meaning is the fundamental basis which cannot be departed from. It also required that the ordinary meaning is to be given to the treaty terms in their context. In other words, the context is also to confine or help decide the ordinary meaning. So when resorting to the context of a treaty term, it is still the ordinary meaning being given in the context of an interpreted term. The use of contextual interpretation does not mean that an interpreter can depart from the ordinary meaning. Article 31.1 also requires that a treaty is interpreted in accordance with the ordinary meaning of a treaty term in light of the object and purpose of the treaty. Therefore, the object-and-purpose is also to confine or help decide the ordinary meaning of an interpreted treaty term.

10.2.4 How to Decide the Ordinariness of a Meaning

Although the contents of the VCLT are customary international law in nature, the text of the VCLT is still a treaty text. Since there is no definition provided in the VCLT concerning various elements for treaty interpretation (including good faith, ordinary meaning, object-and-purpose, and context), the provisions in the VCLT (particularly the term "ordinary meaning" provided in Article 31.1) need a proper interpretation.

The first issue is about the terms used. Although Article 31.1 uses the term "ordinary meaning", there are other terms sometimes used by many people interchangeably, including "plain meaning" and "literal meaning". The term "ordinary meaning" focuses more on the ordinariness of the usage of an interpreted provision. The term "plain meaning" focuses more on the connotation of the interpreted provision. The term "literal meaning" focuses more on the linguistic aspect of the provision. In the context of statutory interpretation and contractual interpretation, the term "plain meaning" is more often used. When referring to specific approach of statutory interpretation, the term "literalism" is often used. In the context of treaty interpretation, the term "ordinary meaning" is constantly used, basically because of the specific provision in Article 31.1 of the VCLT, also partly because the term "ordinary meaning" avoids entering into investigating the connotation and linguistic aspects of a treaty term. But these terms (i.e. ordinary meaning, plain meaning and literal meaning) mutually help each other in clarifying their meanings. Ordinary meaning must not deviate from the literal meaning of a term. Also ordinary meaning must be plain meaning, as opposed to uncommon meaning.

The second issue is about the "ordinary meaning of what". The ordinary meaning is connected to the textual wording actually appeared and used in the treaty. Hence, the reliance on the ordinary meaning can also be called textualism so as to indicate that the primary focus is on the treaty text. An interpreter is not to exercise its interpretation based on words or concepts which cannot be found in the interpreted treaty term. The Appellate Body indicated in *India—Patents (US)* in this regard that:[12]

> The duty of a treaty interpreter is to examine the words of the treaty to determine the intentions of the parties. This should be done in accordance with the principles of treaty interpretation set out in Article 31 of the Vienna Convention. But *these principles of interpretation neither require nor condone the imputation into a treaty of words that are not there or the importation into a treaty of concepts that were not intended.*
>
> (Emphasis added)

The third issue is about the *subjective aspect* of the ordinariness. The essence of the problem is "ordinary to whom": Should it be ordinary to traders/specific group or other people or should it be ordinary to experts or laypersons? In this regard, there is a commonly cited paragraph by Lawrence Solum:

> Some laws are meant for all citizens (e.g., criminal statutes) and some are meant only for specialists (e.g., some sections of the tax code). A text that means one thing in a legal context, might mean something else if it were in a technical manual or a novel. So the plain meaning of a legal text is something like the meaning that would be understood by competent speakers of the natural language in which the text was written who are within the intended readership of the text and who understand that the text is a legal text of a certain type.[13]

This explanation is made in the context of statutory interpretation. It is basically also true in the context of treaty interpretation. For a trade treaty, the ordinary meaning of a term usually must be decided based on the ordinary understanding of the term the field of international trade. For a technical term used in a technical treaty, its ordinary meaning usually should not be based on ordinary people's understanding, but the understanding of the people in the field, of the term.

But the difference between statutory interpretation and treaty interpretation concerning the subjective aspect of the textual interpretation is that for statutory interpretation, the ordinariness is determined based on the intended regulated persons (i.e. the targeted persons), whereas for treaty interpretation, the decision of ordinariness is not based on intended regulated parties (i.e. the contracting parties). It would not be correct to say that the ordinariness is based on some contracting parties' understanding of the term. Because it is likely that a country does not have expertise in a field, but it still signed a treaty in such field. If the ordinariness of a treaty term is decided based on the contracting parties' understanding of the provision, it can undermine the objectiveness of the treaty. So in the context of treaty interpretation, the decision of ordinariness should be based on the ordinary understanding of the people in the respective field.

The fourth issue is about the *objective aspect* of the ordinariness. There are almost always more than one "ordinary meaning" for a term, instead of merely

---

[12]Id.

[13]Solum (2017).

having a single ordinary meaning.[14] Treaty interpretation involves the process of selection of one ordinary meaning from two or more meanings which are all "ordinary". A question to be asked here is how ordinary should the meaning be, for the purpose of using it to understand the interpreted term. There is no specific measure or scale to evaluate the extent of ordinariness. But the requirement should be that a meaning should be ordinary enough so as to be considered for treaty interpretation. The standard of "ordinary enough" should not be a high standard. As long as a meaning is ordinary in the respective field, it is eligible to be considered by the treaty interpreter. For instance, as long as a meaning is included in the dictionary definitions, it could be considered ordinary enough. It must be also noted that the reliance on the ordinary meaning does not mean that the "more ordinary" a meaning is, the more likely such meaning should be used. As long as a meaning can be considered as "ordinary", it is a qualified candidate to be considered by the treaty interpreter in connection with the context and the object-and-purpose.

For instance, as will be explained in Chap. 12 of this book, the "most ordinary" (or the commonly used) meaning for the term "sporting" is conducting "an activity involving physical exertion and skill in which an individual or team competes against another or others for entertainment." But since the dictionary definitions of the term "sporting" include the meaning of "gambling", the meaning of gambling should be "ordinary enough" and is qualified to be considered by the treaty interpreter. When the interpreter has to decide whether the term "sporting" should be understood to refer to playing a game for stakes or to conducting physical exercise in a treaty, he/she has to put the term "sporting" in its context and in the light of the interpreted treaty's object-and-purpose so as to select a proper "ordinary meaning" to be given to the interpreted term.

10.2.5 Different from Other Means: The Process of "Searching"

Again Article 31.1 of the VCLT states: "A treaty shall be interpreted in good faith in accordance with the *ordinary meaning to be given to the terms of the treaty* in their context and in the light of its object and purpose." (Emphasis added) Although Article 31.1 uses the phrase the "ordinary meaning to be given to the terms of the treaty", it is apparent that a treaty interpreter is not to create a meaning and to "give" it to the interpreted term. Since it is the "ordinary meaning" (which should be in existence already) to be given, apparently it is not possible for a treaty interpreter to create an ordinary meaning and then to give it to the treaty term. Instead, it should be the duty of a treaty interpreter to "identify" an "existing" ordinary meaning and then to "give" this ordinary meaning to a treaty term. In other words, the ordinary

[14]Merrills (1968), p. 58. The article is also available at http://www.austlii.edu.au/au/journals/AUYrBkIntLaw/1968/4.html. Accessed 8 Aug 2017.

meaning should have already existed for some extended time before a particular treaty interpretation is carried out. If a meaning did not previously exist or if a previously existing meaning is not ordinary, it can never be considered as the meaning in ordinary sense.

From this perspective, it is clear that the duty of a treaty interpreter is not to formulate the "meaning" of a treaty term, but to "search for", to "find out" or to "identify" the ordinary meaning. Hence, treaty interpretation in this regard is a process of "searching for", "finding out" or "identifying" the ordinary meaning. Since it is a process of "searching for", "finding out" or "identifying" the ordinary meaning, instead of "creating and giving" a meaning to a term, the reliance on the "ordinary meaning" involves a lower extent of judgment and evaluation from the treaty interpreters.

In contrast to such process of treaty interpretation, other methods of interpreting a treaty involve comparatively a higher extent of judgment and evaluation from the treaty interpreters. For instance, in *US—Section 301 Trade Act*, the Panel applied the method of treaty interpretation through looking into the object-and-purpose of relevant agreements and stated the following:

> Providing security and predictability to the multilateral trading system is another central *object and purpose* of the system which could be instrumental to achieving the broad objectives of the Preamble. Of all WTO disciplines, the DSU is one of the most important instruments to protect the security and predictability of the multilateral trading system and through it that of the market-place and its different operators. DSU provisions must, thus, be interpreted in the light of this *object and purpose* and in a manner which would most effectively enhance it. In this respect we are referring not only to preambular language but also to positive law provisions in the DSU itself.[15] (Emphasis added)

In the process of such treaty interpretation, the panel has to evaluate various objects-and-purposes of relevant agreements and choose one of them in order to support a specific interpretation. In the above case, the chosen one is "providing security and predictability to the multilateral trading system" stipulated in Article 3.2 of the DSU. Other objects and purposes, such as "preserving the rights and obligations of Members" provided in the same paragraph, are not chosen by the panel to support the interpretation. The panel than apply this chosen object-and-purpose in order to prevent WTO Members from enacting and implementing their domestic legislations to deviate from such object-and-purpose.

But this does not mean that an interpreter does not have to exercise judgement or evaluation in searching for the ordinary meanings of the interpreted term. For example, the Appellate Body in *US—Shrimp* stated the following concerning the judgement of the equivocalness of the text and the reliance on the context and the object-and-purpose to interpret an agreement:

> A treaty interpreter must begin with, and focus upon, the text of the particular provision to be interpreted. It is in the words constituting that provision, read in their context, that the object and purpose of the states parties to the treaty must first be sought. Where the

[15] US—Section 301 Trade Act Panel Report, *supra* note 9, at para. 7.75.

> meaning imparted by the text itself is equivocal or inconclusive, or where confirmation of the correctness of the reading of the text itself is desired, light from the object and purpose of the treaty as a whole may usefully be sought.[16]

From this statement, it is clear that the treaty interpreter still has to conduct judgment and evaluation about whether meaning imparted by the text itself is equivocal or inconclusive and whether confirmation of the correctness of the reading of the text itself is desired before it resorts to the context and the object-and-purpose for the purpose of interpreting the relevant agreement.

10.3 Methods of Searching for Ordinary Meaning

10.3.1 Adjudicator's Personal Knowledge

There are different ways of ascertaining the ordinary meaning of a treaty term. One way of doing it is merely to rely on the personal knowledge and understanding of the treaty interpreter, instead of relying on any other objective source. For instance, the Arbitrator in *EC—Hormones* (*Article 21.3*) has to decide the reasonable period of time for the compliance of recommendation and ruling of the DSB under Article 21.3(c) of the DSU, which provides that:

> The reasonable period of time shall be: ... (c) a period of time determined through binding arbitration within 90 days after the date of adoption of the recommendations and rulings. In such arbitration, a *guideline* for the arbitrator should be that the reasonable period of time to implement panel or Appellate Body recommendations should not exceed 15 months from the date of adoption of a panel or Appellate Body report. However, that time may be shorter or longer, depending upon the particular circumstances. (Emphasis added)

Concerning the ordinary meaning of the "guideline" provided in this article, the arbitrator held:

> The ordinary meaning of the terms of Article 21.3(c) indicates that 15 months is a 'guideline for the arbitrator', and not a rule. This guideline is stated expressly to be that 'the reasonable period of time... *should not exceed* 15 months from the date of adoption of a panel or Appellate Body report' (emphasis added). In other words, the 15-month guideline is an outer limit or a maximum in the usual case. For example, when implementation can be effected by administrative means, the reasonable period of time should be considerably shorter than 15 months. However, the reasonable period of time could be shorter or longer, depending upon the particular circumstances, as specified in Article 21.3(c).[17]

When relying on the personal belief to decide the ordinary meaning of a treaty term, the situation should be so clear and apparent that even without resorting to

---

[16]US—Shrimp Appellate Body Report, *supra* note 8.

[17]Arbitration Report, *European Communities—Measures Concerning Meat and Meat Products* (*Hormones*) (*Article 21.3*), para. 25, WTO Doc. WT/DS26/15, WT/DS48/13 (circulated 29 May 1998) [hereinafter EC—Hormones (Article 21.3) Arbitration Report].

any other objectively existing source, the term in a treaty would have only one possible reasonable interpretation and no other interpretation could be reasonably made. The above quoted case of *EC—Hormones* (*Article 21.3*) is a useful example. A guideline and a rule of binding nature are vastly different and are even opposite to each other. The ordinary meaning of a "guideline" cannot include a "rule" with binding nature. However, this way of ascertaining the ordinary meaning of a treaty term is not often resorted either in WTO cases or in any other dispute settlement forum.

10.3.2 Usage in Another Treaty

Another way of finding out or searching for the ordinary meaning of a treaty term is to rely on the definition or the usage of the same term in another treaty. For example, the Appellate Body in its report on *US—Shrimp* relied on other international instruments to decide the ordinary meaning of the term "exhaustible natural resources" provided in Article XX(g) of the GATT 1994. It states:

> From the perspective embodied in the preamble of the *WTO Agreement*, we note that the generic term 'natural resources' in Article XX(g) is not 'static' in its content or reference but is rather 'by definition, evolutionary'. It is, therefore, pertinent to note that modern international conventions and declarations make frequent references to natural resources as embracing both living and non-living resources.[18]

In *EC–Approval and Marketing of Biotech Products*, the panel held more clearly about the reliance on relevant rules of international law as the evidence to help understand the ordinary meaning of a treaty term. It states:

> The ordinary meaning of treaty terms is often determined on the basis of dictionaries. We think that, in addition to dictionaries, other relevant rules of international law may in some cases aid a treaty interpreter in establishing, or confirming, the ordinary meaning of treaty terms in the specific context in which they are used. Such rules would not be considered because they are legal rules, but rather because they may provide evidence of the ordinary meaning of terms in the same way that dictionaries do.
>
> In the light of the foregoing, we consider that a panel may consider other relevant rules of international law when interpreting the terms of WTO agreements if it deems such rules to be informative. But a panel need not necessarily rely on other rules of international law, particularly if it considers that the ordinary meaning of the terms of WTO agreements may be ascertained by reference to other elements.[19]

[18]US—Shrimp Appellate Body Report, *supra* note 8, at para. 130.

[19]Panel Report, *European Communities—Measures Affecting the Approval and Marketing of Biotech Products*, paras. 7.92–7.93, WTO Doc. WT/DS291/R, WT/DS292/R, WT/DS293/R (adopted 21 Nov 2006).

10.3.3 Relying on Dictionaries

In addition to the above methods of ascertaining the ordinary meaning of treaty terms, the most often relied-on method by an interpreter is to look into dictionary definitions. The Appellate Body straightforwardly confirmed in *EC—Chicken Cuts* that dictionaries are a "useful starting point" for the analysis of "ordinary meaning" of an interpreted term.[20]

In so many WTO cases, dictionaries are the heavily relied-on tools by panels and the Appellate Body in order to decide the ordinary meaning of terms and provisions in WTO agreements.[21] Just take as an example of the Award on *EC—Hormones (Article 21.3)*. The Arbitrator relied on *The Concise Oxford Dictionary* to define the word "prompt". It reads:

> Article 21.1 stipulates that: '*Prompt compliance* with recommendations and rulings of the DSB is essential in order to ensure effective resolution of disputes to the benefit of all Members' (emphasis added). Article 3.3 states: 'The *prompt* settlement of situations in which a Member considers that any benefits accruing to it directly or indirectly under the covered agreements are being impaired by measures taken by another Member is essential to the effective functioning of the WTO and the maintenance of a proper balance between the rights and obligations of Members' (emphasis added). *The Concise Oxford Dictionary* defines the word, 'prompt', as meaning 'a. acting with alacrity; ready. b. made, done, etc. readily or at once'. Read in context, it is clear that the reasonable period of time, as determined under Article 21.3(c), should be the shortest period possible within the legal system of the Member to implement the recommendations and rulings of the DSB. In the usual case, this should not be greater than 15 months, but could also be less.[22]

Another quick example is in the panel report on *US—Certain EC Products*, which relied on the *Webster New Encyclopedic Dictionary* and the *New Shorter Oxford English Dictionary* in the same paragraph to define the term "seeking" and "to seek" as well as "redress". It states:

> The term 'seeking' or 'to seek' is defined in the *Webster New Encyclopedic Dictionary* as: 'to resort to, … to make an attempt, try'. … The term 'to redress' is defined in the *New Shorter Oxford English Dictionary* as 'repair (an action); atone for (a misdeed); remedy or remove; to set right or rectify (injury, a wrong, a grievance etc.); obtaining reparation or compensation'. …. The term 'redress' implies, therefore, a reaction by a Member against another Member, because of a perceived (or WTO determined) WTO violation, with a view to remedying the situation.[23]

---

[20]Appellate Body Report, *European Communities—Customs Classification of Frozen Boneless Chicken Cuts*, paras. 175–176, WTO Doc. WT/DS269/AB/R, WT/DS286/AB/R, WT/DS269/AB/R/Corr.1, WT/DS286/AB/R/Corr.1 (adopted 27 Sept 2005).

[21]Harris (2008), p. 140.

[22]EC—Hormones (Article 21.3) Arbitration Report, *supra* note 17, at para. 26.

[23]Panel Report, *United States—Import Measures on Certain Products from the European Communities*, para. 6.22, WTO Doc. WT/DS165/R (adopted 10 Jan 2001).

Sometimes there were as many as 10 dictionaries being relied on in a single report to decide the ordinary meanings of various terms. The panel report on *China—Publications and Audiovisual Products* is a pertinent example. The dictionaries being used in the report is listed in Table 10.1.

10.3.4 Instruction from the Interpreted Treaty—Anti-Dumping Agreement as an Example

Although the ordinary of a treaty term is looked for based on the above means, it is still possible that the interpreted treaty has already established certain rules to govern the decision of the ordinary meaning of the terms provided in the treaty. A salient and unique example is that provided in Article 17.6(ii) of the Anti-Dumping Agreement, which requires the panel to find the challenged measure to be in conformity with the Anti-Dumping Agreement, if the panel finds that a relevant provision of the Agreement admits of more than one permissible interpretation and that the measure rests upon one of those permissible interpretations.

Under this provision, there must be more than one permissible interpretation. Otherwise the panel would not be able to apply this rule. It is possible that the situation of two permissible interpretations arises from two possible ordinary meanings for a term in the Anti-Dumping Agreement. It is also possible that the two permission interpretations are because of the different understanding of the contexts of a term in the Anti-Dumping Agreement. But it would be more likely that the two permissible interpretations come from the possible two different ordinary meanings. Hence, although Article 17.6(ii) does not specifically indicate that it is designed to restrict or to guide the selection of an ordinary meaning from multiple possible ordinary meanings, the actual function of this article should be related to choosing a meaning from two or more ordinary meanings of a term or provision in the Anti-Dumping Agreement.

It must also be noted that the possible two interpretations must be "permissible". Otherwise, the interpreter would not be able to select from one of them. Whether or not it is permissible should be decided based on treaty interpretation rules under the VCLT. Only after having exercised the treaty interpretation activity based on treaty interpretation rules the interpreter still has to select and give a proper meaning to the interpreted term, Article 17.6(ii) would have a role to play.

It must also be noted that the two permissible meanings should be the ones which lead to the opposite results concerning whether a measure is in breach of the obligation under the Anti-Dumping Agreement. In such case, the interpreter is obliged to choose the one which would lead to the result of considering the measure being in conformity with the agreement.

Table 10.1 Dictionaries cited in the panel report on *China—publications and audiovisual products*

Dictionary	Terms to be interpreted	Ordinary meanings from the dictionaries	Paragraphs in the panel report
New Shorter Oxford English Dictionary (L. Brown (ed.) (Clarendon Press 1993), Vol. II)	Unify	Make, form into, or cause to become one; reduce to unity or uniformity	Para. 7.50
Shorter Oxford English Dictionary (5th ed. (Clarendon Press 2002), Vol II)	Without prejudice to	Without detriment to any existing claim or right; *spec*. in law, without damage to one's own rights or claims	Para. 7.253
	Regulate	Control, govern, or direct by rule or regulations; subject to guidance or restrictions	Para. 7.256
	Import	something imported or brought in	Para. 7.257
	Related to	Having relation; having mutual relation; connected	Para. 7.268
	Recording	Recorded material; a recorded broadcast, performance	Para. 7.1173
	Recorded material	"Material that is recorded" and not the "recording material"	Para. 7.1175
Black's Law Dictionary (7th ed., B.A. Garner (ed.) (West Group 1999))	Without prejudice to	Without loss of any rights; in a way that does not harm or cancel the legal rights or privileges of a party	Para. 7.253
	Discretionary	Involving an exercise of judgment and choice, not an implementation of a hard-and-fast rule	Para. 7.324
American Heritage Dictionary (*4th ed. Hought*on Mifflin 2000, available at http://www.bartleby.com/61/)	Including	What follows is not an exhaustive, but a partial, list of all covered items	Para. 7.294
Oxford English Dictionary Online available at http://dictionary.oed.com/entrance.dtl	Audiovisual	Pertaining to both hearing and vision	Para. 7.340
	Subscription	A method of bringing out a book, by which the publisher or author undertakes to supply copies of the book at a certain rate to those who agree to take copies before publication	Para. 7.965
	Digital	signals or information represented by discrete numeric values of a physical quantity such as voltage or	Para. 7.1151

(continued)

Table 10.1 (continued)

Dictionary	Terms to be interpreted	Ordinary meanings from the dictionaries	Paragraphs in the panel report
		magnetic polarization (commonly representing the digits 0 and 1)	
Businessdictionary.com	Distribution	Movement of goods *and services* from the source through the distribution channel	Para. 7.1180
The Monash Marketing Dictionary, www.buesco.monash.edu.au/mkt/dictionary/	A distribution channel	The path or route taken by goods *and services* as they move from producer to final consumer	Para. 7.1180
Random House Unabridged Dictionary, (Random House 1997) available at http://dictionary.infoplease.com/distribution	Economics	The system of dispersing goods throughout a community	Para. 7.1457
Webster's New Encyclopedic Dictionary, (Black Dog & Leventhal 1993)	Distribution	Marketing or merchandising of commodities	Para. 7.1457
BNET Business Dictionary, available at http://dictionary.bnet.com/definition/Distribution+Channel.html	Distribution channel	The route by which a product or service is moved from a producer or supplier to customers. A distribution channel usually consists of a chain of intermediaries, including wholesalers, retailers, and distributors, that is designed to transport goods from the point of production to the point of consumption in the most efficient way	Para. 7.1458

10.4 Issues of Relying on Dictionary

10.4.1 Justification of Relying on Dictionary

It is clear that treaty interpretation either under the DSU or other DSMs is not merely a task of checking up the meaning of the terms in dictionaries. However, it is also clear that the definitions provided in dictionaries are the easiest way of finding out the possible solutions. There are some plausible reasons for treaty interpreters to rely on dictionaries for the purpose of searching for or confirming the ordinary meaning of a term in an agreement.

First, about the nature of the dictionary, the compilation of a dictionary usually involves many people in an editing team. Basically, it represents views of people collected by the team who compiled the dictionary. Since a dictionary is published and widely circulated, it could be subject to possible challenges by other people. The process of compiling dictionary is basically of prudence and wariness so as to ensure the credibility about the comprehensiveness of the collection of terms and the correctness of the definitions to prevent it from being challenged.

Second, about the process of treaty interpretation, it would not be reasonable to expect the treaty interpreters to conduct a public survey by themselves for the purpose of collecting people's views about the ordinary meaning of a particular term. Also, although sometimes there could be sound reasons to look at the definition or usage of the same term in another treaty, it might not always be possible, because very often, there is a lack of relevant treaty providing such definition. Also sometimes it simply would not be possible or appropriate to rely on the definition of the same term in another treaty when there are more than one treaty providing different definitions of the same term, or even when the object-and-purpose of another treaty is fundamentally different from the treaty which is subject to interpretation. Resorting to dictionaries by the treaty interpreter is logically a better option in most situations to ascertain the ordinary meaning of a treaty term.

10.4.2 Problems Arising from the Use of Dictionaries

Although there are positive aspects for the use of dictionary to identify the ordinary meaning of a treaty term, it should also be pointed out that if there is no clear rule to guide the use of dictionary, it could be subject to manipulation. Donald McRae states in this regard that "anyone who has pleaded a case knows that you can usually find a dictionary meaning to support the meaning that your client prefers."[24]

Although there were discussions by the Appellate Body about some basic points of using dictionary, as quoted below, there is no comprehensive rule directing the proper application of dictionary for the purpose of deciding the ordinary meaning of a treaty term under the DSU to preclude manipulation by treaty interpreters.

As a matter of fact, there have been disputes arising from the use of dictionaries. For instance, in the above mentioned *China—Publications and Audiovisual Products* case, China challenged the panel report by arguing that the Panel should have proceeded to examine the two possible dictionary meanings in the light of the relevant context and the object-and-purpose of the treaty, instead of relying solely on one dictionary definition, and "should have found that the existence of two possible meanings suggested that the use of dictionary definitions was in fact

[24]McRae (2006), p. 364.

inconclusive."[25] For China, in cases where a panel commences its interpretation by consulting dictionary definitions, it must identify the range of possible meanings. In its view, because the various dictionary definitions were inconclusive, the Panel should have undertaken a careful examination of each possible meaning in the relevant context and in the light of the object and purpose of the treaty.[26]

The Appellate Body in its Report on *China –Publications and Audiovisual Products* summarized its previous decisions concerning the use of dictionary and added additional rationales. Although the previous statements of the Appellate Body are not sufficient to become a comprehensive rule for the application of dictionaries, it is still a useful reference for the purpose of establishing a more comprehensive rule. The Appellate Body's previous statements are listed in Table 10.2.

10.5 Restrictions on the Use of Dictionary and Some Proposed Rules

10.5.1 The Use of Dictionary Has Caused Concerns

There are also some apparent facts concerning the use of dictionaries which we cannot ignore. As pointed out by the Panel Report of *Canada—Certain Measures Affecting the Automotive Industry*, there are very few words which have only one dictionary meaning.[27] Therefore, there is always a need to select an appropriate meaning from various definitions in one or more dictionaries for one treaty term in a particular case. As a matter of fact, as having been indicated in the Panel Reports on *Canada—Certain Measures Affecting the Automotive Industry* (DS139, DS142)[28] and *United States—Anti-Dumping Act of 1916* (DS136, DS162),[29] there is a step of choosing the relevant dictionary meaning in pursuit of the ordinary meaning by treaty interpreters. If every disputing party is happy about the results of selecting

[25]Appellate Body Report, *China—Measures Affecting Trading Rights and Distribution Services for Certain Publications and Audiovisual Entertainment Products*, para. 39, WTO Doc. WT/DS363/AB/R (adopted 19 Jan 2010) [hereinafter China—Publications and Audiovisual Products Appellate Body Report].

[26]Id. at para. 41.

[27]Panel Report, *Canada—Certain Measures Affecting the Automotive Industry*, fn. 807, WTO Doc. WT/DS139/R, WT/DS142/R (adopted 19 June 2000).

[28]Id.

[29]Panel Report, *United States—Anti-Dumping Act of 1916, Complaint by the European Communities*, fn. 435, WTO Doc. WT/DS136/R and Corr. 1 (adopted 26 Sept 2000); and Panel Report, *United States—Anti-Dumping Act of 1916, Complaint by Japan*, fn. 562, WTO Doc. WT/DS162/R and Add. 1 (adopted 26 Sept 2000): "It is evident that while we review the ordinary meaning, our reading of the dictionary is already made selective by the broad context of the term".

Table 10.2 Points expressed by the appellate body concerning the use of dictionary

Rules	Relevant appellate body reports
While a panel may start with the dictionary definitions of the terms to be interpreted, in the process of discerning the ordinary meaning, dictionaries alone are not necessarily capable of resolving complex questions of interpretation because they typically catalogue all meanings of words	Appellate Body report, *US—Gambling*, para. 164; Appellate Body report, *US—Softwood Lumber IV*, para. 59; Appellate Body report, *Canada—Aircraft*, para. 153; and Appellate Body report, *EC—Asbestos*, para. 92
Dictionaries are important guides to, but not dispositive of, the meaning of words appearing in treaties	Appellate Body report, *US—Offset Act (Byrd Amendment)*, para. 248
Under Article 31 of the *Vienna Convention*, the "ordinary meaning" of treaty terms may be ascertained only in their context and in the light of the object and purpose of the treaty	Appellate Body report, *US—Gambling*, paras. 166 and 167
Interpretation pursuant to the customary rule codified in Article 31 of the *Vienna Convention* is ultimately a holistic exercise that should not be mechanically subdivided into rigid components	Appellate Body report, *EC—Chicken Cuts*, para. 176
The Panel also did not quote in its reasoning the alternative dictionary definitions submitted by China and contained in *The American Heritage Dictionary of the English Language*. However, the Panel did consider whether the meaning of the entry "Sound recording distribution services" was limited to the distribution of physical goods or whether it extended to electronic distribution, and it continued to do so in its subsequent analysis of relevant context, and object and purpose, as explained below. We, therefore, do not consider that, in its analysis of the ordinary meaning of "Sound recording distribution services", the Panel disregarded the definitions put forward by China. Neither are we persuaded that the Panel prematurely reached conclusions on the ordinary meaning of "Sound recording distribution services" based only on dictionary meanings before analyzing the relevant context and the object and purpose of the GATS	Appellate Body report, *China—Publications and Audiovisual Products,* para. 357

dictionaries or dictionary meanings, of course people should not bother about exploring any "rule".

Unfortunately, not all disputing parties agree to the results of selection from different dictionaries or dictionary meanings in specific cases. The salient example is in the case of *China—Measures Affecting Trading Rights and Distribution*

Services for Certain Publications for Certain Publication and Audiovisual Entertainment Products. The Appellate Body Report indicates China's non-satisfaction in Panel's selection of different meanings from dictionaries that the Panel "should have found that the existence of two possible meanings suggested that the use of dictionary definitions was in fact inconclusive" and that the Panel should have proceeded to examine the two possible dictionary meanings in the light of the relevant context and the object and purpose of the treaty.[30]

We should not pretend that there is no problem concerning the selection of different dictionaries or different definitions from them. The book is of the view that there is a legitimate ground to tackle or even to remove such concern and that certain clearer rules of the game for disputing parties to argue and to predict the selection process of dictionary meanings for treaty terms could ease their concern and would enhance the credibility of the already very well respected panels and the Appellate Body. The bottom line is that the disputing parties deserve some words about why a dictionary meaning is preferred to another dictionary meaning.

10.5.2 There Have Already Been Some "Rules" Established by AB and Panels

As a matter of fact, the Appellate Body and panels have already been trying to establish some kind of "rules" as the basis for the use of dictionaries or for the selection of dictionary meanings, although they might not call them "rules".

The first "rule" is that searching for a dictionary meaning is a proper method of deciding the ordinary meaning. For example, as quoted above, the Appellate Body states in its Report on *United States—Measures Affecting the Cross-Border Supply of Gambling and Betting Services* (*DS285*) that "[i]n order to identify the ordinary meaning, an interpreter may start with the dictionary definitions of the terms to be interpreted." This has implied that searching for an appropriate dictionary definition is a proper method to identify the ordinary meaning of a treaty term and that it can be a starting point for identifying the ordinary meaning.

The second "rule" is that dictionary is not dispositive. Also in the Appellate Body Report on *United States—Continued Dumping and Subsidy Offset Act of 2000*, it is state that "dictionaries are important guides to, not dispositive statements of, definitions of words appearing in agreements and legal documents."[31] The "rule" reflected in this statement is that the nature of dictionary definition is not to decide the meaning of treaty terms, but to serve as a guidance or reference for deciding the appropriate meaning of them.

---

[30]China—Publications and Audiovisual Products Appellate Body Report, *supra* note 25.

[31]Appellate Body Report, *United States—Continued Dumping and Subsidy Offset Act of 2000*, para. 248, WTO Doc. WT/DS217/AB/R, WT/DS234/AB/R (adopted 27 Jan 2003).

The third "rule" is that due regard must be paid to context when using dictionary. In the Appellate Body Report on *United States—Measures Affecting the Cross-Border Supply of Gambling and Betting Services* (*DS285*), three related "rules" have been specifically or generally established by the Appellate Body. The first "rule" is the requirement of not simply relying on dictionary to find the ordinary meaning to resolve treaty interpretation. It is stated in the report that "[d]ictionaries, alone, are not necessarily capable of resolving complex questions of interpretation, as they typically aim to catalogue all meanings of words—be those meanings common or rare, universal or specialized"[32] and that "[t]o the extent that an interpreter is reasoning simply equates the 'ordinary meaning' with the meaning of words as defined in dictionaries, this is too mechanical an approach."[33] The second "rule" established in the report is to pay due regard to various possible meanings. This "rule" is reflected in a statement in the report that "the Panel failed to have due regard to the fact that its recourse to dictionaries revealed that gambling and betting can, at least in some contexts, be one of the meanings of the word 'sporting'."[34] The third "rule" impliedly established by the Appellate Body should be the requirement of providing necessary explanation for the selection of different meanings. Although when the Appellate Body was making the relevant statement it was talking about the need for the panel to provide explanation for its recourse to the meanings of the French and Spanish words,[35] there should be a similar reason for the panel to provide explanation for its recourse to a specific dictionary meaning over the other meanings. If there is no explanation provided to support the selection of a dictionary meaning over the other meanings, it would not be easy to argue that due regard has been given to various possible meanings.

The panel in *EC—Chicken Classification* also indicated that "while dictionaries are the primary source for determination of the ordinary meaning of treaty terms," it is "necessary in this case to test the appropriateness of those dictionary definitions against the factual context in which the concession in question exists and is being applied".[36]

People cannot pretend that these are not some kinds of "rules" concerning the use of dictionaries, notwithstanding the facts that they might not be comprehensive enough to cover many aspects of dictionary use and that they are more about the confinement of the use of dictionary for the meanings of treaty terms.

Although people can consider these statements being the process or result of applying the VCLT Article 31, the fact still is that these are some "rules" instructing the proper situation to use dictionaries (such as allowing an interpreter to start with

---

[32]Appellate Body Report, *United States—Measures Affecting the Cross-Border Supply of Gambling and Betting Services*, para. 164, WTO Doc. WT/DS285/AB/R (adopted 20 Apr 2005) [hereinafter US—Gambling Appellate Body Report].

[33]Id. at para. 166.

[34]Id.

[35]Id.

[36]Paras. 7.104–105 of panel report in complaint by Brazil; paras. 7.104–105 of panel report in the complaint by Thailand.

the dictionary definitions for the terms to be interpreted) and the manner of using dictionaries (such as requiring the approach of using dictionaries not to be too mechanical and requiring to pay due regard to various meanings).

Also there are some limits indicated by the Appellate Body and the panels. For instance, the Appellate Body indicated in its Report on *US—Softwood Lumber IV* that "dictionary definitions have their limitations in revealing the ordinary meaning of a term. This is especially true where the meanings of terms used in the different authentic texts of the *WTO Agreement* are susceptible to differences in scope."[37] The Appellate Body also indicated in its Report on *US—Gambling* that "In order to identify the ordinary meaning, a panel may start with the dictionary definitions of the terms to be interpreted. But dictionaries, alone, are not necessarily capable of resolving complex questions of interpretation, as they typically aim to catalogue *all* meanings of words—be those meanings common or rare, universal or specialized."[38]

10.5.3 Proposed Rules for Applying Dictionary Based on Good Faith to Be Codified

Due to the lack of comprehensive rules and due to the importance of using dictionaries to find out or to search for the ordinary meanings of treaty terms and taking into account of the previous statements by the Appellate Body, the chapter proposes the following principles to be the possible candidates for codification. In the view of this book, the compliance of the following rules should be considered as having interpreted the terms in a good faith manner under paragraph 1 of Article 31 of the VCLT.

(1) The language of the dictionary: The first principle should be to rely only on the dictionary with the same language of the treaty to be interpreted. Since when the negotiators negotiated an agreement, the meaning of a treaty term in their mind would be that of the language used for the agreement. It would not be appropriate to translate a treaty term into another language and use a dictionary of that other language to find out the ordinary meaning. Although the official languages of the WTO include English, French and Spanish, basically panel and Appellate Body reports were almost always drafted in English[39] and as a result virtually only English dictionaries were used by the panels and the Appellate Body for the purpose of searching for the ordinary meanings of the terms in the WTO agreements.

---

[37]Appellate Body Report, *United States—Final Countervailing Duty Determination with respect to certain Softwood Lumber from Canada*, paras. 58–59, WTO Doc. WT/DS257/AB/R (adopted 17 Feb 2004).

[38]US—Gambling Appellate Body Report, *supra* note 32, para. 164, fn. 191.

[39]Plasai (2010).

(2) The nature of the term to be interpreted: Article 31 of the VCLT does not distinguish different natures of treaty terms for the purpose of deciding their ordinary meanings. Both ordinary words and technical or professional words are subject to the treaty interpretation of ordinary meaning. However, a reasonable question to be asked is whether only ordinary words should be eligible for the method of relying on dictionaries and whether it is appropriate to also rely on technical and professional dictionaries. Theoretically, it is possible to argue that ordinary meaning should be the understood meanings of ordinary people and the meanings provided in technical or professional can never be the understood meanings of the ordinary people. However, the book is of the view that there is no clue to infer from Article 31 of the VCLT that an ordinary meaning should be the understood meaning of the ordinary people. As long as a meaning of a term is ordinary to the potential users, it is the ordinary meaning from the perspective of the VCLT. Thus, although the definitions of terms in Black's Law Dictionary are not used by the ordinary people, it can still be the ordinary meanings of treaty terms. In other words, technical or professional dictionaries, such as *The Monash Marketing Dictionary*, *BNET Business Dictionary*, and *Black's Law Dictionary* used in the Panel Report on *China—Publications and Audiovisual Products* (see Table 10.1), are also eligible to be consulted with for the purpose of finding out ordinary meanings of technical or professional terms. However, it must be noted that when consulting with a technical or professional dictionary for a particular term, it must not be in conflict with the definition or usage of the term in the agreement. For example, there is a definition of the term "most-favored-nation" (MFN) in Black's Law Dictionary, i.e., the contracting nations receiving the same privileges either party grants to its most favored nations.[40] Such definitions should not be applied to the interpretation of WTO's provisions requiring the MFN treatments, because there are already definitions of MFN treatments in Article I of the GATT 1994, in Article II of the GATS and in Article 4 of the TRIPS Agreement.

(3) The form of dictionary: There are different forms to publish dictionaries. It can be published in hard copy, in digital form, in online format or in two or three forms simultaneously. According to the current practice, not only dictionaries in hard copy, but also dictionaries on the internet, such as *Oxford English Dictionary Online*, *The Monash Marketing Dictionary*, and *BNET Business Dictionary* mentioned in Table 10.1 above, are consulted with. The book agrees with the decision of the Appellate Body to rely on both hard copy and online dictionaries.

(4) The credential of dictionary: There are so many dictionaries published either in hard copy, in digital form or on the internet. It should be reasonable to presume that not all of the dictionaries should be eligible for the purpose of providing the ordinary meanings of treaty terms. A dictionary having existed for many years

[40] Black's Law Dictionary (1990), p. 1013.

would generally help building its credibility. Also if a dictionary is compiled by a renowned publisher or a publisher under a renowned university, it should be given a greater weight for the purpose of providing the ordinary meaning of a treaty term. If it is not published by such publisher, there must be evidence to show that the team and process of compilation are academically and practically reliable. Also if a dictionary is only published locally, i.e., merely in a WTO Member, this particular fact would serve as an evidence to show the lack of credibility of such dictionary.

(5) Conflicting definitions in different dictionary: When there are two or more dictionaries providing different definitions of the same term, the treaty interpreter would have to provide plausible reasons about why only one of the dictionaries was selected for the purpose of treaty interpretation. The treaty interpreter should not disregard any one of the dictionaries suggested/proposed by any one of the parties without any explanation. In the above mentioned case of *China –Publications and Audiovisual Products*, the Appellate Body confirmed that the panel did not disregard definitions in different dictionaries which were put forward by China and thus supported the panel's decision regarding the reliance on a dictionary for the purpose of ascertaining the ordinary meaning.

(6) Conflicting definitions in a dictionary: It is almost always the case that two or more definitions are provided in a dictionary for a single term. In such situation, the treaty interpreter should not disregard or exclusively choose any one of such definitions without any proper explanation. If there is no explanation about the selection of one of the conflicting meanings in a dictionary, the interpretation could be considered as in breach of good faith principle.

(7) The scope of dictionaries and the burden of proof issue: According to the practice of the Appellate Body and the panels, it is apparent that the dictionaries used by treaty interpreters are not limited to those suggested by the parties. This is an acceptable position, since treaty interpretation is the power granted to the treaty interpreter, who has the authority and duty of conducting correct and proper interpretation under Article 31. Thus the Appellate Body and the panels are not to rely on the principle of allocation of burden of proof to decide which party should be responsible for submitting dictionaries for the purpose of searching for the ordinary meaning. The treaty interpreters are of the power to select dictionaries on their own initiative. However, if a party has submitted a definition in a dictionary and if the treaty interpreter does not agree with such definition, an explanation about not accepting such definition in the dictionary should be properly provided. Otherwise, the interpretation arising from the ignorance of a definition in a dictionary suggested by a party could be considered as in breach of good faith principle, as mentioned above.

(8) The form of citing dictionaries: The current practice of the Appellate Body and the panels is that when quoting the definition of a dictionary, they just did it, without providing any overall explanation about the reasons of citing the dictionary. The book suggests that in order to conduct a good faith search for ordinary meaning through relying on dictionaries, the Appellate Body and the

panels would have to do the following: First, they must list all cited dictionaries. The current practice about citing previous cases has been that all cases cited by the Appellate Body or the panel reports are listed in a separate table after the table of contents in the report. Sometimes, other items, such as abbreviations are also listed in another table. This would help the parties and others to read and to challenge, if necessary, the reports. In order to help the parties and others to have comprehensive understanding of the dictionaries used in a report, it would be the requirement of good faith principle to list all dictionaries cited and relevant terms interpreted as well as definitions applied in the report. It would also be the requirement under the good faith principle that an overall explanation of the decision about applying certain dictionaries before the Appellate Body or the panels turns to the analysis of substantive issues involved in the dispute in their reports.

10.5.4 Some "Rules" Would not Adversely Affect the Flexibility and the Holistic Interpretation of Treaty Terms

There could be concerns about establishing some "rules" for the use of dictionary could undermine treaty interpreters' flexibility and could change the function of treaty interpretation rules in enabling treaty interpreters to exercise their power and could affect the "holistic exercise" of treaty interpretation.

Concerning the necessary flexibility and the holistic approach, the "rules" proposed above were specifically dealing with the methods of using dictionary and selecting dictionary meanings. It is in line with the 'rule' reflected in *United States —Measures Affecting the Cross-Border Supply of Gambling and Betting Services* (*DS285*) that it is appropriate to search for appropriate dictionary meaning to identify the ordinary meaning. These "rules" are not to change the nature of checking with dictionary definitions as a starting point of identifying the ordinary meaning of treaty terms. The main idea is that when a treaty interpreter starts with checking dictionary definitions, he/she must be mindful about possible controversies involved and pay due regard to various meanings. He/She must also ensure the selection of dictionary definitions to be as transparent as possible through providing some explanations about the selections. In other words, the "rules" are to ensure that when treaty interpreters start with dictionary definition, they will not do it in an arbitrary manner.

The "rules" proposed above are not to expect or require treaty interpreters to merely rely on dictionary to resolve cases. Rather these "rules" are proposed to properly identify dictionary definitions and to guide the appropriate findings of the meaning for treaty terms. After the starting step of properly checking dictionary definitions, treaty interpreters would still have to rely on the holistic approach under Articles 31 and 32 to decide treaty interpretation. In other words, holistic approach is the second step of treaty interpretation coming after the first step of clarifying the ordinary meaning of the interpreted term, the context of it and the object-and-purpose of the treaty. The "rules" is only to assist finding the ordinary meaning of a treaty term. They would not affect necessary flexibility to take into account other factors to interpret treaty terms.

Concerning the enabling and restricting functions, treaty interpretation principles do not necessarily serve an enabling function. It is also restricting treaty interpreters' exercise of their interpreting powers. It is not clear as to whether Articles 31 and 32 can be interpreted as only to enable treaty interpreters to exercise their jobs and not to restrict them. As a matter of fact, it might not be difficult to find from WTO practice that there is such restrictive function imposed on the exercise of treaty interpreters' duties. For instance, the above Appellate Body report on *United States—Measures Affecting the Cross-Border Supply of Gambling and Betting Services* (*DS285*) requiring the use of dictionary definition not to be too mechanical and requiring due regard to be paid to various possible meanings is apparently restricting treaty interpreters' exercise of their power. These are not the enabling functions.

It is apparent that dictionaries will continue to be the most heavily relied-on method of finding out or searching for the ordinary meanings of treaty terms. However, it is also clear that there is a need of establishing some more comprehensive "rules" for the use of dictionary to make treaty interpretation in line with good faith requirement under Article 31.1 of the VCLT. The above proposed "rules" are from various perspectives, including the language of the dictionary, the nature of the term to be interpreted, the form of dictionary, the credential of dictionary, the conflicting definitions in different dictionaries, the conflicting definitions in a dictionary, the scope of dictionaries and burden of proof, and the form of citing dictionaries. It is hoped that such rules would help parties to understand the reasons for the Appellate Body or a panel to rely on certain dictionaries and could enhance the practice of ascertaining the ordinary meanings of the terms of WTO agreements. The book is of the view that the essence of the above mentioned "rules" should be reflected in the codified set of treaty interpretation rules.

References

Black's law dictionary, 6th edn (1990). West, Saint Paul, Minnesota

Harris DP (2008) The honeymoon is over: the U.S.-China WTO intellectual property complaint. Fordham Int Law J 32:96–187

Knox JH (2004) The judicial resolution of conflicts between trade and the environment. Harv Environ Law Rev 28:1–78

Leal-Arcas R, Grasso C, Ríos JA (2016) Energy security, trade and the EU: regional and international perspectives. Edward Elgar Publishing, Cheltenham

Lo C (2010) Good faith use of dictionary in the search of ordinary meaning under the WTO dispute settlement understanding. J Int Dispute Settl 1(2):431–445

Lo C (2012) A clearer rule for dictionary use will not affect holistic approach and flexibility of treaty interpretation—a rejoinder to Isabelle Van Damme. J Int Dispute Settl 3(1):89–94

McRae D (2006) Treaty interpretation and the development of international trade by the WTO appellate body. In: Sacerdoti G, Yanovich A, Bohanes J (eds) The WTO at ten: the contribution of the dispute settlement system. Cambridge University Press, Cambridge, pp 360–371

Merrills JG (1968) Two approaches to treaty interpretation. Aust Year Book Int Law 4:55–82. http://www.austlii.edu.au/au/journals/AUYrBkIntLaw/1968/4.html. Accessed 8 Aug 2017

Plasai V (2010) The WTO dispute settlement system and the customary rules of treaty interpretation: nine years after, p 6. http://www.mfa.go.th/jtepa/asset/a073_Article_on_DSU.pdf. Accessed 4 June 2010

Ruse-Khan HG (2010) A real partnership for development? Sustainable development as treaty objective in European economic partnership agreements and beyond. J Int Econ Law 13:139–180

Solum L (2017) Legal theory lexicon: textualism. http://lsolum.typepad.com/legaltheory/2009/10/legal-theory-lexicon-textualism.html. Accessed 8 Aug 2017

Chapter 11
Ways of Taking into Consideration the Object-and-Purpose and the Possible Codification

Contents

11.1 Some Elaborations on the Object-and-Purpose

11.1.1 Meaning and Functions of the Object-and-Purpose

Article 31.1 of the VCLT requires treaty interpreter to interpret treaty provision by considering the object-and-purpose. It provides: "A treaty shall be interpreted in good faith in accordance with the ordinary meaning to be given to the terms of the treaty in their context and in the light of *its object and purpose*." (Emphasis added)

The term "object-and-purpose" is used not only in Article 31.1 in the VCLT. It is used seven more times in other provisions in the VCLT not related to treaty interpretation.[1] The repetition of the use of the term "object-and-purpose" throughout the VCLT shows the importance of the object-and-purpose of a treaty in its uses and functions. These other provisions include the following:

[1]Jonas and Saunders (2010), pp. 571–577.

C. Lo, *Treaty Interpretation Under the Vienna Convention on the Law of Treaties*,
https://doi.org/10.1007/978-981-10-6866-9_11

(1) Article 18 requires that "A State is obliged to refrain from acts which would defeat *the object and purpose of a treaty* when: (a) it has signed the treaty or has exchanged instruments constituting the treaty subject to ratification, acceptance or approval, until it shall have made its intention clear not to become a party to the treaty; or (b) it has expressed its consent to be bound by the treaty, pending the entry into force of the treaty and provided that such entry into force is not unduly delayed." (Emphasis added)
(2) Article 19 states that "A State may, when signing, ratifying, accepting, approving or acceding to a treaty, formulate a reservation unless: (a) the reservation is prohibited by the treaty; (b) the treaty provides that only specified reservations, which do not include the reservation in question, may be made; or (c) in cases not falling under sub-paragraphs (a) and (b), the reservation is incompatible with *the object and purpose of the treaty*." (Emphasis added)
(3) Article 20.2 states that "When it appears from the limited number of the negotiating States and *the object and purpose of a treaty* that the application of the treaty in its entirety between all the parties is an essential condition of the consent of each one to be bound by the treaty, a reservation requires acceptance by all the parties." (Emphasis added)
(4) Article 33.4 states that "Except where a particular text prevails in accordance with paragraph 1, when a comparison of the authentic texts discloses a difference of meaning which the application of articles 31 and 32 does not remove, the meaning which best reconciles the texts, having regard to *the object and purpose of the treaty*, shall be adopted." (Emphasis added) This provision will be further analyzed in connection with the overall discussion of Article 33 of the VCLT in a later part of the book.
(5) Article 41.1 states in part that "Two or more of the parties to a multilateral treaty may conclude an agreement to modify the treaty as between themselves alone if: … (b) the modification in question is not prohibited by the treaty and: … (ii) does not relate to a provision, derogation from which is incompatible with the effective execution of *the object and purpose of the treaty* as a whole." (Emphasis added)
(6) Article 58.1(b) (ii) states in part that "Two or more parties to a multilateral treaty may conclude an agreement to suspend the operation of provisions of the treaty, temporarily and as between themselves alone, if: … (b) the suspension in question is not prohibited by the treaty and: … (ii) is not incompatible with *the object and purpose of the treaty*." (Emphasis added)
(7) Article 60.3 provides in part that "A material breach of a treaty, for the purpose of this article, consists in: … (b) the violation of a provision essential to the accomplishment of *the object or purpose of the treaty*." (Emphasis added)

The treaty interpretation element/method of the "object-and-purpose" provided in Article 31.1 is not defined in the VCLT. Apparently, the term can be subject to very different views in its meaning and roles for treaty interpretation.

The first issue is whether the two words "object" and "purpose" are two separate terms with distinct meanings or whether they are synonymous and conjoint.

Although the ICJ and many French scholars consider these two words to have different meanings (for instance, the object being the immediate purpose of an act whereas the purpose being the reason of the object),[2] most scholars and other treaty interpreters consider these two words being synonyms.[3] Based on the interpretation in the vast majority of international disputes, the book considers that these two words are synonyms (with the same meaning or nearly the same meaning to each other), which jointly mean the ultimate goal that a treaty intends to achieve. Hence when these words are used in this book, they are used in the form of "object-and-purpose" (unless the phrase "object and purpose" is quoted from the VCLT or from other sources) so as to indicate that these two words are of a single and joint meaning.

Since the ultimate goal is the reason and cause that a treaty is created and put into force, it makes sense that the goal of the treaty plays the key role in the operation of the treaty, including in the interpretation of the treaty. The bottom line is that the operation of a treaty (including its application and interpretation) will not be deviating from the ultimate goal of the treaty. The above quoted articles in the VCLT have shown that the object-and-purpose of a treaty is given with a high weight in the operation of a treaty.

11.1.2 The Object-and-Purpose of What?

In VCLT provisions where the phrase "object and purpose" (or "object or purpose") is used, it is almost always linked to the relevant treaty (such as "the object and purpose of the treaty"). In other word, the phrase in these VCLT provisions is referred to *the overall goal of the treaty* (instead of the goal of *a specific provision* in the treaty) to guide its operation. The provision of Article 31.1 uses different expression, i.e. "its object and purpose". Since the provision uses a singular term "its", apparently and grammatically, it refers to the interpreted treaty's object-and-purpose, instead of the interpreted terms' (or the interpreted provisions') object-and-purpose.

It should be noted that the object-and-purpose of the interpreted treaty and the object-and-purpose of the interpreted provision could be different. The object-and-purpose of a treaty is the overall goal and purpose of concluding such treaty. Since a treaty provision can be an exception to some general principles, the object-and-purpose of such exceptional provision could be very different from the overall object-and-purpose of the entire treaty.

But still, there is an issue about whether or not the object-and-purpose of a specific part or of a specific article/provision in the treaty should also be given with such guiding role in treaty interpretation, in addition to *the object-and-purpose of the entire treaty* which needs to be considered when interpreting a provision in this

[2]Buffard and Zemanek (1998), pp. 318, 325.

[3]Id. at pp. 322–325.

treaty. GATT Article III:1 is an example. In order to understand the whole picture, paragraphs 2 and 4 of the same article are also partly quoted below together with paragraph 1:

1. The contracting parties recognize that internal taxes and other internal charges, and laws, regulations and requirements affecting the internal sale, offering for sale, purchase, transportation, distribution or use of products, and internal quantitative regulations requiring the mixture, processing or use of products in specified amounts or proportions, should not be applied to imported or domestic products so as to afford protection to domestic production.
2. The products of the territory of any contracting party imported into the territory of any other contracting party shall not be subject … to internal taxes or other internal charges of any kind in excess of those applied … to like domestic products. Moreover, no contracting party shall otherwise apply internal taxes or other internal charges to imported or domestic products in a manner contrary to the principles set forth in paragraph 1.
3. The products of the territory of any contracting party imported into the territory of any other contracting party shall be accorded treatment no less favourable than that accorded to like products of national origin in respect of all laws, regulations and requirements affecting their internal sale, offering for sale, purchase, transportation, distribution or use …

GATT Article III:1 sets forth the principle that internal taxes and internal rules should not be applied so as to afford protection to domestic production. There are a number of possible functions served by this paragraph. First, this paragraph can be considered as a separate "obligation" imposed on or an "expectation" from WTO Members not to act in certain way. But the obligation is quite soft, because it uses the term "should", which is usually used in a treaty to indicate that it is not to impose a legal obligation on the related parties. Second, this paragraph can also be considered as the "context" to other provisions in the same article so as to assist the interpretation of other provisions. Third, paragraph 2 of the same article (especially the last sentence "… Moreover, no contracting party shall otherwise apply internal taxes or other internal charges to imported or domestic products in a manner contrary to the principles set forth in paragraph 1") specifically link to paragraph 1 so as to create an obligation for WTO Members, because here the imperative term "shall" is used. Hence literally, the last sentence of paragraph 2 means that WTO Members "shall not" apply internal taxes or other internal charges to imported or domestic products in a manner to afford protection to domestic production. Fourth, it is also theoretically possible to consider paragraph 1 of Article III *as the object-and-purpose of the whole Article III*. That is to say, the whole purpose of national treatment requirement under GATT Article III is to avoid internal taxes and internal rules being used to provide protection for domestic production.

In this regard, the Appellate Body of the WTO has clarified that *the object-and-purpose of a treaty provision* (instead of *the object-and-purpose of the entire treaty*) can still be taken into consideration, but the object-and-purpose of a provision should not be considered in isolation from the object-and-purpose of the entire treaty. The Appellate Body report on *EC—Chicken Cuts* states that[4]:

> We begin our analysis with the question whether the Panel incorrectly distinguished between *the object and purpose of the treaty and that of its individual provisions*. It is well accepted that the use of the singular word "its" preceding the term "object and purpose" in Article 31(1) of the Vienna Convention indicates that the term refers to *the treaty as a whole*; had the term "object and purpose" been preceded by the word "their", the use of the plural would have indicated a reference to particular "treaty terms". Thus, the term "its object and purpose" makes it clear that *the starting point for ascertaining "object and purpose" is the treaty itself, in its entirety. At the same time, we do not believe that Article 31(1) excludes taking into account the object and purpose of particular treaty terms, if doing so assists the interpreter in determining the treaty's object and purpose on the whole.* We do not see why it would be necessary to divorce a treaty's object and purpose from the object and purpose of specific treaty provisions, or vice versa. To the extent that one can speak of the "object and purpose of a treaty provision", it will be informed by, and will be in consonance with, the object and purpose of the entire treaty of which it is but a component.
>
> Having said this, *we caution against interpreting WTO law in the light of the purported "object and purpose" of specific provisions, paragraphs or subparagraphs* of the WTO agreements, or tariff headings in Schedules, *in isolation from the object and purpose of the treaty on the whole*. Even if, arguendo, one could rely on the specific "object and purpose" of heading 02.10 of the EC Schedule in isolation, we would share the Panel's view that "one Member's unilateral object and purpose for the conclusion of a tariff commitment cannot form the basis" for an interpretation of that commitment, because interpretation in the light of Articles 31 and 32 of the Vienna Convention must focus on ascertaining the common intentions of the parties.
>
> For these reasons, we have no difficulty with the Panel's approach in interpreting the tariff commitment at issue in this case in the light of the object and purpose of the WTO Agreement and the GATT 1994.
>
> (Emphases added)

Another related issue is about the possibility of a goal or object-and-purpose set forth in one treaty serving as the goal or object-and-purpose of another treaty in the same treaty system. For instance, the Preamble of the GATT does not explicitly state anything about the sustainable development. But the Agreement Establishing the WTO states in its Preamble the following: "allowing for the optimal use of the world's resources in accordance with *the objective of sustainable development*, seeking both to protect and preserve the environment and to enhance the means for doing so in a manner consistent with their respective needs and concerns at different levels of economic development". (Emphasis added) The "objective of sustainable development" is specifically mentioned and linked to the objective of the WTO. Apparently, sustainable development is an objective of the Agreement Establishing the WTO.

There are two possible understandings on the sustainability provision in the Preamble of the Agreement Establishing the WTO. One possibility is to consider

---

[4]Appellate Body Report, *European Communities—Customs Classification of Frozen Boneless Chicken Cuts*, paras. 238–240, WTO Doc. WT/DS269/AB/R, WT/DS286/AB/R, WT/DS269/AB/R/Corr.1, WT/DS286/AB/R/Corr.1 (adopted 27 Sept 2005).

the preamble of the Agreement Establishing the WTO as the context of the GATT 1994 so as to have the objective of sustainable development being based upon to interpret the GATT provisions. Another possibility is to consider it as not merely the object-and-purpose of the Agreement Establishing the WTO, but also the object-and-purpose of the GATT 1994 so that when interpreting the textual wordings in the GATT 1994, the interpreter will have to consider the provisions in the preamble of the Agreement Establishing the WTO. The Appellate Body has impliedly confirmed in its Report on *US—Shrimp* that the preamble of the Agreement Establishing the WTO can be the object-and-purpose of the GATT 1994[5]:

> We note once more that the preamble of the WTO Agreement demonstrates a recognition by WTO negotiators that optimal use of the world's resources should be made in accordance with the objective of sustainable development. As this preambular language reflects the intentions of negotiators of the WTO Agreement, we believe *it must add colour, texture and shading to our interpretation of the agreements annexed to the WTO Agreement, in this case, the GATT 1994*. We have already observed that Article XX(g) of the GATT 1994 is appropriately read with the perspective embodied in the above preamble.
>
> (Emphasis added)

11.1.3 Terms Other Than "Object-and-Purpose" Are Used for Interpretation Purpose

There are some other terms used more often in "statutory interpretation" to refer to the reliance on or taking into consideration of the object-and-purpose of a statute. One of these terms is the "purposive interpretation". It expects a "statutory interpreter" to look for the purpose of the interpreted legislation. But the "purposive interpretation" for the "statutory interpretation" is broader than the object-and-purpose for "treaty interpretation", because the "statutory interpretation" in different jurisdictions allows the "statutory interpreter" to use various aids/ sources (such as the preparatory works and other documents used or referred to in the legislative process) to identify the legislature's intention,[6] whereas treaty interpretation only allows the treaty interpreter to rely on the treaty text (including the main text of the treaty and its preamble) so as to identify the object-and-purpose. Preparatory works are simply a "supplementary means" for treaty interpretation. The status of preparatory works being a "supplementary means" is provided in VCLT Article 32 that: "Recourse may be had to supplementary means of

[5]Appellate Body Report, *United States—Import Prohibition of Certain Shrimp and Shrimp Products*, para. 153, WTO Doc. WT/DS58/AB/R (adopted 6 Nov 1998) [hereinafter US—Shrimp Appellate Body Report].

[6]The Purposive Approach to Statutory Interpretation. http://www.e-lawresources.co.uk/Purposive-approach.php. Accessed 21 Aug 2017.

interpretation, including *the preparatory work of the treaty and the circumstances of its conclusion*, in order to confirm the meaning resulting from the application of article 31, or to determine the meaning when the interpretation according to article 31: (a) leaves the meaning ambiguous or obscure; or (b) leads to a result which is manifestly absurd or unreasonable." (Emphasis added)

A similar term used in "statutory interpretation" to refer to the object-and-purpose of a legislation is "intentionalism". An intentionalist's interpretation is not merely based on the text of a legislation to determine the legislative intent. Other relevant evidence to show the legislative intent could be used for the "statutory interpretation" purpose.[7] Another similar term used in "statutory interpretation" to refer to the object-and-purpose is the "teleological interpretation", which uses the purpose of a legislation to explain the meaning of the text.

For treaty interpretation, it makes sense not to use those terms which are commonly used in the context of "statutory interpretation" (such as purposive interpretation and intentionalist interpretation) so as to avoid a possible misunderstanding that when identifying the object-and-purpose of a treaty, the preparatory work should also serve as the evidence. For international treaties, there could be new parties joining the treaties at certain later stages long after the treaties have become effective. It would be fairer to all parties (including existing and newly acceded parties) if they are bound by the text and by the object-and-purpose as reflected in the text of the treaty. It would not be fair and appropriate for those new parties to be primarily bound by the preparatory works, in which they did not participate. The exceptions to this general rule about the parties to be bound only by the text and the object-and-purpose as reflected in the text are those mentioned in Article 32 of the VCLT, which allows the introduction of preparatory works as a supplementary means for treaty interpretation.

11.2 Identifying the "Object-and-Purpose" of a Treaty

11.2.1 The Preamble

There could be various parts in a treaty where the "object-and-purpose" of the treaty can be found. As mentioned above, the object-and-purpose of a treaty can be found from the broad text of a treaty. Although the preamble of a treaty does not directly bind the contracting parties (because basically the preambular wording only states the background and reasons or purposes of concluding treaties, but does not include contents of binding nature), still it definitely can serve as an evidence to show the object-and-purpose of the treaty.

[7]Statutory Interpretation in the Supreme Court of Canada. http://aix1.uottawa.ca/~resulliv/legdr/siinscc.html. Accessed 21 Aug 2017.

The Appellate Body Report on the above quoted *US—Shrimp* has the following statement[8] showing that the preamble of a treaty can be the source to identify the object-and-purpose of a treaty:

> We note once more that the preamble of the WTO Agreement demonstrates a recognition by WTO negotiators that optimal use of the world's resources should be made in accordance with the objective of sustainable development. As *this preambular language reflects the intentions of negotiators of the WTO Agreement, we believe it must add colour, texture and shading to our interpretation of the agreements annexed to the WTO Agreement*, in this case, the GATT 1994. We have already observed that Article XX(g) of the GATT 1994 is appropriately read with the perspective embodied in the above preamble.
>
> (Emphasis added)

In practice, many treaties do not include their preambles. But there are also many treaties having preambles to show the backgrounds and their goals for the contracting parties to conclude these treaties. Hence, the preamble should be a constant source to identify the object-and-purpose. A typical example of a preamble to include the object-and-purpose of a treaty can be found in the Agreement on Agriculture, under the WTO which states in part the following:

> *Having* decided to establish a basis for initiating a process of reform of trade in agriculture in line with the objectives of the negotiations as set out in the Punta del Este Declaration;
>
> *Recalling* that their long-term objective as agreed at the Mid-Term Review of the Uruguay Round "is to establish a fair and market-oriented agricultural trading system and that a reform process should be initiated through the negotiation of commitments on support and protection and through the establishment of strengthened and more operationally effective GATT rules and disciplines";
>
> *Recalling* further that "the above-mentioned long-term objective is to provide for substantial progressive reductions in agricultural support and protection sustained over an agreed period of time, resulting in correcting and preventing restrictions and distortions in world agricultural markets";

Hence there is a long-time objective being agreed upon during the negotiations and such long-time objective is included in the preamble of the Agreement of Agriculture to serve as the objective of the agreement.

Another example is in the GATS, the preamble of which indicates the "wishes" and "desires" of the negotiators. These terms are another ways of showing the goals of the treaty. The relevant paragraphs are:

> *Wishing* to establish a multilateral framework of principles and rules for trade in services with a view to the expansion of such trade under conditions of transparency and progressive liberalization and as a means of promoting the economic growth of all trading partners and the development of developing countries;
>
> *Desiring* the early achievement of progressively higher levels of liberalization of trade in services through successive rounds of multilateral negotiations aimed at promoting the interests of all participants on a mutually advantageous basis and at securing an overall balance of rights and obligations, while giving due respect to national policy objectives;

[8]US—Shrimp Appellate Body Report, *supra* note 5, at para. 153.

Here is another example of a preamble using the term "desire" to express the goals of the treaty: In the preamble of the Agreement on Import Licensing Procedure of the WTO, there are two relevant paragraphs of such nature of reflecting the object-and-purpose of the agreement:

> *Desiring* to further the objectives of GATT 1994;
>
> *Desiring* to ensure that import licensing procedures are not utilized in a manner contrary to the principles and obligations of GATT 1994;

Also for instance, in the Agreement on Rules of Origin under the WTO, there are a number of paragraphs showing the desires/goals of the negotiators:

> *Desiring* to further the objectives of GATT 1994;
>
> *Desiring* to ensure that rules of origin themselves do not create unnecessary obstacles to trade;
>
> *Desiring* to ensure that rules of origin do not nullify or impair the rights of Members under GATT 1994;
>
> *Desiring* to ensure that rules of origin are prepared and applied in an impartial, transparent, predictable, consistent and neutral manner;

It must be noted that when the terms "desiring" and "wishing" as well as other words of similar meaning are used, it is easier to confirm that the paragraph following one of these terms is actually reflecting the object-and-purpose of the treaty. But this does not mean that a preambular paragraph not led by such term could not be the object-and-purpose of the treaty. The above mentioned Appellate Body's view is that the preambular language (that optimal use of the world's resources should be made in accordance with the objective of sustainable development) reflects the intentions of negotiators. This statement is actually led by the term "recognizing", instead of desiring or wishing.

11.2.2 The Text Itself

Although it is quite common that the object-and-purpose of a treaty is reflected in its preamble, it is also possible for treaty negotiators to include its object-and-purpose in its main text, either in the first article or in other articles, even when simultaneously there is preambular language to show the goal of the treaty.

For instance, in the TRIPS Agreement under the WTO, there are paragraphs in its preamble showing the goals of the agreement:

> *Desiring* to reduce distortions and impediments to international trade, and taking into account the need to promote effective and adequate protection of intellectual property rights, and to ensure that measures and procedures to enforce intellectual property rights do not themselves become barriers to legitimate trade;
>
> *Emphasizing* the importance of reducing tensions by reaching strengthened commitments to resolve disputes on trade-related intellectual property issues through multilateral procedures;

> *Desiring* to establish a mutually supportive relationship between the WTO and the World Intellectual Property Organization (referred to in this Agreement as "WIPO") as well as other relevant international organizations;

In addition to these preambular paragraphs, Articles 7 and 8 of the TRIPS Agreement are also considered as indicating the object-and-purpose of the agreement. Their respective provisions are as the following:

> Article 7 (entitled "Objectives")
>
> The protection and enforcement of intellectual property rights should contribute to the promotion of technological innovation and to the transfer and dissemination of technology, to the mutual advantage of producers and users of technological knowledge and in a manner conducive to social and economic welfare, and to a balance of rights and obligations.
>
> Article 8 (entitled "Principles")
>
> 1. Members may, in formulating or amending their laws and regulations, adopt measures necessary to protect public health and nutrition, and to promote the public interest in sectors of vital importance to their socio-economic and technological development, provided that such measures are consistent with the provisions of this Agreement.
> 2. Appropriate measures, provided that they are consistent with the provisions of this Agreement, may be needed to prevent the abuse of intellectual property rights by right holders or the resort to practices which unreasonably restrain trade or adversely affect the international transfer of technology.

Paragraph 5(a)of the Declaration on the TRIPS Agreement and Public Health, adopted on 14 November 2001, makes it clear that the contents in these two articles (i.e. Articles 7 and 8) are the object-and-purpose of the TRIPS Agreement. It states: "In applying the customary rules of interpretation of public international law, each provision of the TRIPS Agreement shall be read in the light of *the object and purpose of the Agreement as expressed, in particular, in its objectives and principles*." (Emphasis added) Also, paragraph 19 of the Doha Ministerial Declaration, adopted on 14 November 2001, has similar statement: "In undertaking [the work referred to in that paragraph], the TRIPS Council shall be *guided by the objectives and principles set out in Articles 7 and 8 of the TRIPS Agreement*." (Emphasis added)

Sometimes the object-and-purpose is provided in the first article of a treaty. For instance, the Convention on the Rights of Persons with Disabilities (CRPD) provides in Article 1 (entitled "Purpose") that: "The purpose of the present Convention is to promote, protect and ensure the full and equal enjoyment of all human rights and fundamental freedoms by all persons with disabilities, and to promote respect for their inherent dignity." Since the title has made clear that this provision is the purpose of the convention, apparently it is the "object-and-purpose" of the CRPD for the purpose of treaty interpretation based on VCLT Article 31.1.

Not only a provision with the title of "purpose" can be considered as stating the object-and-purpose of a treaty, those other provisions showing the general principles of a treaty can also be considered as the object-and-purpose for treaty interpretation purpose. For instance, Article 3 (entitled "General principles") of the CRPD provides:

The principles of the present Convention shall be:

a. Respect for inherent dignity, individual autonomy including the freedom to make one's own choices, and independence of persons;
b. Non-discrimination;
c. Full and effective participation and inclusion in society;
d. Respect for difference and acceptance of persons with disabilities as part of human diversity and humanity;
e. Equality of opportunity;
f. Accessibility;
g. Equality between men and women;
h. Respect for the evolving capacities of children with disabilities and respect for the right of children with disabilities to preserve their identities.

These principles are definitely the object-and-purpose of the CRPD and should be taken into consideration when interpreting other provisions in the convention.

11.2.3 To Infer from the Text?

Another issue concerning the identification of the object-and-purpose of a treaty is whether the object-and-purpose can be "inferred" from a treaty provision in the main text or from some general rules of the interpreted treaty.

As explained above, normally the object-and-purpose is "found" in the preamble or in the main text of a treaty. But this does not mean that there should not be implied "object-and-purpose" embedded in the treaty.

For instance, GATT Article XX states in its chapeau that: "Subject to the requirement that such measures are not applied in a manner which would constitute a means of arbitrary or unjustifiable discrimination between countries where the same conditions prevail, or *a disguised restriction on international trade*, nothing in this Agreement shall be construed to prevent the adoption or enforcement by any contracting party of measures …" The requirement of a measure not to constitute a disguised restriction on international trade is basically to expect WTO Members not to adopt a measure that could give rise to any "protective effect".

The inexistence of protective effect for a trade measure is a general principle that can be inferred from the chapeau of GATT Article XX. Such principle can be considered as an implicit object-and-purpose of the entire GATT provisions so as to guide the interpretation of the agreement to ensure that any trade restrictive measure adopted by a WTO Member will not have such undesirable protective effect.

11.3 How to "Consider" the Object-and-Purpose of the Interpreted Treaty

11.3.1 Relation with the "Ordinary Meaning"

It is already explained in the preceding chapter that the starting point for treaty interpretation is to look for an ordinary meaning to be given to the textual wording of a treaty provision. Under Article 31.1 of the VCLT, when identifying a proper ordinary meaning to be given to the text of a treaty, an interpreter must take into account the object-and-purpose of the treaty.

Article 31.1 of the VCLT states: "A treaty shall be interpreted … in accordance with the *ordinary meaning to be given to the terms of the treaty ... in the light of its object and purpose*." (Emphasis added) The identification of an appropriate ordinary meaning is always the primary job for the interpreter. When deciding whether an ordinary meaning is appropriate, the interpreter will have to take into account the object-and-purpose of the interpreted treaty. Hence, under Article 31.1 of the VCLT, the ordinary meaning must be "given to the terms of the treaty in the light of its object and purpose".

So the consideration of the object-and-purpose of the treaty is to ensure that the ordinary meaning being chosen and being given to a term is appropriate. Although the ordinary meaning and the object-and-purpose are two elements or two methods of treaty interpretation, they function jointly so as to find the appropriate ordinary meaning to be given to an interpreted provision.

11.3.2 "Object-and-Purpose" as Guiding Principle

Article 31.1 of the VCLT states: "A treaty shall be interpreted … in accordance with the ordinary meaning to be given to the terms of the treaty … *in the light of* its object and purpose." The phrase "in the light of" in Article 31.1 basically means "in consideration of". Hence, the obligation of a treaty interpreter under this provision is *to consider* the object-and-purpose of the entire interpreted treaty. In the above-quoted Appellate Body Report on *US—Shrimp*, it indicates that the preamble "must add colour, texture and shading to our interpretation".

But the problem is whether the object-and-purpose in the preamble or the preamble as a whole is merely adding colour, texture and shading light to the interpretation of a provision in the treaty.

In this regard, we have to differentiate the preambular language into two types. One type of the preambular language serves as the object-and-purpose of the treaty. Another type of statement in the preamble does not serve as the object-and-purpose of the treaty, but is just explaining the backgrounds of the treaty. The latter type can be considered as "context" for treaty interpretation purpose. This will be further discussed in the next chapter of this book. For the preambular language serving as the object-and-purpose, the treaty interpreter should not merely consider it as "adding colour or texture or shading light to the interpreted provision". It should be given with a higher weight to guide the interpretation of a treaty provision.

This is because the object-and-purpose is the ultimate goal of the treaty. A deviation from the goal of the treaty through treaty interpretation will defeat or undermine the function and operation of the treaty and thus should not be desirable. The way to ensure that the ultimate goal will not be undermined is to make sure that the goal will guide the interpretation of the treaty. In other words, a treaty interpreter will have to give a higher weight to the object-and-purpose of the treaty when he/she takes into consideration of it as required by Article 31.1 of the VCLT.

Also most likely, the goal of a treaty involves certain values chosen by the negotiators. Hence when a treaty interpreter is identifying the object-and-purpose, he/she is confirming the values to be protected or achieved by the treaty. And when he/she is "considering" the object-and-purpose, he/she is actually prioritizing the chosen value and ensuring that the chosen values will be maintained or achieved.

For instance, Article 8 of the TRIPS Agreement includes the protection of public health as an object-and-purpose of the agreement. Public health is a human value of high importance. Such important human value should not merely be of declarative function. It should be given with real use and function in treaty interpretation. The only way of given such chosen value a real use and function is to make it as a guiding principle for treaty interpretation purpose so as to ensure the attainment of the protected value.

To conclude this chapter, it should be useful to indicate in the codified set of rules that the two words "object" and "purpose" are synonymous and conjoint in treaty interpretation to jointly refer to the ultimate goal that a treaty intends to achieve. It is also useful to indicate in the codified set of rules that the object-and-purpose is referred to the "overall goal of the treaty" (instead of the "goal of a specific provision" in the treaty) to guide its operation and that the object-and-purpose of a "treaty provision" (instead of the object-and-purpose of the "entire treaty") can still be taken into consideration, but the object-and-purpose of "a provision" should not be considered in isolation from the object-and-purpose of the entire treaty. It is also useful to include in the codified set of rules that the object-and-purpose of a treaty can be identified from the preamble (if the preambular language reflects the intentions of negotiators) and the text of the interpreted treaty and that it can also be implied in the treaty or inferred from certain treaty provisions. The object-and-purpose of a treaty should not merely be considered as adding colour or texture or shading light to the interpreted provision. It should be given with a higher weight to guide the interpretation of a treaty provision. These guiding rules are the candidates for being considered for the inclusion in the codified rules of treaty interpretation.

References

Buffard I, Zemanek K (1998) The "object and purpose" of a treaty: an enigma? Austrian Rev Int Eur Law 3:311–343

Jonas DS, Saunders TN (2010) The object and purpose of a treaty: three interpretive methods. Vanderbilt J Int Law 43(3):565–609

Statutory Interpretation in the Supreme Court of Canada. http://aix1.uottawa.ca/~resulliv/legdr/siinscc.html. Accessed 21 Aug 2017

The Purposive Approach to Statutory Interpretation. http://www.e-lawresources.co.uk/Purposive-approach.php. Accessed 21 Aug 2017

Chapter 12
Means of Taking into Consideration the Context and the Possible Codification

Contents

12.1 Functions and Scope of Context

12.1.1 Functions of Context in Treaty Interpretation

For the purpose of treaty interpretation, context means other terms or provisions preceding or following the interpreted term or provision in the treaty, or other terms or provisions used together with the interpreted term or provision in the same article or paragraph of the treaty, or other legal instrument concluded in connection with the interpreted treaty, which are identified to help explain the interpreted term or provision's meaning. The process in treaty interpretation is to identify the relevant contextual terms or provisions and then put the interpreted term or provision in the contexts so as to give an ordinary meaning to the interpreted term or provision.

C. Lo, *Treaty Interpretation Under the Vienna Convention on the Law of Treaties*,
https://doi.org/10.1007/978-981-10-6866-9_12

Such way of treaty interpretation is called contextual interpretation. The approach is usually called "systemic interpretation" in statutory interpretation. But, it must be noted that for treaty interpretation, relying on context is not a separate method of interpretation. Context is to be considered by the treaty interpreter so as to help decide the ordinary meaning of an interpreted term or provision. This can be understood from the provision of VCLT Article 31.1, which provides in part that "A treaty shall be interpreted … in accordance with the ordinary meaning to be given to the terms of the treaty in their context…" In other words, the ordinary meaning is to be given to a treaty term in its context. If there are more than one ordinary meanings for a treaty term, the one selected by the interpreter must make sense when it is put in the context of the interpreted term.

The meaning of a term or a provision in a treaty can be objectively and absolutely clear. If this is the situation, the context of the term or provision would not affect its meaning. For instance, a commitment in tariff reduction concerning a "tariff rate" under a trade agreement is mostly clear enough to be understood and to be implemented without the need of resorting to its context. A 10% *ad valorem* tariff binding obligation would not have a meaning other than the binding obligation for 10% *ad valorem* tariff.

But a lot of time, a term or provision in a treaty is unclear or ambiguous because of the nature of the term, because of the fact that the term or provision has too many "ordinary meanings", or because of the term being used in a situation causing it being subject to different meanings. In these situations, the context can affect or help the proper understanding of the term or provision.

For instance, in a WTO dispute between Antigua and Barbuda (as the complainant) and the United States (as the respondant), there involved the interpretation of the United States' commitments concerning the heading of "Other Recreational Services (except sporting)" in its schedule.[1] An important issue here is that if the term "sporting" is interpreted to include "gambling" , then the United States might not have an obligation to open up its internet gambling service market to Antigua and Barbuda (because of wording of "except sporting" in the parenthesis of the heading in the United States' schedule of commitments); whereas if it does not include "gambling", then the United States will have to open up such "recreational

[1]Briefly about the background of the case: Several states in the United States ban internet gambling and some federal laws restrict the use of technology associated with internet gambling. The United States' service commitment as reflected in its schedule of specific commitment indicates under the heading of "Other Recreational Services (except sporting)" that there is no limitation on market access. The Panel found that the United States' schedule of specific commitments has been interpreted to include specific commitments for gambling and betting services under the sub-sector entitled "Other Recreational Services (except sporting)". The Appellate Body upheld the Panel's finding with different reasoning that the United States' Schedule includes a commitment to grant market access in gambling and betting services. The Appellate Body disagreed with the Panel's designation of two documents (i.e. W/120 and the 1993 Scheduling Guidelines) as "context" for the interpretation of Members' Schedules and considered these as "preparatory work" (which are supplementary means of interpretation under VCLT Article 32. See the case summary of the WTO at https://www.wto.org/english/tratop_e/dispu_e/cases_e/ds285_e.htm. Accessed 21 Aug 2017.

service market". There is an ordinary understanding of the term "sporting" to mean conducting "an activity involving physical exertion and skill in which an individual or team competes against another or others for entertainment."[2] This term is normally differentiated from the term "gambling" or "betting" which means an "activity of playing a game for stakes or betting on an uncertain outcome".[3] But dictionary definition of sporting still include gambling. Hence, the "most ordinary" meaning (i.e. the most commonly used meaning) of the term "sporting" could be an activity involving physical exertion. But the "less ordinary" meanings (which are still within the scope of dictionary definitions and hence should still be considered as ordinary meanings, because, as explained in Chap. 10 of this book, the threshold for deciding the ordinariness should *not* be set at a very high level) include the meaning of gambling (i.e. playing a game for stakes or betting on uncertain outcomes). Therefore, gambling should not be directly excluded from the scope of "sporting" for the reason that it is not one of the ordinary meanings of sporting (because it is still within the broader scope of the ordinary meaning of sporting). If gambling is to be excluded from the scope of sporting and hence to be considered as falling within the scope of "other recreational service", it must be because of additional reasons. The Appellate Body indicates in its Report on *US—Gambling* that "the Panel failed to have due regard to the fact that its recourse to dictionaries revealed that gambling and betting can, at least in some contexts, be one of the meanings of the word 'sporting'."[4] According to the Appellate Body, when the context and the preparatory works are taken into consideration, the commitment with respect to "other recreational services (except sporting)" as provided in the United States' schedule must be interpreted as including "gambling and betting services" within its scope.

A treaty interpreter might not be able to identify the correct or appropriate meaning of a treaty term or provision without putting the term or provision in its context of the treaty. If the interpreter takes the interpreted term or provision's context into consideration, he/she might be able to establish the correct or appropriate meaning (which is still one of the ordinary meanings of the interpreted term or provision). So the function of context in treaty interpretation is to help the interpreter identify and select the correct or appropriate ordinary meaning.

For instance, whether or not the term "distribution service" as committed by a WTO Member should include "electronic distribution service" can be properly understood when the term is put in its context. In *China—Publications and Audiovisual Products*, the Appellate Body states:

[2]See Oxford Living Dictionaries, at https://en.oxforddictionaries.com/definition/sport. Accessed 21 Aug 2017.

[3]See The Free Dictionary. http://www.thefreedictionary.com/gambling. Accessed 21 Aug 2017.

[4]Appellate Body Report, *United States—Measures Affecting the Cross-Border Supply of Gambling and Betting Services*, para. 166, WTO Doc. WT/DS285/AB/R, WT/DS285/AB/R/Corr.1 (adopted 20 Apr 2005) [hereinafter US—Gambling Appellate Body Report].

> As we have considered above, while certain elements of context clearly support the Panel's interpretation of "Sound recording distribution services" as extending to the electronic distribution of sound recordings, other elements considered by the Panel are consistent with or do not contradict such an interpretation of the scope of this commitment. On balance, we are persuaded that *the analysis of a number of contextual elements supports the interpretation of China's commitment on "Sound recording distribution services" as including the electronic distribution of sound recordings.*[5] (Emphasis added)

Again, Article 31.1 of the VCLT provides that: "A treaty shall be interpreted in good faith in accordance with the ordinary meaning to be given to the terms of the treaty *in their context* and in the light of its object and purpose." (Emphasis added) It clearly shows the function of context. The ordinary meaning is to be given to an interpreted term in its context. Therefore, the ordinary meaning is not to be given to a term in isolation from the context. Also context is not a separate and independent means of treaty interpretation to be chosen by the interpreter. It is an element needed to be considered by the interpreter to help the proper decision and selection of an appropriate ordinary meaning, which is to be given to an interpreted term or provision.

From the provision of Article 31.1, it is also clear that context is *not the only element to assist a treaty interpreter to decide the ordinary meaning* of a term or provision. In this regard, it is similar to the object-and-purpose in that they are included in Article 31.1 of the VCLT to guide a treaty interpreter's decision of the proper ordinary meaning for a treaty term.

12.1.2 Scope of Context Under VCLT

There are three places in the treaty interpretation provisions of the VCLT mentioning the "context" for treaty interpretation purpose. It has been indicated above that Article 31.1 of the VCLT requires treaty interpreter to give the ordinary meanings to the interpreted terms not in isolation from their context, but in their context. Article 31.2 further defines the scope of context to include the text, the preamble, the annexes, and an agreement or instrument in connection with the conclusion of the interpreted treaty. Article 31.3 requires to take into account a subsequent agreement, subsequent practice or relevant rules of international law.

Concerning the scope of context which includes the main text of the interpreted treaty, its preamble, its annex, and the agreement or instrument in connection with the conclusion of the interpreted treaty, Article 31.2 provides the following:

> The context for the purpose of the interpretation of a treaty shall comprise, in addition to the text, including its preamble and annexes:

---

[5] Appellate Body Report, *China—Measures Affecting Trading Rights and Distribution Services for Certain Publications and Audiovisual Entertainment Products*, paras. 387–388, WTO Doc. WT/DS363/AB/R (adopted 19 Jan 2010).

(a) Any agreement relating to the treaty which was made between all the parties in connexion with the conclusion of the treaty;
(b) Any instrument which was made by one or more parties in connexion with the conclusion of the treaty and accepted by the other parties as an instrument related to the treaty.

Although the scope of context is broad, it is not unlimited. First, for the treaty interpretation purpose under VCLT Article 31, a context should be referred only to "legal context" (i.e. the provision or document "surrounding" or "associated with" the interpreted word) and should not include the "factual context" (i.e. the facts "surrounding" or "associated with" the case).

But sometimes the "factual context" (i.e. putting interpretation in the context of a set of factual background of the case) still needs to be considered in order to decide whether an ordinary meaning being selected fits into the factual context of a dispute. If the "factual context" of the case is not considered, it is possible that an interpretation of a treaty provision could become absurd. For instance, the panel in its report on *EC—Chicken Cuts* indicates that:

> … our starting points in determining the ordinary meaning of the concession contained in heading 02.10 of the EC Schedule is to ascertain the meaning of the term contained in that concession. While dictionaries are the primary source for determination of the ordinary meaning of treaty terms, we consider it necessary in this case to test the appropriateness of those dictionary definitions against the factual context in which the concession in question exists and is being applied. To be clear, when we refer to *factual* context, this is distinct from *legal* context within the meaning of Article 31(2) of the *Vienna Convention*. The factual context could include, for example, aspects associated with the physical characteristics of the products are issue and those that are known to be covered by the concession in question in this dispute. The purpose for taking these aspects into account is to test any claim of ordinary meaning by the parties against the relevant factual setting to ensure that the ordinary meaning that is being considered corresponds to the reality of the factual context at the relevant point in time.[6]

The Appellate Body agrees with the panel in the view of considering the "factual context". It states in its Report on *EC—Chicken Cuts* the following:

> … we would agree with the European Communities that there is no reference in the *Vienna Convention* to "factual context" as a separate analytical step under Article 31. Nevertheless, we do not believe that the Panel was incorrect to consider elements such as the "products covered by the concession contained in heading 02.10", "flavour, texture, [and] other physical properties" of the products falling under heading 02.10, and "preservation" when interpreting the term "salted" as it appears in heading 02.10. The Panel's consideration of these elements under "ordinary meaning" of the term "salted" complemented its analysis of the dictionary definitions of that term. In any event, even if we were to agree with the European Communities that these elements are not to be considered under "ordinary meaning", they certainly could be considered under "context". Interpretation pursuant to the customary rules codified under Article 31 of the *Vienna Convention* is ultimately a holistic exercise that should not be mechanically subdivided into rigid components. Considering particular surrounding circumstances under the rubric of "ordinary meaning" or "in the light

[6]Pane Report, *European Communities—Customs Classification of Frozen Boneless Chicken Cuts —Complaint by Thailand*, para. 7.105, WTO Doc. WT/DS286/R (adopted 27 Sept 2005).

of its context" would not, in our view, change the outcome of treaty interpretation. Therefore, we find no error in the Panel's interpretative approach.[7]

Second, although a language in the preamble, the main text, or the annex, or the agreement or instrument in connection with the conclusion of an interpreted treaty can be broadly included as the context of an interpreted provision in the treaty, in order to be qualified as "context" to be considered by the treaty interpreter, a language provided therein must be "pertinent to" the interpreted term or provision and be "apt to shed light on" the meaning of the term or provision. This requirement is to proper link the "interpreted term" and the "contextual provision" so as to justify the consideration of the context. The Appellate Body has expressed this point in its Report on *China—Auto Part* the following:[8]

> ... The realm of context as defined in Article 31(2) is broad. "Context" includes all of the text of the treaty — in this case, the *WTO Agreement* — and may also extend to "any agreement relating to the treaty which was made between all the parties in connection with the conclusion of the treaty" and "any instrument which was made by one or more parties in connection with the conclusion of the treaty and accepted by the other parties as an instrument related to the treaty". Yet context is *relevant* for a treaty interpreter to the extent that it may shed light on the interpretative issue to be resolved, such as the meaning of the term or phrase at issue. Thus, for a particular provision, agreement or instrument to serve as *relevant* context in any given situation, it must not only fall within the scope of the formal boundaries identified in Article 31(2), *it must also have some pertinence to the language being interpreted that renders it capable of helping the interpreter to determine the meaning of such language*. [Emphasis here is added] Because WTO Members' Schedules of Concessions were constructed using the nomenclature of the Harmonized System, the Harmonized System is *apt to shed light on the meaning of terms used in these Schedules*. [Emphasis here is added] It does not, however, automatically follow that the Harmonized System was context relevant to the interpretative question faced by the Panel in its analysis of the threshold issue in this dispute.

Third, although legal views expressed in the decisions of previous disputes/cases can have practical influence or relevancy, they are not the "context" under Articles 31.1 and 31.2 of the VCLT. In Chap. 2 of this book, it was explained that in international adjudication, there is no such rule of *stare decisis*. But if a previous jurisprudence is persuasive, it is very likely that the future interpreters will follow the jurisprudence. However, there is no basis for a treaty interpreter to consider previous jurisprudence as context. In other words, legal views in previous cases do not have binding effect either based on *stare decisis* or based on any possible argument that they have the status of "context" to the interpreted term. The

---

[7]Appellate Body Report, *European Communities—Customs Classification of Frozen Boneless Chicken Cuts*, para. 176, WTO Doc. WT/DS269/AB/R, WT/DS286/AB/R, WT/DS269/AB/R/Corr.1, WT/DS286/AB/R/Corr.1 (adopted 27 Sept 2005) [hereinafter EC—Chicken Cuts Appellate Body Report].

[8]Appellate Body Report, *China—Measures Affecting Imports of Automobile Parts*, para. 151, WTO Doc. WT/DS339/AB/R, WT/DS340/AB/R, WT/DS342/AB/R (adopted 12 Jan 2009).

Appellate Body Report on *US—Anti-Dumping and Countervailing Duties (China)* indicates in this regard that:[9]

> … China contends that the Panel considered, as part of its *contextual* analysis of Article 1.1 (a)(1) of the *SCM Agreement* a concern explained by the panel in *Korea — Commercial Vessels* regarding what the Panel considered to be a similar issue to the one of the present case. We note that the definition of "context" in Article 31(2) of the *Vienna Convention* makes no mention of jurisprudence. Panel reports in previous disputes do not form part of the context of a term or provision in the sense of Article 31(2) of the *Vienna Convention.* Rather, the legal interpretation embodied in adopted panel and Appellate Body reports become part and parcel of the WTO *acquis* and have to be taken into account as such.

It must be noted that the three elements in the introductory part of Article 31.2, namely the text, the preamble and the annex, are interrelated. They serve as context to each other. In other words, the preamble can be the context of the main text and the annexes. The main text can also be the context of the annexes. And the annexes can be the context of the main text. The preambular language sometimes needs interpretation. But generally speaking, the preamble is to help interpret other parts of the treaty. It is rare that the main text or the annexes become the context for the purpose of interpreting the preamble.

12.2 Various Contexts

12.2.1 Other Parts of the Main Text as the Context

The main text is the source for a treaty interpreter to find the context of an interpreted term or provision so as to help its interpretation. The most closely related context of an interpreted term is the other portions in the same article or paragraph. In other words, when interpreting a term, the article or paragraph containing the interpreted term should first be looked at so as to know the context in which the term is used. In addition to other portion in the same article or the same paragraph, the other articles or parts in the main text of the same agreement also serve as context for the interpreted term or provision.

The Appellate Body uses the term "immediate context" and "broader context" to describe the closeness of the respective locations between the interpreted term or provision and the contextual term or provision. In *EC—Chicken Cuts*, the Appellate Body states in its Report:[10]

> It is clear from these provisions that the context of the term "salted" in heading 02.10 consists of *the immediate, as well as the broader, context* of that term. The *immediate*

---

[9]Appellate Body Report, *United States—Definitive Anti-Dumping and Countervailing Duties on Certain Products from China*, para. 325, WTO Doc. WT/DS379/AB/R (adopted 25 Mar 2011) [hereinafter US—Anti-Dumping and Countervailing Duties (China) Appellate Body Report].

[10]EC—Chicken Cuts Appellate Body Report, *supra* note 7, at para. 193.

> *context* is the other terms of the product description contained in heading 02.10 of the EC Schedule. The *broader context* includes the other headings in Chap. 2 of the EC Schedule, as well as other WTO Member Schedules. (Emphasis added)

An example reflecting that other paragraphs in the same article or other parts in the same agreement can be the context of an interpreted term or provision is in *Canada—Renewable Energy/Canada—Feed-in Tariff Program*, in the Report of which the Appellate Body states:[11]

> Article III:8(a)[12] contains several elements describing the types and the content of measures falling within the ambit of the provision. … We consider that Article III:8(a) should be interpreted holistically. This requires consideration of the linkages between the different terms used in the provision and the contextual connections to *other parts of Article III*, as well as to *other provisions of the GATT 1994*. At the same time, the principle of effective treaty interpretation requires us to give meaning to every term of the provision. (Emphasis added)

Sometimes various articles in a treaty use the cross-reference to show their respective relations. In such situation, these "referring article" and "referred article" mutually serve as context to each other for the purpose of interpreting these articles. Also suppose in a treaty, there are cross-references used in some provisions but is not used in other provisions. The use of cross-reference and the non-use of cross-reference in different parts of a treaty can also serve as context to each other so as to give meaning to the lack of cross-reference in a provision. The Appellate Body has the following statement in its Report on *US—Carbon Steel* in this regard:[13]

> … the technique of cross-referencing is frequently used in the *SCM Agreement*. … These cross-references suggest to us that, when the negotiators of the *SCM Agreement* intended that the disciplines set forth in one provision be applied in another context, they did so expressly. In the light of the many express cross-references made in the *SCM Agreement*, we attach significance to the absence of any textual link between Article 21.3 reviews and the *de minimis* standard set forth in Article 11.9. …

Although cross-referencing wording provided in the respective articles is useful in deciding the context of these articles, it is not a requirement for the purpose of identifying the context. The criterion should be that as long as any part or provision in the treaty are pertinent to or could affect or help decide the meaning of a term or

---

[11] Appellate Body Report, *Canada—Certain Measures Affecting the Renewable Energy Generation Sector/ Measures Relating to the Feed-In Tariff Program*, para. 5.57, WTO Doc. WT/DS412/AB/R, WT/DS426/AB/R (adopted 24 May 2013).

[12] GATT Article III is about "national treatment" requirement. Article III:8(a) is an exception to the national treatment requirement. It provides: "The provisions of this Article shall not apply to laws, regulations or requirements governing the procurement by governmental agencies of products purchased for governmental purposes and not with a view to commercial resale or with a view to use in the production of goods for commercial sale".

[13] Appellate Body Report, *United States – Countervailing Duties on Certain Corrosion-Resistant CarbonSteel Flat Products from Germany*, WT/DS213/AB/R and Corr.1 (adopted 19 December 2002).

provision, such part or provision should be taken into account as context for the purpose of deciding or helping decide the meaning of the interpreted term or provision.

Another aspect about the context is the footnotes in a treaty. It is more and more common to see footnotes to be included in a treaty. If a footnote is to define a term or to list the scope of it in the main text of a treaty, the footnote is the basis to confirm the "ordinary meaning" or the "special meaning" given to the term by the parties.[14] If it is not a definition, but is to elaborate a term or a provision in the main text or to provide some additional situations,[15] then the footnote could be considered as context for the purpose of interpreting the "associated main text" (the main text to which the footnote is attached) of the treaty or even the other parts of the treaty. For instance, Article 3.1(a) of the SCM Agreement provides that "Except as provided in the Agreement on Agriculture, the following subsidies, within the meaning of Article 1, shall be prohibited: (a) subsidies *contingent*, in law or *in fact*, whether solely or as one of several other conditions, upon export performance, including those illustrated in Annex I". (Emphasis added) There is a footnote (i.e. Footnote 4) attached to the requirement of "contingent in fact" stating that: "This standard is met when the facts demonstrate that the granting of a subsidy, without having been made legally contingent upon export performance, is in fact tied to actual or anticipated exportation or export earnings. The mere fact that a subsidy is granted to enterprises which export shall not for that reason alone be considered to be an export subsidy within the meaning of this provision."

Regarding the requirement "contingent … in fact" provided in Article 3.1(a) of the SCM Agreement, the Panel on *Australia—Automotive Leather II* states:

> An inquiry into the meaning of the term 'contingent … in fact' … must … begin with an examination of the ordinary meaning of the word 'contingent'. The ordinary meaning of 'contingent' is 'dependent for its existence on something else', 'conditional; dependent on, upon'. The text of Article 3.1(a) includes footnote 4, which states that the standard of 'in

---

[14]For instance, Footnote 1 of the Agreement on Agriculture is to define the scope of the phrase "any measures of the kind which have been required to be converted into ordinary customs duties" provided in Article 4.2. Footnote 1 reads: "These measures include quantitative import restrictions, variable import levies, minimum import prices, discretionary import licensing, non-tariff measures maintained through state-trading enterprises, voluntary export restraints, and similar border measures other than ordinary customs duties, whether or not the measures are maintained under country-specific derogations from the provisions of GATT 1947, but not measures maintained under balance-of-payments provisions or under other general, non-agriculture-specific provisions of GATT 1994 or of the other Multilateral Trade Agreements in Annex 1A to the WTO Agreement".

[15]For instance, regarding the determination of "dumping" under the Anti-Dumping Agreement, footnote 2 in this agreement elaborates the provision in Article 2.2 (which addresses the situation when there are no sales of the like product in the ordinary course of trade in the domestic market of the exporting country or when, because of the particular market situation or the *low volume of the sales in the domestic market* of the exporting country) and states that: "Sales of the like product destined for consumption in the domestic market of the exporting country shall normally be considered a sufficient quantity for the determination of the normal value if such sales constitute 5 per cent or more of the sales of the product under consideration to the importing Member, provided that a lower ratio should be acceptable where the evidence demonstrates that domestic sales at such lower ratio are nonetheless of sufficient magnitude to provide for a proper comparison".

> fact' contingency is met if the facts demonstrate that the subsidy is 'in fact tied to actual or anticipated exportation or export earnings.' The ordinary meaning of 'tied to' is 'restrain or constrain to or from an action; limit or restrict as to behavior, location, conditions, etc.'. Both of the terms used – 'contingent … in fact' and 'in fact tied to' – suggest an interpretation that requires a close connection between the grant or maintenance of a subsidy and export performance.[16]

Although the panel did not explicitly mention, actually it considers the footnote as a context to help understand the requirement of "contingent … in fact" provided in the main text of the agreement.

12.2.2 An Example of GATT Article XX to Illustrate the Contextual Interpretation

The book uses the requirement of not constituting "disguised restriction on international trade" provided in the chapeau of GATT Article XX as an example to illustrate the consideration of other parts in the chapeau and the provisions in GATT Articles I and III as context to help interpretation of this requirement. The chapeau of GATT Article XX reads:

> "Subject to the requirement that such measures are not applied in a manner which would constitute a means of arbitrary or unjustifiable discrimination between countries where the same conditions prevail, or *a disguised restriction on international trade*, nothing in this Agreement shall be construed to prevent the adoption or enforcement by any contracting party of measures:" (Emphasis added)

The proper interpretations on the requirement of not constituting a "disguised restriction on international trade" and its relations with other requirements in the chapeau of GATT Article XX are difficult and controversial, mainly because of the unclear and ambiguous meaning of this term.

The Appellate Body and some dispute settlement panels have explained the reasons or functions of including the requirement of not constituting "disguised restriction on international trade" in the GATT or similar phrases in other WTO agreements: First, the requirement serves as a qualification: The Appellate Body points out that the Article XX exceptions are "limited and conditional".[17] It is "limited" because they are applied in only a few tightly defined circumstances. It is "conditional" because that government measures get the "safe haven" of GATT Article XX only if the measures do not constitute a means of arbitrary

[16] Panel Report, *Australia—Subsidies Provided to Producers and Exporters of Automotive Leather*, para. 9.55, WTO Doc. WT/DS126/R (adopted 16 June 1999).

[17] Appellate Body Report, *United States—Import Prohibition of Certain Shrimp and Shrimp Products*, para. 157, WTO Doc. WT/DS58/AB/R (adopted 6 Nov 1998) [hereinafter US—Shrimp Appellate Body Report].

discrimination, unjustifiable discrimination, or a disguised restriction of international trade.[18] Second, the requirement prevents the abusive use of exceptions or rights: The Appellate Body states in its Report on *US—Shrimp* that "the purpose and object of the introductory clauses of Article XX is generally the prevention of 'abuse of exceptions of [Article XX]."[19] Third, the requirement balances rights and obligations of the WTO Members: In *US—Shrimp*, the Appellate Body describes the core reason and the ultimate purpose of the chapeau of GATT Article XX being to serve as a balance of rights and obligations of the Member adopting the challenged measure and the Members being affected by the measure. It states: "[A] balance must be struck between the *right* of a Member to invoke an exception under Article XX and the *duty* of that same Member to respect the treaty rights of the other Members."[20]

In previous WTO cases, there were a number of approaches adopted by the Appellate Body and panels for interpreting the requirement of not constituting "disguised restriction on international trade".

Some approaches focus on *the forms of the restrictions* to see whether the restrictions were published or unpublished. For instance, the Appellate Body Report on *US—Gasoline* states in part that: "It is equally clear that *concealed* or *unannounced* restriction or discrimination in international trade does *not* exhaust the meaning of 'disguised restriction.'"[21]

Some focus on the *intention of the restrictions of the measure-taking country.* For instance, the Panel Report on *EC—Asbestos* has the following statement indicating that the main focus of determining this requirement should be on the intention aspect: "...the key to understanding what is covered by 'disguised restriction on international trade' is not so much the word 'restriction', inasmuch as, in essence, any measure falling within Article XX is a restriction on international trade, but the word 'disguised'. ...the verb 'to disguise' implies an *intention*. Thus, 'to disguise' means, 'conceal beneath deceptive appearances, counterfeit', 'alter so as to deceive', 'misrepresent', 'dissimulate'."[22]

Some rely on the terms *"arbitrary discrimination" and "unjustifiable discrimination"* provided in the same chapeau to decide the meaning of the requirement of not constituting "disguised restriction on international trade". For instance, in *US—Gasoline* the Appellate Body held that "arbitrary or unjustifiable discrimination"

---

[18] Id. at para. 150.

[19] Id. at para. 151 (quoting Appellate Body Report, *United States—Standards for Reformulated and Conventional Gasoline*, at 22, WTO Doc. WT/DS2/AB/R (adopted 20 May 1996) [hereinafter US—Gasoline Appellate Body Report]).

[20] US—Shrimp Appellate Body Report, *supra* note 16, at para. 156.

[21] US—Gasoline Appellate Body Report, *supra* note 18, at p. 25.

[22] Panel Report, *European Communities—Measures Affecting Asbestos and Asbestos-Containing Products*, para. 8.236, WTO Doc. WT/DS135/R and Add.1 (adopted 5 Apr 2001) [as modified by Appellate Body Report, *European Communities—Measures Affecting Asbestos and Asbestos-Containing Products*, WTO Doc. WT/DS135/AB/R (adopted 5 Apr 2001)].

and "disguised restriction on international trade" are related concepts which "imparted meaning to one another":

> 'Arbitrary discrimination', 'unjustifiable discrimination' and 'disguised restriction' on international trade may, accordingly, be read side-by-side; they impart meaning to one another. It is clear to us that 'disguised restriction' includes disguised *discrimination* in international trade. It is equally clear that *concealed* or *unannounced* restriction or discrimination in international trade does *not* exhaust the meaning of 'disguised restriction.' *We consider that 'disguised restriction', whatever else it covers, may properly be read as embracing restrictions amounting to arbitrary or unjustifiable discrimination in international trade taken under the guise of a measure formally within the terms of an exception listed in Article XX.* [Emphasis added] Put in a somewhat different manner, the kinds of considerations pertinent in deciding whether the application of a particular measure amounts to 'arbitrary or unjustifiable discrimination', may also be taken into account in determining the presence of a 'disguised restriction' on international trade. The fundamental theme is to be found in the purpose and object of avoiding abuse or illegitimate use of the exceptions to substantive rules available in Article XX.[23]

There is a view of relying on the extent of trade effect of undermining the objective of the measure. The Panel on *Brazil—Tyres* considers that trade effect should be a factor to decide whether there is a disguised restriction on international trade:

> "If such imports were to occur *in significant amounts, they would have the potential to undermine the achievement of the stated objective* of the prohibition on the importation of retreaded tyres, while protecting the retreading industry in the beneficiary countries. If this were the case, the measure would be being applied in a manner that constitutes a disguised restriction on international trade."[24] "In conclusion, the Panel finds that, since *imports of used tyres are taking place* to the benefit of the Brazilian retreading industry *in such quantities as to seriously undermine the achievement of the stated objective* of avoiding the further accumulation of waste tyres in Brazil, the measure at issue is being applied in a manner that constitutes a disguised restriction on international trade."[25] (Emphases added)

Appellate Body on *Brazil—Tyres* disagreed with the Panel Report on *Brazil—Tyres* concerning its view about relying on trade effect to decide the "disguised restriction on international trade" requirement. The Appellate Body states: "… Indeed, the Panel conditioned a finding of a disguised restriction on international trade on the existence of significant imports of retreaded tyres that would undermine the achievement of the objective of the Import Ban. We explained above why we believe that the Panel erred in finding that the MERCOSUR exemption would result in arbitrary or unjustifiable discrimination only if the imports of retreaded tyres from MERCOSUR countries were to take place in such amounts that the achievement of the objective of the Import Ban would be significantly undermined."[26]

---

[23]US—Gasoline Appellate Body Report, *supra* note 18, at p. 25.

[24]Id. at para. 7.353.

[25]Id. at para. 7.355.

[26]Appellate Body Report, *Brazil—Measures Affecting Imports of Retreaded Tyres*, para. 239, WTO Doc. WT/DS332/AB/R (adopted 17 Dec 2007).

The book is of the view that the requirement of not constituting "arbitrary or unjustifiable discrimination between countries where the same conditions prevail" in the same chapeau of GATT Article XX is apparently linked to the discrimination between different WTO Members which are countries other than the country adopting the challenged measure. This requirement is similar to the requirement of GATT Article I (i.e. the most-favoured-nation treatment requirement) which requires not to discriminate between different countries. Textually speaking, the requirement of not constituting "disguised restriction on international trade" should address a "differential treatment", which is in favour of domestic production of the measure-adopting Member. In this regard, the requirement of not constituting "disguised restriction on international trade" is similar to the function and requirement of GATT Article III (i.e. the national treatment requirement), which requires not to protect domestic production.

This interpretation is more in line with the function and the ultimate purpose of the requirement of not constituting "disguised restriction on international trade" in GATT Article XX chapeau, which is to prevent the abusive use of the exceptions or the abusive application of the rights and to balance rights and obligations of the Members. If the requirement is not interpreted so as to prevent giving favours to domestic production, there will be a major leak for the measure-adopting country to disguise its purpose of protecting domestic production in the name of protecting human health or life, or other causes. Such leak would provide the measure-adopting Member with an opportunity to abuse the use of exceptions in GATT Article XX so as to protect domestic production. And this would also break the balance of rights and obligations under the relevant agreements.[27]

The interpretation of the requirement of not constituting "disguised restriction on international trade" in GATT Article XX suggested above is basically conducted in consideration of the context of GATT Articles I and III and also the context of the requirement of not constituting "arbitrary or unjustifiable discrimination between countries where the same conditions prevail" provided in the same chapeau of GATT Article XX.

12.2.3 Annexes as the Context

In practice, annex can be a single treaty or a full set of treaties to be attached to a general treaty. For instance, the Agreement Establishing the WTO has Annexes 1–4, including Multilateral Agreements on Trade in Goods in Annex 1A (such as the GATT 1994, the Agreement on Agriculture, the SCM Agreement, the Anti-dumping Agreement, the Safeguards Agreement, the TBT Agreement, and the SPS Agreement, among others); the GATS in Annex 1B; the TRIPS Agreement in

[27]The discussion in this section can be found in the following article in a detailed manner: Lo (2013).

Annex 1C; the DSU in Annex 2; the Trade Policy Review Mechanism in Annex 3; and the Plurilateral Trade Agreements in Annex 4. Hence, the GATT, the GATS and other agreements thereunder are context to the Agreement Establishing the WTO, and vice versa.

Annex can also be a smaller piece of document to supplement the provisions in the main text. For instance, under the GATS, there are Annex on Article II Exemptions; Annex on Movement of Natural Persons Supplying Services under the Agreement; Annex on Air Transport Services; Annex on Financial Services; Second Annex on Financial Services; Annex on Negotiations on Maritime Transport Services; Annex on Telecommunications; and Annex on Negotiations on Basic Telecommunications. The GATS and its annexes are context to each other for treaty interpretation purpose.

Annex can also be designed to interpret, define or illustrate the terms used in the main text. For instance, under the Agreement on Implementation of Article VII of the GATT 1994 (Customs Valuation Agreement), there is Annex I (entitled "Interpretative Notes") to instruct the application of various customs valuation methods and interpretation of some terms used in the agreement. Also under the TBT Agreement[28] and the SPS Agreements,[29] there are some definitional provisions in their Annexes on certain key terms and phrases used in these agreements. Under the TRIMS Agreement, the only Annex (entitled "Illustrative List") is to illustrate the situations (which can be considered as trade-related investment measures (TRIMs), which are considered as inconsistent with the obligation of the national treatment or the general elimination of quantitative restrictions.

There could be other terms which are different from the term "annex" (as provided in introductory part of VLCT Article 31.2) used in different treaties to refer to their annexes. For instance, in the DSU, there are "Appendixes" to supplement the DSU, including Appendix 1 (Agreements Covered by the Understanding), Appendix 2 (Special and Additional Rules and Procedures Contained in the Covered Agreements), Appendix 3 (Working Procedures), and Appendix 4 (Expert Review Groups). These appendixes are all "annexes" for the purpose of applying Article 31.2 of the VCLT.

It must be also noted that in addition to annexes being the context of the main text of a treaty and the main text being the context of the annexes, an annex could also serve as context of another annex in the same treaty, as long as they are pertinent and related to each other and one of them can shed light to another annex which is to be interpreted.

---

[28]Annex 1 (entitled "Terms and Their Definitions for the Purpose of this Agreement") provides the definitions to the following terms and phrases: technical regulation, standard, conformity assessment procedures, international body or system, regional body or system, central government body; local government body, and non-governmental body.

[29]Annex A (entitled "Definitions") to the SPS Agreement includes definitions on the following terms and phrases: sanitary or phytosanitary measure; harmonization; international standards, guidelines and recommendations; risk assessment; appropriate level of sanitary or phytosanitary protection; pest- or disease-free area; and area of low pest or disease prevalence.

12.2.4 *Provisions in the Preamble of a Treaty Can Be the Context or an Object-and-Purpose*

In the preceding chapter, it is explained that object-and-purpose can be identified from the preamble of the interpreted treaty. It is also provided in Article 31.2 of the VCLT that the preamble can also serve as context to the main text of the treaty. So an issue here is the relation between these two statements, namely the preambular language serving as object-and-purpose and it serving as context.

To answer this question, it must be noted that there could be different kinds of paragraphs in the preamble of a treaty. Usually there are some paragraphs in the preamble reflecting the background of the treaty. For instance, the following paragraphs in the preamble of the FCTC is of the nature describing the reasons and background of the convention. They can serve as the context of the main text of the FCTC for treaty interpretation purpose:

> *Recognizing* that the spread of the tobacco epidemic is a global problem with serious consequences for public health that calls for the widest possible international cooperation and the participation of all countries in an effective, appropriate and comprehensive international response,
>
> *Reflecting* the concern of the international community about the devastating worldwide health, social, economic and environmental consequences of tobacco consumption and exposure to tobacco smoke,
>
> *Seriously concerned* about the increase in the worldwide consumption and production of cigarettes and other tobacco products, particularly in developing countries, as well as about the burden this places on families, on the poor, and on national health systems,

Usually there are also paragraphs showing the goal of the treaty. In the preceding chapter, there have been some examples included there to explain that some preambular languages can be the source for identifying the object-and-purpose of the treaty. In the preamble of the FCTC, the objectives of the convention can also be identified. The following paragraphs in the preamble of the FCTC are of the nature of object-and-purpose:

> *Determined* to give priority to their right to protect public health,
>
> *Recalling also* the preamble to the Constitution of the World Health Organization, which states that the enjoyment of the highest attainable standard of health is one of the fundamental rights of every human being without distinction of race, religion, political belief, economic or social condition,
>
> *Determined* to promote measures of tobacco control based on current and relevant scientific, technical and economic considerations.

12.2.5 Agreement/Instrument in Connection with the Conclusion of a Treaty

Article 31.2 of the VCLT provides that the context shall comprise: (a) "any agreement relating to the treaty which was made between all the parties in connexion with the conclusion of the treaty" and (b) "any instrument which was made by one or more parties in connexion with the conclusion of the treaty and accepted by the other parties as an instrument related to the treaty." Hence, there could be a related "agreement" or a related "instrument" being considered as context of a treaty.

For an *agreement*, the requirements are that it must be relating to the interpreted treaty; that such related agreement must be concluded between all parties to the interpreted treaty, that is to say that there must be a full overlap of the members between the interpreted treaty and the related agreement; and that such agreement must be in connection with the conclusion of the interpreted treaty.

For an *international instrument*, the requirements are that it must be made by one or more parties of the interpreted treaty; that the instrument must be in connection with the conclusion of the interpreted treaty; and that such instrument must be accepted by the other parties as an instrument related to the treaty.

There is an example in a WTO case concerning whether an agreement or instrument can be the context to the interpreted provision. The Appellate Body Report on *US—Gambling* states[30]:

> We note that Article 31(2) refers to the *agreement* or *acceptance* of the parties. In this case, both W/120 and the 1993 Scheduling Guidelines were drafted by the GATT Secretariat rather than the parties to the negotiations. It may be true that, on its own, authorship by a delegated body would not preclude specific documents from falling within the scope of Article 31(2). However, we are not persuaded that in this case the Panel could find W/120 and the 1993 Scheduling Guidelines to be context. Such documents can be characterized as context only where there is sufficient evidence of their constituting an "agreement relating to the treaty" between the parties or of their "accept[ance by the parties] as an instrument related to the treaty".
>
> … therefore, the Panel erred in categorizing W/120 and the 1993 Scheduling Guidelines as "context" for the interpretation of the United States' GATS Schedule. …

The Appellate Body Report on *EC—Chicken Cuts* has indicated that the Harmonized Commodity Description and Coding System ("Harmonized System" or "HS"), which is international product nomenclature developed by the World Customs Organization (WCO) currently being "used by more than 200 countries and economies as a basis for their Customs tariffs and for the collection of international trade statistics", with "Over 98% of the merchandise in international trade

[30]US—Gambling Appellate Body Report, *supra* note 4, at paras. 175, 178.

[being] classified in terms of the HS",[31] can be considered as a related agreement or instrument to serve as context to the interpreted tariff headings. It states[32]:

> The Harmonized System is not, formally, part of the *WTO Agreement*, as it has not been incorporated, in whole or in part, into that Agreement. Nevertheless, the concept of "context", under Article 31, is not limited to the treaty text — namely, the *WTO Agreement* — but may also extend to "any agreement relating to the treaty which was made between all the parties in connection with the conclusion of the treaty", within the meaning of Article 31(2)(a) of the *Vienna Convention*, and to "any instrument which was made by one or more parties in connection with the conclusion of the treaty and accepted by the other parties as an instrument related to the treaty", within the meaning of Article 31(2)(b) of the *Vienna Convention*. …

It must be further noted that if there are two agreements (i.e. the superseded one and the subsequent one), the agreement being superseded does not fall within the scope of Article 31.2(a) of the VCLT, because the superseded agreement (i.e. the earlier treaty) can never be an agreement made in connection the conclusion of the interpreted treaty (i.e. the later treaty). Hence the superseded agreement should not be considered as context for the purpose of interpreting the subsequent agreement based on the provision of Article 31.2(a).

12.3 Extended Contexts—Subsequent Agreement/Practice and Relevant Rules of Int'l Law

12.3.1 The Use of Subsequent Agreement/Practice—To Read into the Text as Context

Article 31.3 of the VCLT instructs that: "There shall be *taken into account*, together with the context …" (Emphasis added) An issue here is the way of taking into account the subsequent agreement and subsequent practice.

The Appellate Body has clarified that this is to require a treaty interpreter to "read the agreement into the interpreted treaty". But it is not to use relevant agreement to replace or override the interpreted term or provisions. Although the Appellate Body's following explanatory statement is related to "subsequent agreement", the same rule should be applied to "subsequent practice". It states the following in its Report on *US—Clove Cigarettes*[33]:

---

[31]What is the Harmonized System (HS)?. http://www.wcoomd.org/en/topics/nomenclature/overview/what-is-the-harmonized-system.aspx. Accessed 21 Aug 2017.

[32]EC—Chicken Cuts Appellate Body Report, *supra* note 7, at para. 195.

[33]Appellate Body Report, *US—Measures Affecting the Production and Sale of Clove Cigarettes*, para. 269, WTO Doc. WT/DS406/AB/R (adopted 24 Apr 2012) [hereinafter US—Clove Cigarettes Appellate Body Report].

> In the light of our characterization of paragraph 5.2 of the Doha Ministerial Decision as a subsequent agreement between the parties within the meaning of Article 31(3)(a) of the *Vienna Convention*, we turn now to consider the meaning of Article 2.12 of the *TBT Agreement* in the light of the clarification of the term "reasonable interval" provided by paragraph 5.2. We observe that, in its commentaries on the *Draft articles on the Law of Treaties*, the ILC states that a subsequent agreement between the parties within the meaning of Article 31(3)(a) "must be read into the treaty for purposes of its interpretation". As we see it, while the terms of paragraph 5.2 must be "read into" Article 2.12 for the purpose of interpreting that provision, this does not mean that the terms of paragraph 5.2 replace or override the terms contained in Article 2.12. Rather, the terms of paragraph 5.2 of the Doha Ministerial Decision constitute an interpretative clarification to be taken into account in the interpretation of Article 2.12 of the *TBT Agreement*.

Since an interpreter is to "read the relevant agreement into the interpreted treaty" and not to use relevant agreement to replace or override the interpreted term or provisions, the requirements are that the textual language should still be the fundamental basis for interpretation and that an interpretation based on the context of a relevant agreement should not serve a ground to deviate from the scope of the ordinary meanings of the interpreted treaty provision.

It is not clear from the text of Article 31.3 of the VCLT concerning whether a subsequent agreement, a subsequent practice and relevant rules of international law are "context" of an interpreted treaty or whether they themselves are not context but they still need to be considered. It just requires treaty interpreters to take into account these agreement, practice and rules "together with context". Article 31.3 reads:

> There shall be taken into account, together with the context:
>
> (a) Any subsequent agreement between the parties regarding the interpretation of the treaty or the application of its provisions;
> (b) Any subsequent practice in the application of the treaty which establishes the agreement of the parties regarding its interpretation;
> (c) Any relevant rules of international law applicable in the relations between the parties.

From the phrase "There shall be taken into account, together with the context: …", a possible understanding is that the "subsequent agreement" , the "subsequent practice" and the "relevant rules of international law" are only to be taken into account "together with context", but they themselves are not "context". However, the text of Article 31.3 does not exclude the possibility that the paragraph is interpreted as the "subsequent agreement", the "subsequent practice" and the "relevant rules of international law" themselves being the context and needed to be taken into account with other context. The book is of the view that there is no need to create a separate category in addition to the category of context to be taken into consideration by the treaty interpreters. Hence, a more appropriate understanding of Article 31.3 should be that this paragraph includes some extended or additional contexts (i.e. subsequent agreement, subsequent practice and relevant rules of international law) which help the interpretation of a treaty provision.

12.3.2 Subsequent Agreement

For a "subsequent agreement" being considered together with context, it must be between the parties. It must also be regarding the interpretation of a treaty or the application of its provision. It must further be "a subsequent agreement" (instead of "an agreement being superseded") to be considered together with the context. The Appellate Body has expressed on this point. In *US—Anti-Dumping and Countervailing Duties (China)*, the Appellate Body indicates that the Subsidies Code concluded in 1979 cannot be the context of a WTO agreement which was concluded in 1994. It states in its Report that[34]:

> In our view, Article 15 of the *Tokyo Round Subsidies Code* cannot be considered as context within the meaning of Article 31 of the *Vienna Convention*. Article 31 does not refer to a predecessor agreement — that is, an agreement on the same matter that has ceased to exist and has been replaced by the agreement being interpreted — as context or as one of the elements to be taken into account together with the context. Rather, a provision in a predecessor agreement may, at most, form part of the circumstances of the conclusion of a treaty under Article 32 of the *Vienna Convention* and thus be considered as supplementary means of interpretation.

The Appellate Body indicates that the term "agreement" here should be understood from its substance, instead of its form. It indicates in its Report on *US—Clove Cigarettes*[35]:

> … the text of Article 31(3)(a) of the *Vienna Convention* does not establish a requirement as to the form which a "subsequent agreement between the parties" should take. We consider, therefore, that the term "agreement" in Article 31(3)(a) of the *Vienna Convention* refers, fundamentally, to substance rather than to form. Thus, in our view, paragraph 5.2 of the Doha Ministerial Decision can be characterized as a "subsequent agreement" within the meaning of Article 31(3)(a) of the *Vienna Convention* provided that it clearly expresses a common understanding, and an acceptance of that understanding among Members with regard to the meaning of the term "reasonable interval" in Article 2.12 of the *TBT Agreement*. …

So a "subsequent agreement" does not limit to a formal agreement concluded between the parties. It also includes an interpretation made by a recognized body entrusted with the power of authoritative interpretation in accordance with the treaty. Hence, an authoritative interpretation issued by an authorized body under a treaty can be considered as "subsequent agreement" with regard to the application of Article 31.3 of the VCLT. This has been mentioned in Chap. 5 of this book. In this regard, the Appellate Body Report on *EC—Bananas III (Article 21.5—Ecuador II)/EC—Bananas III (Article 21.5—US)* states the following:

> Multilateral interpretations of provisions of WTO law are the next method identified above. Article IX:2 of the *WTO Agreement* sets out specific requirements for decisions that may be

[34]US—Anti-Dumping and Countervailing Duties (China) Appellate Body Report, *supra* note 9, at para. 579.

[35]US—Clove Cigarettes Appellate Body Report, *supra* note 32, at para. 267.

> taken by the Ministerial Conference or the General Council to adopt interpretations of provisions of the Multilateral Trade Agreements. Such multilateral interpretations are meant to clarify the meaning of existing obligations, not to modify their content. Article IX:2 emphasizes that such interpretations "shall not be used in a manner that would undermine the amendment provisions in Article X". A multilateral interpretation should also be distinguished from a waiver, which allows a Member to depart from an existing WTO obligation for a limited period of time. We consider that a multilateral interpretation pursuant to Article IX:2 of the *WTO Agreement* can be likened to a subsequent agreement regarding the interpretation of the treaty or the application of its provisions pursuant to Article 31(3)(a) of the *Vienna Convention*, as far as the interpretation of the WTO agreements is concerned.[36]

In *EC—Bananas III (Article 21.5—Ecuador II)/EC—Bananas III (Article 21.5—US)*, the Appellate Body further states concerning authoritative interpretation as subsequent agreement that:

> We further observe that, in its commentary on the Draft Articles on the Law of Treaties, the International Law Commission (the "ILC") describes a subsequent agreement within the meaning of Article 31(3)(a) of the *Vienna Convention* "as a further *authentic element of interpretation* to be taken into account together with the context". In our view, by referring to "authentic interpretation", the ILC reads Article 31(3)(a) as referring to agreements bearing specifically upon the interpretation of a treaty. In the WTO context, multilateral interpretations adopted pursuant to Article IX:2 of the *WTO Agreement* are most akin to subsequent agreements within the meaning of Article 31(3)(a) of the *Vienna Convention*, but not waivers adopted pursuant to Articles IX:3 and 4 of the *WTO Agreement.*
>
> … In our view, the term "application" in Article 31(3)(a) relates to the situation where an agreement specifies how existing rules or obligations in force are to be "applied"; the term does not connote the creation of new or the extension of existing obligations that are subject to a temporal limitation and are to expire. We find the Panel's conclusion that the Doha Article I Waiver extended the duration of the tariff quota concession beyond 31 December 2002, and thereby modified or changed the content of the European Communities' Schedule, difficult to reconcile with its conclusion that the Waiver should be considered an agreement on the *application* of existing commitments contained in that Schedule. As such, we do not consider that the Doha Article I Waiver could be regarded as an agreement on the application of the tariff quota concession in the European Communities' Schedule within the meaning of Article 31(3)(a) of the *Vienna Convention.*[37]

In addition to the authoritative interpretation under the WTO, other decisions adopted by the WTO under its decision-making procedure are also qualified as subsequent agreements for purpose of interpreting WTO agreements. The Appellate Body indicates in its Report on *US—Clove Cigarettes* the following:

> … the United States argued that a decision by the Ministerial Conference that does not conform with the specific decision-making procedures established by Article IX:2 of the *WTO Agreement* cannot constitute a "subsequent agreement between the parties" within

[36]Appellate Body Report, *European Communities—Regime for the Importation, Sale and Distribution of Bananas (Article 21.5—Ecuador II)/(Article 21.5—US)*, para. 383, WTO Doc. WT/DS27/AB/RW2/ECU, WT/DS27/AB/RW/USA, WT/DS27/AB/RW2/ECU/Corr.1, WT/DS27/AB/RW/USA/Corr.1 (adopted 11 Dec 2008/22 Dec 2008).

[37]Id. at paras. 390–391.

the meaning of Article 31(3)(a) of the *Vienna Convention*. We observe that multilateral interpretations adopted pursuant to Article IX:2 of the *WTO Agreement*, on the one hand, and subsequent agreements on interpretation within the meaning of Article 31(3)(a) of the *Vienna Convention*, on the other hand, serve different functions and have different legal effects under WTO law. …

… Article 31(3)(a) of the *Vienna Convention* is a rule of treaty interpretation, pursuant to which a treaty interpreter uses a subsequent agreement between the parties on the interpretation of a treaty provision as an interpretative tool to determine the meaning of that treaty provision. … Interpretations developed by panels and the Appellate Body in the course of dispute settlement proceedings are binding only on the parties to a particular dispute. Article IX:2 of the *WTO Agreement* does not preclude panels and the Appellate Body from having recourse to a customary rule of interpretation of public international law that, pursuant to Article 3.2 of the DSU, they are required to apply.

…

We consider, therefore, that a decision adopted by Members, *other than* a decision adopted pursuant to Article IX:2 of the *WTO Agreement*, may constitute a "subsequent agreement" on the interpretation of a provision of a covered agreement under Article 31(3)(a) of the *Vienna Convention*. …

12.3.3 Subsequent Practice

For a "subsequent practice" to be considered together with context, it must be a "practice". The practice must be subsequent to the interpreted treaty. It must be "concordant, common, consistent, discernible pattern of acts or pronouncements". It must also be in the application of the treaty. The practice must further establishes the agreement of the parties regarding its interpretation. The Appellate Body explains the requirement of "practice" in its Report on *US—Gambling*[38]:

… in order for "practice" within the meaning of Article 31(3)(b) to be established: (i) there must be a common, consistent, discernible pattern of acts or pronouncements; *and* (ii) those acts or pronouncements must imply *agreement* on the interpretation of the relevant provision.

… Although the 2001 Guidelines were explicitly adopted by the Council for Trade in Services, this was in the context of the negotiation of *future* commitments and in order to assist in the preparation of offers and requests in respect of such commitments. As such, they do not constitute evidence of Members' understanding regarding the interpretation of *existing* commitments. Furthermore, as the United States emphasized before the Panel, in its Decision adopting the 2001 Guidelines, the Council for Trade in Services explicitly stated that they were to be "non-binding" and "shall not modify any rights or obligations of the Members under the GATS". Accordingly, we do not consider that the 2001 Guidelines, in and of themselves, constitute "subsequent practice" within the meaning of Article 31(3)(b) of the *Vienna Convention*.

[38]US—Gambling Appellate Body Report, *supra* note 4, at paras. 192–193.

Also a "practice" must be that of "all parties" to the interpreted treaty, instead of "some parties" to the treaty, so as to be qualified as a common and concordant practice for the purpose of Article 31.3(b) of the VCLT. The Appellate Body Report on *EC—Chicken Cuts* states the following[39]:

> … we observe that "subsequent practice" in the application of a treaty may be an important element in treaty interpretation because "it constitutes objective evidence of the understanding of the parties as to the meaning of the treaty".
>
> …
>
> We share the Panel's view that not each and every party must have engaged in a particular practice for it to qualify as *a "common" and "concordant" practice* [Emphasis added here]. Nevertheless, practice by some, but *not all* parties is obviously not of the same order as practice by only one, or very few parties. To our mind, it would be difficult to establish a "*concordant, common and discernible pattern*" [Emphasis added here] on the basis of acts or pronouncements of one, or very few parties to a multilateral treaty, such as the *WTO Agreement*. We acknowledge, however, that, if only some WTO Members have actually traded or classified products under a given heading, this circumstance may reduce the availability of such "acts and pronouncements" for purposes of determining the existence of "subsequent practice" within the meaning of Article 31(3)(b).

A subsequent practice could include many elements. It should be examined in an overall, not partial or sporadic, manner. The Appellate Body Report on *EC—Chicken Cuts* states:[40]

> In our view, as the Panel examined only a subset of salted meat products classifiable under heading 02.10, and it did not examine classification practice with respect to alternative headings such as heading 02.07, it could not draw valid conclusions as to the existence of "subsequent practice" establishing the agreement of the parties within the meaning of Article 31(3)(b) with respect to all salted meat products potentially covered by the tariff commitment under heading 02.10 of the EC Schedule.

In order to establish subsequent practice, there must be some positive actions being identified. A mere lack of action itself does not establish subsequent practice. The Appellate Body Report on *EC—Chicken Cuts* states[41]:

> We recall that, under Article 31(3)(b), agreement of the parties regarding interpretation of a treaty term must be established. This raises the question how to establish agreement of those parties that have not engaged in a practice. …
>
> We agree with the Panel that, in general, agreement may be deduced from the affirmative reaction of a treaty party. However, we have misgivings about deducing, *without further inquiry*, agreement with a practice from a party's "lack of reaction". We do not exclude that, in specific situations, the "lack of reaction" or silence by a particular treaty party may, in the light of attendant circumstances, be understood as acceptance of the practice of other treaty parties. Such situations may occur when a party that has not engaged in a practice has become or has been made aware of the practice of other parties (for example, by means of notification or by virtue of participation in a forum where it is discussed), but does not react

[39]EC—Chicken Cuts Appellate Body Report, *supra* note 7, at paras. 255, 259.

[40]Id. at para. 270.

[41]Id. at paras. 271–272.

to it. However, we disagree with the Panel that "lack of protest" against one Member's classification practice by other WTO Members may be understood, on its own, as establishing agreement with that practice by those other Members. Therefore, the fact that Brazil and Thailand, having actually exported the products at issue, may have accepted the European Communities' import classification practice under heading 02.10, is not dispositive of whether other Members with actual or potential trade interests have also accepted that practice. We, therefore, disagree with the Panel that "subsequent practice" under Article 31(3)(b) has been established by virtue of the fact that the Panel "[had] not been provided any evidence to indicate that WTO Members protested against the EC classification practice in question from 1996 to 2002".

12.3.4 Relevant Rules of International Law

Article 31.3(c) of the VCLT requires treaty interpreters to take into account "any relevant rules of international law applicable in the relations between the parties". The qualifications of this requirement include that they must be rules of international law; that they must be relevant; and that they must be applicable in the relations between the parties.

The Appellate Body explains various requirements in Article 31.3(c) in its Report on *EC and certain member States—Large Civil Aircraft*[42]:

> … To qualify under Article 31(3)(c), the 1992 Agreement would therefore have to be a "rule[] of international law", which is "relevant" and "applicable in the relations between the parties". Moreover, even assuming the 1992 Agreement were to fulfil these conditions, the chapeau to Article 31(3)(c) specifies the normative weight to be ascribed to the 1992 Agreement, namely that it is to be "taken into account" in interpreting the *SCM Agreement*.

The Appellate Body has further elaboration on these requirements. In its Report on *US—Anti-Dumping and Countervailing Duties (China)*, the Appellate Body explained the following[43]:

> We note that Article 31(3)(c) of the *Vienna Convention* … contains three elements. First, it refers to "rules of international law"; second, the rules must be "relevant"; and third, such rules must be "applicable in the relations between the parties". We will address these three elements in turn.
>
> First, the reference to "rules of international law" corresponds to the sources of international law in Article 38(1) of the Statute of the International Court of Justice and thus includes customary rules of international law as well as general principles of law. Second, in order to be relevant, such rules must concern the same subject matter as the treaty terms being interpreted. To the extent that Articles 4, 5, and 8 of the ILC Articles [International Law Commission, Articles on State Responsibility] concern the same subject matter as

[42]Appellate Body Report, *European Communities—Measures Affecting Trade in Large Civil Aircraft*, para. 841, WTO Doc. WT/DS316/AB/R (adopted 1 June 2011) [hereinafter EC and certain member States—Large Civil Aircraft Appellate Body Report].

[43]US—Anti-Dumping and Countervailing Duties (China) Appellate Body Report, *supra* note 9, at paras. 307–308, 311, fn. 222.

Article 1.1(a)(1) of the *SCM Agreement*, they would be "relevant" in the sense of Article 31(3)(c) of the *Vienna Convention*. With respect to the third requirement, the question is whether the ILC Articles are "applicable in the relations between the parties". We observe that Articles 4, 5, and 8 of the ILC Articles are not binding *by virtue of* being part of an international treaty. However, insofar as they reflect customary international law or general principles of law, these Articles are applicable in the relations between the parties.

…

In this context, we observe that the United States acknowledges that the ILC Articles might reflect customary international law to some extent. Yet, the United States contends that given the "fine line distinctions" constructed in Articles 5 to 8 of the ILC Articles, it remains an open and contested question whether all of these details and distinctions have risen to the status of customary international law. Our analysis, however, does not draw on any details or "fine line distinctions" that might exist under Article 5 of the ILC Articles. Rather, we see similarities in the core principles and functions of the respective provisions. Our consideration of Article 5 of the ILC Articles does not contradict our analysis of Article 1.1(a)(1) above. Rather, it lends further support to that analysis. Yet, because the outcome of our analysis does not turn on Article 5, it is not necessary for us to resolve definitively the question of to what extent Article 5 of the ILC Articles reflects customary international law.

Also for the purpose of Article 31.3(c), the rules of international law are not decisive, but are only one of the means to assist treaty interpretation. The Appellate Body has explained this aspect in its Report on *US—Anti-Dumping and Countervailing Duties (China)*[44]:

… In our view, the Panel misconstrued the role of the ILC Articles when it set out to analyze "whether [the ILC Articles] would override [the Panel's] analysis and conclusions based on the text of the SCM Agreement itself". The question is not whether intermediate results of one element of the interpretative exercise "override" the results of another. Rules of international law within the meaning of Article 31(3)(c) are one of several means to ascertain the common intention of the parties to a particular agreement reflected in Article 31 of the *Vienna Convention*.

… The Panel elaborated that, while in some WTO disputes the ILC Articles "have been cited as containing similar provisions to those in certain areas of the WTO Agreement, in others they have been cited by way of contrast with the provisions of the WTO Agreement, as a way to better understand the possible meaning of the provisions of the WTO Agreement". The Panel considered this to indicate that panels and the Appellate Body have not considered the ILC Articles to constitute rules of international law in the sense of Article 31(3)(c). To us, this demonstrates the opposite. If, as the Panel states, certain ILC Articles have been "cited as containing similar provisions to those in certain areas of the WTO Agreement" or "cited by way of contrast with the provisions of the WTO Agreement", this evinces that these ILC Articles have been "taken into account" in the sense of Article 31(3)(c) by panels and the Appellate Body in these cases.

Article 31.3(c) requires that any relevant rules of international law must be applicable in the relations between the "parties". The Appellate Body explains that

[44]Id. at paras. 312–313.

the term basically refers to "all parties" to the interpreted treaty. It explains the reasons in its Report on *EC and certain member States—Large Civil Aircraft*[45]:

> ... the meaning of the term "the parties" in Article 31(3)(c) of the *Vienna Convention* has in recent years been the subject of much academic debate and has been addressed by the ILC. While the participants refer to WTO panels that have addressed its meaning, the Appellate Body has made no statement as to whether the term "the parties" in Article 31(3)(c) refers to *all* WTO Members, or rather to a subset of Members, such as the parties *to the dispute*. The meaning of the term "the parties" in Article 31(3)(c) of the *Vienna Convention* has in recent years been the subject of much academic debate and has been addressed by the ILC. While the participants refer to WTO panels that have addressed its meaning, the Appellate Body has made no statement as to whether the term "the parties" in Article 31(3)(c) refers to *all* WTO Members, or rather to a subset of Members, such as the parties *to the dispute*.
>
> An interpretation of "the parties" in Article 31(3)(c) should be guided by the Appellate Body's statement that "the purpose of treaty interpretation is to establish the *common* intention of the parties to the treaty". This suggests that one must exercise caution in drawing from an international agreement to which not all WTO Members are party. At the same time, we recognize that a proper interpretation of the term "the parties" must also take account of the fact that Article 31(3)(c) of the *Vienna Convention* is considered an expression of the "principle of systemic integration" which, in the words of the ILC, seeks to ensure that "international obligations are interpreted by reference to their normative environment" in a manner that gives "coherence and meaningfulness" to the process of legal interpretation. In a multilateral context such as the WTO, when recourse is had to a non-WTO rule for the purposes of interpreting provisions of the WTO agreements, a delicate balance must be struck between, on the one hand, taking due account of an individual WTO Member's international obligations and, on the other hand, ensuring a consistent and harmonious approach to the interpretation of WTO law among all WTO Members.

To conclude this chapter, it should be useful to clarify that although the "factual context" (as opposed to the "legal context") is not currently provided in the VCLT, it is still a factor for a treaty interpreter to examine the appropriateness of the selection of an ordinary meaning to be given to an interpreted term. Certain codified rules as to the situation and ways of consideration of factual context in treaty interpretation should be useful. It should also be useful to indicate in a codified set of treaty interpretation rules that a preambular language can be considered as context of an interpreted term or as an object-and-purpose of the interpreted treaty, depending on the contexts of the language. It is also useful to indicate in a codified rule that the footnotes in a treaty can be the context for the interpretation of the main texts to which the footnotes are attached and the context for other parts in the interpreted treaty. Still, it is useful to indicate in a codified set of rules that the subsequent agreement and practice and relevant rules of international law are to be "read into the interpreted treaty", but are not to replace or override the interpreted term or provisions.

[45]EC and certain member States—Large Civil Aircraft Appellate Body Report, *supra* note 41, at paras. 844–845.

References

Lo C (2013) The proper interpretation of “disguised restriction on international trade” under the WTO: the need to look at the protective effect. J Int Dispute Settl 4(1):111–137

The Free Dictionary. http://www.thefreedictionary.com/gambling. Accessed 21 Aug 2017

What is the Harmonized System (HS)? http://www.wcoomd.org/en/topics/nomenclature/overview/what-is-the-harmonized-system.aspx. Accessed 21 Aug 2017

Chapter 13
Special Meaning, Supplementary Means and Different Languages as well as the Possible Codification

Contents

13.1 Special Meaning as Opposed to Ordinary Meaning

13.1.1 What to Constitute a Special Meaning and When to Use It

It has been explained in the above discussions that the whole process of treaty interpretation is mainly to identify the ordinary meaning to be given to the interpreted terms or provisions under Article 31.1 of the VCLT. Context (as further elaborated in Articles 31.2 and 31.3) and the object-and-purpose are to help identify and select an appropriate ordinary meaning to be given to the interpreted terms or

C. Lo, *Treaty Interpretation Under the Vienna Convention on the Law of Treaties*,
https://doi.org/10.1007/978-981-10-6866-9_13

provisions under Article 31.1. Although an interpreted term or provision might be subject to various meanings, these meanings must all be "ordinary" ones. In principle, an interpreter is not allow to give a special meaning to an interpreted term, unless the requirements in Article 31.4 are met.

Sometimes it is obvious that a term used in a legal document has a special or technical meaning. For instance, for nautical purpose, the term "skin" refers to the outer part of the hull or the body of a ship and the term "waist" refers to the middle part of the upper deck of a ship between the forecastle and the quarterdeck. If such terms are used in a legal document addressing nautical matters, apparently these terms are not referring to different parts of human body. In the widely cited British case of *Unwin v Hanson*, the judge states the following:

> If the Act is directed to dealing with matters affecting everybody generally, the words used have the meaning attached to them in the common and ordinary use of language. If the Act is one passed with reference to a particular trade, business or transaction, and words are used which everybody conversant with this trade, business or transaction knows and understands to have a particular meaning in it, then the words are to be construed as having that particular meaning though it may differ from the common or ordinary meaning of the words. For instance, the 'waist' or 'skin' are well-known terms as applied to a ship, and nobody would think of their meaning the waist or skin of a person when they are used in an Act of Parliament dealing with ships.[1]

Article 31.4 of the VCLT provides that: "A special meaning shall be given to a term if it is established that the parties so intended." There is no definition in the VCLT on the term "special meaning". It must be understood from its context.

When taking Article 31.1 into consideration, it is clear that the special meaning is used as opposed to the ordinary meaning. Since the "ordinary meaning" refers to the ordinariness of the usage of an interpreted term or provision, a special meaning must refer to an unusual, uncommon or distinctive usage of a term. In practice, sometimes a special meaning could be given to an interpreted term without referring it as a "special meaning".

Sometimes it is not clear as to whether a meaning reflected in the dictionary is an ordinary meaning or a special meaning. For instance, the Appellate Body states in its report on *US—Gambling* that[2]:

> We have three reservations about the 'way in which the Panel determined the ordinary meaning of the word 'sporting' in the United States' Schedule. … Secondly, the Panel failed to have due regard to the fact that its recourse to dictionaries revealed that gambling and betting can, at least in some contexts, be one of the meanings of the word 'sporting'.

It is not clear as to whether the Appellate Body considers "gambling" as one of the *ordinary meanings* of the term "sporting" or whether "gambling" is a *special meaning* of the term "sporting." But based on the discussions in Chaps. 10 and 12

---

[1]Unwin v. Hanson [1891] 2 QB 115.

[2]Appellate Body Report, *United States—Measures Affecting the Cross-Border Supply of Gambling and Betting Services*, para. 166, WTO Doc. WT/DS285/AB/R, WT/DS285/AB/R/Corr.1 (adopted 20 Apr 2005).

of this book, the author argues that the threshold of deciding the ordinariness of the meaning of an interpreted term is not high. Since the meaning of "gambling" is included the dictionary definitions of the term "sporting", the meaning of "gambling" should be "ordinary enough" for the interpreted term "sporting" and is qualified to be considered by the treaty interpreter.

Under VCLT Article 31.4, the only situation where a special meaning is to be given to an interpreted term or provision is "when the parties so intended". In other words, it must be because of the parties having such intention of giving an interpreted term a special meaning, the interpreter will then give such special meaning to the term so as to correspond to the parties' intention. The situation allowing a treaty interpreter to rely on the "special meaning" to interpret a treaty term could be more limited than the situation allowing a statutory interpreter to rely on "special meaning" to interpret a law provision. Depending on jurisdictions, in statutory interpretation, a "trade custom" can also lead to the court's decision to give a "special meaning" to the interpreted law provision. But in treaty interpretation, an interpreter can rely on a "special meaning" and to give it to a treaty term only when the treaty's contracting parties "so intended". A "custom" might help identify the parties' intention of applying a "special meaning". But the "custom" itself and alone cannot be the basis of giving a "special meaning" to an interpreted treaty term.

13.1.2 How to Identify the Parties' Intention and the Special Meaning

Under Article 31.4 of the VCLT, there are a number of tasks for a treaty interpreter to fulfill concerning the use of a special meaning, namely to decide whether the parties have such intention mentioned or implied in the interpreted paragraph, to decide the possible range of special meanings, and to choose one of the special meanings to be given to the interpreted term or provision.

Concerning the decision on whether the parties "so intended", a treaty interpreter must look for an intention of the "parties". In this regard, it should be discussed about the meaning of the term "parties" in Article 31.4 of the VCLT. Article 31.4 does not expressly indicate the meaning or scope of the term "parties". But from the whole paragraph (i.e. "A special meaning shall be given to a term if it is established that the *parties* so intended"), the term "parties" must refer to the whole contracting parties of the interpreted treaty. Since the intention is referred to the interpreted treaty, it would make sense only to interpret that the intention is of the whole contracting parties of the interpreted treaty and hence the term "parties" must mean the whole parties to the interpreted treaty. The term should not be considered as referring to the disputing parties.

Hence, if a dispute is conducted under a multilateral or regional treaty, the two disputing parties are not the whole parties of the treaty. The disputing parties' intent of giving a special meaning to a term would not be sufficient to show that all parties also have such intent.

Although Article 31.4 of the VCLT is a rule for treaty interpretation, the provision itself still needs interpretation. When applying it, the interpreter will have to decide whether the requirement of "when parties so intended" is met. It involves the *finding of the existence of such intention* by the parties. Although it is not *the ordinary fact-finding activity* in a dispute settlement procedure, there should still be sufficient evidence to show the parties' intent of such kind so as to apply Article 31.4. If a disputing party alleges that the parties of the interpreted treaty have such intention and suggests that Article 31.4 should apply, it will need to provide supporting evidence so as to persuade the interpreter for the justification of applying Article 31.4. The parties' intention must show that special meaning has been contemplated at the time when the term was used or at the time when the parties' intention was expressed. But if the disputing party claiming the use of a special meaning is not able to provide sufficient evidence to show that the contracting parties of the treaty had the alleged intent when they concluded the treaty, the treaty interpreter still has to make his/her own research so as to decide whether there was such intent. The interpreter should not purely rely on the rule of burden of proof and decides that since the alleging party fails to provide sufficient evidence to discharge the burden of proof by showing the contracting parties' intent for a special meaning to be given to a term, an adverse conclusion of no such evidence should be inferred.

Concerning the methods of identifying a special meaning, a treaty interpreter can look at the textual language of the treaty for such purpose. The contracting parties' intention can be reflected in a definitional provision which gives a special meaning to a particular term. If there is any definitional provision to show that a special meaning is intended, a treaty interpreter is in no position to interpret in contradiction to the special meaning as defined in the treaty. The contracting parties' intention can also be reflected in a separate document. For instance, the contracting parties of a treaty may issue a ministerial declaration specifying their intention to give a special meaning to a term in the treaty.

An interpreter can also depend on the object-and-purpose of the treaty as revealed in the preamble or in the main text as well as the context so as to ascertain and decide whether the treaty's contracting parties have intended to give a special meaning to a term or provision. However, the interpreter must have a preponderant evidence to show that the object-and-purpose as well as the context would support the fact that the contracting parties had such intention of giving a special meaning to the interpreted term. If the object-and-purpose and the context merely show a *possibility* of such intention, it would not be enough for the interpreter to ascertain that there is such intention.

Preparatory works are also useful material to show the contracting parties' intention of using a term in a special way. However, the interpreter must be careful in relying too much on the preparatory work, because under the VCLT, relying on preparatory works is a supplementary means of interpretation. If preparatory works can be heavily used to decide that a special meaning is to be given to a term, the result would be that Articles 31.1 and 31.2 concerning the primary treaty interpretation method (relying on the ordinary meaning of a textual term, the context and the object-and-purpose) would be reversed by the supplementary means under Article 32 (relying on the preparatory works). Making the secondary means more decisive than the primary means is definitely an undesirable situation. Hence, when an interpreter is to ascertain a special meaning to be given to the interpreted term, he/she should still put the preparatory works in a secondary and supplementary position to be considered and should give lesser weight to the preparatory works in the ascertaining process. Preparatory works should be used to "support" or "confirm" the result of identifying the contracting parties' intent for the use of a special meaning for a term based one the object-and-purpose and the context.

It must also be noted that since a special meaning must be intended at the time when the term is used, it must be careful using subsequent practices to show parties' intention. It is because subsequent practices occur at a time after the term was used. Hence, normally they reflect the position of the parties at the implementation stage. However, subsequent practices can still be useful to serve as supplementing element to assist showing that the contracting parties of the interpreted treaty did have such intention of giving a special meaning to a term, otherwise the parties would not have such subsequent practices.

Having explained that the parties' intention must be the one when the treaty was concluded, it is worth explaining that the parties can still make their intent of giving special meaning to a treaty term clear through a legal instrument (such as a ministerial declaration) which is adopted at a stage which is later than the conclusion of the treaty.

Concerning the possibility of two or more special meanings and the choice from one of them, most of the time when deciding whether "the parties so intended", an interpreter is to find "one" specific "special meaning" to be contemplated by the parties. Hence, normally there would not be two or more "special meanings" to be given to an interpreted term or provision. However, in the situation where the contracting parties' intention is clear about a term not being given with an ordinary meaning, but is unclear as to *which* "special meaning" is intended to be given to the term, an interpreter will have to choose "one" specific "special meaning" for the term. In such situation, the interpreter still has to consider and rely on the object-and-purpose as well as the context so as to decide *the most appropriate special meaning* to be given to the interpreted term.

13.2 Supplementary Means of Interpretation

13.2.1 When to Have Recourse to Supplementary Means

Under the framework of the provisions in Articles 31 and 32 of the VCLT, there are two layers of interpretation means/elements, namely the main means/elements (including the ordinary meaning of the textual language, the context and the object-and-purpose) as the first layer and the supplementary means/elements (including preparatory works and circumstance of conclusion) as the second layer. The main means/elements have been discussed in the previous chapters. Now we turn to the supplementary means, which are provided in Article 32 of the VCLT:

> Recourse may be had to supplementary means of interpretation, including the preparatory work of the treaty and the circumstances of its conclusion, in order to confirm the meaning resulting from the application of article 31, or to determine the meaning when the interpretation according to article 31:
>
> (a) Leaves the meaning ambiguous or obscure; or
> (b) Leads to a result which is manifestly absurd or unreasonable.

So there are two situations when a treaty interpreter can have recourse to the supplementary means, namely, the situation where it is needed "*to confirm the meaning* resulting from the application of Article 31" and the situation where it is needed "*to determine the meaning* when the interpretation according to Article 31 leaves the meaning ambiguous or obscure or leads to a manifestly absurd or unreasonable result." In other words, the supplementary means have two functions, namely the *confirming function* and the *determining function*.

13.2.2 The Confirming Function of the Supplementary Means

For the *confirming function* (i.e. the function of confirming the result of interpretation based on an ordinary meaning being given to a textual wording in its context and in the light of the object-and-purpose), there is no restriction in the application of the supplementary means. An interpreter can always decide to apply or not to apply the supplementary means to support or strengthen his/her interpretation based on Article 31 of the VCLT.

In principle, when an interpretation based on Article 31 is clear, the interpreter does not need to have recourse to the supplementary means. But of course having recourse to the supplementary means could strengthen the interpretation based on the primary means. The Appellate Body indicates in its report on *EC—Fasteners (China)* that when an interpretation based on the text and context is clear, it would not have recourse to the supplementary means of interpretation. It states:

> … based on the text of the provision read in its context, that Article 9.2 of the *Anti-Dumping Agreement* requires the imposition of anti-dumping duties on an individual basis and that the exception in the third sentence of Article 9.2 does not justify the imposition of country-wide duties on non-IT suppliers from NMEs. We, therefore, consider that we do not need to have recourse to supplementary means of interpretation under Article 32 of the

> Vienna Convention, such as the preparatory work of the treaty and the circumstances of its conclusion, in order to confirm or determine the meaning resulting from the application of Article 31.[3]

But the *confirming function* under Article 32 permits a "discretion" to be given to an interpreter to conduct an assessment based on the supplementary means so as to confirm or strengthen the interpretation based on Article 31. Hence, the Appellate Body states in its Report on *US—Large Civil Aircraft (2nd complaint)* that:

> ... under Article 32 of the *Vienna Convention*, preparatory work and the circumstances of a treaty's conclusion are relevant to confirm the interpretation reached under Article 31. In our view, while the negotiating history of the *SCM Agreement* supplies little concrete insight as to how Members intended the Annex V procedure to be initiated, it does confirm our understanding of the reasons why Members considered such a procedure to be a key part of serious prejudice disputes.[4]

Sometimes an interpreter enters into analysis of the supplementary materials so as to address the argument of a party, even though he/she has concluded that there is no ambiguity/obscurity or absurdity/unreasonableness arising from interpretation based on Article 31. In such situation, the supplementary means are used *to refute the argument of a party* in the dispute settlement procedure. The Appellate Body states in its report on *US—Stainless Steel* that[5]:

> We do not consider it strictly necessary in this case to have recourse to the supplementary means of interpretation identified in Article 32 of the Vienna Convention because our analysis under Article 31 has not left the meaning of the relevant provisions of the *Anti-Dumping Agreement* "ambiguous or obscure", nor has it led to a "manifestly absurd or unreasonable" result. Nevertheless, we turn to examine the United States' arguments relating to the historical background of the *Anti-Dumping Agreement.*

13.2.3 The Determining Function of the Supplementary Means

For the *determining function* (i.e. the function of determining the meaning when the interpretation according to Article 31 of the VCLT leaves the meaning ambiguous or obscure or leads to a manifestly absurd or unreasonable result), there are only two situations where an interpreter is permitted to disregard or to deviate from the

[3]Appellate Body Report, *European Communities—Definitive Anti-Dumping Measures on Certain Iron or Steel Fasteners from China*, paras. 352–353, WTO Doc. WT/DS397/AB/R (adopted 28 July 2011).

[4]Appellate Body Report, *United States—Measures Affecting Trade in Large Civil Aircraft (Second Complaint)*, para. 526, WTO Doc. WT/DS353/AB/R (adopted 23 Mar 2012).

[5]Appellate Body Report, *United States—Final Anti-dumping Measures on Stainless Steel from Mexico*, para. 128, WTO Doc. WT/DS344/AB/R (adopted 20 May 2008) [hereinafter US—Stainless Steel (Mexico) Appellate Body Report].

interpretation based on Article 31. These two situations are: (a) where an interpretation according to Article 31 leaves the ambiguity or obscurity and (b) where an interpretation according to Article 31 leads to a result of manifest absurdity or unreasonableness. Only when there is any one of these two situations, an interpreter can resort to the supplementary means to disregard or to reverse the interpretation based on Article 31. In any one of such situations, the supplementary means are used to "determine" the meaning of an interpreted term or provision.

Concerning the situation where an interpretation according to Article 31 still leaves the meaning ambiguous or obscure, it must be noted that there could be different extent of ambiguity and obscurity in an interpreted term. The situation where the extent of ambiguity or obscurity is lower is when the meaning is "general" and "broad" so that the interpreter will have to choose from among these general or broad range of meanings. The situation where the extent of ambiguity and obscurity is higher is when the meaning is vastly unclear so that the interpreter does not have a reasonable clue about the possible range of meanings. In WTO jurisprudence, it seems that as long as a term is still "general" after making assessment under Article 31, an interpreter should be allowed to have recourse to supplementary means provided in Article 32. The Appellate Body indicates in its report on *Canada—Dairy* the following[6]:

> In our view, the language in the notation in Canada's Schedule is not clear on its face. Indeed, the *language is general and ambiguous*, and, therefore, requires special care on the part of the treaty interpreter. For this reason, it is appropriate, indeed necessary, in this case, to turn to "supplementary means of interpretation" pursuant to Article 32 of the Vienna Convention. … (Emphasis added)

Hence, it should be appropriate to argue that the threshold of applying Article 32(a) concerning the use of supplementary means of interpretation to determine the meaning of an ambiguous or obscure treaty term is relatively low.

Concerning the situation when an interpretation according to Article 31 could lead to a manifestly absurd or unreasonable result, it must be noted that the absurdity or unreasonableness must be manifest to any reasonable person under the interpreted treaty. Whether or not a result is manifestly absurd or unreasonable should be primarily decided based on the object-and-purpose of the treaty. If it seems from the language that a treaty term or provision is used in a way that seems to be unusual or unreasonable, but if it is still in line with the object-and-purpose, the interpreter will in principle have to respect the unusual way of its use. Since a treaty is to be interpreted in accordance the ordinary meaning, taking the context and the object-and-purpose into account, it should be rare that the result of interpretation based on the context and the object-and-purpose is still manifestly absurd or unreasonable. As will be further elaborated in the next section, the threshold of

[6]Appellate Body Report, *Canada—Measures Affecting the Importation of Milk and the Exportation of Dairy Products*, para. 138, WTO Doc. WT/DS103/AB/R, WT/DS113/AB/R, WT/DS103/AB/R/Corr.1, WT/DS113/AB/R/Corr.1 (adopted 27 Oct 1999).

applying Article 32(b) concerning the use of supplementary means of interpretation to avoid absurdity or unreasonableness is far higher.

13.2.4 The "Absurdity Principle" Should Be Used in an Exceptionally Limited Way

In regard to the *determining function* of the supplementary means of treaty interpretation, it must be further noted that the two situations lead to different determining effects. For the situation where an interpretation according to Article 31 leaves the meaning *ambiguous or obscure*, the supplementary means becomes "determinative" to the extent that it decides and helps select a meaning from two or more ordinary meanings or decides the reliance on the special meaning. Hence, the supplementary means used in the situation of Article 32(a) should not be considered as an exception to the interpretation under Article 31 of the VCLT.

However, Article 32(b) concerning the situation where an interpretation according to Article 31 could lead to a result of *manifest absurdity or unreasonableness* is different from Article 32(a) in their respective results. The result of applying Article 32(b) would be that the interpretation based on Article 31 (i.e. the ordinary meaning being given to a textual language in its context and in the light of the treaty's object-and-purpose) would be *totally reversed*. In other words, Article 32(b) serves as an *exception* to Article 31.

Since Article 32(b) of the VCLT (which can be called the "absurdity principle") serves as an exception to the treaty interpretation under Article 31, it gives an enormous power to the treaty interpreter to deviate from the result of interpretation conducted under the general principle of Article 31. Hence, the requirement for applying Article 32(b) should be interpreted in a strict manner so as to limit an undesirable discretion being given to the treaty interpreter and even to avoid an unexpected rewriting of the treaty through treaty interpretation process.

As explained above, the threshold of meeting the requirement of ambiguity and obscurity requirement provided in Article 32(a) is not high. As long as a term is still "general" after making assessment under Article 31, an interpreter should be allowed to have recourse to supplementary means provided in Article 32.

Different from Article 32(a), the threshold of meeting the requirement of "manifest absurdity or unreasonableness" provided in Article 32(b) should be vastly higher. The absurdity or unreasonableness must be manifest enough. That is to say, the absurdity or unreasonableness must be so obvious from all aspects. If there is a room for a different interpretation as to whether the result of interpretation based on Article 31 is absurd/unreasonable or not, it should not be considered as manifestly absurd or unreasonable.

Hence, although *the absurdity principle* under VLCT Article 32(b) actually gives a treaty interpreter the power of making or rewriting a treaty provision, the power should be exercised in an exceptionally limited way and only in an extremely extraordinary situation.

13.2.5 Meaning of "Supplementary Means" and the Non-exhaustiveness in Article 32

Supplementary means of treaty interpretation is relied on by an interpreter as a supplement when certain requirements are met. Hence, it is to supplement the interpretation under Article 31 of the VCLT, but not to replace the principles provided in Article 31, unless absurdity [as provided in Article 32(b)] occurs. In any event, an interpreter must have conducted interpretation assessment under Article 31 before a recourse can be have to the supplementary means.

There is another aspect which needs to be borne in mind when resorting to the supplementary means. Article 32 states in part that "Recourse may be had to supplementary means of interpretation, including the preparatory work of the treaty and the circumstances of its conclusion…" Apparently, the preparatory work and the circumstances of the treaty's conclusion are merely illustrative examples. There could be other supplementary means. The Appellate Body states in its Report on *EC—Chicken Cuts* that[7]:

> We stress … that Article 32 does not define exhaustively the supplementary means of interpretation to which an interpreter may have recourse. It states only that they *include* the preparatory work of the treaty and the circumstances of its conclusion. Thus, an interpreter has a certain flexibility in considering relevant supplementary means in a given case so as to assist in ascertaining the common intentions of the parties.

Other supplementary means include, for example, *lex specialis derogat lagi generali* (meaning that a specific rule prevails over a general rule); *lex posterior derogat legi priori* (meaning that a later rule repeals a prior rule); and *expressio unitus est exclusio alterius* (meaning that the expression of one thing is the exclusion of those not mentioned).[8] These interpretation principles are mentioned in Chap. 5 and will be further discussed in the next chapter of this book. These principles are mainly used in "statutory interpretation". But they are also useful supplements to treaty interpretation because they represent the generally accepted rules of interpretation.

Two additional aspects need clarification. First, these principles are used not only for the interpretation of norms, but also for their application. So they guide treaty interpretation as well as treaty application. Second, not all principles

---

[7]Appellate Body Report, *European Communities—Customs Classification of Frozen Boneless Chicken Cuts*, para. 283, WTO Doc. WT/DS269/AB/R, WT/DS286/AB/R, WT/DS269/AB/R/Corr.1, WT/DS286/AB/R/Corr.1 (adopted 27 Sept 2005) [hereinafter EC—Chicken Cuts Appellate Body Report].

[8]Fitzmaurice and Elias (2005), p. 221.

generally used in the interpretation in domestic context are equally useful in treaty interpretation. For instance, there is *contra proferentem* (meaning that the interpretation must be against the one who drafted or proposed the provision). This principle is useful in contractual interpretation. But it is basically not applicable to statutory interpretation, because in statutory interpretation, the drafter or proposal of a statutory provision is the legislative body or the executive body. It does not make much sense to have an interpretation against the legislative body or the executive body in a country in deciding the relations between private parties. Neither is this principle useful for treaty interpretation. Although a treaty term or provision might have been proposed by one of the contracting parties during negotiations, the proposed term or provision becomes the integrated part of the treaty when it is accepted. Parties to a treaty should be equally and non-discriminatorily governed by the term or provision as provided in the treaty. Hence, the principle of *contra proferentem* would not apply in treaty interpretation.

There are some other principles which could also be considered as supplementary means, such as the principle of *ut res magis valeat quam perat* (principle of effectiveness), the principle of *in dubio mitius* (more leniently in case of doubt), and the evolutive interpretation. These principles are more commonly used in treaty interpretation and hence will be further discussed in Chaps. 14 and 15 of this book respectively.

13.2.6 Preparatory Works as Supplementary Means

As indicated above, Article 32 of the VCLT lists two examples of supplementary means of interpretation, one of which is the preparatory works (*travaux préparatoires*) .

For "statutory interpretation", preparatory works (i.e. the materials used in the preparation of a domestic legislation, including congressional reports and records of discussions, hearings and floor debates during the debating, drafting and negotiating stages of the legal document) can be used to decide the intention of the domestic legislature. Hence it could be quite heavily relied on in domestic court proceedings when conducting "statutory interpretation" as *a primary means of interpretation*, instead of being *a supplementary means*. However, in "treaty interpretation", preparatory works are only a *supplementary means*, either to support the interpretation results under Article 31 or to replace the interpretation arising from the use of Article 31 of the VCLT.

There is no definition on the term "preparatory work". From its plain meaning, preparatory works should include all documents produced during the preparing, debating, drafting and negotiating stages of a treaty. They should include "the correspondence (letters, notes, memoranda) between two or more negotiating states during the drafting of a treaty; preliminary drafts or proposals for a treaty together with suggested modifications; records of international conferences; reports, declarations, statements, and other similar documents used at such conferences; and so forth."[9]

However, it is not absolutely clear about the distinction between the *preparatory works* for a treaty and the *circumstances of its conclusion*, both of which are provided in Article 32 of the VCLT. In principle, if a material or document is made in conjunction with the negotiation of a treaty, it should fall within the scope of preparatory works. But if a material or document has existed *before* the negotiation was conducted, it falls within the scope of the circumstances of conclusion. For instance, in the WTO case of *US—Stainless Steel (Mexico)*, the United States argued that certain historical materials (i.e. the materials which pre-existed the establishment of the WTO in 1994, including a 1960 Group of Experts report, two panel reports made under the Antidumping Code of 1979 and some proposals submitted during the Uruguay Round negotiations which led to the conclusion of WTO agreements, including the Anti-Dumping Agreement) constituted the circumstances of the conclusion. The Appellate Body did not consider necessary to resort to such supplementary means. But it still entered into a detailed analysis of the supplementary means and did not reject that historical materials were circumstance of conclusion of the Anti-Dumping Agreement of the WTO. It states in its Report that[10]:

> The United States argues that recourse to the circumstances of the conclusion of the *Anti-Dumping Agreement* is appropriate in this case as a supplementary means of interpretation under Article 32 of the *Vienna Convention*. The United States refers to various historical materials, including the 1960 Group of Experts Report, two pre-WTO panel reports that dealt with the issue of zeroing in the context of the *Tokyo Round Anti-Dumping Code*, and several proposals submitted during the Uruguay Round. According to the United States, the historical materials demonstrate that the negotiators were not able to agree on a general prohibition of zeroing or on a requirement to aggregate individual transactions under Article 9.3 of the *Anti-Dumping Agreement*. The United States submits that, throughout the history of the GATT, it was recognized that zeroing was allowed under Article VI of the GATT 1947, and adds that this Article was not modified during the Uruguay Round. …
>
> We are not persuaded that the aforementioned historical materials provide guidance as to whether simple zeroing is permissible under Article 9.3 of the *Anti-Dumping Agreement*. First, as we see it, the negotiating proposals referred to by the United States reflect the positions of only some of the negotiating parties. …
>
> Secondly, we note that the same historical materials referenced by the United States were examined by the Appellate Body in *US—Softwood Lumber V*, where the Appellate Body concluded that these materials did not resolve the issue of whether the negotiators of the Anti-Dumping Agreement intended to prohibit zeroing. Although the 1960 Group of Experts Report concluded that making an injurious dumping determination based on individual transactions was the "ideal method", it also regarded such method as "clearly impracticable". This report is of little relevance to our analysis and does not shed light on the determination of a margin of dumping under Article 9.3 of the *Anti-Dumping Agreement*. In addition, even if we were to assume that zeroing was permitted under

---

[9]Linderfalk (2007, p. 240).

[10]US—Stainless Steel (Mexico) Appellate Body Report, *supra* note 5, at paras. 129–132.

Article VI of the GATT 1947, Article VI of the GATT 1994 has to be interpreted now in conjunction with the relevant provisions of the *Anti-Dumping Agreement*, such as Articles 2.1, 2.4, 2.4.2, and 9.3.

Thirdly, the *Anti-Dumping Agreement* entered into force in 1995, as part of the results of the Uruguay Round negotiations, long after the 1960 Group of Experts Report. The Panel Reports in *EC—Audio Cassettes* (unadopted) and *EEC—Cotton Yarn* (adopted), referred to by the United States, examined the issue of zeroing under the provisions of the *Tokyo Round Anti-Dumping Code*. The relevance of these panel reports is diminished by the fact that the plurilateral *Tokyo Round Anti-Dumping Code* was legally separate from the GATT 1947 and has, in any event, been terminated. This Code was not incorporated into the WTO covered agreements and, furthermore, it contained provisions that were less detailed than those in the *Anti-Dumping Agreement*. In its arguments on the permissibility of zeroing, the United States relies specifically on Article 2.6 of the *Tokyo Round Anti-Dumping Code*. We note that the corresponding provision in the *Anti-Dumping Agreement*, namely, Article 2.4, has a different wording in that it contains a new first sentence. Moreover, the *Tokyo Round Anti-Dumping Code* contained no provision similar to Article 2.4.2 of the *Anti-Dumping Agreement*. Therefore, whatever the legal status of zeroing under the *Tokyo Round Anti-Dumping Code*, it is of little relevance for the interpretation of differently phrased or new provisions of the *Anti-Dumping Agreement*.

13.2.7 Circumstances of Conclusion as Supplementary Means

In WTO jurisprudence, historical materials/backgrounds, provisions in the predecessor agreement, and unilateral acts and materials can all be considered as circumstance of a treaty's conclusion.

Concerning historical materials or background, the Appellate Body states in its Report on *EC—Computer Equipment* that: "With regard to 'the circumstances of [the] conclusion' of a treaty, this permits, in appropriate cases, the examination of the historical background against which the treaty was negotiated."[11]

Historical background can include other international treaties, as long as such treaties can be considered as a part of the historical background of the interpreted treaty. In *EC—Poultry*, the Appellate Body states in its Report: "… the Oilseeds Agreement may serve as a supplementary means of interpretation of Schedule LXXX pursuant to Article 32 of the Vienna Convention, as it is part of the historical background of the concessions of the European Communities for frozen poultry meat."[12]

[11]Appellate Body Report, *European Communities—Customs Classification of Certain Computer Equipment*, para. 86, WTO Doc. WT/DS62/AB/R, WT/DS67/AB/R, WT/DS68/AB/R (adopted 22 June 1998) [hereinafter EC—Computer Equipment Appellate Body Report].

[12]Appellate Body Report, *European Communities—Measures Affecting Importation of Certain Poultry Products*, para. 83, WTO Doc. WT/DS69/AB/R (adopted 23 July 1998).

If an international treaty is a predecessor treaty, it can basically be considered as part of the circumstances of another (the later) treaty's conclusion. The Appellate Body indicates in its Report on *US—Anti-Dumping and Countervailing Duties (China)* that[13]:

> In our view, Article 15 of the *Tokyo Round Subsidies Code* cannot be considered as context within the meaning of Article 31 of the Vienna Convention. Article 31 does not refer to a predecessor agreement — that is, an agreement on the same matter that has ceased to exist and has been replaced by the agreement being interpreted — as context or as one of the elements to be taken into account together with the context. Rather, a provision in a predecessor agreement may, at most, form part of the circumstances of the conclusion of a treaty under Article 32 of the *Vienna Convention* and thus be considered as supplementary means of interpretation.

Circumstances of conclusion of a treaty include not only multilateral sources, but also unilateral ones, as long as the sources are relevant to the conclusion of the interpreted treaty. The Appellate Body states in its Report on *EC—Chicken Cuts* that[14]:

> … we do not agree with the European Communities that a "direct link" to the treaty text and "direct influence" on the common intentions must be shown for an event, act, or instrument to qualify as a "circumstance of the conclusion" of a treaty under Article 32 of the *Vienna Convention.* An "event, act or instrument" may be relevant as supplementary means of interpretation not only if it has actually influenced a specific aspect of the treaty text in the sense of a relationship of cause and effect; it may also qualify as a "circumstance of the conclusion" when it helps to discern what the common intentions of the parties were at the time of the conclusion with respect to the treaty or specific provision. Moreover, the European Communities has taken the Appellate Body statement out of context; the Appellate Body was speaking of the sum or end-result of treaty interpretation; it should not be misconstrued as introducing a concept that an act, event, or instrument qualifies as a circumstance only when it has influenced the intent of all the parties. Thus, not only "multilateral" sources, but also "unilateral" acts, instruments, or statements of individual negotiating parties may be useful in ascertaining "the reality of the situation which the parties wished to regulate by means of the treaty" and, ultimately, for discerning the common intentions of the parties.

Another example of domestic practice being considered as part of the circumstance of a treaty's conclusion is in *EC—Computer Equipment*, in which the Appellate Body considers that "the classification practice in the European Communities during the Uruguay Round is part of 'the circumstances of [the] conclusion' of the WTO Agreement and may be used as a supplementary means of interpretation within the meaning of Article 32 of the Vienna Convention."[15]

Not only can the external circumstance be considered as the circumstance of the conclusion, but also a domestic court's decision in the negotiating party can be

[13]Appellate Body Report, *United States—Definitive Anti-Dumping and Countervailing Duties on Certain Products from China*, para. 579, WTO Doc. WT/DS379/AB/R (adopted 25 Mar 2011).

[14]EC—Chicken Cuts Appellate Body Report, *supra* note 7, at para. 289.

[15]EC—Computer Equipment Appellate Body Report, *supra* note 11, at para. 92.

considered to form part of the circumstance of a treaty's conclusion. The Appellate Body states in its Report on *EC—Chicken Cuts* the following[16]:

> … the Panel asked whether a Member's court judgments may, in principle, be taken into account as supplementary means of interpretation under Article 32. The Panel concluded that:
>
> This would suggest that a valid distinction cannot be drawn between, on the one hand, EC legislation and, on the other hand, ECJ judgements for the purposes of Article 32 of the Vienna Convention.
>
> We share the Panel's consideration that judgments of domestic courts are not, in principle, excluded from consideration as "circumstances of the conclusion" of a treaty if they would be of assistance in ascertaining the common intentions of the parties for purposes of interpretation under Article 32. It is necessary to point out, however, that judgments deal basically with a specific dispute and have, by their very nature, less relevance than legislative acts of general application (although judgments may have some precedential effect in certain legal systems).

13.3 Treaty Interpretation Concerning Different Authenticated Language Versions

13.3.1 Equal Authoritativeness of Different Versions

It is very common to have a treaty being drafted and adopted in two or more languages. There are issues concerning the authenticity of various versions as well as issues concerning treaty interpretation. Article 33 of the VCLT does not limit to treaty interpretation issues. It also includes the decision of authenticity of different language versions of a treaty.

Articles 33.1 and 33.2 are about the authenticity of treaty versions in different languages. They provide respectively that:

1. When a treaty has been authenticated in two or more languages, the text is equally authoritative in each language, unless the treaty provides or the parties agree that, in case of divergence, a particular text shall prevail.
2. A version of the treaty in a language other than one of those in which the text was authenticated shall be considered an authentic text only if the treaty so provides or the parties so agree.

When a treaty is concluded in one language, it is automatically authenticated. But if it is concluded in two or more languages, the authenticity must be decided by the contracting parties. In principle, the authenticity is decided based on the explicit provision in the treaty. The parties can decide whether the versions in different languages are equally authenticated or one of them should prevail.

[16]EC—Chicken Cuts Appellate Body Report, *supra* note 7, at para. 309.

An additional issue is about the meaning of "languages". The British style and American style of English could be slightly different. For example, in American English, a billion means 1,000,000,000, whereas in British English, a billion means 1,000,000,000,000. In many multilateral treaties, the British style is used. The interpretation is generally based on the British usage of English. But this is not always the case. As opposed to English, there are simplified and traditional Chinese characters and some different Chinese language usages used in Mainland China and Taiwan. Some simplified characters can have more than on corresponding traditional Chinese characters. Both simplified and traditional Chinese are Chinese language. Hence the difference between them is not directly governed by the provisions in Article 33. However, it should be reasonable to argue that the principles in Article 33 should be applied *mutatis mutandis* to the difference between the simplified and traditional Chinese versions of agreements between Mainland China and Taiwan.

13.3.2 Language Differences to Be Removed and Reconciled Through Interpretation

There are two paragraphs in Article 33 directly relevant to treaty interpretation. It provides in paragraphs 3 and 4 the following:

3. The terms of the treaty are presumed to have the same meaning in each authentic text.
4. Except where a particular text prevails in accordance with paragraph 1, when a comparison of the authentic texts discloses a difference of meaning which the application of Articles 31 and 32 does not remove, the meaning which best reconciles the texts, having regard to the object and purpose of the treaty, shall be adopted.

Concerning the presumption of the same meaning in different authenticated language versions, the Appellate Body has stated in *US—Softwood Lumber IV* that a treaty interpreter is expected to adopt a meaning that gives effect to all the terms of the treaty used in each authentic language:

> … in accordance with the customary rule of treaty interpretation reflected in Article 33(3) of the *Vienna Convention on the Law of Treaties* (the "*Vienna Convention*"), the terms of a treaty authenticated in more than one language — like the *WTO Agreement* — are presumed to have the same meaning in each authentic text. It follows that the treaty interpreter should seek the meaning that gives effect, simultaneously, to all the terms of the treaty, as they are used in each authentic language. …

The ultimate goal of dealing with different language versions for treaty interpretation purpose is to remove the difference between provisions in different versions or to reconcile them. There are a number of methods and processes to achieve these goal. First, an interpreter must conduct interpretation of a term or provision based on Articles 31 and 32 of the VCLT. Second, if there is any doubt as to the correct meaning to be given to the interpreted term or provision, the interpreter can look at the language used in another version and conduct interpretation of it based on Articles 31 and 32. Third, the interpreter must make comparison between different versions so as to decide whether there is any difference. Fourth, if there is no apparent difference, a version can be considered as "context" for the interpretation of another version (which is usually the working version in the dispute settlement procedure). Fifth, if the interpreter identifies a difference in their meanings, the interpreter should try to remove it based on Articles 31 and 32. Sixth, in case the difference cannot be removed, it is a real difference between two language versions which need to be reconciled. The reconciliation of the difference should be made in consideration of the object-and-purpose of the treaty.

13.3.3 Different Language Version Serving as Context or Helping Find Ordinary Meaning

When conducting a dispute settlement procedure, the disputing parties and the adjudicator will normally use one language version of a treaty as the working basis. It is when the adjudicator encounters a difficulty in identifying the ordinary meaning of an interpreted term or provision, he/she will probably look into the term or provision used in another language version of the same treaty to find a solution. Conceptually, the terms and provisions in another language version of the same treaty serves as the *context* to the working version of the interpreted treaty. These terms and provisions in another language version also help understand the ordinary meaning of the terms and provisions used in the working version.

The Appellate Body has indicated that different language version can help identify the ordinary meaning of an interpreted term. It states in its Report on *US—Upland Cotton*[17]:

> … We agree, however, that the Panel's description of "price suppression" in paragraph 7.1277 of the Panel Report reflects the ordinary meaning of that term, particularly when read in conjunction with the French and Spanish versions of Article 6.3(c), as required by Article 33(3) of the *Vienna Convention on the Law of Treaties* (the "*Vienna Convention*").

In *Canada—Renewable Energy/Canada—Feed-in Tariff Program*, the Appellate Body makes comparison between different language versions so as to

[17]Appellate Body Report, *United States Subsidies on Upland Cotton*, para. 424, fn. 510, WTO Doc. WT/DS267/AB/R (adopted 21 Mar 2005).

decide which one can achieve a harmonious result. This is actually taking different language versions as *context* to each other. It states in its Report that[18]:

> We further note that the French version of Article III:8(a) refers to "*les besoins des pouvoirs publics*" and the Spanish version of the provision refers to "*las necesidades de los poderes públicos*". The term "purposes" thus corresponds to the terms "*besoins*" and "*necesidades*", respectively, in the French and the Spanish texts. Both the French and the Spanish terms correspond closely to the English term "needs". As such, the French and the Spanish text can be read harmoniously with an interpretation of the word "purposes" in English as referring to purchases of products directed at the government or purchased for the needs of the government in the discharge of its functions. By contrast, the words "*besoins*" or "*necesidades*" cannot be read harmoniously with the definition of the term "purpose" as "objectives" or "aims" of the government, because neither the word "*besoins*" in French, nor the word "*necesidades*" in Spanish, encompasses the notion of an aim or objective.

To conclude this chapter, it should be useful to include in a codified set of rules of interpretation that only when *all contracting parties* of the interpreted treaty "so intended", a special meaning can be given to the interpreted term. A custom might help identify the parties' intention of applying a "special meaning". But the custom itself and alone cannot be the basis of giving a "special meaning" to an interpreted treaty term. The contracting parties' intention can be reflected in a textual language or in the object-and-purpose of the interpreted treaty or even in a separate document. In any event, the interpreter must have a preponderant evidence to show that the object-and-purpose as well as the context would support the fact that the contracting parties had such intention of giving a special meaning to the interpreted term. The interpreter must be careful in relying too much on the preparatory work to decide the contracting parties' intention of special meaning in order not to use the supplementary means to reverse the interpretation result arising from the primary treaty interpretation method of relying on the ordinary meaning of a textual term, the context and the object-and-purpose.

Concerning the application of Article 32(b) of the VCLT, since the result of interpretation under Article 32(b) will be totally different from the result of interpretation under Article 31, Article 32(b) should be seen as an exception to Article 31 and hence its application should be extremely strict and limited. The absurdity or unreasonableness must be obvious from all aspects without a room for a different interpretation as to whether the result of interpretation based on Article 31 is absurd/unreasonable or not before Article 32(b) can be applied.

Concerning different language versions of a treaty, it should also be useful to indicate in a codified set of rules that a treaty interpreter should be permitted to consider the provisions and terms used in different language versions as mutual context to each other so as to help identify the ordinary meaning of and to interpret a treaty term.

---

[18]Appellate Body Report, *Canada—Certain Measures Affecting the Renewable Energy Generation Sector/ Measures Relating to the Feed-In Tariff Program*, para. 5.67, fn. 512, WTO Doc. WT/DS412/AB/R, WT/DS426/AB/R (adopted 24 May 2013).

References

Fitzmaurice M, Elias O (2005) Contemporary issues in the law of treaties. Eleven, Utrecht
Linderfalk U (2007) On the interpretation of treaties—the modern international law as expressed in the 1969 Vienna Convention on the Law of Treaties. Springer, Dordrecht

Chapter 14
Some Other Supplementary Interpretation Principles and the Possible Codification

Contents

14.1 Some Other "Supplementary" Principles and the Non-exclusiveness of Articles 31–33

14.1.1 Some Interpretation Principles of Supplementary Nature

It was mentioned in the preceding chapter and Chap. 5 of this book that there could be other treaty interpretation principles not explicitly listed in Articles 31–33. Many of these principles are Latin maxims, some of which were discussed in international cases, such as some WTO cases. The following examples (which were mentioned in Chap. 5 of this book) are commonly cited Latin maxims, which potentially can serve as supplementary treaty interpretation principles:

C. Lo, *Treaty Interpretation Under the Vienna Convention on the Law of Treaties*,
https://doi.org/10.1007/978-981-10-6866-9_14

(1) *Lex specialis derogat legi generali* (meaning that the special law repeals the general laws);[1]
(2) *Lex posterior derogat legi priori* (meaning that a later law repeals an earlier law);[2]
(3) *Expressio unius est exclusio alterius* (meaning that the inclusion of the one is the exclusion of the other);[3]
(4) *In dubio mitius* (meaning of interpreting more leniently in case of doubt);[4]
(5) *Ut res magis valeat quam pereat* (or the principle of effectiveness; meaning that one should avoid reading the instrument in a manner that would render the language in the instrument redundant, void, or ineffective);[5] and
(6) *Exceptio est strictissimae applicationis* (meaning that an exception is of the strictest application).[6]

These Latin maxims not only are "interpretation" principles (since they help the interpretation of domestic law and international treaty), but also are legal "application" principles (since they also instruct adjudicators to decide the proper application of different domestic law provisions and different international treaties).

In this chapter, discussions will focus on the status and role of some of these additional principles in treaty interpretation. But it must also be noted that the additional treaty interpretation rules are not limited these Latin maxims. As explained in Chap. 5 of this book, maintaining balanced situation of rights and obligations and not trying to restrike a new balance by an interpreter should be a very important principle for interpreting trade agreement. Also as will be explained in Chap. 15 of this book, interpreting human rights treaties might need an evolutive interpretation so as to ensure that they are "living treaties". These are also supplementary means of treaty interpretation.

14.1.2 The Nature and Functions of Latin Maxims

There are three additional aspects to be noted concerning these Latin maxims, which serve as treaty interpretation principles or rules. First, all these "principles"

---

[1]Fellmeth and Horwitz (2011).

[2]Id. https://www.google.com.tw/webhp?sourceid=chrome-instant&ion=1&ie=UTF-8&rct=j#q=lex+posterior+derogat+legi+priori+oxford+reference&*. Accessed 21 Aug 2017.

[3]Id. http://www.oxfordreference.com/view/10.1093/acref/9780199664924.001.0001/acref-9780199664924-e-1494?rskey=S4FPOs&result=1638. Accessed 21 Aug 2017.

[4]Id. http://www.oxfordreference.com/view/10.1093/acref/9780195369380.001.0001/acref-9780195369380-e-910. Accessed 21 Aug 2017.

[5]Id. http://www.oxfordreference.com/view/10.1093/acref/9780195369380.001.0001/acref-9780195369380-e-2062?rskey=5iNIGK&result=2062. Accessed 21 Aug 2017.

[6]Id. http://www.oxfordreference.com/view/10.1093/acref/9780195369380.001.0001/acref-9780195369380-e-731. Accessed 21 Aug 2017.

should be considered as supplementary means which fall within the scope of Article 32 of the VCLT. Hence, such "principles" are to assist the interpretation based on the provisions of the VCLT, especially Article 31.1 of it. These "principles" are not to reverse or undermine the result of interpretation based upon the rules provided in the VCLT.

But noted that, in practice, it is often seen that these principles are *directly applied or argued to be directly applicable* in treaty interpretation without first resorting to Articles 31 and 32. For instance, in a WTO dispute of *China—Publications and Audiovisual Products*, the Appellate Body Report cited the disputing parties' arguments about the application or non-application of the Latin maxim *in dubio mitius*[7]:

> … China claims that the Panel should have found that the application of both Articles 31 and 32 of the Vienna Convention left the issue of whether China's GATS commitment on "Sound recording distribution services" included the distribution of sound recordings by electronic means largely "inconclusive". In China's view, when confronted with such a high level of ambiguity, the Panel should have applied the *in dubio mitius* principle and refrained from adopting the interpretation that was the least favourable to China. The United States responds that there was no basis for applying the *in dubio mitius* principle in this dispute because the Panel correctly interpreted China's GATS specific commitment based on Articles 31 and 32 of the *Vienna Convention.*

Also, the Appellate Body sometimes directly uses the Latin maxims. For instance, the Appellate Body states in its Report on *Japan—Alcoholic Beverages II* that "… A fundamental tenet of treaty interpretation flowing from the general rule of interpretation set out in Article 31 is the principle of effectiveness (*ut res magis valeat quam pereat*)."[8]

However, the means of treaty interpretation are already included in the set of rules provided in Articles 31–33 of the VCLT, which do not explicitly include these Latin maxims. Hence the Latin maxims do not have a "direct position" in the VCLT. The appropriate way to have these maxims being introduced into the treaty interpretation process is through Article 32. Hence, a correct use of such principles should be to use these principles under the instruction of Article 32 only to supplement the interpretation based on the provisions in Article 31.

Second, as explained in the preceding chapter, Article 32 of the VCLT requires that recourse may be had to supplementary means only for two purposes: The first purpose is to *confirm* the meaning resulting from the application of Article 31. The second purpose is to *determine* the meaning of the interpreted term when the interpretation according to Article 31 could still leave the meaning ambiguous or

---

[7]Appellate Body Report, *China—Measures Affecting Trading Rights and Distribution Services for Certain Publications and Audiovisual Entertainment Products*, para. 410, WTO Doc. WT/DS363/AB/R (adopted 19 Jan 2010) [hereinafter China—Publications and Audiovisual Products Appellate Body Report].

[8]Appellate Body Report, *Japan—Taxes on Alcoholic Beverages*, p. 12, WTO Doc. WT/DS8/AB/R, WT/DS10/AB/R, WT/DS11/AB/R (adopted 1 Nov 1996) [hereinafter Japan—Alcoholic Beverages II Appellate Body Report].

obscure, or to *replace and revert* the interpretation based on Article 31 if such interpretation leads to a manifestly absurd or unreasonable result. It is understandable that such Latin maxims or principles can help (1) *confirm* the meaning resulting from the application of Article 31 or (2) *determine* the meaning of the interpreted term when the interpretation according to Article 31 could still leave the meaning ambiguous or obscure. However, it is very unlikely, if not absolutely impossible, that such Latin maxims can be applied so as to suggest that the interpretation based on Article 31 leads to a manifestly absurd or unreasonable result and hence such interpretation should be *replaced and reverted* by the interpretation based on such maxims. In other words, the supplementary functions of these maxims are limited to the *confirming function* provided in the introductory part of Article 32 (to confirm the meaning resulting from the application of Article 31) and the part of the *determining function* provided in Article 32(a) (to determine the meaning when the interpretation according to Article 31 leaves the meaning ambiguous or obscure). But they basically should not be given the *determining function* provided in Article 32(b) (to determine the meaning when the interpretation according to Article 31 leads to a result which is manifestly absurd or unreasonable) so as to produce an opposite result from Article 31.

Third, whether or not a "principle" will be considered as a supplementary means could sometimes be controversial. But at least, there is no need to recognize an interpretation principle (or a Latin maxim) as part of the customary international law rules (or part of the customary rules of treaty interpretation) in order for an interpreter to resort to it as a supplementary means. Since such principles are merely supplementary, as long as any one of these "principles" (or Latin maxims) is useful to support the reasoning of interpretation, an interpreter should be permitted to use it under the requirements provided in Article 32 of the VCLT.

14.1.3 Non-exclusiveness and Open-Endedness of Articles 31–33

It was mentioned in the preceding chapter that Article 32 lists two examples of supplementary means, i.e. the preparatory work of the treaty and the circumstances of its conclusion. These two elements for interpretation are only illustrations. In other words, the provision in Article 32 concerning the scope of supplementary means is broader than the listed examples. Hence, the supplementary means listed in Article 32 are non-exhaustive. It allows various other interpretation principles to be introduced into the procedure as supplementary means either to confirm the interpretation based on Article 31 or to determine the interpretation when an interpretation based on Article 31 would lead to ambiguous situation as described in Article 32(a).

It must be further noted that not only the list in Article 32 concerning the supplementary means is non-exhaustive, the whole provisions in Articles 31–33 of the VCLT can be considered as non-exclusive and open-ended. There are always additional elements to be introduced into the interpretation process. For example, the time factor could affect the interpretation. An interpreter sometimes cannot ignore the time factor so as to adopt an evolutive interpretation. Also holistic interpretation is not explicitly provided in the VCLT, but it plays the key role in treaty interpretation practice. Interpreting a treaty term or provision by giving a formula is not indicated in the VCLT, but it is very often used as an approach for treaty interpretation when an interpreted treaty term is a key requirement in a provision but is so abstract and vastly uncertain.

Hence, it should be appropriate to state that the VCLT concerning its treaty interpretation provisions is non-exclusive in the sense that other relevant and appropriate elements can be introduced for interpretation purpose.

In the following sections of this chapter, discussions will focus on three of the above mentioned Latin maxims concerning their practical applications in the treaty interpretation process.

14.2 Principe of (Maximum) Effectiveness

14.2.1 Meaning of (Maximum) Effectiveness and Its Status in Treaty Interpretation

The *principle of effectiveness* or the *principle of maximum effectiveness (ut res magis valeat quam pereat)* is described by Fitzmaurice as: "texts are to be presumed to have been intended to have a definite force and effect, and should be interpreted so as to have such force and effect rather than so as not to have it and so as to have the *fullest* value and effect consistent with their wording."[9] (Emphasis original) Hence, the key idea here is to give fullest value and effect to the textual wording in the treaty. The result is similar to the interpretation based on the textualism, which emphasizes the textual language as the prime basis for treaty interpretation.

The *principle of maximum effectiveness* has been constantly used in domestic and some regional contexts, for instance in the interpretation of a constitution or in the interpretation and application of European Union rules. For treaty interpretation, the legal status of such principle is not absolutely clear.

For example, the ICJ had once rejected the principle of maximum effectiveness in its 1950 Advisory Opinion, in which the ICJ ruled that peace treaties concluded by eastern European states containing arbitration clauses could not be interpreted in a way to give the UN Secretary General a power to appoint arbitrators, if the states involved had refused to appoint or to give power to the Secretary General to do so.[10]

---

[9]Fitzmaurice (1951), p. 8.

[10]Treaty Interpretation. http://www.judicialmonitor.org/archive_0906/generalprinciples.html. Accessed 21 Aug 2017.

Although the ICJ does not recognize the *principle of maximum effectiveness* in relation to the above mentioned case, it should not be understood to mean that the principle has no legal status in treaty interpretation. Again, Article 32 of the VCLT states in part that "recourse may be had to supplementary means of interpretation … to confirm the meaning, … or to determine the meaning when …." In other words, it is the discretion of the treaty interpreter to decide whether to have recourse to a supplementary means of interpretation. The rejection of the application in a specific case does not necessarily constitute an overall denial of the existence and possible application of the *principle of maximum effectiveness*. It only means that in that particular case, the application of this principle is not appropriate either due to its contradiction to the result of interpretation arising from Article 31 or due to its lack of helpfulness to the interpretation of a treaty term or provision.

Giving the "fullest value and effect" to the textual wordings can be achieved through giving the fullest value and effect to the ordinary meaning of the textual language so as not to negate or undermine the term used or, when the wording is not clear, through the teleological interpretation so as to give fullest value and effect to the object-and-purpose of the treaty based on context of a treaty term or provision. Hence, it is not only a separate/independent supplementary principle, but also a principle to support the interpretation based on the ordinary meaning, context, and the object-and-purpose.

There could be slightly different phrases used to refer to the same or similar rules. For instance, the "principle of effectiveness" very often used by the Appellate Body of the WTO is to consider *every word in the treaty with some meaning intended by the drafter* and also to consider the difference in the words used with some intended meaning. Concerning the possible difference between the *principle of effectiveness* and the *principle of maximum effectiveness*, it could be said that under the *principle of effectiveness*, a higher weight should be given to the textual language, whereas under the *principle of maximum effectiveness*, a higher weight should be given to the object-and-purpose so that the ultimate goal of a treaty can be achieved through interpretation.

14.2.2 Its Application: WTO Jurisprudence as an Example

The WTO Appellate Body does not adopt the same position as the ICJ. Instead, the Appellate Body is actually relying on the principle of effectiveness in its analysis. For instance, in *US—Shrimp-Turtle I*, the Appellate Body states: "We hold that, in line with the principle of effectiveness in treaty interpretation, measures to conserve exhaustible natural resources, whether living or non-living, may fall within Article XX(g)."[11] Although the Appellate Body indicates that it is relying on the *principle*

[11]Appellate Body Report, *United States—Import Prohibition of Certain Shrimp and Shrimp Products*, para. 131, WTO Doc. WT/DS58/AB/R (adopted 6 Nov 1998).

of effectiveness in this case, a commentator considers this approach being more like a “broad interpretation”, i.e. “giving the provisions to be interpreted maximum effect from the standpoint of their legal efficacy.”[12]

There are many other WTO cases, in which the Appellate Body expressed once and again its recognition of the principle of effectiveness. It treats the principle of effectiveness as an important part or as a *corollary* of the general rule of treaty interpretation. For instance, in *Japan—Alcoholic beverages II*, the Appellate Body considered the principle as a fundamental tenet of the general rule of treaty interpretation. It states: “A fundamental tenet of treaty interpretation flowing from the general rule of interpretation set out in Article 31 is the principle of effectiveness (*ut res magis valeat quam pereat*). …”[13]

The principle of effectiveness is closely related to the textual interpretation in the sense that all textual wordings are not to be ignored. For instance, in *US—Gasoline*, the Appellate Body states in its Report that:

> … One of the corollaries of the “general rule of interpretation” in the *Vienna Convention* is that interpretation must give meaning and effect to all the terms of the treaty. An interpreter is not free to adopt a reading that would result in reducing whole clauses or paragraphs of a treaty to redundancy or inutility.[14]

In some cases, the Appellate Body explicitly or impliedly uses this principle to support the textual wording in a treaty. For instance, in *Canada—Dairy*, the Appellate Body states in its Report that:

> … the task of the treaty interpreter is to ascertain and give effect to a legally operative meaning for the terms of the treaty. The applicable fundamental principle of *effet utile* is that a treaty interpreter is not free to adopt a meaning that would reduce parts of a treaty to redundancy or inutility.[15]

Another example of the Appellate Body using the principle of effectiveness is to support the overall reading of the whole treaty provisions. This is basically using the principle to confirm the contextual reading of the treaty provision as provided in Article 32 of the VCLT. In *Argentina—Footwear (EC)*, the Appellate Body has the following explanation in its Report:

> … a treaty interpreter must read all applicable provisions of a treaty in a way that gives meaning to *all* of them, harmoniously. And, an appropriate reading of this “inseparable package of rights and disciplines” must, accordingly, be one that gives meaning to *all* the relevant provisions of these two equally binding agreements.

---

[12]Stern (2006), p. 91.

[13]Japan—Alcoholic Beverages II Appellate Body Report, *supra* note 8.

[14]Appellate Body Report, *United States—Standards for Reformulated and Conventional Gasoline*, p. 23, WTO Doc. WT/DS2/AB/R (adopted 20 May 1996).

[15]Appellate Body Report, *Canada—Measures Affecting the Importation of Milk and the Exportation of Dairy Products*, para. 133, WTO Doc. WT/DS103/AB/R, WT/DS113/AB/R, WT/DS103/AB/R/Corr.1, WT/DS113/AB/R/Corr.1 (adopted 27 Oct 1999).

> Our reading of these prerequisites does precisely this, by making certain that *all* the relevant provisions of the *Agreement on Safeguards* and Article XIX of the GATT 1994 relating to safeguard measures are given their full meaning and their full legal effect. …[16]

Also in *Korea—Dairy*, the Appellate Body has similar points about using the principle of effectiveness to support the overall reading of the related provisions. It states in its Report on this case the following:[17]

> In light of the interpretive principle of effectiveness, it is the *duty* of any treaty interpreter to "read all applicable provisions of a treaty in a way that gives meaning to *all* of them, harmoniously". An important corollary of this principle is that a treaty should be interpreted as a whole, and, in particular, its sections and parts should be read as a whole. Article II:2 of the *WTO Agreement* expressly manifests the intention of the Uruguay Round negotiators that the provisions of the *WTO Agreement* and the Multilateral Trade Agreements included in its Annexes 1, 2 and 3 must be read as a whole.

Another similar statement about using the principle of effectiveness to support the overall reading of the treaty provisions is found in the Appellate Body Report on *US—Upland Cotton*, in which it states:[18]

> … Furthermore, as the Appellate Body has explained, "a treaty interpreter must read all applicable provisions of a treaty in a way that gives meaning to all of them, harmoniously". We agree with the Panel that "Article 3.1(b) of the SCM Agreement can be read together with the Agreement on Agriculture provisions relating to domestic support in a coherent and consistent manner which gives full and effective meaning to all of their terms".

Sometimes the Appellate Body even uses the principle of effectiveness to strengthen the interpretation based on the object-and-purpose of the treaty. In *US—Section 211 Appropriations Act*, the Appellate Body seems to use the principle to support such interpretation:[19]

> Article 8 of the Paris Convention (1967) covers only the protection of trade names; Article 8 has no other subject. If the intention of the negotiators had been to exclude trade names from protection, there would have been no purpose whatsoever in including Article 8 in the list of Paris Convention (1967) provisions that were specifically incorporated into the *TRIPS Agreement*. To adopt the Panel's approach would be to deprive Article 8 of the Paris Convention (1967), as incorporated into the *TRIPS Agreement* by virtue of Article 2.1 of that Agreement, of any and all meaning and effect. …

From the WTO jurisprudence, it is apparent that the principle of effectiveness is a useful principle for treaty interpretation and that it can be used to support the

---

[16] Appellate Body Report, *Argentina—Safeguard Measures on Imports of Footwear*, paras. 81, 95, WTO Doc. WT/DS121/AB/R (adopted 12 Jan 2000).

[17] Appellate Body Report, *Korea—Definitive Safeguard Measure on Imports of Certain Dairy Products*, para. 81, WTO Doc. WT/DS98/AB/R (adopted 12 Jan 2000).

[18] Appellate Body Report, *United States—Subsidies on Upland Cotton*, para. 549, WTO Doc. WT/DS267/AB/R (adopted 21 Mar 2005).

[19] Appellate Body Report, *United States—Section 211 Omnibus Appropriations Act of 1998*, para. 338, WTO Doc. WT/DS176/AB/R (adopted 2 Jan 2002).

textual and teleological interpretations of a treaty provision. But what the WTO jurisprudence fails to address is whether the introduction of the principle of effectiveness should be made through Article 32 of the VCLT.

14.3 Principle of *in Dubio Mitius*

14.3.1 Meaning of in Dubio Mitius *and Its Status in Treaty Interpretation*

The principle of *in dubio mitius* is understood as giving to a term the meaning "which is less onerous to the party assuming an obligation or which interferes less with the territorial and personal supremacy of a party, or involves less general restrictions upon the parties".[20] This is sometimes considered as "restrictive interpretation" in the sense that it requires to interpret treaty obligations in deference to the sovereignty of States.[21] It is also called "restrictive interpretation in favour of state sovereignty".[22]

The reason for having such principle is to protect and to pay deference to the sovereignty of the parties to a treaty.[23] Since almost all international treaties are to impose obligations on States or to limit the exercise of States' sovereignty, the principle of paying deference to the sovereignty cannot be interpreted in a broad manner so as to allow contracting parties escaping their commitments and obligations under a treaty. Nor should it be considered as an absolute rule for treaty law, otherwise, States' responsibilities to faithfully fulfil their obligations as required by a treaty could be seriously undermined.

The principle of *in dubio mitius* is not specified in the VCLT, but it should still be considered as a supplementary means for a treaty interpreter to take into account. For treaty interpretation, such principle can only serve as a supplementary means in its function and application, subject to the requirements provided in Article 32 of the VCLT.

Under Article 32, there are two situations where the principle of *in dubio mitius* can be relevant and applied. First, this principle can be used to confirm the interpretation based on Article 31 of the VCLT so as to strengthen the reasoning of the interpreter. Second, it can also be used to decide the interpretation if the application of Article 31 would lead to ambiguous or obscure situation. But it must be noted again that an interpreter should not apply the principle of *in dubio mitius* so as to

[20]Appellate Body Report, *European Communities—Measures Concerning Meat and Meat Products (Hormones)*, para. 165, fn. 154, WTO Doc. WT/DS26/AB/R, WT/DS48/AB/R (adopted 13 Feb 1998) [hereinafter EC—Hormones Appellate Body Report].

[21]Larouer (2009).

[22]Crema (2010).

[23]Van Damme (2009), p. 61.

decide that because of (or as a result of) such principle, an interpretation based on Article 31 in a particular case should be considered as leading to a manifestly absurd or unreasonable result and that the principle should be applied to replace the interpretation based on Article 31.

14.3.2 Its Application: WTO Jurisprudence as an Example

The Appellate Body has actually applied this principle of *in dubio mitius* to confirm that a far reaching obligation needs to be supported by a very specific and compelling treaty language. So this principle is to support or confirm an interpretation based on the textual language of a treaty provision. It states in its Report on *EC—Hormones* the following:

> … We cannot lightly assume that sovereign states intended to impose upon themselves the more onerous, rather than the less burdensome, obligation by mandating *conformity* or *compliance with* such standards, guidelines and recommendations. To sustain such an assumption and to warrant such a far-reaching interpretation, treaty language far more specific and compelling than that found in Article 3 of the *SPS Agreement* would be necessary.[24]

The principle of *in dubio mitius* might not always be relevant and applicable if an interpretation based on Article 31 of the VCLT is able to lead to a proper conclusion. For instance, in *China—Publications and Audiovisual Products*, the Appellate Body cited the disputing parties' arguments on the application of the principle and concluded by stating that the principle is not applicable in that case. The following quoted sentences have been partly quoted above:[25]

> China claims that the Panel should have found that the application of both Articles 31 and 32 of the *Vienna Convention* left the issue of whether China's GATS commitment on "Sound recording distribution services" included the distribution of sound recordings by electronic means largely "inconclusive". In China's view, when confronted with such a high level of ambiguity, the Panel should have applied the *in dubio mitius* principle and refrained from adopting the interpretation that was the least favourable to China. The United States responds that there was no basis for applying the *in dubio mitius* principle in this dispute because the Panel correctly interpreted China's GATS specific commitment based on Articles 31 and 32 of the *Vienna Convention*.
>
> We have found above that the Panel did not err in its interpretation of "Sound recording distribution services" in accordance with Article 31 of the *Vienna Convention*. We have expressed the view that the Panel's recourse to Article 32 of the *Vienna Convention* was not in error, but that it was also not necessary, given that the application of Article 31 yielded a conclusion on the proper interpretation of this entry in China's GATS Schedule. We have also observed that we see no error in the Panel's analysis under Article 32. We therefore do not accept China's contention that the Panel should have found that the meaning of the

---

[24]EC—Hormones Appellate Body Report, *supra* note 20, at para. 165, fn. 154.

[25]China—Publications and Audiovisual Products Appellate Body Report, *supra* note 7, at paras. 410–411.

> entry "Sound recording distribution services" remains inconclusive or ambiguous after its analysis under Articles 31 and 32 of the *Vienna Convention*. Consequently, even if the principle of *in dubio mitius* were relevant in WTO dispute settlement, there is no scope for its application in this dispute.

Hence, in this case, the principle of *in dubio mitius* was not applied by the Appellate Body not because of the lack of a status of the principle in the VCLT, but because of its irrelevancy in this particular case.

14.4 Exception to Be Interpreted Narrowly?

14.4.1 Meaning and Status of the "Principle" Under Treaty Interpretation

Similar to domestic law, an international treaty also contains some general rules and, possibly, certain exceptions to the general rules. There is an issue about whether exceptions should be subject to a different rule of interpretation. In domestic context, the *principle of exception to be interpreted narrowly* is a commonly applied rule for statutory interpretation. For instance, the German Federal Supreme Court considers the exemptions under the copyright law as exceptions which must be interpreted narrowly.[26]

In international context, a possible view on the status of such *principle of exception to be interpreted narrowly* is that the general rules in a treaty set forth the guiding principles so as to support the achievement of the treaty, whereas the exceptions are to deviate from the achievement of the goal of the treaty; hence the exceptions need to be interpreted narrowly or more strictly so as to reduce the possible hindrance of the achievement of the objective of the treaty. On the other hand, there could also be a possible opposite view against such *principle of exception to be interpreted narrowly* that the exceptions also contain special rules which are generally applicable if the facts provided for in the treaty do exist; hence the validity of such *principle of exception to be interpreted narrowly* should be rejected.[27]

In the pre-WTO age, the practice of the GATT 1947 has been that the general exceptions provided in Article XX of the GATT (which are exceptions to, for example, the most-favoured-nation treatment in GATT Article I, the national treatment in GATT Article II, and the general elimination of quantitative restrictions in GATT Article XI) must be interpreted narrowly. For instance, the GATT 1947 panel in *Tuna I* stated in its Report that:

> … previous panels had established that Article XX is a limited and conditional exception from obligations under other provisions of the General Agreement, and not a positive rule

[26]Holzapfel and Werner (2009), p. 103.

[27]Conrad (2011), p. 266.

establishing obligations in itself. Therefore, the practice of panels has been to interpret Article XX narrowly.[28]

But the GATT 1947's panels did not explain much in its reasoning of applying such principle of exception to be interpreted narrowly.[29] As a commentator mentioned: "This interpretation rule can be explained with the relatively common perception that exceptions mitigate the effectiveness of the rules to which they form an exception and thus impede the attainment of the law's objectives."[30]

14.4.2 Its Application: WTO Jurisprudence as an Example

Although there is the Latin maxim of *exceptio est strictissimae applicationis* (meaning that an exception is of the strictest application), the Appellate Body does not apply such *principle of exceptions to be interpreted narrowly or strictly*. Instead, it focuses on the ordinary meaning to be given to the textual language in its context and in the light of the object-and-purpose of the treaty, as required by the provisions in Article 31 of the VCLT. The Appellate Body states in its report on *EC – Hormones* the following:[31]

> [M]erely characterizing a treaty provision as an "exception" does not by itself justify a "stricter" or "narrower" interpretation of that provision than would be warranted by examination of the ordinary meaning of the actual treaty words, viewed in context and in the light of the treaty's object and purpose, or, in other words, by applying the normal rules of treaty interpretation.

The Appellate Body's view of "not by itself justify[ing] a stricter or narrower interpretation" should not be seen as totally excluding the possible application and usefulness of the *principle of exceptions to be interpreted narrowly*. First, the Appellate Body's position is in line with Article 32 of the VCLT in that principles other than those provided in Article 31 are only supplementary in their nature and functions. Hence, all supplementary means, including the *principle of exceptions to be interpreted narrowly*, can only be applied so as to confirm the interpretation under Article 31 or, when the result under Article 31 will be ambiguous or obscure, to determine the interpretation. In other words, all supplementary means do not "by themselves" justify any *direct and independent use* for treaty interpretation purpose.

---

[28] Report of the Panel, *United States—Restrictions on Imports of Tuna*, para. 5.22, DS21/R (3 Sept 1991), GATT B.I.S.D. (39th Supp.) at 155.

[29] See for instance, Report of the Panel, European Economic Community—Restrictions on Imports of Apples—Complaint by the United States, para. 5.13, L/6513 (9 June 1989), GATT B.I.S.D. (36th Supp.) at 135; United States—Countervailing Duties on Fresh, Chilled and Frozen Port from Canada, para. 4.4, DS7/R (18 Sept 1990), GATT B.I.S.D. (38th Supp.) at 30. Also see Feichtner (2012), p. 243.

[30] Id.

[31] EC—Hormones Appellate Body Report, *supra* note 20, at para. 104.

They can only be considered together with the principles provided in Article 31. So the *principle of exceptions to be interpreted narrowly* is of no difference from other supplementary principles. But this does not mean that this principle cannot be used to support or supplement the application of Article 31.

Second, actually, in the above case of *EC—Hormones*, the Appellate Body was able to come to a conclusion of interpretation based on Article 31. Therefore, there was no need to use this *principle of exception to be interpreted narrowly* to confirm the conclusion. Neither was there a need to use this principle to *determine* the interpretation, because the result of interpretation under Article 31 of the VCLT did not lead to ambiguous or obscure situation. Hence it is understandable for the Appellate Body not to consider the *principle of exception to be interpreted narrowly* in this case. The Appellate Body's view should not be used to deny the possible use and usefulness of this principle in supplementing Article 31, under the conditions provided in Article 32 of the VCLT.

To conclude this chapter, it should be useful to clarify in a codified set of treaty interpretation rules that the two situations listed in Article 32 of the VCLT (i.e. the preparatory work of the treaty and the circumstances of its conclusion) are non-exhaustive and that Latin maxims (especially *lex specialis derogat legi generali*; *lex posterior derogat legi priori*; *expressio unius est exclusio alterius*; *in dubio mitius*; *ut res magis valeat quam perat*; and *exceptio est strictissimae applicationis*) can be considered by a treaty interpreter as supplementary means when he/she conducts treaty interpretation. However, these principles are only supplementary means as provided in VCLT Article 32. More specifically, such Latin maxims can help *confirm* the meaning resulting from the application of Article 31 or *determine* the meaning of the interpreted term when the interpretation according to Article 31 could still leave the meaning ambiguous or obscure. However, an interpreter should avoid applying these Latin maxims to suggest that the interpretation based on Article 31 leads to a manifestly absurd or unreasonable result and hence such interpretation should be *replaced and reverted* by these Latin maxims.

It should also be useful to indicate in the codified set of rules that the whole provisions in Articles 31–33 of the VCLT should be considered as non-exclusive and open-ended. There could be additional elements (such as the time factor and the holistic interpretation) to be introduced into the interpretation process.

References

Conrad CR (2011) Processes and production methods (PPMs) in WTO law: interfacing trade and social goals. Cambridge University Press, Cambridge

Crema L (2010) Disappearance and new sightings of restrictive interpretation(s). http://ejil.oxfordjournals.org/content/21/3/681.full. Accessed 21 Aug 2017

Feichtner I (2012) The law and politics of waivers—stability and flexibility in public international law. Cambridge University Press, Cambridge

Fellmeth AX, Horwitz M (2011) Guide to latin in international law. http://www.oxfordreference.com/view/10.1093/acref/9780195369380.001.0001/acref-9780195369380-e-1303. Accessed 21 Aug 2017

Fitzmaurice GG (1951) The law and procedure of the international court of justice: treaty interpretation and certain other treaty points. Br Yearb Int Law 28:1–28

Holzapfel H, Werner G (2009) Interpreting exceptions in intellectual property law. In: Prinz zu Waldeck und Pyrmont W, Adelman MJ, Brauneis R, Drexl J, Nack R (eds) Patents and technological progress in a globalized world: Liber Amicorum Joseph Straus. Springer, Berlin, pp 99–114

Larouer CJ (2009) In the Name of Sovereignty? The Battle over in Dubio Mitius Inside and Outside the Courts. In: Paper presented at Cornell law school inter-University graduate student conference papers. http://scholarship.law.cornell.edu/cgi/viewcontent.cgi?article=1050&context=lps_clacp. Accessed 21 Aug 2017

Stern B (2006) DS 58: United States—import prohibition of certain Shrimp and Shrimp products. In: Stern B, Fabri HR (eds) The case-law of the WTO: 1998-2. Springer, Leiden, pp 64–105

Treaty Interpretation. http://www.judicialmonitor.org/archive_0906/generalprinciples.html. Accessed 21 Aug 2017

Van Damme I (2009) Treaty interpretation by the WTO appellate body. Oxford University Press, Oxford

Chapter 15
Time Factor, Technological Development, Evolutive Interpretation and the Possible Codification

Contents

15.1 The Time Factor in Treaty Law

There are many dimensions where the time factor could have implications for or could even directly affect the operation of a treaty.

The first dimension of the time factor is about a treaty's timewise application. It is to decide a treaty's scope of application in terms of time. In other words, whether the time at which a fact occurred is within or beyond the reach of a treaty needs to be decided by the adjudicator based on certain principles. As oppose to the issue of "territorial reach" or "territorial scope" of a treaty (which is provided in Article 29 of the VCLT that unless a different intention appears from the treaty or is otherwise established, a treaty is binding upon each party in respect of its entire territory), the aspect of timewise treaty application can be called the issue of "timely reach" of a treaty.

C. Lo, *Treaty Interpretation Under the Vienna Convention on the Law of Treaties*,
https://doi.org/10.1007/978-981-10-6866-9_15

If a fact occurred at a time after the entry into force of a treaty, the application of the treaty to the fact does not give rise to a retroactive problem. However, if the fact occurred (and had completed) at a time prior to the entry into force of a treaty, the application of the treaty to the fact becomes a retroactive application. Article 28 of the VCLT (entitled "Non-retroactivity of treaties") basically does not allow a retroactive application of a treaty. It provides: "Unless a different intention appears from the treaty or is otherwise established, its provisions do not bind a party in relation to any act or fact which took place or any situation which ceased to exist before the date of the entry into force of the treaty with respect to that party."

The second dimension of the time factor concerns a "specific point in time" at which certain legal effects are given to a treaty or to its provisions. For instance, in Article 24.1 of the VCLT (regarding the entry into force of a treaty), a specific point in time agreed upon by the negotiating parties is set to decide the commencement date for a treaty. It provides: "A treaty enters into force in such manner and upon such date as it may provide or as the negotiating States may agree." Also Article 24.3 of the VCLT specifies the commencement date for a State to be bound by a treaty. It states: "When the consent of a State to be bound by a treaty is established on a date after the treaty has come into force, the treaty enters into force for that State on that date, unless the treaty otherwise provides."

It is also possible that, based on specific treaty provisions, a domestic practice or law having existed prior to a specific point in time could affect the application of a treaty based on its "grandfather clause". For instance, in the age of GATT 1947 (which was the age prior to the establishment of the WTO in 1994), there was the *Protocol of Provisional Application* (PPA) adopted by the original contracting parties to the GATT in 1947, which stated in part that "Part II of the GATT" (which includes, for instance, Article III of the national treatment requirement and Article XI of general elimination of quantitative restrictions among many other provisions from Articles III to XXIII) would be applied "to the fullest extent not inconsistent with existing legislation". This provision actually permitted the continuance of the then-existing national legislations which were supposed to be in violation of the GATT provisions in Part II. This provision in the PPA was called the "grandfather clause".

A related aspect is a modified legal effect of treaty application to be given at a specific point in time. The above mentioned PPA is an example. It provides in part that "The Governments … undertake … to apply provisionally on and after 1 January 1948: (a) Parts I and III of the General Agreement on Tariffs and Trade, and (b) Part II of that Agreement to the fullest extent not inconsistent with existing legislation." The specific point in time (i.e. 1 January 1948) was the time to give an effect of provisional application (instead of definitive application) of the certain parts of the GATT 1947.

The third dimension of the time factor is the "time limit" or "time period" for the contracting parties to a treaty to complete certain required actions or for certain parties to enjoy certain rights or privileges created in the treaty. There could be the general procedures for all contracting parties to complete some acts or works together (either jointly or separately) within a specified period of time. For instance, the negotiating parties can collectively decide to set a target date to complete their commitments for reducing emissions of carbon or pollution under an environmental treaty; for removing certain trade barriers under a trade agreement; or for implementing the progressive reduction of tariffs according to the committed stages and timeframe. There could also be a time limit for an individual contracting party, a disputing party, an organization or its body to complete certain actions. For instance, a party in a dispute could be required to present its submissions, responses or appeal within a certain specified time period. A WTO dispute settlement panel and the Appellate Body are also expected to complete their procedures within certain time periods. For instance, Article 12.8 of the DSU specifies the time period for a panel to complete its procedures: "In order to make the procedures more efficient, the period in which the panel shall conduct its examination, from the date that the composition and terms of reference of the panel have been agreed upon until the date the final report is issued to the parties to the dispute, shall, as a general rule, not exceed six months..." Article 17.5 of the DSU specifies the time period for the Appellate Body to complete its procedures: "As a general rule, the proceedings shall not exceed 60 days from the date a party to the dispute formally notifies its decision to appeal to the date the Appellate Body circulates its report...".

There could also be a specified time period (such as a grace period, a transition period, or a flexibility in terms of implementation time) within which certain contracting parties are given with a right or privilege to continue certain existing practices or to perform certain existing actions. For instance, in the TRIPS Agreement, there are different transition periods provided for all Members, for developing country Members, and for Members in economic transition to implement their respective obligations under the agreement.[1] Also for instance, Article 1 (f) of the Agreement on Agriculture under the WTO defines the implementation period for the commitments made by WTO Members as "the six-year period commencing in the year 1995, except that, for the purposes of Article 13, it means the nine-year period commencing in 1995".

The fourth dimension is the time lapse as a cause or a variation in treaty application or interpretation. For example, a change of circumstance after the lapse

---

[1]For example, paragraphs 1–3 of Article 65 of the TRIPS Agreement (entitled "Transitional Arrangements") provides:

1. Subject to the provisions of paragraphs 2, 3 and 4, no Member shall be obliged to apply the provisions of this Agreement before the expiry of a general period of one year following the date of entry into force of the WTO Agreement.
2. A developing country Member is entitled to delay for a further period of four years the date of application, as defined in paragraph 1, of the provisions of this Agreement other than Articles 3, 4 and 5.
3. Any other Member which is in the process of transformation from a centrally-planned into a market, free-enterprise economy and which is undertaking structural reform of its intellectual property system and facing special problems in the preparation and implementation of intellectual property laws and regulations, may also benefit from a period of delay as foreseen in paragraph 2.

of certain time periods can affect the application or operation of certain treaty provisions. Article 62.1 of the VCLT provides in this regard that:

> A fundamental change of circumstances which has occurred with regard to those existing at the time of the conclusion of a treaty, and which was not foreseen by the parties, may not be invoked as a ground for terminating or withdrawing from the treaty unless: (a) the existence of those circumstances constituted an essential basis of the consent of the parties to be bound by the treaty; and (b) the effect of the change is radically to transform the extent of obligations still to be performed under the treaty.

The evolution of time can become a factor to decide the consideration of treaty interpretation approaches, such as whether to adopt contemporaneous or evolutive interpretation. Sometimes the evolution of time itself is a factor to affect the treaty interpretation approach; sometimes the evolution of time coupled with other factors (such as technological innovation) serves as a collective element to affect treaty interpretation approach. These will be further discussed in the later parts of this chapter.

The fifth dimension is the time factor to be directly integrated into the treaty interpretation rules. For instance, Article 31.2 of the VCLT is about any agreement or instrument made "in connexion with the conclusion of the treaty". If an agreement or instrument is to be considered as being made in connection with the conclusion of the treaty, it must be made *at the time which can be linked to the conclusion of the interpreted treaty*. Also for instance, Article 31.3 of the VCLT requires "any subsequent agreement" (provided in Article 31.3(a)) and "any subsequent practice" (provided in Article 31.3(b)) to be taken into account. The term "subsequent" implies that an agreement or practice must exist *later in time after the conclusion of the interpreted treaty*.

Article 31.3(c) also requires "any relevant rules of international law applicable in the relations between the parties" to be taken into account. "It does not limit this reference to other rules of international law to those that existed *at the time of conclusion* of the treaty, nor does it explicitly include other law that had developed *at the time of application*."[2] Hence, it is a reasonable understanding that such "rules of international law" can include the rules which have already existed at the time when the interpreted treaty was concluded as well as the rules which came to exist after the conclusion of the treaty. The key requirement is that such rules must be "relevant" to the interpretation of the interpreted treaty. Hence, Article 31.3(c) does not exclude the "evolutive" or "contemporaneous" principle in the sense that both the previously and currently existing "rules of international law" can be taken into account.

The two examples (i.e. the preparatory work and the circumstances of conclusion) provided in Article 32 of the VCLT also have the time factors involved. The

---

[2]Pauwelyn J, The Nature of WTO Obligations. http://www.jeanmonnetprogram.org/archive/papers/02/020101-02.html#P296_86702. Accessed 21 Aug 2017.

preparatory works must be those works prepared or existed prior to the time of the conclusion of the interpreted treaty. The circumstances of conclusion must also be the circumstances *at the time* or *reasonably immediately prior to the time* when the interpreted treaty was concluded.

15.2 Evolution of Time as a Factor to Affect Treaty Interpretation

15.2.1 Does the Evolutive or Contemporaneous Interpretation Relate to the Application of "Ordinary Meaning" and Others?

As mentioned above, a pure evolution of time itself can be a factor to affect the treaty interpretation approach. The main issue is whether a treaty interpreter would have to interpret a treaty term based on the understanding *at the time when the term was used in the treaty* or based on the evolutionary understanding *at the time when the dispute arises* or *when the treaty provision is interpreted*. An *evolutive or evolutionary interpretation* is to interpret a treaty term by giving an "evolutive meaning" to it based on the current understanding, whereas a *contemporaneous interpretation* is to interpret a term by giving an "static meaning" to it based on the understanding of the term at the time of treaty conclusion.

Hence, an evolutive interpretation is an approach which allows a term to be interpreted differently when time evolves. As a result, a term can be interpreted to mean something in a dispute being handled many years ago, but interpreted to mean another thing in a current dispute. It is also possible that in the future time, the term can be further interpreted to have another meaning which is different from the current understanding of the term so as to meet the development or the change of circumstances. The essence is that the meaning of a term can be evolved and changed.

The main issue concerning the evolutive or contemporaneous interpretation is on the proper "ordinary meaning" to be given to a treaty term or provision. That is to say, the issue is whether it should be "the *ordinary meaning* commonly understood at the time when the treaty was concluded" or "the *ordinary meaning* commonly understood at the time when a dispute arises or when the treaty provision is interpreted" to be given to the interpreted term or provision based on Article 31.1 of the VCLT.

It must be noted that although the decision on whether to adopt the evolutive or contemporaneous interpretation mainly concerns the identification of an ordinary meaning to be given to a treaty term or provision, it does not mean that such issue does not exist in connection with the contextual and teleological interpretations. Actually, the relevance of the evolutive or contemporaneous interpretation with the "context" of the interpreted term and the "object-and-purpose" of the interpreted treaty also exists.

Contextual interpretation sometimes involves an evolutive or contemporaneous interpretation. For example, Article 31.3(c) concerns the "relevant rules of international law" to be taken into account together with context. Such rules could include the evolutive and contemporaneous rules of international law, as explained above. Also other contexts (such as other parts in the main text of a treaty, the preamble, and the annexes which serve as context to the interpreted term or provision) can also be understood evolutively or contemporaneously so that an "evolutive or contemporaneous understanding of the context" can be taken into account when interpreting a term or provision.

Teleological interpretation can also involve an evolutive or contemporaneous interpretation. For instance, before considering the object-and-purpose of a treaty so as to interpret a term or provision, a treaty interpreter would have to interpret "the provision specifying the object-and-purpose" (such as the provisions in Articles 7 and 8 of the TRIPS Agreement). When interpreting such "provision specifying the object-and-purpose of the treaty", the interpreter might encounter the problem of whether to adopt an evolutive or contemporaneous interpretation.

15.2.2 A General Tendency to Consider Evolutive Interpretation

The VCLT does not set a general rule concerning whether to adopt an evolutive or contemporaneous interpretation of a treaty term or provision. Although a contemporaneous interpretation (to interpret a term or provision based on the general understanding at the time when the treaty was negotiated and concluded) would be more in line with the understanding of the treaty negotiators, international adjudicators generally do not reject considering a treaty term or provision based on the understanding at the time of dispute.

There is a widely discussed case of ICJ on the *Dispute regarding Navigational and Related Rights* (*Costa Rica v. Nicaragua*), the dispute of which involved a section of the San Juan River, which flows along the Nicaragua–Costa Rica border into the Caribbean Sea.[3] The disputed section of the River belongs to Nicaragua. Costa Rica claimed that Nicaragua had violated its obligations to allow Costa Rican vessels and their passengers to navigate freely on the River, and not to impose charges or fees, and other obligations concerning the non-imposition of impediments to these rights. The governing treaty was the Treaty of Limits of 1858 between the two countries, which granted Costa Rica "a perpetual right of free

[3]http://www.britannica.com/place/San-Juan-River-Central-America. Accessed 21 Aug 2017.

navigation '*con objetos de comercio*'". One of the issues in the dispute was whether the term "*con objetos de comercio*" ("for the purpose of commerce") merely applied to commerce with articles (i.e. tangible goods). The ICJ found in part that Costa Rica had the right of free navigation on the San Juan River for purposes of commerce, including the transport of passengers and tourists. The Court interpreted the term "for the purposes of commerce" to mean not merely the "commerce with articles" and hence Costa Rica's right of free navigation applied to the transport of persons.[4] The Court interpreted the term *comercio* in an evolutive manner to include commerce of goods (i.e. trade in goods) and commerce without goods (i.e. trade in services),[5] the latter one of which (i.e. trade in services) was not in practice when the treaty was concluded.

Another pertinent example is the WTO dispute in *US—Shrimp*, the Appellate Body interpreted the term "exhaustible natural resources" provided in GATT Article XX(g)[6] in an evolutionary manner to cover "living natural resources". It states in its Report that[7]:

> The words of Article XX(g), "exhaustible natural resources" , were actually crafted more than 50 years ago. They must be read by a treaty interpreter in the light of contemporary concerns of the community of nations about the protection and conservation of the environment. While Article XX was not modified in the Uruguay Round, the preamble attached to the WTO Agreement shows that the signatories to that Agreement were, in 1994, fully aware of the importance and legitimacy of environmental protection as a goal of national and international policy. The preamble of the WTO Agreement—which informs not only the GATT 1994, but also the other covered agreements—explicitly acknowledges "the objective of *sustainable development*"...
>
> From the perspective embodied in the preamble of the WTO Agreement, we note that the generic term 'natural resources' in Article XX(g) is not "static" in its content or reference but is rather "by definition, evolutionary"....
>
> Given the recent acknowledgement by the international community of the importance of concerted bilateral or multilateral action to protect living natural resources, and recalling the explicit recognition by WTO Members of the objective of sustainable development in the preamble of the WTO Agreement, we believe it is too late in the day to suppose that Article XX(g) of the GATT 1994 may be read as referring only to the conservation of exhaustible mineral or other non-living natural resources.

---

[4]The Hague Justice Portal. ICJ Judgment in Costa Rica v. Nicaragua. http://www.haguejusticeportal.net/index.php?id=10811. Accessed 21 Aug 2017.

[5]Judgment, 2009 I.C.J. Rep. at p. 30, para. 66.

[6]Article XX(g) of the GATT provides: "Subject to the requirement that such measures are not applied in a manner which would constitute a means of arbitrary or unjustifiable discrimination between countries where the same conditions prevail, or a disguised restriction on international trade, nothing in this Agreement shall be construed to prevent the adoption or enforcement by any contracting party of measures: … (g) relating to the conservation of exhaustible natural resources if such measures are made effective in conjunction with restrictions on domestic production or consumption".

[7]Appellate Body Report, *United States—Import Prohibition of Certain Shrimp and Shrimp Products*, paras. 129–131, WTO Doc. WT/DS58/AB/R (adopted 6 Nov 1998).

15.2.3 Making "Living Treaty" Through Evolutive Interpretation?

Here, the term "living treaty" (or "living instrument") refers to a treaty (or international instrument) which is understood and interpreted in an evolutive way so as to ensure its adaptation to the new circumstances or new developments without formally revising the treaty by its contracting parties.

Although it is not always the case, most likely a treaty is concluded for a long or unspecified period of duration so as to govern the continuous relations between the contracting parties or to regulate the possibly recurring behaviours. It is unrealistic to have a treaty subject to constant and repeated revisions so as to ensure that it keeps up with the evolution of ideas, concepts, social and economic developments, and technological evolutions, etc. Also a revision of the treaty can be procedurally, substantively and politically complicated and difficult because that an international procedures will have to be initiated; that there could be a long period of time needed for the negotiating parties to come to the conclusion on the revisions; that a possibly difficult balance of new concessions/commitments will have to be struck again during the negotiations; and that a domestic procedure will have to be completed after the new negotiations. In addition, after a certain period, such procedures will have to be restarted and completed all over again so as to keep up with the further new developments. Hence, it is generally desirable that a treaty should not become obsolete immediately after its conclusion or after certain limited period of time of its conclusion, even the treaty is not formally revised by the parties.

An important way to ensure that a treaty is a "living treaty", instead of letting it becoming a "dead treaty", is through an evolutive interpretation so that new ideas and concepts can be introduced into the understanding of the ordinary meaning of the interpreted terms or provisions. If a "living treaty" is desirable, then an evolutive approach for treaty interpretation cannot be ruled out.

15.2.4 Specific Types of Treaties (Such as Human Rights Treaties) Would Require Evolutive Interpretation?

The idea/principle of the living treaty (living instrument) accompanied by the evolutive interpretation is closely relevant to human rights treaties. This is because most human rights treaties specify relevant fundamental rights to be given to human beings and to be protected by States. Most of such treaties have been concluded for decades. It is not practicable to "constantly" revise such treaties. It is almost equally unrealistic merely to make a "limited number of amendments" to the existing human rights treaties because any negotiation to revise an existing human rights treaty could give rise to the need of redefining some protection standards, which could attract long debates and different opinions. Hence, to a lager extent, the interpretation and the proper operation of the human rights treaties need to rely on the idea of "living treaty" and the evolutive method of treaty interpretation.

For instance, it is explained that: "The 'living instrument' doctrine allows the [European Human Rights] Court to update the application of Convention rights to reflect the increasingly high standard being required in the area of the protection of human rights and fundamental liberties."[8] The European Human Rights Court is clearly in favour of such approach and rejects the reliance on the intention of the negotiators of the European Convention on Human Rights (ECHR).[9] In regard to the interpretation of the ECHR, it states in *Tyrer v United Kingdom* (1979)[10]:

> The Convention is a *living instrument* which … must be interpreted in the light of present-day conditions. In the case now before it the Court cannot but be influenced by the developments and commonly accepted standards in the penal policy of the member States of the Council of Europe in this field.

(Emphasis added)

15.2.5 *Requirements for the Use of the Evolutive Interpretation*

Although not all cases which applied the evolutive interpretation specify the requirements for the application of such interpretation, the ICJ has developed a very useful explanation in this regard. It states in *Costa Rica v. Nicaragua* that there are a number of "requirements" for the interpreter to resort to the evolutive interpretation:

> … where the parties have used *generic terms* in a treaty, the parties necessarily having been aware that the meaning of the terms was likely to *evolve over time*, and where the treaty *has been entered into for a very long period or is 'of continuing duration'*, the parties must be presumed, as a general rule, to have intended those terms to have an *evolving meaning* (Emphasis added).[11]

There can be some elaborations for these requirements. First, the interpreted term (which is considered by the interpreter to be subject to the evolutive interpretation) should be generic in nature. In other word, the term must be general and descriptive of an entire and broad group or class of things. If a treaty term is very specific, the room for an evolutive interpretation could be limited or even excluded.

[8]Lee KYR, Expansive Interpretation of the European Convention on Human Rights and the Creative Jurisprudence of the Strasbourg's Court. Mercury – HKU Journal of Undergraduate Humanities 1(1):70–82. http://www.artsfac.hku.hk/mercury/wp-content/uploads/Rosa_Lee1.pdf. Accessed 21 Aug 2017.

[9]The text of the ECHR is available at http://www.echr.coe.int/Documents/Convention_ENG.pdf. Accessed 21 Aug 2017.

[10]25 April 1978, § 31, Series A no. 26 (quoted in *supra* note 8, at p. 72).

[11]*Supra* note 5.

Second, there must be a long period of time or continuing duration for the operation of a treaty for the purpose of justifying the adoption of the evolutive interpretation. If a treaty is concluded for a short duration or for a specific event, an evolutive interpretation would not be applicable. A related issue is the "needed length of time" to justify the use of the approach. The phrases "a very long period" and "continuing duration" suggest that the time period must be long enough so that there have been important new developments or changes of circumstances. It is possible that there has been an important and apparent change of circumstance not very long after the conclusion of a treaty. If this is the case and if not applying an evolutive interpretation would lead to making the treaty obsolete, such circumstance could still justify the application of the evolutive approach to interpret the treaty.

Third, the effect of meeting the above mentioned two requirements (i.e. the term being generic and the duration being continuing) is to presume the parties to have intended the evolutive interpretation. Since this is only a presumption, an adjudicator should be able to rely on a strong and overwhelming evidence to show the clear intent of the parties not to have an evolutive meaning to be given to their treaty term. An interpreter will have to be very careful in overturning the presumption, because it is likely that a treaty can become obsolete or become a dead treaty if an evolutive interpretation is completely excluded.

15.3 Evolution of Time Coupled with the Factor of Technological Innovation to Affect Treaty Interpretation

As mentioned above, an evolution of time itself can be an important factor to affect treaty interpretation approach. Also sometimes the evolution of time *coupled with other factors* (such as *technological innovation*) serves as a collective element to affect treaty interpretation approach. The most apparent example is the change or improvement of science and technologies.

It must be noted that the scientific and technological development has two aspects relating to treaty interpretation. The first aspect is "the time factor involved in the scientific and technological development" which affects treaty interpretation. The second aspect is its relations with the technological neutrality issues, which in turn could also affect treaty interpretation.

Concerning the time factor involved in the scientific and technological development, the most possibly seen situation should be a "technical term" for a technological product being constantly changed to mean something else when time evolves and hence a treaty interpreter is put in a situation to necessarily address the evolutive aspect of the technical term.

In the WTO case of *EC–IT Products*,[12] there involved certain EC measures pertaining to the tariff classifications, and consequent tariff treatments, of certain information technology products, which mainly include *flat panel display devices* ("FPDs") (including those with digital DVI connectors that are capable of connecting to computers and other equipment); *set-top boxes which have a communication function* ("STBCs") (including those that access the Internet and have recording capabilities); and *multifunctional digital machines* ("MFMs") (which are capable of printing, scanning, copying and/or faxing). A fundamental issue here is whether such new products (with new technological functions) should fall within scope of EC's tariff concessions made under the Information Technology Agreement (ITA) because of the functions performed by the new products were similar to the functions performed by the more traditional products which were covered by the concessions or whether they were new products and hence should fall outside the scope of EC's tariff concessions.

The EC basically argued that some information technology products did not exist at the time when the concessions were negotiated and hence they were new products.[13] But the Panel found that: Concerning FPDs, these products should fall within the scope of the "narrative description" and/or within the scope of the CN code 8471 60 90 (which pertains to "input or output units" of "automatic data-processing machines" (ADP)) and hence they should be subject to the duty-free status. Concerning STBCs, they should also fall within the scope of the duty-free commitment in the "narrative description" included in the EC's Schedule. Concerning MFMs that work with ADP machines and certain MFMs that do not work with ADP machines, they should respectively fall within HS1996 subheadings 8471 60 (for "input or output units" of ADP machines) and 8517 21 (for "facsimiles"), both of which should be subject to duty-free status in EC's Schedule. The Panel also found that the type of technology MFMs used to make "copies" is not "photocopying" and, as such, the products could never fall within the dutiable heading under which the EC was classifying these products (HS1996 subheadings 9009 12).[14]

Although the Panel did not explicitly indicate that it was relying on an evolutive interpretation of the EC's tariff concessions, actually the approach adopted by the Panel reflected the essence of the evolutive interpretation and the adoption of such approach was basically because of the development of technologies.

---

[12]Panel Report, *European Communities and its Member States—Tariff Treatment of Certain Information Technology Products*, WTO Doc. WT/DS375/R, WT/DS376/R, WT/DS377/R (adopted 21 Sept 2010); the summary concerning the IT products and their classifications is found at https://www.wto.org/english/tratop_e/dispu_e/cases_e/1pagesum_e/ds376sum_e.pdf. Accessed 21 Aug 2017.

[13]EC's First Written Submission for *EC—Tariff Treatment of Certain Information Technology Products*, paras. 30–49, WT/DS/375, WT/DS/376, WT/DS/377 (2 Apr 2009). Quoted from Peng (2012), p. 411.

[14]See the summary of the case by the WTO Secretariat at https://www.wto.org/english/tratop_e/dispu_e/cases_e/1pagesum_e/ds377sum_e.pdf. Accessed 21 Aug 2017.

15.4 Treaty Interpretation Concerning Technological Development Not Involving a Time Factor

15.4.1 Technological Neutrality

Concerning the technological neutrality, it must be noted that the concept of technological neutrality can involve a time factor, but it does not necessarily have such involvement.

"Technological neutrality" or "technology neutrality" is a widely accepted principle for enacting regulations, particularly in the fields of information and communications technologies.[15] The general meaning of such term is that a regulation should neither favor nor discriminate against a particular technology so that different technologies are ensured with equivalent treatment. It is basically referring to the idea that "different technologies offering essentially similar services should be regulated in similar manners"[16] and "regulators should let the market decide which technology should be used for a particular purpose".[17] Although the definition of "technological neutrality" could still be ambiguous and not precise enough,[18] such definitional explanation is still useful in helping understand the essence of the principle.

Regulatory framework can affect the development of different technologies in a positive or negative way. The principle of technological neutrality is basically applied to the treatment of different technologies. The principle plays an important role in ensuring free development of different technologies. Because of such principle, various technologies are not discriminated and thus are subject to the same footing to enjoy development potentials in the market.

In many jurisdictions, technological neutrality has been considered as a guiding principle for the regulation of various technologies, such as information and communications technologies.[19] Such regulatory principle was specifically mentioned in the report "Framework for Global Electronic Commerce" issued by the United States Government in 1997 that: "rules should be technology-neutral (i.e., the rules should neither require nor assume a particular technology) and forward looking (i.e., the rules should not hinder the use or development of technologies in

---

[15]Reed (2007), p. 267. The paper is also available at http://www.law.ed.ac.uk/ahrc/script-ed/issue8-2.asp. Accessed 21 Aug 2017.

[16]ICT Regulation Toolkit. http://www.ictregulationtoolkit.org/en/Section.1833.html. Accessed 21 Aug 2017.

[17]Editorial. EBU Tech Rev 312 (Oct 2007). http://www.ebu.ch/en/technical/trev/trev_312-editorial.html. Accessed 21 Aug 2017.

[18]*Supra* note 15.

[19]Id. at p. 264.

the future)."[20] In 1998, the same term was also used in the European Union legislative proposals.[21]

In EU, the Directive 2002/21/EC of the European Parliament and of the Council of 7 March 2002 on a "common regulatory framework for electronic communications networks and services" (Framework Directive) includes a paragraph in its recital to indicate the essence and desirability of having such principle:

> The requirement for Member States to ensure that national regulatory authorities take the utmost account of the desirability of making regulation technologically neutral, that is to say that it neither imposes nor discriminates in favour of the use of a particular type of technology, does not preclude the taking of proportionate steps to promote certain specific services where this is justified, for example digital television as a means for increasing spectrum efficiency.[22]

There are different rationales for countries to adopt technological neutrality when they formulate their regulations. First, if a particular technology is favored over the other, it could reduce the competition in the technology market. Second, if the technological neutrality is adopted, regulation will be "flexible, time-proof and open to technological change concerning with the scope of application of these regulations." Third, under the principle of technological neutrality, "regulation can be maintained, imposed or withdrawn depending on the competitive state of the market." And fourth, the principle helps universal service "be available to consumers, irrespective of the technology used."[23]

Notwithstanding the advantages of adopting the technological neutrality and its role as a guiding principle for the formulation of regulations, the principle itself does not have binding effect and does not impose legal obligations on the governments and legislative bodies when they enact their regulations or laws to govern the use of technologies in the economic activities. As a matter of law, countries still have their legislative discretion to decide whether and to what extent such principle will be applied when they enact their regulations, unless international treaties specifically require the adoption of technological neutrality. However, it must be noted that such principle is still a very important policy option for countries to formulate their policies and enact their rules. The adoption of such principle is to form a better environment for different technologies to properly develop and compete in the market.

Having said the above, the status of technological neutrality in treaty interpretation is not clear. Such principle was sometimes raised in dispute settlement cases

---

[20]http://clinton4.nara.gov/WH/New/Commerce/read.html. Accessed 21 Aug 2017.

[21]*Supra* note 15, at p. 264.

[22]The text of the Framework Directive is available at http://eur-lex.europa.eu/LexUriServ/LexUriServ.do?uri=OJ:L:2002:108:0033:0050:EN:PDF. Accessed 21 Aug 2017.

[23]Ali (2009), pp. 11–12.

of the WTO, such as *China—Measures Affecting Trading Rights and Distribution Services for Certain Publications and Audiovisual Entertainment Products*[24] and *US—Measures Affecting the Cross-Border Supply of Gambling and Betting Services.*[25] But the panels preferred not to address the status of technological neutrality under the WTO or under various methods of treaty interpretation based on the VCLT. Thus, certain clear rules concerning the proper application of such principle to help the interpretation of treaty terms are yet to be established.

From WTO perspective, the principle of technological neutrality should also serve as a useful guiding principle for the negotiation of some WTO rules. However, again, it is also not a binding rule to directly affect the rights and obligations of WTO Members.

It is argued that in the telecommunications sector, the principle of technological neutrality can have impacts under the WTO in three different ways:

> 1. It could help to identify regulatory measures that create a restriction on access or national treatment, within the meaning of the criteria set out in Articles XVI (market access) and XVII (national treatment) of the GATS. These measures would then have to be listed in the schedules of specific commitments, otherwise they would be in breach of the GATS. 2. It could rank as part of the regulatory disciplines imposed through Article VI of the GATS. These disciplines concern regulatory measures that do not fall under Articles XVI and XVII of the GATS, but nonetheless affect the position of suppliers of services. In that sense, Article VI of the GATS imposes limits on what a state can do once it decides (in its discretion) to intervene. 3. It could also be part of the regulatory measures that re necessary to give meaning to the specific commitments regarding market access (Article XVI of the GATS) and national treatment (Article XVII of the GATS) such as are listed in the Reference Paper attached as an additional commitment (pursuant to Article XVII of the GATS) by most signatories to the Fourth Protocol. For example, the obligation listed in the Reference Paper concerning competitive safeguards, interconnection and the independence of the regulatory authority go much beyond regulatory disciplines, and actually create a positive obligation on the part of the signatories to put in place certain regulatory provisions which are seen as essential to ensuring that market access and national treatment commitments are not frustrated by private action.
>
> At this point in time, technological neutrality has not reached such a significance that departures from it would breach Articles XVI or XVII of the GATS. It does not fall within any of the items on the black list of Article XVI on market access. As for Article XVII on national treatment, it would come into play if measures were to depart from technological neutrality in such a way that they would favour local suppliers to the detriment of suppliers from other WTO Members, or distort competition so as to reach that result.[26]

Although the principle of technological neutrality can impacts of the operation of the WTO, its role in the interpretation of WTO treaties is yet to be elaborated.

---

[24]Panel Report, *China—Measures Affecting Trading Rights and Distribution Services for Certain Publications and Audiovisual Entertainment Products*, WTO Doc. WT/DS363/R (adopted 19 Jan 2010).

[25]Panel Report, *United States—Measures Affecting the Cross-Border Supply of Gambling and Betting Services*, WTO Doc. WT/DS285/R (adopted 20 Apr 2005).

[26]Larouche (2004), pp. 412–413.

15.4.2 Technological Neutrality and Treaty Interpretation

The book considers that it is desirable not only to treat technological neutrality merely as a guiding principle for rule-making, but also a "factor" for a treaty interpreter to consider when conducting treaty interpretation.

First, an interpretation *not* favoring a particular technology would allow more competition between different technologies and hence could create a friendly environment for the overall technological development. Second, an interpretation in line with technological neutrality would be more in conformity with the negotiation principle which was the basis for the parties to conclude their treaty and hence should be more in line with the expectation of the parties. Third, an interpretation taking the technological neutrality into account would be more in line with the non-discrimination treatments. Actually Article 27 of the TRIPS Agreement (requiring patents to be available for any inventions in "all fields of technology" and without discrimination as to the "field of technology") already has such non-discrimination principle for different fields of technology. A similar principle could be inferred from this provision that within the "same broad field" of technology, there should not be a discrimination against different specific technologies.

The methods to take into consideration of technological neutrality are multiple in the treaty interpretation process. When deciding a technological term or provision or a technological product or services, the technological neutrality could help the interpreter decide its ordinary meaning. Also the technological neutrality could help decide the object-and-purpose of a treaty or a provision of technological nature, because such principle could have been the negotiating principle, which can be considered as an object-and-purpose of the treaty if it can be found or elaborated from the preamble or from the text of the treaty.

If the desirability can be accepted, an interpretation based on or taking into consideration of the principle of technological neutrality could also be justified under Article 32 of the VCLT, which permits a treaty interpreter to have recourse to the supplementary means of interpretation in order to confirm the meaning resulting from the application of Article 31 or to determine the meaning when the interpretation according to Article 31 would lead to ambiguous or unreasonable result.

To conclude this chapter, it should be useful to include the requirements of relying on the evolutive interpretation into a codified set of treaty interpretation rules. The requirements of applying the evolutive interpretation include that the interpreted term should be generic in nature; that there must be a long period of time or continuing duration for the operation of a treaty for the purpose of justifying the adoption of the evolutive interpretation; and that the effect of meeting of the above mentioned two requirements (i.e. the term being generic and the duration being continuing) is to presume the parties to have intended the evolutive interpretation. An interpreter should be very careful in overturning the presumption so as not to make a treaty become obsolete. Technology development and the technological neutrality are also factors which can be considered by the treaty interpreter to help decide whether to adopt an evolutive interpretation.

References

Ali R (2009) Technological neutrality. Lex Electronica 14(2):1–15

Editorial. EBU Tech Rev 312 (Oct 2007). http://www.ebu.ch/en/technical/trev/trev_312-editorial.html. Accessed 21 Aug 2017

http://clinton4.nara.gov/WH/New/Commerce/read.html. Accessed 21 Aug 2017

http://www.echr.coe.int/Documents/Convention_ENG.pdf. Accessed 21 Aug 2017

http://eur-lex.europa.eu/LexUriServ/LexUriServ.do?uri=OJ:L:2002:108:0033:0050:EN:PDF. Accessed 21 Aug 2017

http://www.britannica.com/place/San-Juan-River-Central-America. Accessed 21 Aug 2017

https://www.wto.org/english/tratop_e/dispu_e/cases_e/1pagesum_e/ds376sum_e.pdf. Accessed 21 Aug 2017

https://www.wto.org/english/tratop_e/dispu_e/cases_e/1pagesum_e/ds377sum_e.pdf. Accessed 21 Aug 2017

ICT Regulation Toolkit. http://www.ictregulationtoolkit.org/en/Section.1833.html. Accessed 21 Aug 2017

Larouche P (2004) Dealing with convergence at the international level. In: Geradin D, Luff D (eds) The WTO and global convergence in telecommunications and audio-visual service. Cambridge University Press, Cambridge, pp 390–422

Lee KYR Expansive interpretation of the European convention on human rights and the creative Jurisprudence of the Strasbourg's Court. Mercury—HKU J Undergrad Humanit 1(1):70–82. http://www.artsfac.hku.hk/mercury/wp-content/uploads/Rosa_Lee1.pdf. Accessed 21 Aug 2017

Pauwelyn J The nature of WTO obligations. http://www.jeanmonnetprogram.org/archive/papers/02/020101-02.html#P296_86702. Accessed 21 Aug 2017

Peng S (2012) Renegotiate the WTO "Schedule of Commitments"? Technological Development and Treaty Interpretation, Cornell Intl Law J, 45: 403–430

Reed C (2007) Taking sides on technology neutrality. SCRIPT-ed—J Law Technol Soc 4(3):263–284. http://www.law.ed.ac.uk/ahrc/script-ed/issue8-2.asp. Accessed 21 Aug 2017

The Hague Justice Portal. ICJ Judgment in Costa Rica v. Nicaragua. http://www.haguejusticeportal.net/index.php?id=10811. Accessed 21 Aug 2017

Chapter 16
The Formula Approach for Indefinite Legal Concepts and the Possible Codification

Contents

16.1 Some Terms and Concepts are Intrinsically Abstract and Indefinite and Need Formulas for Their Interpretation

16.1.1 The Intrinsically Abstract Terms and "Indefinite Legal Concepts"

In domestic context, there are situations where the drafter of a legal provision would not be able to avoid using the abstract or vague terms or the "indefinite legal concepts".[1] The first situation is where a term or concept (such as "necessary" and

[1]There are many commonly used legal terms (such as public welfare, public interest, need, public need, public safety, public order, reliability, urgency, unreasonable, good moral) which can be categorized as "indefinite legal concepts". See Singh (1985), p. 96.

C. Lo, *Treaty Interpretation Under the Vienna Convention on the Law of Treaties*,
https://doi.org/10.1007/978-981-10-6866-9_16

"public interest") which needs to be incorporated into a legislation is by its nature abstract and hence the drafter is unable to alternatively use a clearer or more concrete term or concept in the provision. In such case, the drafter can include some "definitional provisions" in the legal document so as to avoid or reduce the extent of abstractness, vagueness or indefiniteness in the term or concept and make it more easily to be applied. The drafter can also use some illustrative examples to indicate the possible meanings of them (such as listing some examples of "public interest" to indicate the kinds and extents of "public interest" being required in the provision). But such potential methods are not necessarily useful. For instance, it could be difficult to provide a precise definition or some illustrative examples for the term "necessary" in the legal document.

The second situation is where a governed matter is complicated or is of higher scientific uncertainty and the drafter can only use a more general term (such as the term "safe") to regulate the subject matter.[2] In order to avoid or reduce the abstractness and vagueness of such term, the drafter can provide some criteria or benchmarks to help adjudicators to properly understand such term and to correctly apply it in real cases.

The third situation is where the drafter deliberately gives the law certain flexibility and hence an administrative discretion (i.e. the space of discretion given to the implementing body) could be permitted to the government agencies which are in charge of the administration and implementation of such law.[3] Of course, the fact that the law gives flexibility to the administering agency does not mean that the implementing measures cannot be subject to judicial review. Hence although the administrating agency will enjoy some discretion in its implementation of such term, its interpretation could still be subject to review by the court.[4]

In international context, although the phrase "indefinite legal concept" is not commonly used, abstract and vague terms are still not always avoidable. The situations of using vague terms or indefinite legal concepts are similar to the domestic situations in that some treaty terms are abstract and vague by their nature and no clearer alternative terms can be used to replace the vague terms, and that sometimes it is unavoidable to use certain more general terms so as to regulate some specific subject matters. But concerning whether or not and to what extent there should also be a discretion to be given to the contracting parties to a treaty for them to implement the provisions, some clarifications are needed. This will be explained in

[2]Knill (2001), p. 66.

[3]Maxeiner (2013), p. 28.

[4]For instance, for German law, it is indicated that "When a statutory term is determined to be an indefinite legal concept, e.g., "the needs of the public,' 'necessity,' 'reliability,' 'fitness for a purpose,' its interpretation is regarded as a question of law and therefore subject to complete review by the courts." Pakuscher (1976), p. 98, fn. 18.

the following section. After having explained the possible discretion to be given to the contracting parties to a treaty, this chapter will further explain the need and desirability of creating some formulas for the purpose of interpreting certain vague terms or indefinite legal concepts in international treaties.

16.1.2 "Margin of Appreciation" Should not Have a Role in Addressing General Treaty Provisions Other Than Those in ECHR

As mentioned in the preceding section of this chapter, vague terms in domestic legal provisions are sometimes purposely used so as to give necessary discretion to the administrating agencies. But in international context, whether or not certain discretion is given to the contracting parties to a treaty by using vague or general terms is an issue that needs to be further explained. This relates to the term "margin of appreciation" which is used in connection with the European Convention on Human Rights (ECHR).

The ECHR was concluded among culturally and legally diverse Member States in Europe and hence certain uniform standards of human rights for the European countries were not easy to be identified and agreed upon. For this reason, the ECHR was created as the "lowest common denominator" so that there will be certain degrees of deference to the sovereignty of the Member States. The ECHR gives some flexibilities to the Member States and allow them to derogate from their obligations provided in the Convention. This is also to avoid confrontations between the European Court of Human Rights and the Member States of the ECHR so as to enable the Court "to balance the sovereignty of Member States with their obligations under the Convention".[5] Such derogation is called the "margin of appreciation" . It basically indicates that there is "the room for manoeuvre the Strasbourg institutions [including the European Court of Human Rights] are prepared to accord national authorities in fulfilling their obligations under the European Convention on Human Rights."[6]

Concerning the scope of application of the "margin of appreciation", the following situations can be noted.[7] Article 15 of the ECHR (entitled "Derogation in

---

[5]Council of Europe. The Margin of Appreciation. https://www.coe.int/t/dghl/cooperation/lisbonnetwork/themis/echr/paper2_en.asp. Accessed 21 Aug 2017.

[6]Greer (2000), p. 5. The monograph is available at http://www.echr.coe.int/LibraryDocs/DG2/HRFILES/DG2-EN-HRFILES-17(2000).pdf. Accessed 21 Aug 2017.

[7]Id. at pp. 5–6.

tine of emergency")[8] already has its own derogation provision. The "margin of appreciation" is also applied to Article 8 (entitled "Right to respect for private and family life"),[9] Article 9 (entitled "Freedom of thought, conscience and religion"),[10] Article 10 (entitled "Freedom of expression"),[11] and Article 11 (entitled "Freedom

[8]Article 15 of the ECHR reads:

1. In time of war or other public emergency threatening the life of the nation any High Contracting Party may take measures derogating from its obligations under this Convention to the extent strictly required by the exigencies of the situation, provided that such measures are not inconsistent with its other obligations under international law.
2. No derogation from Article 2, except in respect of deaths resulting from lawful acts of war, or from Articles 3, 4 (paragraph 1) and 7 shall be made under this provision.
3. Any High Contracting Party availing itself of this right of derogation shall keep the Secretary General of the Council of Europe fully informed of the measures which it has taken and the reasons therefor. It shall also inform the Secretary General of the Council of Europe when such measures have ceased to operate and the provisions of the Convention are again being fully executed.

[9]Article 8 of the ECHR reads:

1. Everyone has the right to respect for his private and family life, his home and his correspondence.
2. There shall be no interference by a public authority with the exercise of this right except such as is in accordance with the law and is necessary in a democratic society in the interests of national security, public safety or the economic well-being of the country, for the prevention of disorder or crime, for the protection of health or morals, or for the protection of the rights and freedoms of others.

[10]Article 9 of the ECHR reads:

1. Everyone has the right to freedom of thought, conscience and religion; this right includes freedom to change his religion or belief and freedom, either alone or in community with others and in public or private, to manifest his religion or belief, in worship, teaching, practice and observance.
2. Freedom to manifest one's religion or beliefs shall be subject only to such limitations as are prescribed by law and are necessary in a democratic society in the interests of public safety, for the protection of public order, health or morals, or for the protection of the rights and freedoms of others.

[11]Article 10 of the ECHR reads:

1. Everyone has the right to freedom of expression. This right shall include freedom to hold opinions and to receive and impart information and ideas without interference by public authority and regardless of frontiers. This Article shall not prevent States from requiring the licensing of broadcasting, television or cinema enterprises.
2. The exercise of these freedoms, since it carries with it duties and responsibilities, may be subject to such formalities, conditions, restrictions or penalties as are prescribed by law and are necessary in a democratic society, in the interests of national security, territorial integrity or public safety, for the prevention of disorder or crime, for the protection of health or morals, for the protection of the reputation or rights of others, for preventing the disclosure of information received in confidence, or for maintaining the authority and impartiality of the judiciary.

of assembly and association").[12] But it is not clear as to whether the doctrine also applies to, for instance, Article 2 (entitled "Right to life"),[13] Article 3 (entitled "Prohibition of torture"),[14] and Article 4 (entitled "Prohibition of slavery and forced labour").[15]

A question to be addressed here is whether the "margin of appreciation", which is commonly used in interpreting the ECHR by the European Court of Human Rights, is also applicable in interpreting other international treaties by other international adjudicators, especially when the treaty provisions are vague or general. Based on the explanations below, the simple answer to this question should be "no".

According to the explanation in the previous chapters of the book, the VCLT requires the treaty interpreters to interpret treaty terms in accordance with the ordinary meanings in the context of the interpreted term and in the light of the

[12]Article 11 of the ECHR reads:

1. Everyone has the right to freedom of peaceful assembly and to freedom of association with others, including the right to form and to join trade unions for the protection of his interests.
2. No restrictions shall be placed on the exercise of these rights other than such as are prescribed by law and are necessary in a democratic society in the interests of national security or public safety, for the prevention of disorder or crime, for the protection of health or morals or for the protection of the rights and freedoms of others. This Article shall not prevent the imposition of lawful restrictions on the exercise of these rights by members of the armed forces, of the police or of the administration of the State.

[13]Article 2 of the ECHR reads:

1. Everyone's right to life shall be protected by law. No one shall be deprived of his life intentionally save in the execution of a sentence of a court following his conviction of a crime for which this penalty is provided by law.
2. Deprivation of life shall not be regarded as inflicted in contravention of this Article when it results from the use of force which is no more than absolutely necessary:

   (a) in defence of any person from unlawful violence;
   (b) in order to effect a lawful arrest or to prevent the escape of a person lawfully detained;
   (c) in action lawfully taken for the purpose of quelling a riot or insurrection.

[14]Article 3 of the ECHR reads: "No one shall be subjected to torture or to inhuman or degrading treatment or punishment.".

[15]Article 4 of the ECHR reads:

1. No one shall be held in slavery or servitude.
2. No one shall be required to perform forced or compulsory labour.
3. For the purpose of this Article the term "forced or compulsory labour" shall not include:

   (a) any work required to be done in the ordinary course of detention imposed according to the provisions of Article5 of this Convention or during conditional release from such detention;
   (b) any service of a military character or, in case of conscientious objectors in countries where they are recognised, service exacted instead of compulsory military service;
   (c) any service exacted in case of an emergency or calamity threatening the life or well-being of the community;
   (d) any work or service which forms part of normal civic obligations.

treaty's object-and-purpose. The interpreters can consider other methods of treaty interpretation not listed in Article 31 of the VCLT as supplementary means based on Article 32. Since the "margin of appreciation" is not provided in Article 31 of the VCLT, the only "possibility" is to consider it as a supplementary means. However, the book argues that the "margin of appreciation" should not be considered as a supplementary means of interpretation for the following reasons.

First, there was a special background for the ECHR to allow the "margin of appreciation" so as to give flexibility to the Member States of the Convention concerning their fulfilment of the obligations under the ECHR. Such background is "treaty-specific" to the ECHR. Other treaties do not have such background to allow a treaty interpreter to take the same approach in his/her exercise of treaty interpretation.

Second, even if there is a similar background to allow certain discretion for the contracting parties to derogate from their obligations under a specific treaty, such discretion must be reflected implied in the interpreted text, in the context for the interpreted provision or in the object-and-purpose of the treaty. If such discretion is intended by the contracting parties or can be drawn from the text, the context or the object-and-purpose, an interpreter certainly must interpret the treaty provision so as to give the discretion to the contracting parties. In such case, the interpreter does not have to resort to the "margin of appreciation" for the purpose of giving such discretion to the contracting parties. On the other hand, if there is no clue from the text, the context and the object-and-purpose that a discretion should be given to the contracting parties, the interpreter must interpret the treaty provision so as not to give the discretion to the contracting parties so that there will not be undesirable deviations from the textual wording or the object-and-purpose of the treaty. In such case, the interpreter does not have any position to apply the "margin of appreciation" so as to allow a deflection from the general interpretation principle provided in Article 31 of the VCLT.

Third, as having been explained in Chap. 14 of this book, there is the principle of *in dubio mitius*. This principle expects treaty interpreters to give a term the meaning which is less burdensome to the contracting party assuming an obligation so as to be in deference to the sovereignty of such party. There is a similar aspect between the principle of *in dubio mitius* and the "margin of appreciation" in that both of them expect treaty interpreters to pay deference to the contracting parties. However, the principle of *in dubio mitius* is a principle of Latin maxim. Hence the source of this principle is not attached to any specific treaty. On the other hand, the "margin of appreciation" was developed specifically in connection with the ECHR. Hence, it is a "treaty-specific" principle not to be generally applied in the context of other treaties. This distinction helps explain the reason that the principle of *in dubio mitius* can be a supplementary means of treaty interpretation, but the "margin of appreciation" cannot be considered as enjoying such status. Also the principle of *in dubio mitius* is more precise in its meaning. The essence of the principle is that if there are two possible interpretations, the less onerous interpretation should be adopted concerning the assumption of an obligation of a contracting party. On the other hand, the "margin of appreciation" is not precise concerning its scope of application even within the ECHR. It is possible that the "margin of appreciation" can be applied in a generally way so as to create a loophole for contracting parties to escape from their treaty obligations.

To conclude this part of discussion, since the "margin of appreciation" is created and developed in specific connection with the ECHR, there is no room for it to be generally applied to other treaties. Also since there is the principle of *in dubio mitius* serving as a supplementary means of interpretation, there is no need to introduce the "margin of appreciation" (which has a function similar to that of the principle of *in dubio mitius*) . And since the "margin of appreciation" is unclear in its scope, it is not appropriate to consider it as a supplementary means of interpretation under Article 32 of the VCLT.

Having said the above, the issue concerning the method of interpreting the vague and general treaty terms or the indefinite legal concepts in treaty provisions must still be addressed. In the following sections, discussions will focus on the need, desirability and possibility of creating some formulas for the purpose of interpreting such kind of treaty terms and concepts.

16.1.3 Desirability of "Formula Approach" for the Interpretation of Abstract Terms

Article 31 of the VCLT suggests that there must be ordinary meanings that can be identified for an interpreted term and the treaty interpreter is to select one from several possible ordinary meanings to give to the term in its context and in the light of the interpreted treaty's object-and-purpose. But in real situations, even when a term is given with an ordinary meaning, the exact meaning is still unclear. This is particularly true when a treaty term is very abstract and very general in nature.

In such situation, a treaty interpreter might need to develop a more detailed formula for the purpose of elaborating the essence, the meaning and the application of such term, especially when such term is so critical in the operation of a treaty provision. The apparent examples of the treaty terms of such kind are the terms of "necessary" and "public moral" provided in many trade agreements.

As will be explained in the next chapter, the set of treaty interpretation rules is not a formula. In other words, treaty interpretation rules should never be a fixed or step-by-step procedure to be strictly followed by an interpreter when conducting treaty interpretation. It is rather a set of interpretation rules incorporating various elements and principles to be considered by a treaty interpreter and to help the interpreter conduct an overall and holistic assessment based on these elements and principles of consideration. Hence, the set of rules provided in Articles 31 to 33 of the VCLT collectively should not be considered as a "formula" in its strict sense. To be more specific, there should not be a "formula" to strictly guide a step-by-step procedure for treaty interpretation.

However, it does not mean that there should never be some kind of "formulas" being developed by treaty interpreters to consistently and transparently interpret certain specific treaty terms.

In domestic context of statutory or constitutional interpretation, it is a common practice of establishing some kind of formulas for those terms which are abstract but are legally important in the operation of the legal provisions. For instance, in the constitutions of many countries, there is the principle of "proportionality" or the "necessity" requirement which is either explicitly provided in the constitutional texts[16] or is considered as being embodied in the constitutions as underlying principles to limit the statutory restriction on the constitutional rights of the people. Take the German and Canadian jurisprudence concerning the use of the concept of proportionality or necessity requirement as examples, Dieter Grimm explains the following steps of analysis of the requirement:

> In essence, both jurisdictions [i.e. Germany and Canada] follow the same path when they apply the proportionality test. Since the test requires a means-ends comparison, both courts [i.e. the German Constitutional Court and the Canadian Supreme Court] start by ascertaining the purpose of the law under review. Only a legitimate purpose can justify a limitation of a fundamental right. The three-step proportionality test follows. While the Canadian Court requires a rational connection between the purpose of the law and the means employed by the legislature to achieve its objective in the first step, the German Court asks whether the law is suitable to reach its end. In the second step, the Canadian Court asks whether, in pursuing its end, the law minimally impairs the fundamental right, whereas the German Court asks whether the law is necessary to reach its end or whether a less intrusive means exists that will likewise reach the end. The third step in both countries is a cost-benefit analysis, which requires a balancing between the fundamental rights interests and the good in whose interest the right is limited. In Germany it is mostly called 'proportionality,' in the narrower sense, but is also called 'appropriateness,' 'reasonable demand' (*Zumutbarkeit*), and so on."[17]

In international context, such "formula approach" is also used in connection with some treaty provisions, as will be explained in the following discussions. The issue to be addressed here is whether the "formula approach" is necessary and desirable.

The book argues that such approach to cope with the interpretation of certain abstract and general terms is necessary and unavoidable. First, the meanings and definitions of the vague and general terms or the indefinite legal concepts provided in a treaty can certainly be found from various dictionaries. However, the dictionary definitions could be of limited value in the actual application of the provisions. Using certain abstract and vague words to indicate or replace an abstract and vague interpreted term might not be very useful for treaty interpretation purpose. For

---

[16]For instance, Article 23 of the Constitution of Taiwan (ROC) provides: "All the freedoms and rights enumerated in the preceding Articles shall not be restricted by law except by such as may be necessary to prevent infringement upon the freedoms of other persons, to avert an imminent crisis, to maintain social order or to advance public welfare." Hence there is the requirement of legal restriction being "necessary". The Constitutional Court has developed its formula to interpret this necessity requirement.

[17]Grimm (2007), pp. 387–388.

instance, the dictionary definitions for the term "necessary" include "being essential", "indispensable", or "requisite".[18] But whether or not a measure is "necessary" for the protection of human health concerns the level of and the factors to decide indispensableness. The definitions of "being essential", "indispensable", and "requisite" as shown in dictionaries do not provide the needed benchmark or concrete guidance for the treaty interpreters to follow.

Second, since the dictionary definitions do not provide needed benchmark or more concrete guidance to help interpret such treaty terms, it is likely that different treaty interpreters could come up with different understandings of the interpreted terms in the same treaty based on the same dictionary definitions. The consistency and predictability of interpretation of the same treaty provisions could be undermined because of the lack of operable guidance to be followed by the treaty interpreters. Apparently, it is desirable for treaty interpreters to develop certain formulas for certain specific abstract treaty terms or provisions so as to make the treaty interpretation more consistent and predictable and to make the treaty provisions more operable.

Developing formulas for certain specific abstract treaty terms or provisions are not only desirable, but also possible. The formula approach has be very common in many jurisdictions concerning their statutory and constitutional interpretations. As will be explained in the following sections in this chapter, there have been some examples of treaty interpreters also having developed formulas for the interpretation of certain treaty terms.

16.1.4 Formula Approach Is Both for Treaty Interpretation Under Article 32 and for Treaty Application

It must be noted that the formula approach is both for treaty interpretation and for treaty application purposes. As explained in Chap. 6 of this book, conceptually, treaty interpretation and treaty application are of different meanings and functions. But practically, treaty interpretation and treaty application could be intertwined in the adjudication process. The formula approach is in the intertwined area of treaty interpretation and treaty application.

The formula approach is for treaty interpretation because it helps clarify the meaning and essence of an abstract treaty term. But it is somewhat different from merely giving an ordinary meaning in the form of a single word, a single phrase or a single sentence to a treaty term. Instead, the formula approach is to establish a step-by-step rule to be attached to the interpreted term so that the essence of the interpreted treaty term is revealed. Broadly speaking, the formula approach is still

[18]See the definition by Dictionary.com, for instance, at http://www.dictionary.com/browse/necessary. Accessed 21 Aug 2017.

used to find the ordinary meaning of the abstract term. But its ordinary meaning is expressed in the form of a systemically arranged elements, not in the form of a single word or a few words.

The formula approach can be considered as a supplementary means of treaty interpretation provided in Article 32 of the VCLT. The approach is not used for a wide range of treaty terms. It is used in relation to a very limited number of treaty terms. The potential candidates for applying the formula approach are those terms which are abstract and vague by their nature or which are indefinite legal concepts. Concrete and precise legal terms (such as "tariff" and "non-tariff barrier") would not need to rely on the formula approach. Also if there has already been a treaty provision to decide the meaning of a term, the term would not need to rely on the formula approach. For instance, since GATT Article I has elaborated the contents of the Most-Favoured-Nation (MFN) treatment, the term "MFN" would not need to rely on the formula approach to decide its meaning. Also the terms which are suitable for developing formulas for their interpretations must be the "key requirements" in the interpreted provisions. But the concept of "key requirement" must be understood in a broad manner. As long as the term would critically affect the application of a treaty provision, it should be considered as the key requirement for the purpose of developing a formula for its interpretation. But this does not mean that all key requirements in a treaty need to be interpreted by creating formulas for them. It must be that a key requirement is so abstract and that if no formula is developed for it, its interpretation and application could be very difficult and inconsistent.

The formula approach is also for "treaty application" because its ultimate purpose is to help the adjudicator for a treaty dispute decide whether to apply a specific provision, and if the specific provision should be applied, how to apply it.

In the following sections, the book uses the terms "necessary" and "public moral" provided in Article XX of the GATT 1994 as examples to illustrate the use of the formula approach in real situations. It must also be noted that the formula approach can also help interpret the structural issue of a provision, if such provision could theoretically be subject to two or more possible interpretations. The book will use the whole GATT Article XX as an example to explain the use of a formula to help understand the structure of the article.

16.2 Using a Formula to Interpret the Whole Structure of GATT Article XX

16.2.1 The Whole Structure of GATT Article XX

Article XX of the GATT 1994 is entitled "General exceptions". The article includes its chapeau and 10 listed items of exceptions under which WTO Members may be exempt from GATT obligations. These exceptions serve as defences to the obligations under other GATT articles.

Specifically, Article XX provides in part that:

> Subject to the requirement that such measures are not applied in a manner which would constitute a means of arbitrary or unjustifiable discrimination between countries where the same conditions prevail, or a disguised restriction on international trade, nothing in this Agreement shall be construed to prevent the adoption or enforcement by any contracting party of measures:
>
> (*a*) necessary to protect public morals;
>
> (*b*) necessary to protect human, animal or plant life or health;
>
> ...
>
> (*d*) necessary to secure compliance with laws or regulations which are not inconsistent with the provisions of this Agreement, including those relating to customs enforcement, the enforcement of monopolies operated under paragraph 4 of Article II and Article XVII, the protection of patents, trade marks and copyrights, and the prevention of deceptive practices;
>
> ...

So the requirements in the chapeau include that a measure is not applied in an arbitrarily discriminatory manner; that it is not applied in an unjustifiably discriminatory matter and it does not become a disguised restriction on international trade. And for the listed exceptions, their respective requirements are different. As will be explained below, the formula approach can be used in understanding the whole structure of the article and the relations between the requirements in the chapeau and those in the listed exceptions. It can also be used to understand the essence of the term "public moral" in paragraph (a) and the term "necessary" in paragraphs (a), (b) and (d).

16.2.2 Formulas to Address the Whole Structure of Article XX

There is an issue about how to perceive the whole structure of GATT Article XX so that a panel or the Appellate Body can properly apply it. The first formula developed by the WTO jurisprudence for the whole structure of GATT Article XX is the balancing consideration of the right of a Member invoking an exception under Article XX and the duty of that Member to respect other Members' rights under other provisions in the GATT 1994.

The Appellate Body in its Report on *US—Shrimp* explains the essence of the whole provisions in Article XX of the GATT 1994. It states:

> [A] balance must be struck between the right of a Member to invoke an exception under Article XX and the duty of that same Member to respect the treaty rights of the other Members.

> The task of interpreting and applying the chapeau is, hence, essentially the delicate one of locating and marking out a line of equilibrium between the right of a Member to invoke an exception under Article XX and the rights of the other Members under varying substantive provisions (e.g., Article XI) of the GATT 1994, so that neither of the competing rights will cancel out the other and thereby distort and nullify or impair the balance of rights and obligations constructed by the Members themselves in that Agreement. The location of the line of equilibrium, as expressed in the chapeau, is not fixed and unchanging; the line moves as the kind and the shape of the measures at stake vary and as the facts making up specific cases differ.[19]

The Appellate Body's suggestion of drawing the line of equilibrium and balancing the rights and obligations can be considered as creating a rough formula to instruct WTO Members and the interpreters to take the balancing elements into consideration when perceiving and applying GATT Article XX.

The second formula created by the Appellate Body is the "two-tier analysis" (or "two-tier test") which is more specific and easier to be applied by the treaty interpreter concerning the relation between the chapeau and the specific paragraphs under Article XX. This two-tier analysis addresses the proper understanding of the whole structure of Article XX of the GATT as well as the sequence of analysing the chapeau and the listed exceptions (to require analysing the listed exceptions first and then analysing the requirements in the chapeau).

The Appellate Body states in its Report on *US—Gasoline* in connection with Article XX (g) that:

> In order that the justifying protection of Article XX may be extended to it, the measure at issue must not only come under one or another of the particular exceptions — paragraphs (a) to (j) — listed under Article XX; it must also satisfy the requirements imposed by the opening clauses of Article XX. The analysis is, in other words, two-tiered: first, provisional justification by reason of characterization of the measure under XX(g); second, further appraisal of the same measure under the introductory clauses of Article XX.

So the two-tier analysis requires the panel to analyse the cited paragraphs in Article XX of the GATT as the first and provisional step. It also requires, as the second step, to analyse whether the requirements in the chapeau are met.

The Appellate Body further emphasized in its Report on *US—Shrimp* the importance of the sequence and indicated that a reversed sequence of analysis would not be appropriate:

> The sequence of steps indicated above in the analysis of a claim of justification under Article XX reflects, not inadvertence or random choice, but rather the fundamental structure and logic of Article XX. The Panel appears to suggest, albeit indirectly, that following the indicated sequence of steps, or the inverse thereof, does not make any difference. To the Panel, reversing the sequence set out in *United States — Gasoline* 'seems equally appropriate.' We do not agree.
>
> The task of interpreting the chapeau so as to prevent the abuse or misuse of the specific exemptions provided for in Article XX is rendered very difficult, if indeed it remains

[19]Appellate Body Report, *United States—Import Prohibition of Certain Shrimp and Shrimp Products*, paras. 156, 159, WTO Doc. WT/DS58/AB/R (adopted 6 Nov 1998).

> possible at all, where the interpreter (like the Panel in this case) has not first identified and examined the specific exception threatened with abuse. The standards established in the chapeau are, moreover, necessarily broad in scope and reach: the prohibition of the *application* of a measure 'in a manner which would constitute a means of *arbitrary* or *unjustifiable discrimination* between countries where the same conditions prevail' or 'a *disguised restriction* on international trade.' (emphasis added) When applied in a particular case, the actual contours and contents of these standards will vary as the kind of measure under examination varies.[20]

The Appellate Body re-emphasized again in its Report on *Brazil—Retreaded Tyres* that the analysis of a measure by a panel under Article XX is two-tiered: first to examine whether a measure falls under one of the exceptions listed in any one of the paragraphs of Article XX and second to examine whether the measure in question satisfies the requirements of the chapeau of Article XX.[21]

16.3 Some Requirements in GATT Article XX as Examples

16.3.1 The Necessity Requirement and the Formula

As stated above, paragraphs (a) ("necessary to protect public morals"), (b) ("necessary to protect human, animal or plant life or health") and (d) ("necessary to secure compliance with laws or regulations which are not inconsistent with the provisions of this Agreement, including those relating to customs enforcement, the enforcement of monopolies operated under paragraph 4 of Article II and Article XVII, the protection of patents, trade marks and copyrights, and the prevention of deceptive practices") all include the requirement of "necessary". The term "necessary" is one of the key requirements in these paragraphs. But the requirement is of the nature of "indefinite legal concept" and is very abstract. Hence, it is the perfect example of a treaty term which should be subject to the formula approach for its interpretation.

The Appellate Body and some panels were able to develop some approaches (including a "weighing and balancing" process) to be used to understand and apply the necessity requirement in these paragraphs.

The Panel in its Report on *EC—Tariff Preferences* considered the ordinary meaning of the term "necessary" and cited the Appellate Body's view. It states:

---

[20] Id. at paras. 119–120.

[21] Appellate Body Report, *Brazil—Measures Affecting Imports of Retreaded Tyres*, para. 139, WTO Doc. WT/DS332/AB/R (adopted 17 Dec 2007).

> The Panel recalls the Appellate Body ruling in *Korea — Various Measures on Beef* that 'the term "necessary" refers, in our view, to a range of degrees of necessity. At one end of this continuum lies "necessary" understood as "indispensable"; at the other end, is "necessary" taken to mean as "making a contribution to". We consider that a "necessary" measure is, in this continuum, located significantly closer to the pole of "indispensable" than to the opposite pole of simply "making a contribution to".' In order to determine where the Drug Arrangements are situated along this continuum between 'contribution to' and 'indispensable', the Panel is of the view that it should determine the extent to which the Drug Arrangements contribute to the European Communities' health objective. This requires the Panel to assess the benefits of the Drug Arrangements in achieving the objective of protecting life or health in the European Communities.[22]

But in a number of cases, the panels and the Appellate Body mainly relied on the "weighing and balancing" formula to further interpret the term "necessary" provided in various paragraphs in GATT Article XX. For instance, the Appellate Body in its Report on *Korea—Various Measures on Beef* stated that:

> In sum, determination of whether a measure, which is not 'indispensable', may nevertheless be 'necessary' within the contemplation of Article XX(d), involves in every case a process of weighing and balancing a series of factors which prominently include the contribution made by the compliance measure to the enforcement of the law or regulation at issue, the importance of the common interests or values protected by that law or regulation, and the accompanying impact of the law or regulation on imports or exports.[23]

The Panel of *Brazil—Retreaded Tyres* has a very good summary in its Report about the "weighing and balancing" formula and the application of the approach:

> … the term 'necessary', as contained in paragraphs (b) and (d) of Article XX of GATT 1994 and paragraph (a) of Article XIV of the GATS, has been interpreted in a number of previous cases by the Appellate Body[24]: the necessity of a measure should be determined through 'a process of weighing and balancing a series of factors', which usually includes the assessment of the following three factors: the relative importance of the interests or values furthered by the challenged measure, the contribution of the measure to the realization of the ends pursued by it and the restrictive impact of the measure on international commerce.[25] Once all those factors have been analyzed, the Appellate Body said a comparison should be undertaken between the challenged measure and possible alternatives. In performing this comparison, the Appellate Body also stated that the weighing and balancing process of the factors informs the determination of whether a WTO-consistent

---

[22]Panel Report, *European Communities—Conditions for the Granting of Tariff Preferences to Developing Countries*, para. 7.211, WTO Doc. WT/DS246/R (adopted 20 Apr 2004).

[23]Appellate Body Report, *Korea—Measures Affecting Imports of Fresh, Chilled and Frozen Beef*, para. 164, WTO Doc. WT/DS161/AB/R, WT/DS169/AB/R (adopted 10 Jan 2001).

[24]E.g. *Korea—Various Measures on Beef, EC—Asbestos, Dominican Republic—Imports and Sales of Cigarettes* and *US—Gambling* (cited in Panel Report, *Brazil—Measures Affecting Imports of Retreaded Tyres*, para. 7.104, fn. 1173, WTO Doc. WT/DS332/R (adopted 17 Dec 2007) [hereinafter Brazil—Retreaded Tyres Panel Report]).

[25]Appellate Body Report on *Korea—Various Measures on Beef*, para. 164; Appellate Body Report on *EC—Asbestos*, para. 172; Appellate Body Report on *US—Gambling,* para. 306; Appellate Body Report on *Dominican Republic—Import and Sale of Cigarettes*, para. 70 (cited in Brazil—Retreaded Tyres Panel Report, *supra* note 24, para. 7.104, fn. 1174).

alternative measure, or a less WTO-inconsistent measure, which the Member concerned could reasonably be expected to employ, is available.[26,27]

To summarize the discussions in this section, the term "necessary" provided in GATT Article XX can be more properly perceived and understood based on a formula which include the following elements for a step-by-step analysis:

(1) The weighing and balancing process of three factors:
   (i) The relative importance of the interests or values furthered by the challenged measure,
   (ii) The contribution of the measure to the realization of the ends pursued by it, and
   (iii) The restrictive impact of the measure on international commerce;
(2) A comparison between the challenged measure and possible alternatives: whether a WTO-consistent alternative measure, or a less WTO-inconsistent measure (which the responding Member could reasonably be expected to employ) is available.

16.3.2 The "Public Moral" Requirement and the Formula

As stated above, Article XX(a) provides that a measure necessary to protect "public morals" can also be an exception to the general obligations under other provisions in the GATT 1994. The term "public morals" is also abstract and can be considered as an indefinite legal term. The WTO jurisprudence has also developed a formula for its interpretation.

The Panel in its Report on *China—Publications and Audiovisual Products* adopted the interpretation of "public morals" developed by the panel in *US—Gambling*, indicates the following:

> '[T]he term "public morals" denotes standards of right and wrong conduct maintained by or on behalf of a community or nation' … 'the content of these concepts for Members can vary in time and space, depending upon a range of factors, including prevailing social, cultural, ethical and religious values' … Members, in applying this and other similar societal concepts, 'should be given some scope to define and apply for themselves the concepts of "public morals" … in their respective territories, according to their own systems and scales of values.'
>
> The Panel recalled that "the content and scope of the concept of "public morals" can vary from Member to Member, as they are influenced by each Member's prevailing social, cultural, ethical and religious values" and it proceeded with its analysis on the assumption that "each of the prohibited types of content listed in China's measures is such that, if it

---

[26]Appellate Body Report on *Dominican Republic – Import and Sale of Cigarettes*, para. 70 (cited in Brazil—Retreaded Tyres Panel Report, *supra* note 24, para. 7.104, fn. 1175).

[27]Brazil—Retreaded Tyres Panel Report, *supra* note 24, at para. 7.104.

were brought into China as part of a physical product, it could have a negative impact on 'public morals' in China within the meaning of Article XX(a) of the GATT 1994.[28]

To summarize from the above panel report, the formula to perceive the term "public morals" under GATT Article XX(a) include the following elements and process. The group of these elements can be collectively considered as a formula developed for the purpose of properly perceiving the ordinary meaning of the term "public morals":

(1) It is the right and wrong standards by a community or nation.
(2) The range of factors, including prevailing social, cultural, ethical and religious values, should be considered in deciding the standards.
(3) The time and space factors need to be considered as well, because the right and wrong standards can vary in time and space.
(4) Members should be given some latitude to define their own concepts for their territories.
(5) But when deciding their own standards, the decision must be made in accordance to their own system and scales of values.

To conclude this chapter, although interpreting a treaty term or provision by giving a formula is not indicated in the VCLT, it is very often used as an approach for treaty interpretation when an interpreted treaty term is a key requirement in a provision but is so abstract and vastly uncertain. It should be useful to indicate in a codified set of rules that for the interpretation of some abstract terms or indefinite legal concepts and even for the interpretation of provisions with more complicated structures, it could be appropriate to develop formulas to specify the sequence and elements to be analyzed so as to correctly perceive and understand the essence of the terms or provisions. Such formula approach can be justified under Article 32 of the VCLT.

References

Council of Europe. The Margin of Appreciation. https://www.coe.int/t/dghl/cooperateon/lisbonnetwork/themis/echr/paper2_en.asp. Accessed 21 Aug 2017

Greer S (2000) The margin of appreciation: interpretation and discretion under the European Convention on Human Rights. Council of Europe Publishing, Strasbourg. http://www.echr.coe.int/LibraryDocs/DG2/HRFILES/DG2-EN-HRFILES-17(2000).pdf. Accessed 21 Aug 2017

Grimm D (2007) Proportionality in Canadian and German Constitutional Jurisprudence. Univ Toronto Law J 57:383–397

http://www.dictionary.com/browse/necessary. Accessed 21 Aug 2017

[28]Panel Report, *China—Measures Affecting Trading Rights and Distribution Services for Certain Publications and Audiovisual Entertainment Products*, paras. 7.759, 7.763, WTO Doc. WT/DS363/R (adopted 19 Jan 2010).

Knill C (2001) The Europeanisation of national administrations: patterns of institutional change and persistence. Cambridge University Press, Cambridge

Maxeiner JR (2013) Scalia & Garner's reading law: a civil law for the age of statutes? J Civil Law Stud 6:1–35

Pakuscher EK (1976) The use of discretion in German Law. Univ Chicago Law Rev 44:94–109

Singh MP (1985) German administrative law in common law perspective. Springer, Berlin

Chapter 17
Sequence, Hierarchy, Good Faith, Holistic Interpretation and the Possible Codification

Contents

17.1 Relations Between Different Interpretation Methods/Elements—Not a Formula of Technical Nature

In the above chapters, discussions focused on the individual methods and elements of treaty interpretation, including the ordinary meaning of textual language, the context of the interpreted provision, the object-and-purpose of the treaty, the special meaning, and the supplementary means of interpretation. There could be four possible perspectives to understand the relations among these methods and elements.

The first perspective is about whether there should be a "sequence" for their application so as to decide which one of them will be used or applied in the first place and which one will be decided in a later stage in the exercise of treaty interpretation. The only sequence that is explicitly provided in the VCLT is the

C. Lo, *Treaty Interpretation Under the Vienna Convention on the Law of Treaties*,
https://doi.org/10.1007/978-981-10-6866-9_17

relationship between Articles 31 and 32. Since Article 32 provides additional means to supplement the application, an appropriate understanding of the sequence between Articles 31 and 32 should be that Article 32 should be applied after an assessment has been made based on Article 31. Hence, the supplementary means of interpretation (whether they are used to confirm the meaning resulting from the application of Article 31, or to determine the meaning when the interpretation according to Article 31 leaves the meaning ambiguous or obscure or leads to a result which is manifestly absurd or unreasonable) should be placed in the second position for the purpose of applying it to interpret treaty terms. Concerning the relation between the ordinary meaning of textual language, the context and the object-and-purpose, legally speaking, there is no sequence required by the VCLT, nor should there be a rigid sequence adopted by an interpreter. But practically, a treaty interpreter must always begin with some methods/elements of interpretation and then conduct further exercises of interpretation based on other methods/elements.

The second perspective is about whether there should be a hierarchy of their application so as to decide whether any one of the methods/elements of treaty interpretation should be prioritized in its use or application over the others. As will be explained below, concerning the elements provided in Article 31 of the VCLT, it is possible and could be generally desirable to give a higher weight to the object-and-purpose of the interpreted treaty in real cases so that the result of treaty interpretation will not be deviating from the ultimate goal of the treaty. But there should not be a hierarchical priority being given to any one of the elements provided in Article 31. However, specifically concerning the relation between Articles 31 and 32, there is a hierarchical priority being given to Article 31.

The third perspective is about whether all methods/elements are subject to a higher principle/requirement of good faith requirement. The book argues that the good faith requirement as the fundamental principle of treaty law should be followed by a treaty interpreter and that there must be certain elements to decide the conformity of the good faith principle.

The fourth perspective is about the holistic assessment or overall assessment of various methods/elements of treaty interpretation. In conducting an overall assessment of the relevant methods/elements, flexibility must be given to the treaty interpreter. However, it does not mean that there should never be clearer rules for the interpreter to exercise his/her holistic assessment.

Having explained the above, it must also be noted that the whole treaty interpretation provisions in VCLT Articles 31 to 33 are not a formula of technical nature. As Gardiner explained:

> … the Vienna rules … are *not a step-by-step formula for producing an irrebuttable interpretation in every case.* They do indicate what is to be taken into account (in the sense of text, preamble, annexes, related agreements, preparatory works, etc.) and, to some extent, how to approach this body of material (using ordinary meaning in context, in the light of the treaty's object and purpose, distinguishing a general rule from supplementary means,

> and so on). There is in the rules a certain inherent logical sequence. They are not, however, all of use every time or always sequentially applicable.[1]
>
> (Emphasis added)

But it must also be noted that this does not mean that there could never be any formula for treaty interpretation purpose. As explained in Chap. 16 of this book, it is desirable and possible for an interpreter to create some formulas so as to help understand the very essence of some abstract treaty terms (such as "necessary" and "public morals"). Hence the understandings that the VCLT's treaty interpretation provisions are not a step-by-step formula and that the elements provided in Article 31 should not be mechanically subdivided into rigid component must not exclude the possibility of having some useful rules or formula to help apply the VCLT provisions.

17.2 Sequence and Hierarchy?

17.2.1 Rigid Sequence: "No" Within Art. 31 (Only Loosely-Understood Sequence) But "Yes" Between Arts. 31 and 32

Article 31.1 of the VCLT does not indicate the sequence of the use of the ordinary meaning, the context and the object-and-purpose. The panel on *US—Section 301 Trade Act* states in its Report that "the elements referred to in Article 31—text, context and object-and-purpose as well as good faith—are to be viewed as one holistic rule of interpretation rather than a sequence of separate tests to be applied in a hierarchical order."[2] The Appellate Body also states in its Report on *EC—Chicken Cuts* that: "… Interpretation pursuant to the customary rules codified under Article 31 of the *Vienna Convention* is ultimately a holistic exercise that should not be mechanically subdivided into rigid components…".[3]

Hence from the perspective of the overall assessment of the result of treaty interpretation under Article 31 of the VCLT, there is no legally required sequence between these elements, nor is there any inherent rigid sequence to guide the treaty interpreter under Article 31. It is even suggested that:

> … this range of material (i.e. text, context and objects and purposes, as indicated in Article 31 of the VCLT) is intended to facilitate a holistic approach to interpretation, and may even

---

[1]Gardiner (2015), p. 10.

[2]Panel Report, *United States—Sections 301–310 of the Trade Act 1974*, para. 7.22, WTO Doc. WT/DS152/R (adopted 27 Jan 2000) [hereinafter US—Section 301 Trade Act Panel Report].

[3]Appellate Body Report, *European Communities—Customs Classification of Frozen Boneless Chicken Cut*, para. 176, WTO Doc. WT/DS269/AB/R, WT/DS286/AB/R, WT/DS269/AB/R/Corr.1, WT/DS286/AB/R/Corr.1 (adopted 27 Sept 2005) [hereinafter EC—Chicken Cuts Appellate Body Report].

be characterized as a description of one. Thus, any level of sequencing between the text, context, and objects and purposes as a *modus operandi* in interpretation, if it involves or results in exclusion and hierarchy among these materials, is controversial.[4]

However, the exclusion of any rigid sequencing of these elements of treaty interpretation does not mean that an interpreter will have to and be able to start with a holistic assessment *in the very beginning* of his/her exercise of treaty interpretation, at the time when he/she is yet to have the preliminary results arising from identifying and analyzing the ordinary meanings of the interpreted term, the contexts of the term and the objects-and-purposes of the treaty. Hence, practically speaking, a treaty interpreter must begin analyzing one element before going into analyzing the other elements and before entering into an overall assessment. So there is actually a loosely-understood "practical" sequence in the use of these elements.

This loosely-understood sequence is not a rigid rule of any kind, nor a hierarchical order, but a process of practical usefulness to assist streamlining the series of thought and process in treaty interpretation.

The first step in the loosely-understood sequence is the beginning of looking at the textual wording. As explained in the previous discussions, a treaty interpreter always begins with the textual language so as to identify its most appropriate ordinary meaning. The Appellate Body states in its Report on *US—Shrimp* that: "A treaty interpreter must begin with, and focus upon, the text of the particular provision to be interpreted."[5] This is because the text is the basis to govern the parties. Understanding the textual meaning should be the prime job for the treaty interpreter. The context of the interpreted term is the perspective or attitude of looking at the textual language for the purpose of giving a proper ordinary meaning to the treaty term or provision from a broader perspective. The object-and-purpose of the interpreted treaty is an important factor to be considered when deciding the ordinary meaning to be given to the term or provision. Hence, practically, the general sequence is to identify the interpreted textual language first, then to collect possible ordinary meanings, and then deciding one the meanings to be given to the term or provision from its context, taking into consideration of the object-and-purpose of the interpreted treaty. Although the loosely-understood "sequence" mentioned here is not a mechanical process, it should be a useful and practical consideration.

The second step in the loosely-understood sequence is about the identification of the ordinary meaning. There are a number of ways of searching for and identifying the ordinary meaning of an interpreted term or provision. But a practical way of searching and identifying the ordinary meaning is to use dictionaries, as explained

[4]Qureshi (2015), p. 205.

[5]Appellate Body Report, *United States—Import Prohibition of Certain Shrimp and Shrimp Products*, para. 114, WTO Doc. WT/DS58/AB/R (adopted 6 Nov 1998).

in Chap. 9 of this book. The Appellate Body states in its Report on *US—Gambling* case that[6]:

> ... *In order to identify the ordinary meaning, a panel may start with the dictionary definitions of the terms to be interpreted.* But dictionaries, alone, are not necessarily capable of resolving complex questions of interpretation, as they typically aim to catalogue all meanings of words — be those meanings common or rare, universal or specialized. (Emphasis added)

So practically, it is useful (and sometimes even desirable) for an interpreter to start with checking the dictionaries when he/she has to conduct a treaty interpretation process. When deciding the meaning of a textual language, an interpreter will have to pay attention to the possibility of the contracting parties' intention of giving a special meaning to the term or provision. If there is such intention, then Article 31.4 will apply so as to give special meaning to the interpreted term.

But again, this loosely-understood sequence is not "dispositive". So the Appellate Body indicates in its Report on *EC—Chicken Cuts* that "dictionaries are a 'useful starting point' for the analysis of "ordinary meaning" of a treaty term, but they are *not necessarily dispositive*." (Emphasis added)[7]

Concerning the identifying the context of the interpreted term, although there is no formal sequence for this, it should also be practically useful to look at other paragraphs in the same article, other provisions in the main text of the same treaty, the preamble and the annexes in the interpreted treaty first, before looking at an agreement or instrument made in connection with the conclusion of the interpreted treaty as provided in subparagraphs (a) and (b) of Article 31.2 of the VCLT. This is because other paragraphs in the same article, other provisions in the main text, the preamble and the annexes of the interpreted treaty are the most closely connected context for an interpreted term or provision. After having considered the agreement or instrument in connection with the conclusion of the interpreted treaty, an interpreter can also look at subsequent agreement or practice, and then look at the relevant rules of international law, as provided in Article 31.3. But again, this practical "sequence" is not a rigid one. Its function is to help streamline the series of thought for treaty interpreters in discharging their jobs.

17.2.2 Hierarchy: "No" Within Art. 31 But "Yes" Between Arts. 31 and 32

As explained above, the elements of the ordinary meaning of the interpreted term, the context of the interpreted term, and the object-and-purpose of the interpreted

---

[6]Appellate Body Report, *United States—Measures Affecting the Cross-Border Supply of Gambling and Betting Services*, para. 164, fn. 191, WTO Doc. WT/DS285/AB/R, WT/DS285/AB/R/Corr.1 (adopted 20 Apr 2005).

[7]EC—Chicken Cuts Appellate Body Report, *supra* note 3, at para. 175.

treaty are *practically* used/applied in certain sequence. However, these elements should be applied equally concerning their priority positions. No one of these elements should be used so as to exclude the "consideration" of the others. Although the final result could be that the object-and-purpose of the interpreted treaty is given more weight so as to ensure that the ultimate goal of the treaty would not be undermined or frustrated, this does not mean that any one of the elements is prioritized. In other words, under Article 31, there is no "hierarchical priority" between the elements of the ordinary meaning of the interpreted term, the context of the term and the object-and-purpose of the interpreted treaty in the sense that one could *systemically* exclude or overturn the others. However, the situation between Articles 31 and 32 is different.

Under the VCLT, there are two layers of interpretation means/elements, namely the main means/elements (including the ordinary meaning in the textual language, the context and the object-and-purpose) and the supplementary means/elements (including the preparatory works, the circumstance of conclusion and other supplement means). A treaty interpreter is expected to apply Article 31 first, before he/she can resort to Article 32 when certain conditions or requirements are met. The conditions or requirements of applying Article 32 of the VCLT include the situation when an interpreter needs to confirm the meaning resulting from the application of Article 31 and the situation when the interpretation according to Article 31 will leave the meaning ambiguous or obscure or will lead to a manifestly absurd or unreasonable result.

Hence, the provisions in Article 31 are prioritized to be applied by the interpreter over Article 32, and the provisions in Article 32 are at the second level in the hierarchy of application by the treaty interpreter.

17.3 Good Faith Principle in Treaty Interpretation

17.3.1 A Separate Principle or an Element to Help Apply Ordinary Meaning, Context or Object-and-Purpose?

The good faith requirement is a fundamental principle in treaty law. The VCLT uses the term "good faith" in five different provisions. In addition to the provision in Article 31.1, the preamble of the VCLT indicates the nature of universal recognition of the good faith requirement by stating that the parties note that "that the principles of free consent and of good faith and the *pacta sunt servanda* rule are universally recognized". Article 26 of the VCLT requires treaties to be performed in a good faith manner. It reads: "Every treaty in force is binding upon the parties to it and must be performed by them in good faith." Article 46.2 uses the good faith requirement as the basis to decide a manifest violation of a provision of a party's internal law regarding competence to conclude treaties as invalidating its consent. It reads: "A violation is manifest if it would be objectively evident to any State conducting itself in the matter in accordance with normal practice and in good faith." Also under Article 69.2(b), in case of a treaty being established as invalid and void, acts performed in good faith before the invalidity should not be rendered unlawful. It reads: "If acts have nevertheless been performed in reliance on such a treaty: ... (b) acts performed in good faith before the invalidity was invoked are not rendered unlawful by reason only of the invalidity of the treaty."

The good faith requirement in connection to treaty interpretation was briefly mentioned in Chap. 9 of this book. In that chapter, the good faith requirement under VCLT Article 31.1 was compared with the good faith requirement under the CISG concerning their respective functions in treaty interpretation. Specifically for the VCLT, Article 31.1 provides: "A treaty shall be interpreted *in good faith* in accordance with the ordinary meaning to be given to the terms of the treaty in their context and in the light of its object and purpose." (Emphasis added) Hence, there is the good faith requirement in this paragraph to mandate treaty interpreters to follow when conducting treaty interpretation.

The relation between the "good faith" requirement and the three other elements (i.e. the ordinary meaning, the context and the object-and-purpose) are thus of importance. As quoted above, the Panel on *US—Section 301 Trade Act* states in its Report that "the elements referred to in Article 31—text, context and object-and-purpose as well as good faith—are to be viewed as one holistic rule of interpretation rather than a sequence of separate tests to be applied in a hierarchical order."[8] Since all these elements are to be viewed in one holistic rule, it would be a reasonable interpretation that these three elements (i.e. the ordinary meaning of the text, the context and the object-and-purpose) should all be subject to the good faith principle. This conclusion can also be drawn from the sentence of Article 31, which not only requires a treaty to "be interpreted in good faith", but also "in accordance with the ordinary meaning to be given to the terms of the treaty in their context and in the light of its object and purpose". If the giving of certain "meaning" to the terms of the treaty or the reliance of the context and the object-and-purpose is not made in good faith manner, it would not meet the requirement that the treaty should be interpreted in good faith. A writer also held similar view and commented: "All of those elements are operating within the boundaries of the good faith safeguard of giving effect to the treaty terms."[9]

Although the good faith requirement is provided in Article 31.1 of the VCLT, it does not mean that the good faith requirement is relevant only when Article 31.1 is applied. The good faith requirement should be considered as a fundamental element in the whole treaty interpretation process. So when deciding the application of Articles 31.2 and 31.3 concerning whether there is an agreement or instrument in connection with the conclusion of the interpreted treaty or whether there is a subsequent agreement or practice or relevant international law rule to be taken into account, the good faith requirement should still be observed. Even when deciding

[8]US—Section 301 Trade Act Panel Report, *supra* note 2, at para. 7.22.

[9]Ruse-Khan (2010), p. 164.

the scope of the supplementary means or deciding the requirement of ambiguity/obscurity or absurdity/unreasonableness under Article 32, an interpreter will still have to be abide by the good faith requirement.

17.3.2 A Subjective or Objective Criterion for Good Faith and Elements to Decide the Good Faith Requirement

The good faith requirement under Article 31 of the VCLT suggests that a treaty interpreter "must conduct treaty interpretation in a good faith manner". Apparently, the good faith requirement is imposed on the treaty interpreter for his/her treaty interpretation activity. An issue arises here concerning whether the interpreter should observe the good faith requirement from subjective or objective perspective. From the perspective that this requirement is imposed on the treaty interpreter, it seems that he/she must act in a *subjectively* good faith manner and that whether or not an interpreter is acting in a good faith manner must be decided based on the situation of the mind of the interpreter.

However, a subjective criterion to decide the situation of the mind of the interpreter is not practical, because it would be difficult to examine whether there is a subjective bad faith intention borne by the interpreter when he/she is conducting interpretation. There must be some objective criteria serving as the basis to decide whether the good faith requirement is observed.

The possible objective criteria should include: Fairness/unfairness of the result (to see whether the result of interpretation will be manifestly unfair or uneven to one of the disputing parties); honesty/malice (to see whether there is any objective fact to reflect that an interpreter has been acting in an un-honest manner); reasonableness/unreasonableness (to see whether the interpretation is supported by proper reasons and whether the result is reasonable to the related international community or the affected parties); consistency/inconstancy (to see whether an *obvious* and *manifest* inconsistency from previous interpretation is created without proper reason); and whether being against the goal of the treaty (to see whether the interpreted term or the object-and-purpose of the interpreted treaty is obviously disregarded or an evasion of treaty obligation by a disputing party is thus created).

In *US—Anti-Dumping and Countervailing Duties (China)*, the Appellate Body states in its Report that[10]:

> … according to Article 31 of the *Vienna Convention*, a treaty is to be interpreted in good faith. That means, *inter alia*, that terms of a treaty are not to be interpreted based on the assumption that one party is seeking to evade its obligations and will exercise its rights so as to cause injury to the other party. Yet, the United States' argument … pleads for an interpretation founded on this very assumption, and the above statement by the Panel

---

[10]Appellate Body Report, *United States—Definitive Anti-Dumping and Countervailing Duties on Certain Products from China*, para. 326, WTO Doc. WT/DS379/AB/R (adopted 25 Mar 2011).

> reveals an interpretation on this basis. A proper interpretation in accordance with Article 31 of the Vienna Convention, however, cannot proceed based on such an assumption. ...

This indicates that a treaty interpretation leading to the evasion of a party's treaty obligations is one type of treaty interpreter not acting in good faith. Although there is no jurisprudence concerning the other objective criteria as suggested in the above paragraph, this book argues that the Appellate Body's consideration of an interpretation leading to an evasion of a treaty obligation constituting a breach of the good faith requirement shows that the objective criteria need to be adopted. The above suggested elements (including whether a result being manifestly unfair or uneven, whether an un-honest manner being reflected by an objective fact, whether a result being reasonable to the related international community or the affected parties, whether an *obvious* and *manifest* inconsistency from previous interpretation being created without proper reason, and whether the interpreted treaty being obviously disregarded or an evasion of treaty obligation being created) are all objective criteria and are of the similar seriousness with the criterion suggested by the Appellate Body. Hence, it should be reasonable to include these criteria as the basis to decide the observance of the good faith requirement by a treaty interpreter.

17.4 Holistic Interpretation and Necessary Flexibility

17.4.1 Holistic Interpretation

Article 31 of the VCLT sets forth some rules, principles and elements for an interpreter to conduct treaty interpretation. Although these rules/elements are *practically* applied in sequences, a treaty interpreter is expected to conduct an overall assessment after having assessed each elements provided in these articles. In other words, an interpreter is supposed to conduct a "holistic interpretation" taking into consideration all related elements. The approach of "holistic interpretation" should be understood as *an overall assessment of all elements* provided in Article 31 by considering these *elements as mutually supportive and reinforcing* (as suggested in the Appellate Body report on *US—Continued Zeroing* quoted below).

This holistic approach has been clearly explained by the Appellate Body in a number of cases. In *EC—Chicken Cuts*, the Appellate Body states in its Report the following[11]:

> ... Interpretation pursuant to the customary rules codified in Article 31 of the *Vienna Convention* is ultimately a holistic exercise that should not be mechanically subdivided into rigid components. Considering particular surrounding circumstances under the rubric of "ordinary meaning" or "in the light of its context" would not, in our view, change the outcome of treaty interpretation....

[11]EC—Chicken Cuts Appellate Body Report, *supra* note 3, at para. 176.

The holistic interpretation is closely related to and works together with harmonious and coherent interpretation. It must also be noted that such holistic interpretation should be applied not only among the elements provided in Article 31, but also between Articles 31 and 32. It was explained above that there is a sequence and hierarchical arrangement between Articles 31 and 32 in the sense that Article 32 should be applied only to supplement the interpretation under Article 31. But this does not mean that Articles 31 and 32 should not be applied in a holistic manner. In *US—Continued Zeroing*, the Appellate Body explains the essence of the holistic interpretation as well as its application in the relation between Articles 31 and 32 of the VCLT. It states in its Report that[12]:

> The principles of interpretation that are set out in Articles 31 and 32 are to be followed in a *holistic fashion*. The interpretative exercise is engaged so as to yield an interpretation that is *harmonious and coherent* and fits comfortably in the treaty as a whole so as to render the treaty provision legally effective. A word or term may have more than one meaning or shade of meaning, but the identification of such meanings in isolation only commences the process of interpretation, it does not conclude it. … a treaty interpreter is required to have recourse to context and object and purpose to elucidate the relevant meaning of the word or term. This logical progression provides a framework for proper interpretative analysis. At the same time, it should be kept in mind that treaty interpretation is *an integrated operation*, where interpretative rules or principles must be understood and applied as *connected and mutually reinforcing components of a holistic exercise*. (Emphases added)

17.4.2 How Much Flexibility Is Desirable?

There are two flexibility aspects in connection with VCLT Articles 31 to 33. The first aspect is the rules provided in these articles are quite flexible so as to allow treaty interpreter a wide space to conduct a treaty interpretation exercise. The Study Group of the International Law Commission for "Fragmentation of International Law" indicated that:

> Articles 31 and 32 of the VCLT are, of course, widely assumed to reflect customary international law. Their appeal may be attributable to the fact that they adopt a set of practical considerations that are familiar from the national context and at the same time *general and flexible enough to provide a reasonable response to most interpretative problems*. The Convention avoids taking a stand on any of the great doctrinal debates on interpretation. The articles adopt both an 'ordinary meaning' and a 'purposive' approach; they look for party consent as well what is in accordance with good faith. It is in fact hard to think of any approach to interpretation that would be excluded from articles 31–32. Yet the Convention does not purport to be an exhaustive statement of interpretative techniques – there is not mention, for example, of *lex specialis* or *lex posterior*.[13]

---

[12]Appellate Body Report, *United States—Continued Existence and Application of Zeroing Methodology*, para. 268, WTO Doc. WT/DS350/AB/R (adopted 19 Feb 2009).

[13]Pronto and Wood (2010), p. 784.

The second aspect of flexibility in treaty interpretation is the wide space given to the interpreter in applying the VCLT provisions and in deciding the final overall assessment of the interpretation activities. More specifically, in order to conduct a holistic assessment based on Articles 31 and 32, a treaty interpreter must have certain extent of flexibility in making his/her conclusion. The Appellate Body indicates the flexibility in the context of Article 32 of the VCLT. It states in its Report on *EC—Chicken Cuts* that[14]:

> We stress ... that Article 32 does not define exhaustively the supplementary means of interpretation to which an interpreter may have recourse. It states only that they *include* the preparatory work of the treaty and the circumstances of its conclusion. Thus, an interpreter has a certain flexibility in considering relevant supplementary means in a given case so as to assist in ascertaining the common intentions of the parties.

Although this statement about treaty interpreter's flexibility is made in connection with Article 32, it is general understood that flexibility must be given to the interpreter so as to conduct a holistic exercise of interpretation.

It must also be noted that the necessary flexibility to be given to an interpreter and the holistic approach conducted by him/her are not to prevent some possible more detailed rules to decide the application of Articles 31 and 32. For instance, establishing some rules to decide the use of dictionaries is helpful in making the treaty interpretation process more transparent and can lead to a more predictable result of interpretation. The use of dictionary is merely the part of the first *practical step* (the starting step) in the exercise of treaty interpretation for the purpose of identifying the possible ordinary meanings to be given to a term or provision. The second *practical step* includes clarifying the ordinary meaning of a treaty term in its context and in the light of the object-and-purpose of the treaty. Establishing some rules to use dictionaries would not harm the overall and holistic assessment of all related interpretation elements/factors by the interpreter. The holistic assessment is the last *practical step* in the interpretation process.

Also Articles 31–33 are rules not only to enable treaty interpreters to conduct their interpretation exercises, but also to restrict their interpretation activities. This also means that a treaty interpreter is not given with unrestricted flexibilities. Treaty interpretation is ultimately bound by the rules set forth in the VCLT and hence the flexibility would not exceed the good faith requirement and other elements provided therein. Hence the flexibility can be considered as "qualified flexibility" in the sense that the flexible exercise of treaty interpretation is bound by the fundamental rules provided in VCLT Articles 31 to 32.

To conclude this chapter, it should be useful to include in a codified set of treaty interpretation rules that the elements and principles provided in Article 31 are not to be applied in a strictly sequential order and there is no hierarchical priority given to any one of these elements. But this does not mean that a treaty interpreter is prevented from conducting treaty interpretation starting from analyzing the ordinary meaning of the textual wording and from checking dictionaries to look for the range

[14]EC—Chicken Cuts Appellate Body Report, *supra* note 3, at para. 283.

of the ordinary meanings for the interpreted term. But such practical sequence is not a rigid or dispositive order in any way. An interpreter is expected to conduct an overall assessment of interpretation in a holistic manner after having conducted the interpretation exercises based on Articles 31 and 32. When conducting the holistic analysis, the interpreter should be given with some flexibility. However, such flexibility should still be subject to the provisions of VCLT Articles 31 and 32. It is also useful to include in a codified set of principles some illustrative examples to show the objective criteria of determining the good faith requirement provided in Article 31 of the VCLT.

References

Gardiner RK (2015) Treaty interpretation, 2nd edn. Oxford University Press, Oxford

Pronto A, Wood M (2010) The International Law Commission: 1999–2009, Volume IV: treaties, final draft articles, and other materials. Oxford University Press, Oxford

Qureshi AH (2015) Interpreting WTO agreements: problems and perspectives, 2nd edn. Cambridge University Press, Cambridge

Ruse-Khan HG (2010) A real partnership for development? Sustainable development as treaty objective in European economic partnership agreements and beyond. J Int Econ Law 13: 139–180

Part III
New Issues and Perspectives

Chapter 18
Introducing Fundamental Values into Treaty Interpretation and the Possible Codification

Contents

18.1 Treaty Interpretation not a Mechanical Process

18.1.1 Examples of Non-mechanicalness in Selecting an Ordinary Meaning

Treaty interpretation must be as objective as possible so that the result will not be departing from the interpreted text, the context of the interpreted term and the object-and-purpose of the interpreted treaty. It must also be able to maintain the highest level of predictability so that the treaty provisions can be applied and operated in a consistent manner. However, it is also true that treaty interpretation is not a mechanical procedure, which could always result in exactly same conclusions.

C. Lo, *Treaty Interpretation Under the Vienna Convention on the Law of Treaties*,
https://doi.org/10.1007/978-981-10-6866-9_18

The followings are some examples showing that treaty interpretation should not be a purely mechanical procedure.

Treaty interpretation process involves various elements of evaluation and selections of values. There could be two or more "ordinary meanings" for a treaty term defined in the dictionary. A treaty interpreter will have to decide the "most appropriate ordinary meaning" to be applied to the text. When deciding the "most appropriate ordinary meaning" for an interpreted term, the interpreter is actually conducting an evaluation process from various perspectives. The process commonly involves the interpreter's discernment and even a selection of different values.

For instance, the term "pest" is usually used to refer to the dictionary definition of "an insect or other small animal that harms or destroys garden plants, trees, etc."[1] But it can also be used to refer to "an annoying or troublesome person, animal, or thing; nuisance."[2] If the first definition is applied, apparently the term "pest" would refer to "animal" (i.e. an insect or other small animal) and the animal must be a living one. Such definition would exclude "plants" and "non-living organisms". But if the second definition is applied, the term would cover not only animals, but also other "things" (such as plants and even other non-living organisms).

The Panel for *EC—Approval and Marketing of Biotech Products* chose the second definition and explained in its report that the selection of such definition was based on the context of Annex A of the SPS Agreement.[3] The Panel Report states the reasons for choosing such definition:

---

[1]http://www.dictionary.com/browse/pest. Accessed 13 Aug 2017.

[2]Id.

[3]Annex A (entitled "definitions") of the SPS Agreement has the following provisions in paragraph 1.

The term "pest" is provided in subparagraphs (a), (c) and (d).

1. Sanitary or phytosanitary measure—Any measure applied:
    a. to protect animal or plant life or health within the territory of the Member from risks arising from the entry, establishment or spread of pests, diseases, disease-carrying organisms or disease-causing organisms;
    b. to protect human or animal life or health within the territory of the Member from risks arising from additives, contaminants, toxins or disease-causing organisms in foods, beverages or feedstuffs;
    c. to protect human life or health within the territory of the Member from risks arising from diseases carried by animals, plants or products thereof, or from the entry, establishment or spread of pests; or
    d. to prevent or limit other damage within the territory of the Member from the entry, establishment or spread of pests.

In addition to the definition provided in paragraph 1 of the Annex A, there is "Footnote 4" attached to the title of this annex: "For the purpose of these definitions, 'animal' includes fish and wild fauna; 'plant' includes forests and wild flora; 'pests' include weeds; and 'contaminants' include pesticide and veterinary drug residues and extraneous matter."

> The Panel notes at the outset that three of the subparagraphs of Annex A(1) to the SPS Agreement, namely, Annex A(1)(a), A(1)(c) and A(1)(d), identify 'pests' as a possible source of risks. *The word 'pest' ordinarily means 'a troublesome, annoying or destructive person, animal, or thing'.* In applying this definition to Annex A(1), *we find two contextual elements in particular to be noteworthy. The first is the previously mentioned footnote to the definitions provided in Annex A of the SPS Agreement. It specifies that, for the purposes of the SPS Agreement, the term "pest" includes weeds. Weeds are plants. Therefore, we consider that the term 'pest' in Annex A(1) must be understood to cover plants in addition to animals. The other element which we find instructive are the references in Annex A(1)(a) and A(1)(c) to 'animal or plant life or health' and 'human life or health' as well as the reference in Annex A(1)(d) to 'other damage'. It is apparent from these references that the SPS Agreement is intended to be applicable, not just to measures taken to protect against risks which pose a threat to the life, and thus the very existence, of animals, plants or humans, but also to measures taken to protect against risks to the 'health' of animals, plants or humans, and to measures taken to prevent other 'damage' within the territory of a Member.* In the light of this, we consider that the term 'pest' should be interpreted to cover 'destructive' animals or plants — that is animals or plants which destroy the life and threaten the very existence of other animals, plants or humans. Equally, however, we think that, for the purposes of the SPS Agreement, the term 'pest' should be interpreted to cover animals and plants which cause other, less serious, deleterious effects, namely, animals and plants which cause harm to the health of animals, plants or humans or which cause other harm.[4]
>
> The European Communities has argued that a pest must be a living organism. We have previously noted that the term 'pest' in Annex A(1) encompasses plants which are destructive, or which cause harm to the health of other animals, plants or humans. While it may be true that many organisms will lose their ability to act as pests if they are no longer alive, we are not persuaded that this is necessarily always the case. In particular, we are not convinced that all plants which are pests as living organisms cease to be destructive or harmful to health immediately after being harvested.[5]
>
> (Emphasis added)

18.1.2 Examples of Non-mechanicalness in Selecting an Object-and-Purpose and Context

It is also possible that there are two or more objectives specified in a treaty which by their natures are in conflict with each other. An interpreter will have to evaluate these objectives so as to decide the "most suitable" one to help interpret a treaty clause. Also there could be two or more provisions relevant to the interpreted clause in the same treaty or in another treaty within the same treaty system. An interpreter will have to decide which one should be the "most relevant context" to the

---

[4]Panel Report, *European Communities—Measures Affecting the Approval and Marketing of Biotech Products*, paras. 7.238–7.239, WTO Doc. WT/DS291/R, WT/DS292/R, WT/DS293/R (adopted 21 Nov 2006).

[5]Id. at para. 7.351.

interpreted clause. For instance, the first recital in the Preamble of the Agreement Establishing the WTO reads:

> *Recognizing* that their relations in the field of trade and economic endeavour should be conducted with a view to raising standards of living, ensuring full employment and a large and steadily growing volume of real income and effective demand, and expanding the production of and trade in goods and services, while allowing for the optimal use of the world's resources in accordance with the objective of sustainable development, seeking both to protect and preserve the environment and to enhance the means for doing so in a manner consistent with their respective needs and concerns at different levels of economic development,

At least there are the following various "objects-and-purposes" that can be identified from this paragraph: (1) raising standards of living, (2) ensuring full employment, (3) ensuring a large and steadily growing volume of real income, (4) ensuring an effective demand, (5) expanding the production of and trade in goods and services, (6) allowing for the optimal use of the world's resources in accordance with the objective of sustainable development, (7) seeking both to protect and preserve the environment and to enhance the means for doing so in a manner consistent with their respective needs and concerns at different levels of economic development. The objective of "expanding the production of and trade in goods and services" can be very different from the objectives of "sustainable development" and "protection/preservation of environment", because the expansion of production implies that there will be more use of resources, whereas the sustainable development entails a limited used of resources. This preambular paragraph in the Agreement Establishing the WTO has some elements which are also mentioned in the Preamble of the GATT, but it also has some other elements which are different from those provided in the GATT Preamble. The first recital provided in the GATT Preamble reads:

> Recognizing that their relations in the field of trade and economic endeavour should be conducted with a view to raising standards of living, ensuring full employment and a large and steadily growing volume of real income and effective demand, developing the full use of the resources of the world and expanding the production and exchange of goods,

The common elements included in both preambles include raising standards of living, ensuring full employment and a large and steadily growing volume of real income and effective demand, and expanding the production and exchange of goods. The most obvious difference is that in the Preamble of the Agreement Establishing the WTO, there is the inclusion of environmental protection and sustainable development, whereas in the GATT Preamble, the focus is on the full use of the resources of the world. When addressing the GATT issues, the Appellate Body decided to rely on the Preamble of the Agreement Establishing the WTO (instead of the GATT Preamble) and to rely on the objective of sustainable development provided in the Preamble of the Agreement Establishing the WTO (instead of the expansion of production of and trade in goods provided in the same preamble).

Since the Appellate Body treated the preambular wordings as reflecting the objects-and-purposes and as contexts for the interpretation of WTO agreements, when deciding the use of particular terms in the Preamble of the Agreement Establishing the WTO, the Appellate Body is actually selecting an object-and-purpose over the other objects-and-purposes or selecting one context over the other contexts.

The Appellate Body in its Report on *US—Shrimp* indicates the following:

> The words of Article XX(g), 'exhaustible natural resources', were actually crafted more than 50 years ago. They must be read by a treaty interpreter in the light of contemporary concerns of the community of nations about the protection and conservation of the environment. While Article XX was not modified in the Uruguay Round, *the preamble attached to the WTO Agreement shows that the signatories to that Agreement were, in 1994, fully aware of the importance and legitimacy of environmental protection as a goal of national and international policy.* The preamble of the WTO Agreement — which informs not only the GATT 1994, but also the other covered agreements — explicitly acknowledges 'the objective of sustainable development'...[6]
>
> At the end of the Uruguay Round, negotiators fashioned an appropriate preamble for the new WTO Agreement, which strengthened the multilateral trading system by establishing an international organization, inter alia, to facilitate the implementation, administration and operation, and to further the objectives, of that Agreement and the other agreements resulting from that Round. In recognition of the importance of continuity with the previous GATT system, negotiators used the preamble of the GATT 1947 as the template for the preamble of the new WTO Agreement. *Those negotiators evidently believed, however, that the objective of 'full use of the resources of the world' set forth in the preamble of the GATT 1947 was no longer appropriate to the world trading system of the 1990s.* As a result, they decided to qualify the original objectives of the GATT 1947 with the following words:
>
> ... while allowing for the optimal use of the world's resources in accordance with the objective of sustainable development, seeking both to protect and preserve the environment and to enhance the means for doing so in a manner consistent with their respective needs and concerns at different levels of economic development,...'
>
> We note once more that this language demonstrates a recognition by WTO negotiators that optimal use of the world's resources should be made in accordance with the objective of sustainable development. *As this preambular language reflects the intentions of negotiators of the WTO Agreement, we believe it must add colour, texture and shading to our interpretation of the agreements annexed to the WTO Agreement,* in this case, the GATT 1994. We have already observed that Article XX(g) of the GATT 1994 is appropriately read with the perspective embodied in the above preamble....
>
> It is proper for us *to take into account, as part of the context of the chapeau, the specific language of the preamble to the WTO Agreement,* which, we have said, gives colour, texture and shading to the rights and obligations of Members under the WTO Agreement, generally, and under the GATT 1994, in particular.[7]

---

[6] Appellate Body Report, *United States—Import Prohibition of Certain Shrimp and Shrimp Products*, para. 129, WTO Doc. WT/DS58/AB/R (adopted 6 Nov 1998).

[7] Id. at paras. 152–153, 155.

18.1.3 The Possibility of an Interpreter's Value to Play a Role in Treaty Interpretation

Since a treaty interpreter will have to make decisions in searching for and selecting the "right" meaning or the "most appropriate" understanding of a treaty term in discharging his/her duty, it is not possible to exclude the situation that the values or positions regarding the subject matter held by the interpreter will affect the whole outcome of interpretation. In the above examples, the Panel of *EC—Approval and Marketing of Biotech Products* selected the meaning of "things" including plaints and non-living organisms for the term "pest" so as to protect against risks to the "health" of animals, plants or humans, and to measures taken to prevent other "damage" within the territory of a Member. The Appellate Body selected the context or object-and-purpose of sustainable development in *US—Shrimp* so as to enhance the environmental protection.

From this perspective, treaty interpretation is not a mechanical process, nor merely a linguistic process to identify a meaning of the interpreted term. It is sometimes unavoidable to have certain values being intentionally/unintentionally or directly/indirectly introduced into the process and the results of treaty interpretation. Since it is sometimes not likely to avoid the direct or indirect introduction of certain selected values into the process, also since it could be a positive direction to have some fundamental values to be considered in the treaty interpretation process, a further question to be addressed is whether the introduction of values into the process can be made in a systemic and transparent manner so that the result of treaty interpretation will still be objective and predictable.

In the following discussions, the WTO agreements will be used as an example to show that there are internal and external values which are relevant to treaty interpretation process of WTO provisions. Internal values can be introduced through resorting to the text, the context and the object-and-purpose, whereas external values can be introduced into treaty interpretation process *mainly* through interpreting the textual meaning of treaty terms, or sometimes through considering the adoption of certain new treaties as subsequent state practice. An introduction of external values can still be objective and predictable, and should be acceptable under international law.

18.2 Fundamental Human Values Relevant to Treaty Interpretation

18.2.1 Scope of Fundamental Human Values

There are certain human values which are so fundamental so that they are universally accepted (i.e. the universal values) or they help shape a society and are deeply embedded in it (i.e. the domestic or local values). Both domestic and international legal systems will have to respect these values and to support them.

In order to be considered as fundamental human values, they must be of the trait that they are the deeply held beliefs and the highest priorities of the domestic or international society. Since they are so fundamental, they should have the function of guiding human practices, including the practices in domestic and international matters.

Some human values are by their natures fundamental. For instance, the protection of human life and health and the respect of dignity of others are by their nature fundamental. Some other human values are recognized and protected by various international treaties or instruments. For instance, there are treaties and instruments confirming the protection of certain categories of human rights. The International Covenant on Civil and Political Rights and the International Covenant on Economic, Social and Cultural Rights include the right to self-determination; right to liberty; the right to due process of law; the right to freedom of movement; the right to freedom of thought; the right to freedom of religion; the right to freedom of expression; the right to peaceable assembly; and the right to freedom of association. These human rights should constitute the very important parts of the core human values and should be respected not merely in the international disputes arising directly from these human rights instruments, but also in other international disputes, including trade disputes.

18.2.2 Internal Values

The terms "internal" and "external" are used to refer to the distinction between the situation where a human value is explicitly provided in the text of an interpreted treaty and the situation where a human value is not explicitly incorporated in the treaty text, but should be introduced into the treaty through interpretation.

Most treaties or treaty systems have explicitly incorporated certain values to be pursued, guarded or protected. This is also the case of the WTO system, in which some fundamental values have already been built in the WTO rules. The following are the salient examples of fundamental human values which have been explicitly recognized and incorporated into the WTO rules:

(1) Human life and health: GATT Article XX(b)[8] and GATS Article XIV(b)[9] include the protection of human life or health as an exception to the obligations or as a justification the violation of the obligations under these agreements.

[8]Article XX(b) of the GATT reads: "Subject to the requirement that such measures are not applied in a manner which would constitute a means of arbitrary or unjustifiable discrimination between countries where the same conditions prevail, or a disguised restriction on international trade, nothing in this Agreement shall be construed to prevent the adoption or enforcement by any contracting party of measures: … (b) necessary to protect human, animal or plant life or health;…"

[9]Article XIV(b) of the GATS reads: "Subject to the requirement that such measures are not applied in a manner which would constitute a means of arbitrary or unjustifiable discrimination between countries where like conditions prevail, or a disguised restriction on trade in services, nothing in

Human life, including the sanctity of life, should be the highest fundamental value, which should be respected by both domestic and international legal systems. Human health is also a core human value of key importance. The Constitution of the World Health Organization states in its Preamble and in Article 1 very clearly that "The enjoyment of the highest attainable standard of health is one of the fundamental rights of every human being" and that the objective of the WHO shall be "the attainment by all peoples of the highest possible level of health." Since human life and health are important justifications for breaching GATT and GATS obligations, they are placed in a *superior position* over trade obligations. GATT Article XX and GATS Article XIV reflect the high respect of the fundamental values of human life and health.

The WTO jurisprudence also recognizes human life and health as the highest degree of the human values. In *European Communities—Measures Affecting Asbestos and Asbestos-containing Products* (*EC—Asbestos*), the Appellate Body Report states: "the objective pursued by the measure is the preservation of human life and health through the elimination, or reduction, of the well-known, and life-threatening, health risks posed by asbestos fibres. The value pursued is *both vital and important in the highest degree*."[10] (Emphasis added)

(2) Public morals and public order: GATT Article XX(a)[11] includes the protection of public morals. GATS Article XIV(a)[12] also includes the protection of both public morals and public order. These values can be applied to justify the trade measures which are otherwise in breach of GATT or GATS rules if there were no such exceptions. Hence, public morals and public order are placed in a higher position over trade obligations.

WTO jurisprudence clarifies the meaning of public morals and public order. In *United States—Measures Affecting the Cross-Border Supply of Gambling and Betting Services*[13] (hereinafter *US—Gambling*), it concerns Antigua and Barbuda's

(Footnote 9 continued)

this Agreement shall be construed to prevent the adoption or enforcement by any Member of measures: … (b) necessary to protect human, animal or plant life or health;…"

[10]Appellate Body Report, *European Communities—Measures Affecting Asbestos and Products Containing Asbestos*, para. 172, WTO Doc. WT/DS135/AB/R (adopted 5 Apr 2001).

[11]Article XX(a) of the GATT reads: "… nothing in this Agreement shall be construed to prevent the adoption or enforcement by any contracting party of measures: (a) necessary to protect public morals;…"

[12]Article XIV(a) of the GATS reads: "… nothing in this Agreement shall be construed to prevent the adoption or enforcement by any Member of measures:… (a) necessary to protect public morals or to maintain public order;…"

[13]Appellate Body Report, *United States—Measures Affecting the Cross-Border Supply of Gambling and Betting Services*, WTO Doc. WT/DS285/AB/R (adopted 20 Apr 2005) [hereinafter US—Gambling Appellate Body Report]; Panel Report, *United States—Measures Affecting the Cross-Border Supply of Gambling and Betting Services*, WTO Doc. WT/DS285/R (adopted 20 Apr 2005).

complaint against the United States. The complainant alleged that certain U.S. federal and state laws had a cumulative impact of preventing the supply of gambling and betting services from another WTO Member to the United States on a cross-border basis. The Panel states that "the term 'public morals' denotes *standards of right and wrong* conduct maintained by or on behalf of a community or nation".[14] (Emphasis added) It also decides that the dictionary definition of the word "order", read together with GATS footnote 5,[15] suggests that "'public order' refers to the preservation of the *fundamental interests of a society*, as reflected in public policy and law. These fundamental interests can relate, inter alia, to standards of law, security and morality."[16] (Emphasis added)

(3) Protection of exhaustible natural resources/endangered species: GATT Article XX(g) also includes measures "relating to the conservation of exhaustible natural resources" as an exception to other obligations in the GATT.[17] The WTO jurisprudence has indicated that both "mineral" or "non-living" resources and living species which are susceptible to depletion could be exhaustible natural resources. The protection of endangered species has been a very important human value due to the biodiversity crisis of a large amount of species being threatened with extinction.[18] This threatening trend can be reversed if appropriate efforts are put forth. GATT Article XX(g) is a solid recognition of a very important human value of protecting endangered species and preserving biodiversity.

It must be borne in mind that, there are other items listed in GATT Article XX and GATS Article XIV, and many of them are not of the nature of fundamental values (but are of economic and other considerations). For instance, measures relating to the importations or exportations of gold or silver [as provided in GATT Article XX(c)] or those necessary to secure compliance with laws or regulations [as provided in GATT Article XX(d)] per se are not for the protection of fundamental human values. They are included to ensure the financial stability and compliance of domestic law.

(4) Sustainability: The "sustainable development" is specifically mentioned in the preamble of the Establishing Agreement of the WTO. It states that Members recognize that "their relations in the field of trade and economic endeavour

[14]Para. 6.465 in the Panel Report.

[15]GATS footnote 5 provides: "The public order exception may be invoked only where a genuine and sufficiently serious threat is posed to one of the fundamental interests of society."

[16]Para. 6.467 in the Panel Report.

[17]Article XX(g) of the GATT reads: "… nothing in this Agreement shall be construed to prevent the adoption or enforcement by any contracting party of measures: … (g) relating to the conservation of exhaustible natural resources if such measures are made effective in conjunction with restrictions on domestic production or consumption; …"

[18]Protecting Biodiversity. http://www.davidsuzuki.org/issues/wildlife habitat/science/endangered-species-legislation/protecting-biodiversity/. Accessed 13 Aug 2017.

should be conducted with a view to … expanding the production of and trade in goods and services, while allowing for the optimal use of the world's resources in accordance with the objective of sustainable development".

Sustainable development is defined in "Our Common Future" (i.e. the Brundtland Report) as the "development that meets the needs of the present without compromising the ability of future generations to meet their own needs." It includes two key concepts: "the concept of needs, in particular the essential needs of the world's poor, to which overriding priority should be given"; and "the idea of limitations imposed by the state of technology and social organization on the environment's ability to meet present and future needs."[19] Although the concept of "sustainable development" has not become an international law principle, it should be considered as a built-in fundamental human value because of the explicit inclusion of the concept in the WTO Agreement as an important objective of the WTO.

(5) Public health: Public health is about the health of the population, whereas human health mentioned above is about the health of individuals. Public health is defined as "all organized measures (whether public or private) to prevent disease, promote health, and prolong life among the population as a whole" with the aim to "provide conditions in which people can be healthy and focus on entire populations, not on individual patients or diseases."[20] Since it is to promote a healthier population, it is of pivotal importance in all society and should be properly regarded in all legal systems. In the TRIPS Agreement, public health is explicitly incorporated in the text. Article 8.1 of the TRIPS Agreement states: "Members may, in formulating or amending their laws and regulations, adopt measures necessary to protect public health and nutrition …, provided that such measures are consistent with the provisions of this Agreement." Hence public health is an internal value of the TRIPS Agreement. However, for other WTO agreements (such as the GATT), public health is not a built-in value. But it should still be considered as an external value due to its high importance in protecting the population as a whole.
(6) Procedural fairness and due process: There are two due process requirements in GATT Article X. They include Article X:3(a) (which requires uniform application of laws and regulations) and Article X:3(b) (which requires WTO Members to maintain "judicial, arbitral or administrative tribunals or procedures for the purpose, inter alia, of the prompt review and correction of administrative action relating to customs matters").[21] Due process is about an

[19]World Commission on Environment and Development (WCED) (1987), p. 43.

[20]http://www.who.int/trade/glossary/story076/en/. Accessed 13 Aug 2017.

[21]The complete provisions of Article 10:3(a) and (b) of the GATT are quoted here: "(a) Each contracting party shall administer in a uniform, impartial and reasonable manner all its laws, regulations, decisions and rulings of the kind described in paragraph 1 of this Article. (b) Each contracting party shall maintain, or institute as soon as practicable, judicial, arbitral or administrative tribunals or procedures for the purpose, inter alia, of the prompt review and correction of

individual (including a business) being treated fairly and efficiently by the State or its government agencies. This should be the single most important fundamental value of procedural nature.

One potentially controversial issue could be whether trade liberalization under the GATT and the GATS and the protection of intellectual property under the TRIPS Agreement are also internal fundamental values of the WTO. The answer should be both positive and negative. Trade liberalization and intellectual property rights protection are important values under the WTO system. However, these are "contractual values". Trade liberalization is to be carried out only to the extents which have been committed by WTO Members. Also the protection of intellectual property rights should be implemented only to the extents required under minimum standards of the TRIPS Agreement. These are, by their nature, not fundamental human values to be fully respected under all circumstances. Having said these (that trade liberalization and intellectual property protection are not fundamental human values), they are still very important objects-and-purposes for the WTO agreements (as reflected in the Preamble of the Agreement Establishing the WTO that "the substantial reduction of tariffs and other barriers to trade and to the elimination of discriminatory treatment in international trade relations" is desirable) and for the TRIPS Agreement (as reflected in its Preamble that it is desirable "to promote effective and adequate protection of intellectual property rights").

18.2.3 External Values

There are other values which are not built into the WTO text but are relevant to the operation of the WTO. These can be seen as external values for the trade rules under the WTO. These values should at least include the following:

(1) Human rights: Since human rights and fundamental freedoms are supposed to be respected, promoted and fulfilled by all States, it is unimaginable that the interpretation and application of WTO rules will result in infringing human rights or in disrespecting the dignity of the people.[22]

(Footnote 21 continued)

administrative action relating to customs matters. Such tribunals or procedures shall be independent of the agencies entrusted with administrative enforcement and their decisions shall be implemented by, and shall govern the practice of, such agencies unless an appeal is lodged with a court or tribunal of superior jurisdiction within the time prescribed for appeals to be lodged by importers; Provided that the central administration of such agency may take steps to obtain a review of the matter in another proceeding if there is good cause to believe that the decision is inconsistent with established principles of law or the actual facts."

[22]It must be noted that for some human rights treaties, there are certain provisions which are subject to the reservations by some contracting States. For such parts, apparently there could be different views about whether they still constitute the core human values.

(2) Core labour standards: The International Labour Organization (ILO) has set forth five minimum standards for all workers throughout the world. These minimum standards are laid out in eight conventions. They include the freedom of association (as provided in Conventions No. 87 & No. 98); the effective recognition of the right to collective bargaining (as provided in Conventions No. 87 & No. 98); the elimination of all forms of forced and compulsory labour (as provided in Conventions No. 29 & No. 105); the effective abolition of child labour (as provided in Conventions No. 138 & No. 182); and the elimination of discrimination in respect of employment and occupation (as provided in Conventions No. 100 & No. 111).[23] Although these minimum standards are not mentioned in the WTO agreements, they also have similar nature with other human rights and should be considered as so important to be universally accepted.
(3) Animal welfare: Animal welfare concerns the well-being and proper treatment of animals, including animals in laboratories, companion animals, farm animals, marine life, and wildlife. Although animals do not enjoy the same extent of protection of the fundamental rights which are enjoyed by human beings, it is still the brightest human nature to treat animals in a humane way. Although GATT Article XX (b) and GATS Article XIV (b) mention animal life and health, these are of different nature from the protection of animal welfare. The WTO does not explicitly include the protection of animal welfare as a fundamental value which is superior over trade measures, but the WTO jurisprudence has included animal welfare into the scope of public morals. This will be explained below.

18.2.4 Domestic and Universal Values

There are certain values which should be understood and defined in the local context. Among the values mentioned above, public morals and public order as well as animal welfare are the salient examples of domestic values, the local recognition of which still needs to be respected.

(1) Public morals and public orders: These are important values. But the contents can be understood only in a domestic context. For some countries, gambling might not be a moral problem at all; but for many other countries, gambling can be in serious violation of their local moral standards. Also for some countries, very broad range of pornographic products can become seriously against public

---

[23]What Are ILO Conventions and Core Labour Standards? http://www.cleanclothes.org/issues/faq/ilo. Accessed 13 Aug 2017.

morals; but for some other countries, regulations of pornography are much more relaxed. Although neither GATT Article XX(a) nor GATS Article XIV(a) has mentioned that public morals and public order should be understood and interpreted in a domestic context, it is apparent the provisions allow countries to maintain domestic values and hence if there are domestic morals and local public order to be maintained, the restrictive measures can be justified as long as other requirements in these provisions are fully met.

In the above quoted Panel Report of *US—Gambling*, the Panel indicates clearly that the term "public morals" denotes standards of right and wrong conduct maintained by or on behalf of "a community or nation" and the term "public order" refers to the preservation of the fundamental interests of "a society". Apparently, these exceptions concern the value of a country, a community or a society. Although maintaining public morals and public order is a universally recognized principle, the contents of public morals and public order of a jurisdiction do not have to be universally accepted. The concepts of morality and public order under GATT Article XX and GATS Article XIV should be decided in the context of the country where a disputed restrictive measure is adopted.

(2) Animal welfare: There has not been a set of universally accepted standards for treating animals. But, regionally, there has been Article 13 of the Treaty on the Functioning of the European Union (TFEU), which provides that: "In formulating and implementing the Union's agriculture, fisheries, transport, internal market, research and technological development and space policies, the Union and the Member States shall, since animals are sentient beings, pay full regard to the welfare requirements of animals, while respecting the legislative or administrative provisions and customs of the Member States relating in particular to religious rites, cultural traditions and regional heritage." Hence, for European Union countries, the protection of animal welfare has become an important value, which is put "on equal footing with other key principles mentioned in the same title i.e. promote gender equality, guarantee social protection, protect human health, combat discrimination, promote sustainable development, ensure consumer protection, protect personal data" provided in Title II of the TFEU.[24] Although animal welfare is of high importance for European countries, it does not enjoy the equally high recognition in all other regions or countries outside the European Union.

Many other fundamental values are universal both in their meanings and contents. They should not be modified to meet individual country's situation. For instance, human life and health as well as public health concern the values of highest degree. The protection of them should not be different from society to

[24]Animal Welfare. http://ec.europa.eu/food/animal/welfare/policy/index_en.htm. Accessed 13 Aug 2017.

society. Also, human rights and the minimum labour standards are included in many universally accepted treaties. Their contents and requirements have been universally accepted.[25] Countries are not supposed to deviate from these standards based on their different stages of economic development, different cultural backgrounds and different social structures. These universally recognized values should also play important roles in the operation of WTO rules.

18.3 The Operation of "Internal Values" for Treaty Interpretation

Among the provisions in Articles 31 through 33 of the VCLT, Article 31 is most relevant provision to the discussion here. For the above mentioned "internal values" of WTO, they are incorporated in the text of the agreements and should have the function as a context and the object-and-purpose for an interpreted provision.

As explained above, treaty interpretation always begins with the text of treaty provisions. The protections of public morals, public order, human life and health and exhaustible natural resources are explicitly included in GATT Article XX and GATS Article XIV as exceptions to other obligations in these agreements and as defences and justification for the violation of other obligations under these agreements. These fundamental values should play their roles as instructed by the text of the agreements.

The sustainability is included in the Preamble of the Agreement Establishing the WTO. Sustainable development can be considered as a very important object-and-purpose of all WTO agreements or as a context for the interpretation of various WTO provisions. Public health is included in TRIPS Article 8.1, which is entitled "Principles". So public health can also be considered as the object-and-purpose of the TRIPS Agreement or a context of other TRIPS provisions.

In short, if an internal value has been given a specific role in a treaty [such as the protection of "public moral" being given the role of serving as an exception under GATT Article XX(a)], such value should play the role as instructed by the treaty. If an internal value can be considered as constituting an object-and-purpose, it should also have the role of guiding the interpretation as expected by VCLT Article 31. And if an internal value can be considered as a context of an interpreted provision, the interpreter must take it into consideration when interpreting the provision.

---

[25] Unless any one of the human rights contents in a treaty has been reserved by a specific country as permitted by the treaty.

18.4 External Values Being Introduced Through Treaty Interpretation Process

18.4.1 To Incorporate External Values Through Textual Interpretation

Since the external values have such nature of fundamentality and high importance for human beings, it is desirable to have certain appropriate extent of respect to them by WTO agreements. For treaty interpreters, whenever it is possible, they should choose the way of interpretation which is more in line with the protection of such fundamental values, such as the protection of human rights, the core labour standards, public health and animal welfare.

This does not mean that the WTO should be transformed into a human rights organization with the main objective of promoting better protection of human rights, labour rights and animal welfare. For instance, a WTO Member is not permitted to impose trade sanctions against a particular WTO Member for the mere reason that there is a lack of sufficient protection of human rights or animal welfare in this country. However, if the lack of protection of human rights or animal welfare in an exporting country would lead to undermining or adversely affecting the *fundamental values in the importing country* and if the traded product relates to infringement of human rights or animal welfare, it should be possible for the importing country to adopt trade measures to protect its fundamental values in the protection of human rights and animal welfare. For instance, it should be possible for the importing country to claim that since the imported product (such as diamond) has been produced by a group of workers in the exporting country who had been treated in a seriously inhuman manner during the production process, the permission of sale and consumption of such product in the importing country would be vastly against the moral requirement there. Hence it should be allowed to refuse the importation of such product based on the provision in GATT Article XX(a) (concerning the necessary protection of its public morals).

The protection of fundamental values which are external to the WTO should be made possible through different interpretation methods, mainly through the interpretation of the textual wordings of WTO rules. The following are some examples to show the appropriateness of incorporating the external values into the operation of the WTO through textual interpretation of existing WTO provisions:

(1) To incorporate the value of "public health" into the GATS through the textual interpretation of the ordinary meaning of "public morals" and "public order": In *US—Gambling*, the Appellate Body elaborated the concepts of public morals and public order and confirmed that the interests and concerns which relate to these concepts in this case include: organized crime (because it is easier to use remote gambling as a clearinghouse and is easier for organized criminals to hide their involvement in gambling and evade law enforcement); money laundering (because the volume, speed and international reach of remote

gambling transactions combined with the offshore locations of most remote suppliers and the virtual anonymity of such transactions mean that the "layering and integration" stages of money laundering are effectively facilitated); risks to children (including underage gambling); fraud (because the barriers to establishing an online gambling operation are low so that unscrupulous operators can appear and disappear within minutes); and public health risk (such as pathological gambling).[26] Among these four concerns, public health relates to the above mentioned fundamental human values. It was explained above that public health is an internal value for the TRIPS Agreement, but it is an external value for other WTO agreements. The concept of public health cannot be directly applied in other WTO agreements, including the GATS. It can only be incorporated into the operation of the GATS through an approach of interpreting the meaning and scope of the terms "public morals" and "public order", as adopted by the Appellate Body in its Report on *US—Gambling*.

(2) To incorporate the value of "animal welfare" into the GATT through the textual interpretation of the ordinary meaning of "public morals": In *European Communities—Measures Prohibiting the Importation and Marketing of Seal Products* (*EC—Seal Products*),[27] "the European Union seeks to address the public moral concerns on seal welfare through the EU Seal Regime." The Panel confirms the existence of the EU public concerns on seal welfare in general and finds that such concerns are "of a moral nature within the European Union."[28] "The European Union submits that the 'moral concern with regard to the protection of animals' is regarded as a value of high importance in the European Union." The Panel considers, and the parties do not dispute, that "the protection of such public moral concerns is indeed an important value or interest."[29] Thus although animal welfare is an external value to the WTO and hence the concept of "animal welfare" cannot be *directly applied* by treaty interpreters of WTO law, it can still be incorporated into the operation of the GATT through interpreting the meaning and scope of the term "public morals" provided in GATT Article XX(a) so as to safeguard the moral standards in the European Union.

(3) To incorporate the value of "human rights" and "core labour standards" into the GATT through the textual interpretation of the ordinary meaning of "public morals": Human rights and core labour standards concern the fundamental welfare and interests of human beings. They definitely should be given a higher extent of recognition in legal regimes than the concept of animal welfare. Since the concept of animal welfare is interpreted as falling within the scope of the term "public morals", there should not be of any difficulty of interpreting

---

[26]US—Gambling Appellate Body Report, *supra* note 13, paras. 278–284.

[27]Panel Report, *European Communities—Measures Prohibiting the Importation and Marketing of Seal Products*, WTO Doc. WT/DS400/R, WT/DS401/R (adopted 18 June 2014).

[28]Id. at para. 7.631.

[29]Id. at para. 7.632.

human rights and core labour standards also belonging to the concept of "public morals" provided in GATT Article XX(a). The above mentioned diamond importation is an example of such kind.

Also for instance, a developed country includes the criteria of human rights protection or minimum labour standards in its Generalized System of Preferences (GSP)[30] to exclude those developing countries not meeting these criteria from enjoying its GSP. This is a discriminatory practice against some economically similarly situated developing countries and could be alleged as being in breach of the MFN obligation in GATT Article I. However, such discriminatory measure might be justified under the "public morals" exception of GATT Article XX(a), if other requirements under Article XX [including the requirements in the Chapeau of this article and the necessity requirement in paragraph (a)] are also met. This is because the importing country might be able to argue that there are public concerns on human rights and core labour standards, which are of a moral nature within its territory. Such public concerns fall within the scope of GATT Article XX(a).

(4) To incorporate the value of "public health" into the GATT through the textual interpretation of the ordinary meaning of "human life and health": For instance, there are the Framework Convention on Tobacco Control (FCTC), its supplementing protocol and some sets of implementing Guidelines under the FCTC to prioritize the protection of public health and to remove the spread of the tobacco epidemic, which is a global problem with serious consequences for public health.[31] The measures required or recommended by the FCTC and its instruments closely relate to trade rules. For instance, the recommended price and tax measures for the control of tobacco products concern the national treatment requirement for internal taxes under GATT Article III:2.[32] The recommended regulations of contents, tobacco disclosures, packaging and labelling of tobacco products are about the national treatment requirement for internal regulations under GATT Article III:4[33] and about the technical barriers

[30]GSP is a preferential scheme authorized by the Enabling Clause (i.e. the "Decision on Differential and More Favourable Treatment, Reciprocity and Fuller Participation of Developing Countries"), which was adopted under GATT in 1979, to enable developed countries to give differential and more favourable treatment to developing countries. "Under the GSP, developed countries offer non-reciprocal preferential treatment (such as zero or low duties on imports) to products originating in developing countries. Preference-giving countries unilaterally determine which countries and which products are included in their schemes." See WTO website at https://www.wto.org/english/tratop_e/devel_e/dev_special_differential_provisions_e.htm. Accessed 13 Aug 2017.

[31]See the Preamble of the FCTC.

[32]GATT Article III:2 provides in part that: "The products of the territory of any contracting party imported into the territory of any other contracting party shall not be subject, directly or indirectly, to internal taxes or other internal charges of any kind in excess of those applied, directly or indirectly, to like domestic products…"

[33]GATT Article III:4 provides in part that: "The products of the territory of any contracting party imported into the territory of any other contracting party shall be accorded treatment no less

to trade under the TBT Agreement. The recommended regulations on tobacco advertising, promotion and sponsorship of tobacco products are also about the internal regulation under GATT Article III. Regulations on illicit trade in tobacco products are about the TBT Agreement and the internal regulations under GATT Article III as well as the import restrictions under GATT Article XI. Although human life and health are different from public health and although the FCTC is designed to protect public health, apparently the ultimate purpose is also to protect human life and health due to the nature of tobacco products being very hazardous to human life and health. Thus the tobacco control measures can fall within the scope of GATT Article XX(b) and TBT Article 2.2,[34] and can be justified if other requirements under GATT Article XX and TBT Article 2.2 are met.

18.4.2 To Incorporate External Values Through Object-and-Purpose and Subsequent Practice

In addition to relying on textual interpretation so as to incorporate external values into the operation of a treaty, it is also possible to rely on a broader understanding of the object-and-purpose or a subsequent practice of a treaty to achieve such purpose. The following examples show such possibility:

(1) To incorporate the value of the "right to health" into the WTO agreements (including the TRIPS Agreement) through the consideration of the object-and-purpose: Human rights have multiple dimensions with regard to their legal functions and statuses. They are both rights and obligations, depending on the perspectives of the respective parties. From individuals' perspective, they are the "rights" enjoyed by the people so as to defend themselves from the infringement (or possible infringement) of the States or other people and to request States to fulfill their positive obligations. They are also the "obligations" assumed by the people so that they would have to respect others' human rights. From States' perspective, human rights are "obligations",

(Footnote 33 continued)

favourable than that accorded to like products of national origin in respect of all laws, regulations and requirements affecting their internal sale, offering for sale, purchase, transportation, distribution or use…"

[34]Article 2.2 of the TBT Agreement provides in part that: "Members shall ensure that technical regulations are not prepared, adopted or applied with a view to or with the effect of creating unnecessary obstacles to international trade. For this purpose, technical regulations shall not be more trade-restrictive than necessary to fulfil a legitimate objective, taking account of the risks non-fulfilment would create. Such legitimate objectives are, *inter alia:* national security requirements; the prevention of deceptive practices; protection of human health or safety, animal or plant life or health, or the environment…"

under which States have to *respect*, to *protect* and to *fulfill* human rights. This includes State's responsibility to make health related resources available, accessible and affordable to the people.

Although the WTO does not explicitly recognize the overall status of human rights (including the right to health) under the organization, the Preamble of the Agreement Establishing the WTO seems to provide workable clue of recognizing the right to health for treaty interpretation purpose. The first sentence of the Preamble already indicates clearly WTO Members' recognition of their relations in the field of trade and economic endeavour to be conducted "with a view to raising standards of living, ensuring full employment". The objective of raising livelihood coincides with the State's responsibility of "protecting" and "fulfilling" human rights so as to ensure that the health related resources, including food and medicines, are available, accessible and affordable to the people. Such objective could be useful in interpreting the fair or legitimate use of certain intellectual property rights concerning pharmaceutical products.

(2) To incorporate the value of the "right to health" into the WTO through subsequent practice: The Appellate Body sets forth a high standard for a practice being considered as a subsequent practice in *Japan—Alcoholic Beverages* that it must be "… a 'concordant, common and consistent' sequence of acts or pronouncements which is sufficient to establish a discernible pattern implying the agreement of the parties [to a treaty] regarding its interpretation."[35] One might be able to argue that if a treaty (such as the FCTC, which promotes public health) has its contracting parties largely overlapping with the Members of the WTO, such treaty has established a *discernible pattern of prioritizing public health for the disputing Members under the WTO* if both of them are also Parties to the FCTC. This subsequent practice should be useful in interpreting the possible justification of restrictive measures (which are recommended by the FCTC and adopted for tobacco control purpose) under the WTO.

In sum, there are some fundamental values which need to be respected by the WTO and its Members. Some of the values have already been explicitly included in the WTO rules, some others are not explicitly included, but can be incorporated through treaty interpretation. The main method for incorporating external values into the WTO system is through interpreting the textual meaning of treaty terms. The lesser possibility is to rely on subsequent state practice. Since the incorporation of external values is made through treaty interpretation, which is subject to certain objective rules, it should not have added any element of unpredictability to the whole process.

The objectivity and predictability could also be secured by properly defining the external values. The above suggestion is to divide the fundamental values into universal and domestic or local values. Both values must be fundamental enough in

[35]Appellate Body Report, *Japan—Taxes on Alcoholic Beverages*, para. 107, WTO Doc. WT/DS8/AB/R, WT/DS10/AB/R, WT/DS11/AB/R (adopted 1 Nov 1996).

the relevant geographic context (global or local). For universal values, they must be universally accepted. This definition would help limit the scope to those values being included in international treaties. For the domestic values, they must help shape a society and deeply embedded in it. The scope of domestic values would be decided based on the evidence (such as domestic legislations) showing the local recognition of the high importance of such values. They could be much broader than universal values, but their decision is still objective.

An introduction of external values into treaty interpretation generally or specifically with respect to WTO is necessary and workable. And such approach can still be objective and predictable. Treaty interpretation can (and sometimes should) go beyond linguistic analysis of a treaty term.

To conclude this chapter, it should be useful to codify in a set of treaty interpretation rules that when an interpreter has to choose an ordinary meaning from among two or more ordinary meanings, he/she should select the one which is more in line with the object-and-purpose of the interpreted treaty in protecting fundamental human values, taking into consideration the context of protecting human values for the interpreted provision. For a fundamental human value which has been incorporated into the text of the interpreted treaty, an interpreter should give a higher weight to it for him/her to consider such human value as the important object-and-purpose of the treaty or the context of the interpreted term. For a fundamental value which is not explicitly incorporated into the text of the interpreted treaty, an interpreter should consider the possibility of including such value as falling within the scope of the ordinary meanings of some existing terms in the interpreted treaty (such as "public morals" or "human health" in the GATT) or through considering such external values as important objects-and-purposes or subsequent practices so as to give an appropriate role to the external value in the operation of the interpreted treaty.

References

Animal Welfare. http://ec.europa.eu/food/animal/welfare/policy/index_en.htm. Accessed 13 Aug 2017

http://www.dictionary.com/browse/pest. Accessed 13 Aug 2017

http://www.who.int/trade/glossary/story076/en/. Accessed 13 Aug 2017

https://www.wto.org/english/tratop_e/devel_e/dev_special_differential_provisions_e.htm. Accessed 13 Aug 2017

Protecting Biodiversity. http://www.davidsuzuki.org/issues/wildlife-habitat/science/endangered-species-legislation/protecting-biodiversity/. Accessed 13 Aug 2017

What Are ILO Conventions and Core Labour Standards? http://www.cleanclothes.org/issues/faq/ilo. Accessed 13 Aug 2017

World Commission on Environment and Development (WCED) (1987) Our common future. Oxford University Press, Oxford

Chapter 19
Coordination Between Different Treaties Through Treaty Interpretation and the Possible Codification

Contents

19.1 The Concept of Externality of International Regime

In this chapter, discussions will turn to the problem arising from the possible overlap and concurrent application of two or more treaties (or treaty systems) which address the same issue and the potential conflict between them. The book will look into the possible coordination between two potentially conflicting treaties through treaty interpretation.[1]

Prior to the substantive discussions, a clarification on the "external" and "internal" aspects should be needed. These two terms were used in the preceding chapter to refer to the respective human values from the perspective of whether the values can or cannot be found in the interpreted treaty. These two terms are further used in this chapter to refer to the conflict or consistency which is occurred within a treaty or between two or more treaties.

[1]This chapter is revised from Lo (2012b).

C. Lo, *Treaty Interpretation Under the Vienna Convention on the Law of Treaties*,
https://doi.org/10.1007/978-981-10-6866-9_19

The term "external" and "internal" are two relative concepts. Within a treaty system, there could be many agreements, and the relations between different agreements within the treaty system can be considered as external matters in the sense that such relations are between separate treaties. But from the perspective of the whole treaty system, it is still a matter of internal conflict or consistency issue. Here the term "external" is used to refer to the conflicts or tensions between different treaty systems and the need to have coherent steps to deal with such tensions.

There could be issues concerning the internal consistency "within a treaty". For instance, the relation between Article 5.7[2] and Article 2.2[3] of the SPS Agreementis that Article 5.7 operates as a qualified exemption from the obligation under Article 2.2 of the SPS Agreement, which requires States not to maintain SPS measures without sufficient scientific evidence.[4] There could also be issues concerning the internal consistency "within a treaty system". For instance, Article XIX of the GATT 1994 is about the temporary protection available for an importing Member to protect its industry which suffers from the increased import,[5] and the Agreement on Safeguards is basically to implement GATT Article XIX.[6] The Appellate Body

---

[2]Article 5.7 of the SPS Agreement reads: "In cases where relevant scientific evidence is insufficient, a Member may provisionally adopt sanitary or phytosanitary measures on the basis of available pertinent information, including that from the relevant international organizations as well as from sanitary or phytosanitary measures applied by other Members. In such circumstances, Members shall seek to obtain the additional information necessary for a more objective assessment of risk and review the sanitary or phytosanitary measure accordingly within a reasonable period of time."

[3]Article 2.2 of the SPS Agreement reads: "Members shall ensure that any sanitary or phytosanitary measure is applied only to the extent necessary to protect human, animal or plant life or health, is based on scientific principles and is not maintained without sufficient scientific evidence, except as provided for in paragraph 7 of Article 5."

[4]In the Appellate Body Report on *Japan—Agricultural Products II*, the Appellate Body addressed the relationship between the requirement of sufficient scientific evidence under Article 2.2 and Article 5.7. It states that "Article 5.7 operates as a *qualified* exemption from the obligation under Article 2.2 not to maintain SPS measures without sufficient scientific evidence. An overly broad and flexible interpretation of that obligation would render Article 5.7 meaningless." Appellate Body Report, *Japan—Measures Affecting Agricultural Products*, para. 80, WTO Doc. WT/DS76/AB/R (adopted 19 Mar 1999).

[5]Article XIX:1(a) of the GATT 1994 reads: "If, as a result of unforeseen developments and of the effect of the obligations incurred by a contracting party under this Agreement, including tariff concessions, any product is being imported into the territory of that contracting party in such increased quantities and under such conditions as to cause or threaten serious injury to domestic producers in that territory of like or directly competitive products, the contracting party shall be free, in respect of such product, and to the extent and for such time as may be necessary to prevent or remedy such injury, to suspend the obligation in whole or in part or to withdraw or modify the concession."

[6]Article 1 of the Agreement on Safeguards read respectively: "This Agreement establishes rules for the application of safeguard measures which shall be understood to mean those measures provided for in Article XIX of GATT 1994." Article 2.1 reads: "A Member may apply a safeguard measure to a product only if that Member has determined, pursuant to the provisions set out below, that

of the WTO clarifies the relation between GATT Article XIX and the Agreement on Safeguards and indicates that Article XIX of the GATT 1994 continues in full force and effect and the safeguard measures must be in conformity with both the provision of Article XIX and that of the Safeguards Agreement.[7] The problems of coordinating "different provisions in an agreement" as well as coordinating "different agreements within a treaty system" can be and have been generally dealt with through treaty interpretation methods.

In addition to these internal coherence problems, the WTO also has experiences dealing with its external relationship. In Doha Round,[8] many discussions were on the trade related environmental protection measures. Members discussed the possible ways to maintain "a harmonious co-existence" between the WTO rules and the specific trade obligations in multilateral environmental agreements. Countries also recognized that "environmental problems often transcend national borders, the response must involve concerted action at the international level" and they "have long recognized the need for coherence amongst international institutions in addressing global environmental challenges."[9] This was a very positive experience to have a comprehensive examination on the external relations of the WTO with the environmental agreements. The external tension does not merely exist between the trade norms and the environmental treaties. It also exists between many other different treaty systems. The tension between the WTO and the FCTC is of much seriousness.[10] Hence the book uses the potential conflict between the WTO (which includes the fundamental trade norms) and some investment treaties on the one hand, and the FCTC (which is the set of international norms to control the use of tobacco products) on the other hand, as an example to show the nature of the issue

(Footnote 6 continued)

such product is being imported into its territory in such increased quantities, absolute or relative to domestic production, and under such conditions as to cause or threaten to cause serious injury to the domestic industry that produces like or directly competitive products."

[7]Appellate Body Report on *Argentina—Footwear (EC)*, clarifies the relations between GATT Article XIX and the Safeguards Agreement that: "… Article XIX continues in full force and effect, and, in fact, establishes certain prerequisites for the imposition of safeguard measures. Furthermore, in Article 11.1(a), the ordinary meaning of the language 'unless such action *conforms with the provisions of that Article applied in accordance with this Agreement*' … clearly is that any safeguard action must *conform with* the provisions of Article XIX of the GATT 1994 *as well as* with the provisions of the *Agreement on Safeguards*. Neither of these provisions states that any safeguard action taken after the entry into force of the *WTO Agreement* need only conform with the provisions of the *Agreement on Safeguards*." Appellate Body Report, *Argentina—Safeguard Measures on Imports of Footwear*, para. 83, WTO Doc. WT/DS121/AB/R (adopted 12 Jan 2000).

[8]See The Doha Round. http://www.wto.org/english/tratop_e/dda_e/dda_e.htm. Accessed 13 Aug 2017.

[9]An Introduction to Trade and Environment in the WTO. http://www.wto.org/english/tratop_e/envir_e/envt_intro_e.htm. Accessed 13 Aug 2017.

[10]Some people also addressed similar problems from different perspective. See Liberman and Mitchell (2010), p. 162. See also Baumgärtner (2011).

and the desirability and possibility of addressing such issue through treaty interpretation.

19.2 WTO's Past Experiences in Addressing Deadly Tobacco Products—Some Internal Coherence Problems

Tobacco products are very unique from many perspectives. They are the only products that, when used as intended, will contribute to the death of at least one half of all users.[11] However, tobacco products are not separately treated and are still subject to normal trade and investment rules.

Although under the GATT 1947 and the WTO, cigarettes had been the focus of a number of cases, all of them were about discriminatory and unnecessarily restrictive domestic measures adopted by the importing countries. There is not much difference between tobacco products and other products from the perspective that they are subject to same review standards under the trade rules.

1. The 1990 case of *Thailand—Restrictions on Importation of and Internal Taxes in Cigarettes*[12] was about Thailand's import restriction of tobacco seeds, plants, leaves, and tobacco. The measures were examined under GATT Article XI, among other GATT rules, and were found inconsistent with the provision.
2. The 1994 case of *United States—Measures Affecting the Importation, Internal Sale and Use of Tobacco*[13] concerned the U.S. measure requiring its domestic manufacturers to certify that they used in the manufacture of cigarettes at least 75 percent domestic tobacco on an annual basis. The measure was examined under GATT Article III and was considered inconsistent with the provision.
3. The 2004 case of *Dominican Republic—Measures Affecting the Importation and Internal Sale of Cigarettes*[14] concerned certain general measures of the Dominican Republic related to import charges and fees, as well as other measures specific to the import and sale of cigarettes. There was the requirement that tax stamps must be affixed to cigarette packets "in the territory of the Dominican

[11]Cigarettes—The Only Legal Product. http://www.tobacco-facts.net/2009/04/cigarettes-the-only-legal-product. Accessed 13 Aug 2017.

[12]See Report of the Panel, *Thailand—Restrictions on Importation of and Internal Taxes on Cigarettes*, DS10/R (7 Nov 1990), GATT B.I.S.D. (37th Supp.) at 200.

[13]See Report of the Panel, *United States Measures Affecting the Importation, Internal Sale and Use of Tobacco*, DS44/R (4 Oct 1994), GATT B.I.S.D. (41st Supp.) at 131.

[14]See Panel Report, *Dominican Republic—Measures Affecting the Importation and Internal Sale of Cigarettes*, WTO Doc. WT/DS302/R (adopted 19 May 2005) (as modified by Appellate Body Report); see also Appellate Body Report, *Dominican Republic—Measures Affecting the Importation and Internal Sale of Cigarettes*, WTO Doc. WT/DS302/AB/R (adopted 19 May 2005).

Republic and under the supervision of the local tax authorities". It was held that it was a violation of GATT Article III because the complainant has shown that there were some "additional steps" performed by the importers associated with the tax stamp requirements related to unpacking and repacking of boxes in order to affix the stamps that were not necessary for the domestic producers.

4. The 2010 case of *Thailand—Customs and Fiscal Measures on Cigarettes from the Philippines*[15] concerned various Thai customs and fiscal measures affecting cigarettes imported from the Philippines. The customs measures dealt with "customs valuation" of certain imported cigarettes. In particular, there was the alleged rejection by Thai customs authority of the use of "transaction values" of the imported cigarettes for customs purposes, but to use the "deductive value" instead. Thai measure was found inconsistent with Articles 1.1 and 1.2(a) of the Customs Valuation Agreement in rejecting the transaction value.[16]

---

[15]*See* Panel Report, *Thailand—Customs and Fiscal Measures on Cigarettes from the Philippines*, WTO Doc. WT/DS371/R (adopted 15 July 2011) (adopted as modified by Appellate Body); see also Appellate Body Report, *Thailand—Customs and Fiscal Measures on Cigarettes from the Philippines*, WTO Doc. WT/DS371/AB/R (adopted 15 July 2011).

[16]Articles 1.1 and 1.2(a) of the Customs Valuation Agreement under the WTO basically require that when the customs authorities decide to collect a customs duty based on a percentage of the value of the imported product, the value should be the prices "actually paid or payable". These paragraphs provide detailed rules to decide the calculation:

1. The customs value of imported goods shall be the transaction value, that is the price actually paid or payable for the goods when sold for export to the country of importation adjusted in accordance with the provisions of Article 8, provided:
   (a) that there are no restrictions as to the disposition or use of the goods by the buyer other than restrictions which:
      (i) are imposed or required by law or by the public authorities in the country of importation;
      (ii) limit the geographical area in which the goods may be resold; or
      (iii) do not substantially affect the value of the goods;
   (b) that the sale or price is not subject to some condition or consideration for which a value cannot be determined with respect to the goods being valued;
   (c) that no part of the proceeds of any subsequent resale, disposal or use of the goods by the buyer will accrue directly or indirectly to the seller, unless an appropriate adjustment can be made in accordance with the provisions of Article 8; and
   (d) that the buyer and seller are not related, or where the buyer and seller are related, that the transaction value is acceptable for customs purposes under the provisions of paragraph 2.
2. (a) In determining whether the transaction value is acceptable for the purposes of paragraph 1, the fact that the buyer and the seller are related within the meaning of Article 15 shall not in itself be grounds for regarding the transaction value as unacceptable. In such case the circumstances surrounding the sale shall be examined and the transaction value shall be accepted provided that the relationship did not influence the price. If, in the light of information provided by the importer or otherwise, the customs administration has grounds for considering that the relationship influenced the price, it shall communicate its grounds to the importer and the importer shall be given a reasonable opportunity to respond. If the importer so requests, the communication of the grounds shall be in writing.

5. The 2011 case of *United States—Measures Affecting the Production and Sale of Clove Cigarette*[17] concerned a U.S. tobacco-control measure prohibiting cigarettes with "characterizing flavors" other than tobacco or menthol flavor under the Federal Food, Drug and Cosmetic Act, as amended by the Family Smoking Prevention and Tobacco Control Act. It was concluded that by banning clove cigarettes while exempting menthol cigarettes from the ban, the U.S. law did accord imported clove cigarettes less favorable treatment than that it accorded to domestic menthol cigarettes for the purpose of Article 2.1 of the TBT Agreement and thus the U.S. was in breach of its WTO obligations.

Although tobacco products are the disputed subjects in the above five GATT/WTO cases, the focus of these disputes was purely on the application of rules on trade in goods, including the GATT, the Customs Valuation Agreement and the TBT Agreement.

But the issue to be further discussed in this chapter is more complex because it involves different and potentially conflicting sets of international obligations assumed by States. The issue is also broader because it is about the relations between different treaty systems. Before entering into the discussion of treaty interpretation issues, a brief review of these different regimes is needed.

19.3 Relevant Treaty Systems and Tensions Between Them

19.3.1 Relevant Treaty Systems

Here the relevant treaty systems are the WTO treaties, the bilateral investment treaties (BITs), and the international health treaties.

For the WTO, it is a very comprehensive and complicated treaty system, including tens of basic legal instruments to require liberalization in the areas of trade in goods and trade in services, and to require non-discrimination for foreign goods, services and service suppliers. It also requires its Members to provide minimum standards of protection for intellectual property rights possessed by nationals of other WTO Members under the TRIPS Agreement. The WTO also has the well-established legal culture of Members abiding by the dispute settlement decisions under the DSU.

For BITs, there are more than 3000 treaties dealing with investment liberalization and the protection of foreign investors and their investments. There are also many FTAs incorporating the liberalization and protection of investment into their

[17]See Panel Report, *United States—Measures Affecting the Production and Sale of Clove Cigarettes*, WTO Doc. WT/DS406/R (adopted 24 Apr 2012) (adopted as modified by Appellate Body); see also Appellate Body Report, *United States—Measures Affecting the Production and Sale of Clove Cigarettes*, WTO Doc. WT/DS406/AB/R (adopted 24 Apr 2012).

investment chapters, which substantively are another form of BITs.[18] Although these treaties do not belong to a single treaty system, they have a lot of commonalities, especially concerning the protection of foreign investments. These treaties can be collectively called "treaty networks", the term of which is used to refer to the wide and overlapping coverage of the countries and the extended scope of activities being regulated by these treaties.

For international health treaties, there is the new trend in recent years of WHO exercising its rarely exercised legislative power under Articles 19 and 21 of the WHO Constitution[19] to enact international legal instruments through the World Health Assembly. The results of the exercise of its legislative power include the enactments of the International Health Regulations of 2004 (IHR) and the FCTC. Such new practice has already shown very wide positive impacts respectively in the areas of confining infectious diseases and controling tobacco use. Although both sets of rules are enacted under WHO, each of them can still be considered as a separate treaty system due to the different natures of their subject matters and the different approaches dealing with the problems. So there are the FCTC treaty system and the IHR system under WHO.

As a general rule, a treaty system is a closed and self-sufficient regime. They have their own substantive norms and dispute settlement rules. They are applied and interpreted separately and independently, with the very important exception that all treaty systems are subject to the customary rules of treaty interpretation embodied in the VCLT.

However, it is also apparent that a treaty system can be affected by another treaty system in its application and even its operation. The two most salient examples are the conflict between the WTO treaty system and the FCTC treaty system, and between the BITs treaty networks and the FCTC system.

---

[18]For instance, the United States has included the Investment Chapters in many of its FTAs. Free Trade Agreements. http://www.ustr.gov/trade-agreements/free-trade-agreements. Accessed 13 Aug 2017. See also the discussion of FTA's investment chapter and BITs in Lo (2008).

[19]See Forrest (2000), p. 154. Article 19 of the WHO Constitution reads: "The Health Assembly shall have authority to adopt conventions or agreements with respect to any matter within the competence of the Organization. A two-thirds vote of the Health Assembly shall be required for the adoption of such conventions or agreements, which shall come into force for each Member when accepted by it in accordance with its constitutional processes." Article 20 reads: "Each Member undertakes that it will, within eighteen months after the adoption by the Health Assembly of a convention or agreement, take action relative to the acceptance of such convention or agreement. Each Member shall notify the Director-General of the action taken, and if it does not accept such convention or agreement within the time limit, it will furnish a statement of the reasons for non-acceptance. In case of acceptance, each Member agrees to make an annual report to the Director-General in accordance with Chapter XIV."

19.3.2 Tobacco Control Approaches Under FCTC as an Example

Before the discussion of such tension, a brief introduction about the FCTC and the approaches adopted by the Convention is needed. The FCTC was entered into force in 2005 and was the first international treaty negotiated under the auspices of WHO. It was developed in response to the globalization of the tobacco epidemic and is considered an evidence-based treaty.[20] It is only a "framework convention", which is to be implemented by additional guidelines and protocols. Therefore it includes a number of supplementing or implementing rules, most of which are non-binding recommendations, in the form of guidelines; some of which will be binding protocols, including the current Protocol to Eliminate Illicit Trade in Tobacco Products (which is the first Protocol to the FCTC) adopted on 12 November 2012 at the fifth session of the Conference of the Parties.[21] There have been eight sets of guidelines concluded under the FCTC up to 2017 to encourage or urge countries to take steps for tightening the control of tobacco use.[22]

The FCTC is said to represent "a paradigm shift in developing a regulatory strategy to address addictive substances; in contrast to previous drug control treaties, the FCTC asserts the importance of demand reduction strategies as well as supply issues."[23] The main approaches adopted by the FCTC are to control both the demand and the supply of tobacco use. One way of controlling the demand is to make the tobacco product packaging very unattractive. So there are two sets of guidelines dealing with tobacco packaging and tobacco advertising suggesting FCTC Parties to impose the wildly-known plain packaging or generic packaging requirement, i.e., to require tobacco companies to use a single unattractive color (for

---

[20]See FCTC. WHO Framework Convention on Tobacco Control—Overview. http://www.who.int/fctc/text_download/en/. Accessed 13 Aug 2017.

[21]The text of the Protocol can be found at http://www.who.int/fctc/protocol/en/. Accessed 13 Aug 2017.

[22]They are: the Guidelines for implementation of Article 5.3 of the WHO FCTC (Protection of public health policies with respect to tobacco control from commercial and other vested interests of the tobacco industry); the Guidelines for implementation of Article 6 of the WHO FCTC (Price and tax measures to reduce the demand for tobacco); the Guidelines for implementation of Article 8 of the WHO FCTC (Protection from exposure to tobacco smoke); the Partial guidelines for implementation of Article 9 and 10 of the WHO FCTC (Regulation of the contents of tobacco products and regulation of tobacco product disclosures); the Guidelines for implementation of Article 11 of the WHO FCTC (Packaging and labeling of tobacco products); the Guidelines for implementation of Article 12 of the WHO FCTC (Education, communication, training and public awareness); the Guidelines for implementation of Article 13 of the WHO FCTC (Tobacco advertising, promotion and sponsorship); and the Guidelines for implementation of Article 14 of the WHO FCTC (Demand reduction measures concerning tobacco dependence and cessation). See Adopted Guidelines. http://www.who.int/fctc/treaty_instruments/adopted/en/. Accessed 13 Aug 2017.

[23]See *supra* note 20.

instance, black and white or olive color) for packaging purpose.[24] Such plain packaging requirement is considered to have the functions of making tobacco product less attractive, enhancing the noticeability and effectiveness of health warnings on the plain packages, preventing package design techniques to mislead consumers that some products are less harmful than others, and bringing to the attention of smokers the possible negative health effects arising from smoking. Also the large pictorial warning on the packets of cigarettes, preferably 50% or more of the principal display areas, is urged by FCTC Article 11(b).[25]

Plain packaging is basically composed of two elements, namely the restrictive element (to restrict the use of trademark or design) and the positive mandatory element (to require the use of certain uniform designs). And the large pictorial warning requirement also works to greatly restrict the use of trademark or design. In other words, under such requirements, the promotional function arising from the use of trademark or the use of design of tobacco packaging will be vastly removed.

Although plain packaging method and the large pictorial warning are only "suggested" in the Framework Convention and the above mentioned guidelines under the FCTC and there is no binding effect arising from them, countries are still strongly encouraged or even urged to adopt such measures for more effective and comprehensive tobacco control. However, such measures encouraged by the FCTC have encountered problems under the WTO treaty system and under the BIT networks. To simplify the complicated situation, the issue can be understood as: What is strongly proposed under the FCTC might not be legally or practically workable under the WTO and BITs. This is an enormous challenge to the FCTC and it could also be a serious challenge to the WTO and BITs.

19.3.3 Tension Between WTO and FCTC

There are a couple of examples to illustrate the tension between different treaty systems. The first example of the tension is between the FCTC and the WTO, especially the TRIPS Agreement under the WTO.

Article 20 of the TRIPS Agreement provides in part that: "The use of a trademark in the course of trade shall not be unjustifiably encumbered by special requirements, such as … use in a special form or use in a manner detrimental to its capability to distinguish the goods or services of one undertaking from those of

[24]These two sets of guidelines are the Guidelines for implementation of Article 11 of the WHO FCTC (Packaging and labeling of tobacco products) and the Guidelines for implementation of Article 13 of the WHO FCTC (Tobacco advertising, promotion and sponsorship).

[25]FCTC, Article 11(b) provides: "Each unit packet and package of tobacco products and any outside packaging and labeling of such products also carry health warnings describing the harmful effects of tobacco use, and may include other appropriate messages. These warnings and messages: … (iv) should be 50% or more of the principal display areas but shall be no less than 30% of the principal display area".

other undertakings." This is part of the minimum protection of trademark rights required by the TRIPS Agreement.

Although it can be argued otherwise, there is still a possibility that the plain packaging and large pictorial warning requirements are considered as some kind of "special requirements" that would cause detriment to the trademarks' capacity to distinguish their tobacco products from others' tobacco products. The key problem is whether the plain packaging requirement and the large pictorial warning requirement can be considered as "justifiable" encumbrance under the TRIPS Agreement.

One might argue that the requirements of plain packaging and large pictorial warning are justified encumbrances because of the serious health concerns of tobacco use and because that the plain packaging requirement and the larger pictorial warning requirement are among the effective ways for tobacco control. But there is still a risk that the plain packaging and large pictorial warning requirements which are strongly urged by the FCTC could be effectively challenged under the WTO system for the possible violation of the TRIPS Agreement.

Some WTO Members expressed concerns about the possible violation of TRIPS obligation as a result of plain packaging requirement. Ukraine, Honduras, Dominican Republic, Cuba and Indonesia[26] have challenged such requirement imposed by Australia at the WTO alleging that Australia's measure is incompatible with some provisions in the TRIPS Agreement,[27]some provisions in the TBT

[26]DS434: *Australia—Certain Measures Concerning Trademarks and Other Plain Packaging Requirements Applicable to Tobacco Products and Packaging* complained by Ukraine; DS435: *Australia—Certain Measures Concerning Trademarks, Geographical Indications and Other Plain Packaging Requirements Applicable to Tobacco Products and Packaging* complained by Honduras; DS441: *Australia—Certain Measures Concerning Trademarks, Geographical Indications and Other Plain Packaging Requirements Applicable to Tobacco Products and Packaging* complained by Dominican Republic; DS458: *Australia—Certain Measures Concerning Trademarks, Geographical Indications and Other Plain Packaging Requirements Applicable to Tobacco Products and Packaging* complained by Cuba; DS467: *Australia—Certain Measures Concerning Trademarks, Geographical Indications and Other Plain Packaging Requirements Applicable to Tobacco Products and Packaging* complained by Indonesia.

Note that on 28 May 2015, Ukraine requested the panel to suspend its proceedings in accordance with Article 12.12 of the DSU. On 30 May 2016, pursuant to Article 12.12 of the DSU, the panel's jurisdiction lapsed because it had not been requested to resume its work within the 12 months following the suspension of the panel proceedings. See https://www.wto.org/english/tratop_e/dispu_e/cases_e/ds434_e.htm. Accessed 13 Aug 2017.

[27]These include the following TRIPS articles (among others): Article 2.1: "In respect of Parts II, III and IV of this Agreement, Members shall comply with Articles 1 through 12, and Article 19, of the Paris Convention (1967)." Article 3.1: "Each Member shall accord to the nationals of other Members treatment no less favourable than that it accords to its own nationals with regard to the protection of intellectual property…" Article 15.4: "4. The nature of the goods or services to which a trademark is to be applied shall in no case form an obstacle to registration of the trademark." Article 16.1: "The owner of a registered trademark shall have the exclusive right to prevent all third parties not having the owner's consent from using in the course of trade identical or similar signs for goods or services which are identical or similar to those in respect of which the trademark is registered where such use would result in a likelihood of confusion. …" Article 16.3: "Article

Agreement[28]and GATT Article III:4 (national treatment requirement).[29] The Panel Reports were originally supposed to be issued at the first half of 2016. There were a number of extensions requested by the Panel and granted by the DSB. The Panel was expected to issue its Reports not before the end of 2017.

19.3.4 Tensions Between BITs and FCTC

The second example concerns the conflict between BITs and the FCTC. One of the main purposes for most BITs is to protect investors and their investments from some government measures. An important protection provided for investors is to prevent themselves from mistreatment and to prevent their investments from unjustified direct or indirect expropriation by the host States. Under the vast majority of BITs, the host countries can exercise an expropriation only in the public interest or for public purpose, and only when it is necessary and proportionate. Even though an expropriation is for public purpose and is necessary, the investors must still be compensated for the loss of their property. These rules not only apply

(Footnote 27 continued)

6*bis* of the Paris Convention (1967) shall apply, *mutatis mutandis*, to goods or services which are not similar to those in respect of which a trademark is registered, provided that use of that trademark in relation to those goods or services would indicate a connection between those goods or services and the owner of the registered trademark and provided that the interests of the owner of the registered trademark are likely to be damaged by such use." Article 20: "The use of a trademark in the course of trade shall not be unjustifiably encumbered by special requirements, such as use with another trademark, use in a special form or use in a manner detrimental to its capability to distinguish the goods or services of one undertaking from those of other undertakings. This will not preclude a requirement prescribing the use of the trademark identifying the undertaking producing the goods or services along with, but without linking it to, the trademark distinguishing the specific goods or services in question of that undertaking."

[28]These TBT provisions include: Articles 2.1: "Members shall ensure that in respect of technical regulations, products imported from the territory of any Member shall be accorded treatment no less favourable than that accorded to like products of national origin and to like products originating in any other country." And Article 2.2: "Members shall ensure that technical regulations are not prepared, adopted or applied with a view to or with the effect of creating unnecessary obstacles to international trade. For this purpose, technical regulations shall not be more trade-restrictive than necessary to fulfil a legitimate objective, taking account of the risks non-fulfilment would create. Such legitimate objectives are, inter alia: national security requirements; the prevention of deceptive practices; protection of human health or safety, animal or plant life or health, or the environment. In assessing such risks, relevant elements of consideration are, *inter alia*: available scientific and technical information, related processing technology or intended end-uses of products."

[29]GATT Article III:4 provides in part that: "The products of the territory of any contracting party imported into the territory of any other contracting party shall be accorded treatment no less favourable than that accorded to like products of national origin in respect of all laws, regulations and requirements affecting their internal sale, offering for sale, purchase, transportation, distribution or use…".

to the direct taking of foreign investors' property, but also to the indirect expropriation, which is generally referred to the host countries enacting or applying administrative or legislative procedures to provoke "a unilateral change in contract conditions such that the investor is unable to recover the expected quasi rents of the business"[30] or interfering with the use of the invested property.[31]

Trademark rights held by foreign investors are considered by most BITs as a type of investment of such foreign investors and thus are subject to protection from unjustified direct or indirect expropriation without proper compensation. If a host country is to take a foreigner's trademark right or to enact a legislation to interfere with the use of its right, arguably it must meet the requirements that the taking must be for public purpose; that it must be necessary and proportionate; and that it must be compensated.

From the perspective of trademarks, the function of indicating the origin of products will be minimized by a plain packaging or large pictorial warning scheme. Consumers' ability to make choices between different brands will be reduced as a result of restricting the use of brand logos and colors, and thus the function of the indication of origin is greatly impaired. Also the function of conveying messages of brand image will be substantially reduced.

On the appearance, it is quite plausible for tobacco companies to argue that a plain packaging requirement or a large pictorial warning requirement will cause serious deprivation of the essential commercial value and the core function of their trademarks. They might argue that these requirements are measures tantamount to indirect expropriation of their intellectual properties.

In 2012, the world biggest tobacco company, Philip Morris, launched an investor-state arbitration proceeding for billions of dollars against Australia for its Tobacco Plain Packaging Act 2011 and the related implementing regulations of the Tobacco Plain Packaging Regulations 2011. The legal action was brought by Philip Morris Asia Ltd, Hong Kong, which is the owner of the Australian affiliate. The arbitration was initiated based on and hence the tribunal was constituted under the 1993 Agreement between the Government of Hong Kong and the Government of Australia for the Promotion and Protection of Investments. The arbitration proceedings were conducted by an arbitral tribunal administered by the Permanent Court of Arbitration in accordance with the 2010 UNCITRAL arbitration rules.[32] The arbitral tribunal upheld one of Australia's objections and concluded that:

> … the initiation of this arbitration constitutes an abuse of rights, as the corporate restructuring by which the Claimant acquired the Australian subsidiaries occurred at a time when

[30]Abdala and Spiller (2003), p. 449.

[31]See OECD, "Indirect Expropriation" and the "Right to Regulate" in International Investment Law. http://www.oecd.org/investment/investmentpolicy/33776546.pdf. Accessed 13 Aug 2017.

[32]Permanent Court of Arbitration Press Release (16 May 2016). https://www.pcacases.com/web/sendAttach/1713. Accessed 13 Aug 2017.

> there was a reasonable prospect that the dispute would materialise and as it was carried out for the principal, if not sole, purpose of gaining Treaty protection. Accordingly, the claims raised in this arbitration are inadmissible and the Tribunal is precluded from exercising jurisdiction over this dispute.[33]

Also Philip Morris' Uruguayan subsidiary initiated an investor-state arbitration proceeding in 2010 against Uruguay based on the Switzerland–Uruguay BIT, alleging that Uruguay requirements on tobacco companies to sell only one pack variation per cigarette brand (i.e. the so-called "Single Presentation Requirement" or the SPR), its expansion of the size of warning labels on cigarette packaging from 50 to 80%, and its requirement to include repulsive and shocking pictures constitute an expropriation and are in violation of fair and equitable treatment. The tobacco company requested Uruguay to withdraw the regulations and asked for compensation for its losses.[34]

Concerning whether Uruguay's measures amounted to "indirect expropriation," the arbitral tribunal noted that the tobacco company "remained the registered owner or licensee of the relevant trademarks and continued to be entitled to protect them by an action for infringement". But it also noted that both Uruguayan law and international conventions do not give the trademark holder an "absolute right of use, free of regulation." They only grant an exclusive right to the holder "so that only the trademark holder has the possibility to use the trademark in commerce, subject to the State's regulatory power." Since the tobacco company's brand and "other distinctive elements" continued to appear on cigarette packs and were recognizable and also the tobacco company's overall business in Uruguay had grown more profitable since 2011, the arbitral tribunal did not find expropriation in this case. It concluded that "the challenged measures were a valid exercise by Uruguay of its police powers for the protection of public health".

Concerning whether Uruguay violated the requirement of "fair and equitable treatment" of investments under the BIT, the arbitral tribunal was of the view that the State's conduct must be "arbitrary, grossly unfair, unjust or idiosyncratic, is discriminatory and exposes the claimant to sectional and racial prejudice." Taking into consideration of Uruguay's participation in the FCTC negotiations and implementation, its domestic scientific and technical research on tobacco control, the legitimate aim of the measures, and the relatively minor impact on the company's business, the majority of the tribunal's members concluded that the measures were reasonable and adopted in good faith.[35]

---

[33]Id.

[34]See Posting of Hunter JM and Essex Court Chambers to Kluwer Arbitration Blog (29 Jan 2012). http://kluwerarbitrationblog.com/blog/2012/01/29/investor-state-arbitration-and-plain-packaging-the-new-%E2%80%98anti-tobacco-movement%E2%80%99-has-begun/. Accessed 13 Aug 2017.

[35]International Centre for Trade and Sustainable Development (14 July 2016).

These are not single isolated incidences reflecting the tensions between different treaties, especially between treaties of economic nature and the FCTC. Actually, tobacco companies' previous threats of bringing legal actions against host countries had made these countries very cautious about firmly and swiftly moving toward adopting stricter tobacco control measures. For instance, Phillip Morris International Inc. had previously protested the plain packaging proposal by the Canadian Government on the basis of Chapter 11 of the NAFTA, arguing that, "the ban would be tantamount to an expropriation of tobacco trademarks containing descriptive terms." As a result, the proposed plain packaging requirement was not adopted in Canada.[36]

These examples are not merely another investment arbitration cases between the investors and the host states. It is about the cause promoted by the FCTC treaty system being directly challenged and possibly prevented by the BIT treaty networks. Tobacco companies' bringing huge compensation claims against host countries could have some apparent chilling effects: First, countries could give up the idea of adopting the plain packaging or larger pictorial warning requirements, notwithstanding such requirements are recommended and urged by the FCTC. Actually many countries were closely observing the development of the above-mentioned cases during the legal proceedings so as to decide whether to consider adopting such measures. This could render the FCTC ineffective in realizing its objects and purposes of controlling tobacco use. Second, countries might consider not to include any investor-state arbitration procedures in future BITs so as to prevent tobacco companies from using it for claiming compensation of such kind. Neither of such potential outcomes would be desirable from the FCTC perspective and from the perspective of promoting BITs.

The above tensions between FCTC and WTO and between FCTC and BITs have become apparent and need to be seriously addressed.

On 22 March 2012, the WHO Director-General Margaret Chan urged countries to "stand shoulder to shoulder" against tobacco companies' attempts to overturn the new tobacco control legislation to require plain packaging.[37] This means that WHO will have to back up countries adopting tobacco control measures recommended by the FCTC and its guidelines to fight the legal battles under the WTO and under BITs. There is clear tension between the trade and investment regimes on the one hand and the public health regime on the other hand, as implied by DG Chan.

---

[36]Salazar (2010), p. 70.

[37]Chan to World: Stand with Australia—WHO's Director-General Applauds Australia's Determination in Fighting Tobacco Industry Intimidation. http://www.who.int/mediacentre/news/releases/2012/tobacco_20120322/en/index.html. Accessed 13 Aug 2017.

19.4 Available Options

19.4.1 Relying on Treaty Interpretation to Reduce the Tensions

There are a number of options to deal with such external tensions. These options are not perfect, but a combination of these options could provide a more optimal outcome.

The first option is to rely on proper treaty interpretation. As mentioned above, most treaties are self-sufficient and closed regimes. Take the WTO as an example, non-WTO treaties are not to be applied by WTO dispute settlement panels or the Appellate Body. In other words, the FCTC and its guidelines are not directly applicable in WTO dispute settlement procedures. However, there is still a likelihood that the FCTC and its guidelines are taken into consideration when the WTO rules (including the TRIPS Agreement) are interpreted.

Article 31.1 of the VCLT requires treaty terms being interpreted in good faith in accordance with the ordinary meaning to be given to the terms of the treaty in their context and in the light of its object and purpose. Article 31.3(c) provides that there shall be taken into account, together with the context: any relevant rules of international law applicable in the relations between the parties. The key issues to be addressed here are whether the FCTC rules are "relevant rules" and whether the FCTC guidelines of non-binding nature are "rules of international law". Since it is generally understood that the rules international law are those accepted as binding to govern the behaviors of and relations between States and since those FCTC guidelines suggesting the adoption of plain packaging measures are non-binding, there are apparently high hurdles to be overcome for the purpose of arguing that the FCTC guidelines are relevant rules of international law. In other words, it might not be workable to rely on Article 31.3(c) of the VCLT to bring the FCTC's guidelines (which recommend its parties to adopt plain packaging requirement and large pictorial warning) into the interpretation process of the TRIPS Agreement.

However, as suggested in the preceding chapter of this book, it is possible for one to argue that since the FCTC has its contracting parties largely overlapping with the Members of the WTO, such treaty has established a "discernible pattern of prioritizing public health" for the disputing Members under the WTO. This "subsequent practice" should be a useful context under Article 31.3(b) in interpreting the possible justification of tobacco control measures recommended by the FCTC under the WTO.

Also it is possible to interpret the ordinary meaning of the term "unjustifiably" provided in TRIPS Article 20 ("The use of a trademark in the course of trade shall not be *unjustifiably* encumbered by special requirements…") by requiring the interpreter to consider other international treaties or documents (such as the FCTC and its instruments). In other words, when interpreting the term "unjustifiably" provided in TRIPS Article 20, the interpreter must not only check with the dictionaries to collect the possible ordinary meanings, he/she must also take into account the FCTC and its relevant instruments so as to understand the proper meaning of this term in the context of a dispute involving tobacco products and the relevant trademarks. If there is such expectation that a relevant international treaty should be taken into consideration when interpreting the term "unjustifiably", it will naturally be interpreted in a narrower manner so as not to include the tobacco control measures (which are recommended by the FCTC and its instruments) within the scope of unjustified measures.

Turning to the BITs, there are three groups of requirements for a host country to exercise direct or indirect expropriation, namely the public interest or public purpose requirement, the necessary and due process requirement, and the compensation requirement. It would "not" be difficult to interpret that the plain packaging requirement is for a public interest and meets the due process and necessary requirements. However to interpret that such indirect expropriation is not compensable is of greater difficulty.

One possible argument could be that the host country has an inherent power to impose plain packaging requirement and that the inherent "right to regulate" serves as an exception to compensable expropriation.[38]

From the legal standpoint, the right to regulate by the host States should be deemed as an inherent power of sovereign States, even though there is no explicit granting of such a right in any international agreement. Thus, even if a BIT at issue does not specifically provide the power of the host State to conduct necessary regulation, the host State still has such a right to do so.

The book is of the view that the State's right to regulate can help interpret a BIT by serving as an exception to and a defense against the compensation claim of indirect expropriation. This is because if a regulation does not severely interfere in the exercise of the invested property right to the extent that the essential value or core function is deprived, it would not constitute an indirect expropriation and, accordingly, the host State would not need to rely on the State's inherent right to regulate for the purpose of escaping from the compensation obligation. Hence, the only meaningful function that can be played by the State's right to regulate should be to defend a regulatory measure which is otherwise in breach of the State's obligation.

In the above mentioned investment arbitration case between Phillip Morris and Uruguay, the arbitral tribunal was in support of the State's right to regulate being introduced into the interpretation of the BIT. The arbitral award granted a certain extent of discretion (or margin of appreciation) to the host State so as to allow it making its public policy determination. The award states in paragraphs 398 and 399 the following:

> 398. The remark of a general character relates to the "margin of appreciation" to be recognized to regulatory authorities when making public policy determinations. According to the Claimants, the "margin of appreciation" has no application in the present proceeding

[38] Lo (2012a).

> as being a concept applied by the ECHR for interpreting the specific language of Article 1 of the Protocol to the Convention, no analogous provision being contained in the BIT.
>
> 399. The Tribunal agrees with the Respondent that the "margin of appreciation" is not limited to the context of the ECHR but "applies equally to claims arising under BITs," at least in contexts such as public health. 566 The responsibility for public health measures rests with the government and investment tribunals should pay great deference to governmental judgments of national needs in matters such as the protection of public health. In such cases respect is due to the "discretionary exercise of sovereign power, not made irrationally and not exercised in bad faith … involving many complex factors." As held by another investment tribunal, "[t]he sole inquiry for the Tribunal… is whether or not there was a manifest lack of reasons for the legislation.[39]

Of course there must be criteria to decide whether the exercise of such inherent power to regulate (through certain measures, such as the plain packaging requirement) should be permitted. In the view of the book, the criteria include whether the measure (such as the plain packaging requirement) is to protect a fundamental interest and one of the highest values of the civilized society and whether the values and interests that are intended to be protected apparently outweigh the affected interests. It is desirable for treaty interpreters of BITs to pay higher respect and deference to the host State's sovereign power concerning its right to regulate the hazardous products (such as tobacco products) for this legitimate purpose by introducing an effective measure (such as the plain packaging requirement) without compensating the affected investors (such as the tobacco company).

The above suggested methods of interpretation should have some solid basis. Because if different interpretations are adopted (i.e. to interpret the compensable indirect expropriation to cover the plain packaging requirement or to interpret the term "unjustifiably" in a broader way so that the FCTC recommended measures will become unjustifiable), there could be an absurd outcome, which is undesirable under VCLT Artcile 32(b). That is to say, on the one hand, countries are so strongly encouraged by a multilateral treaty and its related guidelines to adopt the plain packaging requirement, but on the other hand, they could be effectively prevented from adopting such requirement due to the prohibition in the TRIPS Agreement or due to the BIT's investor-to-state arbitration which could result in huge amounts of damages to compensate the economic losses of tobacco companies.

19.4.2 Relying on Another Treaty as a "Factual Reference"

There could be two functions for a treaty to help the application/operation of another treaty. One function is to have a treaty helping interpret the provision in another treaty. This was explained above. The other function is to rely on a treaty to find the fact so as to help apply the other treaty.

---

[39]The arbitral award can be found at http://icsidfiles.worldbank.org/icsid/ICSIDBLOBS/OnlineAwards/C1000/DC9012_En.pdf. Accessed 13 Aug 2017.

Hypothetically, if a treaty (Treaty A) requires that a measure must be adopted in a good faith and non-arbitrary manner so that the measure can be justified. Suppose there is another treaty (Treaty B), the contents and the negotiation backgrounds of which show that the challenged measure was actually adopted in a good faith and non-arbitrary manner. Then Treaty B serves as a *factual reference* to prove that the requirements in Treaty A have been met.

In the above investment dispute between Phillip Morris and Uruguay, the arbitral tribunal had to decide whether the requirement of "fair and equitable" (FET) treatment under the BIT was breached by Uruguay's tobacco control measures. The tribunal states that when a State's conduct is "arbitrary, grossly unfair, unjust or idiosyncratic, is discriminatory and exposes the claimant to sectional or racial prejudice", the conduct should be found in breach of the FET treatment.[40] The tribunal further explains that "According to the international law standard set forth by the ICJ Chamber in the ELSI case, 'arbitrariness' is defined as 'a wilful disregard of due process of law, an act which shocks, or at least surprises, a sense of juridical propriety.'"[41] The tribunal was persuaded by a number of facts (many of which related to the FCTC) that Uruguay was not arbitrary when adopting the challenged measures. For instance, the tribunal states the following:

> 393. For a country with limited technical and economic resources, such as Uruguay, adhesion to the FCTC and involvement in the process of scientific and technical cooperation and reporting and of exchange of information represented an important if not indispensable means for acquiring the scientific knowledge and market experience needed for the proper implementation of its obligations under the FCTC and for ensuring the fulfilment of its tobacco control policy. …
>
> 395. Following ratification of the FCTC in 2004 and its entry into force on 27 February 2005, Uruguay started the process of complying with the resulting obligations. All legal measures taken internally for implementing tobacco control were expressly adopted in conformity with the FCTC. …
>
> 396. In the Tribunal's view, in these circumstances there was no requirement for Uruguay to perform additional studies or to gather further evidence in support of the Challenged Measures. Such support was amply offered by the evidence-based FCTC provisions and guidelines adopted thereunder. …[42]

Apparently, the FCTC and its instruments as well as the surrounding circumstances were applied by the arbitral tribunal as the *factual references* to support that Uruguay was not acting in an arbitrary manner. The function of the FCTC is *factual reference* for the purpose of applying the FET requirement and deciding Uruguay's compliance with such requirement. This is different from the function of a treaty helping the interpretation of a provision in another treaty.

---

[40]See para. 323 in the award. Id. at para. 323.

[41]Id. at para. 390.

[42]Id. at paras. 393, 395–396.

19.4.3 Fixing Relevant Treaties

The third option is to fix the relevant treaties. For instance, the BITs can be fixed in a number of ways. One way of fixing the BITs is to carve out the tobacco sector from the scope of investment and from the application of the BITs. However, there could be enormous pressure coming from the vested interest groups to prevent this carving out policy and at the most a carve-out can only apply to new BITs, not the existing BITs.

Another approach is not to include the investor-to-state arbitration in the BITs. Australia has started such policy of not including the investor-to-state arbitration provisions in its new BITs, mainly because of the specific legal proceedings mentioned above. The shortcomings are that this policy only applies to new investment agreements and would not affect the existing 3000 BITs and that the abolishment of the investor-state arbitration would reduce the attractiveness of BITs to foreign investors, many of which basically consider investor-to-state arbitration as important protection mechanism for their investments.

Yet another way of fixing the BITs is to include provisions into the BITs to prioritize the application of rules that protect public health and other public policies (such as FCTC rules) when they are relevant. There are precedents of such type of arrangement. In some FTAs, there are provisions prioritizing the application of environmental treaties over the FTA provisions. Theoretically, similar approach can be adopted for prioritizing the FCTC. Nevertheless, again, this could only affect new BITs unless countries can negotiate some kind of document to modify the existing BITs. Also, the pressures coming from tobacco industry could be high.

In addition, the current approach of the FCTC can also be modified. The current FCTC approach relies very much on the non-binding guidelines to encourage countries to adopt certain measures or strategies. Plain packaging is recommended by two sets of non-binding FCTC guidelines. If the plain packaging measure becomes mandatory under the FCTC, it would help the interpretation of plain packaging rules as "any relevant rules of international law applicable in the relations between the parties" under VCLT Article 31.3 (c) and help justify the encumbrance for the purpose of TRIPS Article 20, and to consolidate State's inherent power to regulate for the purpose of exempting from compensation requirement.

As to the WTO, a very important option for the WTO would be to have a "second" Ministerial Declaration on TRIPS Agreement and Public Health or to have a "more general declaration" on trade rules and public health. The general reason for having an even more general declaration to prioritize public health protection is that both the TRIPS Agreement and other agreements on trade in goods could get involved. For instance, a country adopting the plain packaging requirement would also prohibit those foreign tobacco products which fail to meet this requirement from being imported into the country. This is an import prohibition issue that could be examined under GATT Articles XI and XX. Hence, the public health issue does not limit to the TRIPS issues.

There are a number of substantive reasons for having either a "second" Ministerial Declaration on TRIPS Agreement and Public Health or to have a "more general declaration" on trade rules and public health:

First, WTO Members had specific experience in dealing with the maintenance of "a harmonious co-existence" between WTO rules and the trade obligations in multilateral environmental agreements. Such precedent is useful for us to consider the relations between the WTO and the FCTC. With this experience, there would not be a problem for WTO Members to also look at the "harmonious co-existence" between the trade rules under the WTO and the tobacco control measures required or suggested by the FCTC.

Second, ministers of WTO Members were able to successfully issue the Declaration on the TRIPS Agreement and Public Health in 2001.[43] Although the focus was on compulsory licensing, the general themes have been to recognize the gravity of the public health problems afflicting many developing and least-developed countries, the need for the TRIPS Agreement to be part of the wider national and international action to address these problems, and the need for the TRIPS Agreement not to prevent members from taking measures to protect public health. Tobacco problems are no less serious than other epidemics, which need higher degree of flexibility for drug licensing. The FCTC preamble acknowledges that "the spread of the tobacco epidemic is a global problem with serious consequences for public health that calls for the widest possible international cooperation and the participation of all countries in an effective, appropriate and comprehensive international response". The solution of the problem of tobacco use apparently deserves another declaration.

There could be a different view about the need to have a second Ministerial Declaration on TRIPS Agreement and Public Health. People might argue that the existing declaration has already clearly recognized "the gravity of the public health problems afflicting many developing and least-developed countries, especially those resulting from HIV/AIDS, tuberculosis, malaria and other epidemics" and that countries have agreed that "the TRIPS Agreement does not and should not prevent members from taking measures to protect public health" and "the Agreement can and should be interpreted and implemented in a manner supportive of WTO members' right to protect public health and, in particular, to promote access to medicines for all."[44] In other words, the general statements about the TRIPS Agreement being interpreted to support Members' right to protect public health are useful and enough to support the interpretation of the TRIPS Agreement so as to make it coherent with the FCTC. However, the main purpose of this declaration was to help developing countries to have better access to medicine. The purpose is very different from the current need of making the TRIPS Agreement and other WTO

[43]See Declaration on the TRIPS Agreement and Public Health. http://www.wto.org/english/thewto_e/minist_e/min01_e/mindecl_trips_e.htm. Accessed 13 Aug 2017.

[44]World Trade Organization, Ministerial Declaration on the TRIPS Agreement and Public Health, paras. 1, 4, WTO Doc. WT/MIN(01)/DEC/2 (20 Nov 2001).

rules supportive of the implementation of the FCTC. Therefore, the book still argues that having a second declaration of similar kind to address the relations between the TRIPS Agreement and other WTO agreements on the one hand and the FCTC on the other hand would help the coherent development of these two treaty systems. Such declaration could also serve as a subsequent agreement between the WTO Members regarding the interpretation of the treaty or the application of WTO's provisions (under VCLT 31.3(a)).

Third, WTO is a well-balanced outcome of series of negotiations. It might be too much to expect from the mere reliance of the method of treaty interpretation to decide the proper co-existence between the WTO and the FCTC under the WTO dispute settlement procedure, especially when there are countries considering that certain ways of interpretation to achieve external coherence would change the contractual relations among the Member and the balance of rights and obligations achieved by them when they negotiate the existing treaty terms. If there is a second declaration on the TRIPS Agreement and Public Health, or a more general declaration as mentioned above, it would represent a new balance of rights and obligations agreed upon and achieved by WTO Members. This would provide a more stabled and desirable relations between the WTO and the FCTC.

To conclude this chapter, it should be useful to note in a codified set of treaty interpretation rules that an external treaty can be a useful interpretation reference to help interpret a treaty as well as a useful factual reference to help apply a treaty. A treaty interpreter should endeavor to interpret a treaty by considering other relevant treaties to help understand the ordinary meaning or by considering them as context so as to ensure the coordination and harmonious co-existence between different treaties.

References

Abdala MA, Spiller PT (2003) Damage valuation of indirect expropriation in international arbitration cases. Am Rev Int Arbitr 14:447–460

Adopted Guidelines. http://www.who.int/fctc/treaty_instruments/adopted/en/. Accessed 13 Aug 2017

An Introduction to Trade and Environment in the WTO. http://www.wto.org/english/tratop_e/envir_e/envt_intro_e.htm. Accessed 13 Aug 2017

Baumgärtner H (2011) Patents, Power, and Rhetoric: Intellectual Property Rights and the Politics of Regime Complexity. http://www.unilu.ch/files/Patents-Power-Rhetoric-wp04.pdf. Accessed 13 Aug 2017

Chan to world: stand with Australia—WHO's director-general applauds Australia's determination in fighting tobacco industry intimidation. http://www.who.int/mediacentre/news/releases/2012/tobacco_20120322/en/index.html. Accessed 13 Aug 2017

Cigarettes—The Only Legal Product. http://www.tobacco-facts.net/2009/04/cigarettes-the-only-legal-product. Accessed 13 Aug 2017

Declaration on the TRIPS Agreement and Public Health. http://www.wto.org/english/thewto_e/minist_e/min01_e/mindecl_trips_e.htm. Accessed 13 Aug 2017

FCTC. WHO Framework convention on tobacco control—overview. http://www.who.int/fctc/text_download/en/. Accessed 13 Aug 2017

Forrest M (2000) Using the power of the World Health Organization: The International Health Regulations and the Future of International Health Law. C J Law Soc Probl 33:153–179
Free Trade Agreements. http://www.ustr.gov/trade-agreements/free-trade-agreements. Accessed 13 Aug 2017
http://icsidfiles.worldbank.org/icsid/ICSIDBLOBS/OnlineAwards/C1000/DC9012_En.pdf. Accessed 13 Aug 2017
http://www.who.int/fctc/protocol/en/. Accessed 13 Aug 2017
https://www.wto.org/english/tratop_e/dispu_e/cases_e/ds434_e.htm. Accessed 13 Aug 2017
International Centre for Trade and Sustainable Development (14 July 2016) Investor-State Tribunal Dismisses Philip Morris Case Against Uruguay Cigarette Packaging. BRIDGES 20 (26). http://www.ictsd.org/bridges-news/bridges/news/investor-state-tribunal-dismisses-philip-morris-case-against-uruguay. Accessed 13 Aug 2017
Liberman J, Mitchell A (2010) In search of coherence between trade and health: inter-institutional opportunities. Md J Int Law 25:143–186
Lo C (2008) A comparison of BIT and the investment chapter of free trade agreement from policy perspective. Asian J WTO Int Health Law Policy 3(1):147–170
Lo C (2012a) Plain packaging and indirect expropriation of trademark rights under BITs: does FCTC help establish a right to regulate tobacco products? Med Law 31(4):521–551
Lo C (2012b) External regime coherence: WTO/BIT and Public Health Tension as an illustration. Asian J WTO Int Health Law Policy 7(1):263–283
OECD. "Indirect expropriation" and the "right to regulate" in international investment law. http://www.oecd.org/investment/investmentpolicy/33776546.pdf. Accessed 13 Aug 2017
Permanent Court of Arbitration Press Release (16 May 2016). https://www.pcacases.com/web/sendAttach/1713. Accessed 13 Aug 2017
Posting of Hunter JM and Essex Court Chambers to Kluwer Arbitration Blog (29 Jan 2012). http://kluwerarbitrationblog.com/blog/2012/01/29/investor-state-arbitration-and-plain-packaging-the-new-%E2%80%98anti-tobacco-movement%E2%80%99-has-begun/. Accessed 13 Aug 2017
Salazar V (2010) NAFTA chapter 11, regulatory expropriation, and domestic counter-advertising law. Arizona J Int Comp Law 27:31–82
The Doha Round. http://www.wto.org/english/tratop_e/dda_e/dda_e.htm. Accessed 13 Aug 2017
World Trade Organization, Ministerial Declaration on the TRIPS Agreement and Public Health, WTO Doc. WT/MIN(01)/DEC/2 (20 Nov 2001)

Chapter 20
Conclusion—Features and Perspectives of the New Codified Rules of Treaty Interpretation

Contents

20.1 Summary of Arguments for a Second Round of Codification

In previous chapters, there have been explanations about the treaty interpretation provisions in the VCLT (especially the provisions in Articles 31 and 32) being the codified rules of customary international law for treaty interpretation. The codification in the VCLT was conducted in 1960s. It can be considered as the first round of codification.

After the codification of the customary rules of treaty interpretation into the VCLT, there have been new developments in the past decades, including the proliferation of treaties, the expansion of treaty coverages and the proliferation of international dispute settlement cases. The proliferation of international disputes results in the increasing demand of interpreting the disputed treaties. The accompanying development is that the treaty interpretation rules provided in Articles 31 to 33 of the VCLT are more and more constantly and heavily relied upon by international adjudicators (or sometimes by domestic courts).

However, the provisions in Articles 31 to 33 are not all clear enough. They themselves needs interpretation. Also since it has been about 60 years since the VCLT was drafted, there have been new situations and developments which were not expected at the time of drafting the convention. There have also been some valuable views of treaty interpretation expressed by international treaty interpreters. It should be useful to select the most valuable ones and to codify them into a more comprehensive set of rules so that the future interpreters will be able to follow certain clearer rules additional to the existing VCLT provisions to ensure that treaty

C. Lo, *Treaty Interpretation Under the Vienna Convention on the Law of Treaties*,
https://doi.org/10.1007/978-981-10-6866-9_20

interpretation will be conducted in a proper and consistent manner. Hence the book argues that it is desirable to have a second round of codification so as to update the existing VCLT rules. The question is how to select the contents to be codified.

The book has suggested in the discussions in previous chapters that there could be much detailed and comprehensive rules to address various treaty interpretation issues. But of course, the needed balance between the detailed rules and the flexibility should be struck and some kind of period review mechanism could be established to ensure the appropriateness and progressiveness of treaty interpretation rules. The additional rules to be codified should include those arising from previous international dispute settlement decisions which can be considered as having already achieved the status of customary rules of treaty interpretation. Also there are some other doctrines or rules which are either widely used or are useful. They can also be considered as qualified to be included in the codified rules. These should all be codified so as to make treaty interpretation more appropriate, transparent and predictable.

20.2 Suggested Contents of the Codified Rules

The additional treaty interpretation principles to be codified in the new set of rules are shown in the following table, in which not only the proposed codified rules are added (in *gray*), but the existing rules are also included, so that readers can have an overall picture of the complete set of rules of treaty interpretation.

The existing and suggested codified rules (The sentences and inserted wordings in italics and being shaded are the suggested new codified rules.)	Reasons for the additional rules
VCLT Part III—Observance, Application and Interpretation of Treaties Section 3. Interpretation of Treaties	
Article 30-1.1 *The rules of treaty interpretation provided in this Section apply to the interpretation of all categories of treaties, except those provided in paragraph 5 of this article, conducted by all international adjudicating bodies and by national courts.*	This is to define the scope of application for the treaty interpretation rules. Chapter 8 of the book has explained that the rules are to be applied not only by international adjudicators, but also by national courts when they interpret a treaty.

(continued)

(continued)

	This is to clarify the existing rules in the VCLT.
Article 30-1.2 *The whole provisions in this Section should be considered as non-exclusive and open-ended. There could be additional elements which can be introduced to supplement the rules and to help interpretation, provided that they are not inconsistent with the provisions in this Section.*	The non-exclusiveness and open-endedness of the VCLT has been discussed in Chap. 14 of this book. This is a clarification of the completeness of the existing rules in the VCLT.
Article 30-1.3 *If there is any authoritative interpretation mechanism created under a treaty, the substantive and procedural requirements as well as the effect of such interpretation will be decided based on the treaty provision which creates such authoritative interpretation. The treaty interpretation rules provided in this Section will not apply to the exercise of such interpretations.*	This is to define the scope of application of the rules. The accompanying explanation is in Chap. 8 of this book. This is to clarify the limit of applying treaty interpretation rules.
Article 30-1.4 *The treaty interpretation rules provided in this Section applies mutatis mutandis to the interpretation of codified rules of customary international law even though such rules are yet to be adopted as a treaty in the sense of this Convention.*	This also defines the scope of application of the rules It has been explained in Chap. 1 of this book that not only those treaties which meet the treaty requirements as provided in VCLT Article 2.1(a) need interpretation. If a set of customary international rules has been codified and if it has not been adopted as a treaty, the codified rules still need interpretation. The interpretation rules in the VCLT should also apply. This is an additional rules to clarify the existing rules.
	The need and contents of special rules for the interpretation of treaties for private matters are discussed in Chap. 9 of this book. This is a

(continued)

(continued)

Article 30-1.5 *For the treaties for private matters, their interpretation will be conducted in consideration of the international character of the matter, the promotion of uniformity and consistency of the interpreted treaty, the good faith requirement, and the general principles based upon by the interpreted treaty, in addition to the consideration of the plain meaning of the interpreted terms and the systemic interpretation.*	new rule to govern interpreters of treaties for private matters.
Article 30-2 *Interpretation shall not lead to adding to or diminishing the rights and obligations provided in the treaty. Nor shall it lead to rebalancing the negotiation deals if the interpreted treaty is to govern the commercial and economic relations between the contracting parties.*	Although the first sentence is only shown in the DSU, it should be a useful principle to govern treaty interpretation. The second sentence should be an important principle for the interpretation of treaties of economic nature. These are new rules to govern treaty interpreters.
Article 30-3.1 *When it is unclear as to whether a provision is relevant and applicable to a dispute, an interpreter is expected to conduct interpretation of the potentially applicable provision so as to decide its legal applicability.*	These rules are to address the relations between conflicting treaty provisions and between treaty interpretation and treaty application, as explained in Chap. 6 of the book. These are new rules to guide treaty interpreters.
Article 30-3.2 *When there are different provisions in a treaty or within a treaty system, there must be a presumption against treaty conflict. There provisions should be presumed to co-exist and the contracting parties are supposed to cumulatively comply with the respective obligations.*	

(continued)

(continued)

Article 30-3.3 *When there is a real conflict between two provisions in a treaty or within a treaty system, the interpreter will consider, among others, the mutual contexts of the conflicting provisions and the ultimate object and purpose of the whole treaty so as to resolve such conflict.*	
Article 30-4 *An interpreter has a broader and more flexible latitude to interpret the procedural rules which govern the dispute before it (including the rules for the fact finding and fact assessment as well as the evidential rules) and that when it has to decide its range of authorities in conducting the dispute settlement proceeding, an interpretation of the procedural rules governing the handling of dispute should be conducted in consideration of the treaty as a whole so as to make the dispute settlement mechanism envisaged by the contracting parties work.*	The need of flexibility in interpreting procedural rules (including the rules for fact finding and fact assessment) should be reflected in the codified rules. This has been explained in Chap. 7 of the book. This is a new rules to guide interpretation of procedural rules.
	This has been explained in Chap. 5 of the book. This is a clarification.

(continued)

(continued)

Article 30-5 *For those dispute settlement mechanisms where there is no rule of stare decisis, previous interpretation of the same provisions by an interpreter is a subsidiary but useful means to assist treaty interpretation and should still be taken into account when they are relevant to the dispute so as to enhance the security and predictability of the treaty. Before citing jurisprudence of a separate dispute settlement mechanism, the interpreter has to discuss whether the interpretation adopted under that other dispute settlement mechanism is plausible and convincing in serving as a secondary means to assist interpretation.*	
	The added sentences concern the sequence and hierarchy of the elements provided in Article 31.1 and the holistic interpretation. They have been discussed in Chap. 17 of this book. These have already been very important and universally accepted parts of treaty interpretation. They can be

(continued)

(continued)

Article 31.1 A treaty shall be interpreted in good faith in accordance with the ordinary meaning to be given to the terms of the treaty in their context and in the light of its object and purpose. *These elements are not to be applied in a strictly sequential order and there is no hierarchical priority given to any one of these elements. An interpreter is also expected to conduct an overall assessment of interpretation in a holistic manner after having conducted the interpretation exercises based on Articles 31 and 32. When conducting the holistic analysis, the interpreter should be given with some flexibility. However, such flexibility should still be subject to the provisions of this Section. The meeting of the good faith requirement can be assessed by considering the fairness of the result, the reasonable basis to adopt an interpretation, the consistency with previous interpretation with or without a reason, the situation of disregarding the objective of the treaty and any other facts to show the existence of malice of the treaty interpreter.*	considered as having achieved the status of customary rules of treaty interpretation and hence needed to be codified in the VCLT. The good faith principle has been discussed in Chap. 17 of this book. This is a new rule to guide the practice of treaty interpreters.
	The issues of the use of dictionary have been discussed in Chap. 10 of this book. These are new rules to guide the interpreters' actual practice of interpretation.

(continued)

(continued)

Article 31.1-1 *Notwithstanding the provisions in the preceding paragraph, a treaty interpreter is usually expected to begin with, and focus upon, the text of the particular provision to be interpreted. It is also a useful starting point for an interpreter to check with dictionary definitions for the purpose of identifying the ordinary meanings of an interpreted term. When checking with dictionaries, the interpreter should rely only on the dictionaries with the same language of the interpreted treaty. The interpreter must also consider the credibility of a dictionary before it. When there are different definitions in one or more dictionaries, the interpreter should provide plausible reasons to explain its selection. Also when the selection of dictionaries or the selection of definitions by the interpreter is different from that suggested by the disputing parties, an explanation about not accepting the suggestion should be provided. If there are a number of dictionaries used, the interpreter should be expected to provide a list of all cited dictionaries so as to make the treaty interpretation more transparent.*	
Article 31.1-2 *The two words "object" and "purpose" provided in paragraph 1 of this article are synonymous and conjoint in treaty interpretation to jointly refer to the ultimate and overall goal that the entire interpreted treaty intends to achieve. The object and purpose of a treaty provision, as opposed to the object and purpose of the entire treaty, can still be taken into consideration, but it should not be considered in isolation from the object and purpose of the entire treaty.*	The object-and-purpose of the interpreted serving as an important element for treaty interpretation has been explained in Chap. 11 of the book. These should be useful clarifications.

(continued)

(continued)

Article 31.1-3 *The object and purpose of a treaty can be identified from the preamble (if the preambular language reflects the intentions of negotiators) and from the text of the interpreted treaty. It can also be implied in the treaty or inferred from the treaty.*	
Article 31.1-4 *The object and purpose of a treaty should not merely be considered as adding colour or texture or shading light to the interpreted provision. It should be given with higher weight to guide the interpretation of a treaty provision.*	
Article 31.1-5 *A "factual context", as opposed to the "legal context", is a factor for a treaty interpreter to test the appropriateness of the selection of an ordinary meaning to be given to an interpreted term so as to correspond to the reality of the factual context.*	The issue of factual context has been explained in Chap. 12 of this book. This should be a useful clarification.
	The issues of introducing fundamental values into treaty interpretation have been discussed in Chap. 18 of this book. These are new rules to guide the possible incorporation of certain human values of high importance into the interpreted treaty through interpretation.

(continued)

(continued)

Article 31.1-6 *When an interpreter has to choose an ordinary meaning from among two or more ordinary meanings, she should select the one which is more in line with the object and purpose of the interpreted treaty in protecting fundamental human values, taking into consideration the context of protecting human values for the interpreted provision. For a fundamental human value which has been incorporated into the text of the interpreted treaty, an interpreter will give a higher weight to the consideration of such human value as the important object and purpose of the treaty or as the context of the interpreted term. For a fundamental value which is not explicitly incorporated into the text of the interpreted treaty, an interpreter should consider the possibility of including such value as falling within the scope of the ordinary meanings of some existing terms in the interpreted treaty or through considering such external values as important objects and purposes or subsequent practices so as to give an appropriate role to the external value in the operation of the interpreted treaty.*	
Article 31.2 The context for the purpose of the interpretation of a treaty shall comprise, in addition to the text, including its preamble and annexes: (a) Any agreement relating to the treaty which was made between all the parties in connexion with the conclusion of the treaty; (b) Any instrument which was made by one or more parties in connexion with the conclusion of the treaty and accepted by the other parties as an instrument related to the treaty	

(continued)

(continued)

Article 31.2-1 *Footnotes in a treaty can be the context for the interpretation of the main texts to which the footnotes are attached and the context for other parts in the interpreted treaty.*	The issue of footnotes serving as context has been explained in Chap. 12 of this book. This rule should be a useful clarification.
Article 31.3 There shall be taken into account, together with the context: (a) Any subsequent agreement between the parties regarding the interpretation of the treaty or the application of its provisions; (b) Any subsequent practice in the application of the treaty which establishes the agreement of the parties regarding its interpretation; (c) Any relevant rules of international law applicable in the relations between the parties	
Article 31.3-1 *Subsequent agreement and practice and relevant rules of international law are to be read into the interpreted treaty, but are not to replace or override the interpreted term or provisions.*	The related issues have been discussed in Chap. 12 of the book. This is to clarify the existing provision in Article 31.3.
Article 31.3-2 *A treaty which is separate from the interpreted treaty can be a useful interpretation reference to help treaty interpretation as well as a useful factual reference to help treaty application. A treaty interpreter should endeavor to interpret a treaty by considering other relevant treaties to help understand the ordinary meaning of an interpreted term or by considering them as context so as to ensure the coordination and harmonious co-existence between different treaties.*	The potential conflict and the need of coordination between treaties have been discussed in Chap. 19. These are new rules to guide treaty interpreters.

(continued)

(continued)

Article 31.3-3 *An interpreter might find it necessary to rely on an evolutive interpretation for interpreting certain treaty provisions. The requirements of applying an evolutive interpretation include that the interpreted term should be generic in nature; that there must be a long period of time or continuing duration for the operation of a treaty for the purpose of justifying the adoption of the evolutive interpretation; and that the effect of meeting of the above mentioned two requirements (i.e. the term being generic and the duration being continuing) is to presume the parties to have intended the evolutive interpretation. But an interpreter should be careful in overturning the presumption so as not to make a treaty become obsolete. Technology development and the technological neutrality are also factors which can be considered by the treaty interpreter to help decide whether to adopt an evolutive interpretation.*	The adoption of an evolutive interpretation has been discussed in Chap. 15 of this book. These are new rules to guide the use of the evolutive interpretation.
Article 31.3-4 *For the interpretation of abstract terms or indefinite legal concepts and also for the interpretation of provisions with more complicated structures, an interpreter can develop formulas to specify the sequence and elements to be analyzed so as to correctly perceive and understand the essence of the terms or provisions.*	The formula approach for indefinite legal concepts has been discussed in Chap. 16 of this book. This is a new rule to guide treaty interpreter.
Article 31.4 A special meaning shall be given to a term if it is established that *all* the *contracting* parties so intended.	The suggestion is to modify the existing provision in Article 31.4 so as to make it clear that the intention must be that of all

(continued)

(continued)

	contracting parties, not just that of the disputing parties. This was discussed in Chap. 13 of this book.
Article 31.4-1 *The contracting parties' intention of giving a special meaning to an interpreted term can be reflected in a textual language or in the object and purpose of the interpreted treaty or even in a separate document. But the interpreter must have a preponderant evidence to show that the object and purpose and the context would support the fact that the contracting parties had such intention of giving a special meaning to the interpreted term.*	The identification of an intention of giving special meaning to a term was discussed in Chap. 13 of this book. These are new rules to guide the use of special meaning to interpret a treaty term.
Article 31.4-2 *The interpreter must be careful in relying on the preparatory work to decide the contracting parties' intention of special meaning so as to avoid using the supplementary means to reverse the interpretation result arising from the primary treaty interpretation method of relying on the ordinary meaning of a textual term, the context and the object and purpose.*	
Article 31.4-3 *A custom might help identify the parties' intention of applying a "special meaning". But the custom itself and alone cannot be the basis of giving a "special meaning" to an interpreted treaty term.*	
Article 32 Recourse may be had to supplementary means of interpretation, including the preparatory work of the treaty and the circumstances of its conclusion, in order to confirm the meaning resulting from the application of article 31, or to determine the meaning when the interpretation according to article 31: (a) Leaves the meaning ambiguous or obscure; or (b) Leads to a result which is manifestly absurd or unreasonable	
	The non-exhaustiveness and the nature of Latin maxims have been discussed in

(continued)

(continued)

Article 32.1 *The two supplementary means of the preparatory work of the treaty and the circumstances of its conclusion listed in Article 32 are non-exhaustive. Some Latin maxims, such as lex specialis derogat legi generali; lex posterior derogat legi priori; expressio unius est exclusio alterius; in dubio mitius; ut res magis valeat quam perat; and exceptio est strictissimae applicationis, can also be considered as supplementary means. These principles help confirm the meaning resulting from the application of Article 31 or determine the meaning of the interpreted term when the interpretation according to Article 31 could still leave the meaning ambiguous or obscure. However, an interpreter should avoid applying these Latin maxims to suggest that the interpretation based on Article 31 leads to a manifestly absurd or unreasonable result and hence such interpretation should be replaced and reverted by these Latin maxims.*	Chap. 14 of this book. These rules are to clarify the existing rules provided in the current introductory provision of Article 32.
Article 32.2 *Sub-paragraph (b) in paragraph 1 of this article is an exception to Article 31. Accordingly, its application should be extremely strict and limited. The absurdity or unreasonableness must be obvious from all aspects without a room for a different interpretation as to whether the result of interpretation based on Article 31 is absurd or unreasonable or otherwise before subparagraph (b) of the preceding paragraph is applied.*	The absurdity and unreasonableness issues have been discussed in Chap. 13 of this book. These are new rules to guide the application of the exception provided in the current Article 32(b).
Article 33.1 When a treaty has been authenticated in two or more languages, the text is equally authoritative in each language,	

(continued)

(continued)

unless the treaty provides or the parties agree that, in case of divergence, a particular text shall prevail	
Article 33.2 A version of the treaty in a language other than one of those in which the text was authenticated shall be considered an authentic text only if the treaty so provides or the parties so agree	
Article 33.3 The terms of the treaty are presumed to have the same meaning in each authentic text	
Article 33.3-1 *A treaty interpreter should be permitted to consider the provisions and terms used in different language versions as mutual context to each other so as to help identify the ordinary meaning of and to interpret a treaty term.*	The issue of different language versions serving as mutual context to each other was discussed in Chap. 13 of this book. This is a new rule to guide treaty interpreters.
Article 33.4 Except where a particular text prevails in accordance with paragraph 1, when a comparison of the authentic texts discloses a difference of meaning which the application of articles 31 and 32 does not remove, the meaning which best reconciles the texts, having regard to the object and purpose of the treaty, shall be adopted	

20.3 The Perspectives

Definitely there could be different views about the need of having another round of codification of treaty interpretation rules and about the appropriate contents to be codified. However, the book is of the view that the transparency and predictability of treaty interpretation should be of higher importance, as long as the needed flexibility for such interpretation is not extinguished.

In order to achieve the objective of transparency and predictability of treaty interpretation, the rules must not be too general and too vague. The current rules of interpretation under the VCLT Articles 31 to 33 are practically too general and vague.

Although the new rules suggested by the book make the current rules in the VCLT more detailed and comprehensive, it is hoped that the balance between the detailed rules and the needed flexibility has been struck in the above suggestions.

Index

C. Lo, *Treaty Interpretation under the Vienna Convention on the Law of Treaties*,
https://doi.org/10.1007/978-981-10-6866-9

FSC
www.fsc.org
MIX
Papier | Fördert
gute Waldnutzung
FSC® C083411

Kolibri 360 GmbH
Ferdinand-Jühlke-Straße 7
99095 Erfurt, Deutschland
produktsicherheit@kolibri360.de